Artefacts in Roman Britain

Their Purpose and Use

Roman Britain has given us an enormous number of artefacts, yet few books available today deal with the province's whole material culture as represented by these artefacts. This introduction, aimed primarily at students and general readers, begins by explaining the process of identifying objects of any period or material. Themed chapters, written by experts in their particular area of interest, then discuss artefacts from the point of view of their use. The contributors' premise is that every object was designed for a particular purpose, which may have been to satisfy a general need or the specific need of an individual. If the latter, the maker, the owner and the end user may have been one and the same person; if the former, the manufacturer had to provide objects that others would wish to purchase or exchange. Understanding this reveals a fascinating picture of life in Roman Britain.

LINDSAY ALLASON-JONES is Director of the Centre for Interdisciplinary Artefact Studies and Reader in Roman Material Culture at the University of Newcastle upon Tyne, and has published eight books and over a hundred academic papers on themes related to the archaeology of the Roman Empire. She is the author of two previous textbooks, *Women in Roman Britain* (1989; 2nd edn 2005) and *Daily Life in Roman Britain* (2008).

Artefacts in Roman Britain

Their Purpose and Use

Edited by LINDSAY ALLASON-JONES

CAMBRIDGE
UNIVERSITY PRESS

CAMBRIDGE UNIVERSITY PRESS
Cambridge, New York, Melbourne, Madrid, Cape Town, Singapore,
São Paulo, Delhi, Dubai, Tokyo, Mexico City

Cambridge University Press
The Edinburgh Building, Cambridge CB2 8RU, UK

Published in the United States of America by Cambridge University Press, New York

www.cambridge.org
Information on this title: www.cambridge.org/9780521860123

First published 2011

Printed in the United Kingdom at the University Press, Cambridge

A catalogue record for this publication is available from the British Library

Library of Congress Cataloguing in Publication data
Artefacts in Roman Britain : their purpose and use / [edited by] Lindsay Allason-Jones.
    p.   cm.
Includes index.
ISBN 978-0-521-86012-3 (hardback)
1. Great Britain – Antiquities, Roman.   2. Material culture – Great Britain.   3. Romans – Great
Britain.   I. Allason-Jones, Lindsay.   II. Title: Artefacts in Roman Britain.   III. Title.
DA145.A78   2010
936.2′04 – dc22   2010038773

ISBN 978-0-521-86012-3 Hardback
ISBN 978-0-521-67752-3 Paperback

Contents

Illustrations

Plates

Figures

Tables

Preface

In 2001 I was approached by Cambridge University Press with the proposal that I should edit a volume on the 'small finds' from Roman Britain. The suggestion was that there was a need for a volume to assist students of archaeology to identify the smaller objects found in excavations. However, mature consideration and discussion with a number of colleagues indicated that such a book would not fill an identifiable gap; what was required was a book that helped students to understand the significance of finds and how they fit into our understanding of Roman Britain. Such a volume, it was hoped, would still help students to learn how to identify objects but in a more meaningful way.

The thinking behind this decision was based on a number of considerations. Firstly, vast numbers of artefacts have been discovered on Roman sites in Britain. Any volume detailed enough, and well enough illustrated, to be useful would have to be very large and unwieldy and thus too costly for the proposed purchasers. Furthermore, for those students wishing to learn how to identify small finds there are a number of books on specific types of finds, e.g. Martin Henig on intaglios (1978), Bill Manning on ironwork (1976; 1985), Glenys Lloyd-Morgan on mirrors (1981), which provide the details necessary to make an accurate identification of an individual artefact. It was also the opinion of finds specialists that anyone wishing to get a general idea of the range of objects to be found in Roman Britain would learn more by looking through several of the larger excavation reports and catalogues, e.g. Nina Crummy on Colchester (1983) or Allason-Jones and Miket on South Shields (1984) than by using a single general volume, however comprehensive.

Artefacts are three-dimensional, have weight and are in colour. Successful identification of objects depends on building up a body of knowledge, which can best be done through museum visits and by handling as many artefacts as possible. Learning to recognise artefacts through books alone tends to lead to fundamental mistakes. There is also the problem that Britain was part of a large and very cosmopolitan Empire in which goods were traded or transferred from province to province. One could not hope to produce a volume which dealt adequately with the full range of artefacts to be found across the whole Roman Empire and, indeed, it would be difficult to commission specialists who would feel comfortable with such a task. Finds from excavations often vary greatly between the different Roman provinces but there is a core of objects which can be found anywhere; for the latter group there are basic principles which can aid identification, whilst for the more unusual artefacts familiarity with the publications of colleagues throughout the Empire is necessary (see, for example, Cool 2004a).

Colleagues are in agreement that what has proved to be particularly difficult for the average student to understand is how the objects found in excavations fitted into the everyday lives of the cultures we study. Instead, there is often a tendency to regard artefacts as merely *objets d'art*. Recent work on finds, however, has progressed beyond merely identifying the objects and preparing detailed catalogues to using the objects to illuminate our understanding of Roman Britain by studying the objects and their contexts together. Examples of this approach can be found in Peter Wilson's recent publication of the excavations at Catterick (2002a; 2002b) and Hilary Cool's appraisal of the excavations at Brougham (2004a).

It was, therefore, decided that a volume that looked at finds from the point of view of their possible use was required. In this volume a series of themed chapters will be found, such as Funerary contexts, Commerce, etc., each chapter written by an expert in the artefacts that relate to that specific theme. The principle behind this method is the premise that throughout history every object found by archaeologists was originally designed for a particular purpose. This purpose may have been to satisfy a general need of a mass of people or the specific need of an individual. If the latter, the maker, the owner and the end user may have been one and the same person; if the former, the manufacturer had to provide objects which were well designed for their purpose so that others would wish to purchase them or exchange other items for them. Being aware of this not only makes the identification of objects easier for archaeologists and museum curators but also puts those objects into their social and economic contexts.

Pottery vessels, glass vessels and coins are mentioned in this volume but possibly not in the detail some colleagues would have preferred. There are many volumes which assist a student to study such artefacts so they have only been included when they are an essential ingredient to complete a scenario; for example, in a funerary context the offerings or equipment might include pots, glass vessels and coins, so merely to discuss the small finds in such a context would hamper understanding. They have also been discussed if they show images that throw light on different aspects of life in Roman Britain, such as the pottery and glass vessels decorated with scenes of gladiatorial combat.

The contributors have attempted to confine their discussions of the artefacts to within the themed topics rather than by the presumed contexts from which they are derived – it is too easy for objects from a fort to be considered as 'military' or those from a temple to be 'sacred' without thought being given to the actual use of the individual objects. Because of this, some artefacts, such as bells, may well be discussed by several of the authors rather than forced into one section. This is not a weakness but a strength as it is important that students understand that an object may have had several uses, depending on both context and user.

The authors hope that readers of this volume will find it a useful aid to learning more about the material culture of Roman Britain. We hope that it will provide an insight into the processes involved in identifying objects as well as introduce students and colleagues to the importance of artefacts in Romano-British studies. We also hope that the essays will offer an unusual view of everyday life in Roman Britain and encourage our readers to reassess what is known of the people of the province.

All the ancient sources cited in the text have used the translations in the Loeb Classical Library series, Cambridge (Mass.): Harvard University Press; London: William Heinemann, unless otherwise stated.

Acknowledgements

The authors are grateful to Paul Sealey of Colchester Museum, Rosalind Sherris of the Museum of London, Dr Graeme Lawson, Rob Collins of the Portable Antiquities Scheme and Glyn Goodrick of CIAS, Newcastle University for all their help.

Photographs

Glyn Goodrick, Centre for Interdisciplinary Artefact Studies (CIAS), Newcastle University (Pls. 1, 2, 4, 5, 8, 18, 20–3, 25–9, 31–6, 41, 43, 45, 47, 50, 51, 54)

Carlisle Museum and Arts Services (Pls. 3, 30, 53)

Portable Antiquities Scheme (Pls. 6, 7, 38)

The Vindolanda Trust (Pls. 9, 42)

Colchester Archaeological Trust (Pl. 10)

Museum of London (Pls. 11, 12)

National Museums of Scotland (Pls. 13, 15, 55)

Reading Museum Service (Reading Borough Council) (Pls. 14, 16, 44)

The Trustees of the British Museum (Pls. 17, 24, 37, 46, 48, 52)

Sussex Archaeological Society (Pl. 19)

Ralph Jackson (Pls. 39, 49)

Colchester Museums (Pl. 40)

Figures

All the figures, with the exception of Figure 22, which is reproduced courtesy of Surrey Archaeological Society, and Figure 24, which is reproduced courtesy of the Centre for Archaeology, English Heritage, were drawn by Mike Bishop.

Abbreviations

AE	*L'Année Épigraphique*
ANRW	*Aufstieg und Niedergang der römischen Welt* ed. H. Temporini and W. Haase. Berlin and New York
DCMS	Department of Culture, Media and Sport
MoLAS	Museum of London Archaeological Service
RCHM York	*An Inventory of the Historical Monuments of the City of York*, vol. I: *Eburacum, Roman York* (1962) Royal Commission on Historical Monuments England. London
RIB	*The Roman Inscriptions of Britain* I: *Inscriptions on Stone* (1965) ed. R. G. Collingwood and R. P. Wright. Oxford
RIB II.3	*The Roman Inscriptions of Britain* II.3: *Instrumentum Domesticum* (1991) ed. S. S. Frere and R. S. O. Tomlin. Stroud
RIB II.4	*The Roman Inscriptions of Britain* II.4: *Instrumentum Domesticum* (1992) ed. S. S. Frere and R. S. O. Tomlin. Stroud
RIB II.5	*The Roman Inscriptions of Britain* II.5: *Instrumentum Domesticum* (1993) ed. S. S. Frere and R. S. O. Tomlin. Stroud
RIB II.8	*The Roman Inscriptions of Britain* II.8: *Instrumentum Domesticum* (1993) ed. S. S. Frere, R. S. O. Tomlin and R. P. Wright. Stroud
RIB III	*The Roman Inscriptions of Britain* III: *Inscriptions on Stone Found or Notified between 1 January 1955 and 31 December 2006* (2009) ed. R. S. O. Tomlin, R. P. Wright and M. W. C. Hassall. Oxford
Tab. Vindol. I	*Vindolanda: The Latin Writing Tablets* (1983) A. K. Bowman and J. D. Thomas. London
Tab. Vindol. II	*The Vindolanda Writing Tablets: Tabulae Vindolandenses II* (1994) A. K. Bowman and J. D. Thomas. London
Tab. Vindol. III	*The Vindolanda Writing Tablets: Tabulae Vindolandenses III* (2003) A. K. Bowman and J. D. Thomas. London
ZPE	*Zeitschrift für Papyrologie und Epigraphik*

Introduction

LINDSAY ALLASON-JONES

Archaeology is the study of our predecessors, using the evidence of artefacts and a wide range of other techniques. It can cover every period from the earliest prehistory to the present day, and in every period artefacts can be found which can be described as diagnostic to that period whilst others appear regularly throughout time. What all these artefacts have in common is that they were all made or adapted by a human being, with or without the help of machinery or tools.

In order for an artefact to assist us in our quest to discover as much as we can about our ancestors it must be correctly identified. In order to do this, certain questions need to be asked which will aid not only identification but also our ability to use the resulting information constructively. These questions divide into six groups:

- Appearance: what does the object look, feel or smell like? What are its colour, shape and size? What material is it made from? Is it made from one material or several? Is it complete? Has it been well used, altered, adapted or repaired?
- Construction: has the object been made by hand or by machine? Which techniques have been involved in its manufacture? Was more than one person involved? How has the object been finished?
- Function: for what purpose was the artefact made? Was its use changed at any time?
- Design: is the object well designed? Was it made with the most appropriate materials available at the time? Is it decorated and, if so, how and why? Is the decoration functional or merely aesthetic?
- Significance: is this a symbolic and/or practical object? Would it have had sentimental or social significance for its owner? Does it provide any clues as to its owner's economic or social status or gender?
- Context of discovery: where was the object found? Is this likely to indicate the object's primary or secondary use or does it represent a post-depositional context which will throw no light on the object's intended function?

Many of these questions are inter-related. Some demand accurate observation on the part of the archaeologist, others require the application of previous observations and an individual's databank of experience, whilst others rely on the archaeologist being able to empathise with the people of the past.

Before considering those artefacts that tell us about life in Roman Britain, let us consider what any artefact can tell us, regardless of period. Let us, as an exercise, use the six groups of questions to discuss a modern ballpoint pen.

Appearance

In order to answer the first group of questions it is necessary to use all five senses. Touch and sight are the most important of these in identifying an object but smell and sound may also be required; the ring of a fragment of stone when tapped against a hard surface, for example, is very different from the sound of a sherd of pottery similarly handled, whilst the smell of excavated leather can be very distinctive. It is not recommended that the sense of taste is brought in to play as a regular methodological tool, for obvious reasons, but there are occasions when the taste of an object has aided an initial identification of its material. Discovering the material an object is made from is usually a simple matter of assessing its colour, weight and texture, based on experience, to arrive at a superficial conclusion that an object is of iron, stone or bone, etc. At a more detailed level, however, scientific analysis may be required; for example, whilst it is often reasonably easy to identify that an object is made from a copper alloy, to state precisely which metals and trace elements make up that alloy needs further assessment in a laboratory. Such evidence can be essential in dating an artefact. In the 1990s, an iron helmet of Anglo-Saxon type, found in a river in Northumberland, was only proved to be of nineteenth-century manufacture by the discovery of manganese in its surface treatment, a metal only introduced into metal-working in the 1870s. In the case of jet, it is only through scientific analysis that black, shiny artefacts can be confidently identified as being carved from jet, shale or cannel coal; even burnt bone and dried leather can fool the casual eye. Accurate identification of the various black materials has only been possible in recent years, and through this identification archaeologists have been able to recognise previously unknown sources of the raw materials, individual workshops and trade patterns (Allason-Jones 2002a; Allason-Jones and Jones 2001).

Observation of a ballpoint pen reveals that it is made from several different materials, some of which might survive better in the ground than others. How easy will it be for archaeologists in the future to identify such a pen if all that survives is the plastic cap or the metal tip? Archaeological artefacts can also be composite objects and a great deal of lateral thought may be required in order to work out what the missing components were made from or looked like. The excavations at Elginhaugh fort, for example, produced a copper-alloy bar 92 mm long, 11.5 mm wide and 5.5 mm thick, with a T-sectioned channel down one face. The back of the channel had a series of transverse angled ribs. Both terminals were broken but appeared to continue only on the flat face and each had been pierced by a large circular hole. To work out what this had been used for one had to presume that it was just one element in a composite item and then go through each part of the object to work out how those parts would relate to the complete object. The flat, pierced terminals indicated that the object had been attached to another material by rivets; the T-sectioned channel suggested that a rod or bar with a T-shaped end had been fitted into it, but loosely so that it could move up and down; the angled ribs at the back of the channel implied that the T-bar could be arrested at various stages. All these observations led to the conclusion that the object was some sort of ratchet. Consideration of which artefacts in the Roman period might require such a ratchet led to the identification of the Elginhaugh piece as a linear ratchet for a catapult. As this was the first linear catapult ratchet to have been found in the Roman world, looking for parallels would have been fruitless – deduction was the only available tool (Allason-Jones 2007: 405–7, pl. 10.5).

Catapults are very large wooden objects but when the wood decays the various metal elements are all that are left. Most of these provide valuable recycling material and thus may be melted down, leaving little trace of the original catapult. Even quite small objects may have fragments or vital pieces missing, either because they were made from a different, more fragile material or because they were made up of individual elements that have become separated; the various sections of a bone composite comb or the individual tesserae of a mosaic are cases in point. In the latter case, the discovery of tesserae suggests that a mosaic was present but unless a section is found *in situ* the patterns and motifs are impossible to reconstruct. It may not even be possible to tell if the mosaic was on a floor, wall or ceiling, or even if it formed a decorative feature on furniture.

Ballpoint pens can be made from a variety of materials – precious metals, enamelled bronze, even wood – but are mostly made from plastic because that is an easily obtainable material that can be mass-produced through moulding, yet is still hard enough to withstand the pressures applied during writing. For most modern objects different materials are used for the different elements that make up the whole because each material has its own characteristics that make it fit for purpose. This is not always so with archaeological objects, because the ideal material either had not yet been discovered or was not available. This did not necessarily matter for the appearance and usefulness of the final object, but can lead the unwary archaeologist into making false judgements. As has already been mentioned, black shiny artefacts usually look as if they are all made from jet. Today the various materials may look different because they have not reacted in the same way to the ravages of age or burial in the ground; while good-quality jet will look exactly as it did when first sold, shale will often have lost its shine and split along its bedding planes, cannel coal may have disintegrated into small blocks, and the surface of poor-quality jet may have 'crazed'. This difference in long-term appearance does not seem to have concerned Romano-British jewellers; indeed they were probably not aware of it. They were quite happy to use jet, shale and cannel coal beads to create a necklace and even make up numbers with grey/black glass if necessary (Allason-Jones 1996; 2002a).

Often an archaeologist has to rely on the shape and size of the object plus its material to identify it. Ballpoint pens can vary in size but are mostly about 16 cm long and 1 cm thick because that makes them comfortable to hold and to use. A ballpoint pen only a centimetre long would be impossible to hold comfortably and would not contain enough ink to make it useful; equally a pen a metre long would make writing a letter an unwieldy matter.

When considering the colour of an object it is important to remember that it may not be its original colour after its sojourn in the ground or even after conservation treatment. The patina acquired by bronzes, for example, can vary considerably from black to brown to dark green, and this can distract us from recalling that when new the object would have resembled gold and that it would have been this mock gold appearance that would have attracted the customer. The use of inlays would also have depended on contrasting colours to have an effect; even the simple use of niello on bronze would have been more striking when both metals were fresh (la Niece 1983). Enamel decoration on brooches and studs can often be missing or have changed tone through the archaeological process; white enamel, for example, often takes a green tinge through its association with copper alloys. Larger objects may also bear little resemblance to their original appearance – stone altars, tombstones and architectural details would often have been painted in bright colours. The Mithraic altars found at Carrawburgh in

1949 still had traces of red, green and pink pigments on their surfaces when they were first excavated; sadly, these colours quickly faded on exposure to light and air (Richmond and Gillam 1951). It is, therefore, important to imagine what the original appearance might have been when considering why an object was made or bought.

Archaeological objects may appear to have been worn with use if they were found in contexts which were continually disturbed, such as plough soils or riverbeds, even if they were in pristine condition when deposited. If they show signs of wear before deposition this may be because they were essential for day-to-day living or because they happened to be favourite items of the user and thus often used or handled. Wear patterns can, however, provide important information when identifying objects. Whetstones, for example, often show distinct dishing on their surfaces as a result of iron blades being stropped back and forth. Techniques using high-resolution microscopes have been used more with prehistoric objects, such as flints and antler tools, but can still provide useful evidence for Roman objects.

Evidence of wear, or even repair, need not indicate the status of an object's owner. In today's market it is very easy to buy a new ballpoint pen if one's old one falls to pieces or runs dry. In Roman Britain it may not always have been so easy to replace one's belongings if they were lost or damaged, particularly if they were imported or if the supply chain was disrupted. A writing tablet from Vindolanda reminds us that even something as simple as bad weather and poor road surfaces could make it difficult to acquire even the most basic commodities (*Tab.Vindol. I*, no. 343). Cracked pots have been found repaired, rather roughly, with lead cramps (Plate 1; Allason-Jones and Miket 1984, nos. 8.74–91) and several paterae have been found with replacement handles riveted into position. These repairs are not always very attractive but serve to remind us that even the most basic domestic artefacts had an importance to their owners.

Construction

The people of the past used the best materials available to them when making artefacts, but often they were limited by the techniques of the time. A case in point is the working of iron. Iron requires a steady temperature of 1,540 °C in order to reach the pouring consistency required for making an object in a mould and this was not easily achievable until the introduction of the blast furnace in the fifteenth century; consequently, Roman objects of iron were mostly hammered into shape and any iron object with clear

Pl. 1 Cooking pot from South Shields fort, which has been repaired with lead cramps

evidence that it has been made in a mould is likely to have been produced after the fifteenth century (Tylecote 1962: 300–2; see also Chapter 3). On the other hand, iron could provide a good edge, which was sharper and more lasting than was possible with a copper-alloy blade. The hardness of iron, and the fact that it is possible to make very large objects from it, makes it perfect for tools – a fact the Romans were well aware of and used to advantage in making agricultural implements (see Chapter 4).

Mould marks can also be instructive when found on the edges of coins. Roman coins were made by placing a blank of metal between two dies and bringing them smartly together – a method known as hammering (see Chapter 1). Signs of a mould line around the edge of a coin, or file marks suggesting that such a line has been removed, indicate that it has been made in a mould. This may not prove that the object is a modern forgery as there were many counterfeiters active in Roman Britain (Reece 1970: 69–70, 110, 127; see also Chapter 1). Coins also may have had their surfaces treated by dipping them in another, usually more precious, metal. This was not necessarily a practice confined to coin forgers but was a common feature of the coinage of some emperors, often when the economy was under stress. Similar surface treatment of other finds, such as copper-alloy brooches which often have their surfaces silvered or tinned, was usually intended to make the final product look more expensive.

It is all too easy to fall into the error of presuming that if an object is handmade it must be older or more primitive than examples made by machine or by mass-production. Even today craftworkers often prefer to make their tools themselves in order to ensure that their equipment precisely fits their needs. There is also the economic argument that it is cheaper to make what one requires oneself or adapt what is already available. However, it is a feature of the Roman economy that mass-production, particularly of pottery, became increasingly cost-effective. Samian ware is an obvious example of factory production, involving a considerable number of people as the process progressed from the makers of the wooden motif stamps, to the mould makers, to the potters, to the adders of foot-rings, to those who dipped the products in coloured slip, and so to the final firing.

The manufacturing techniques used to make objects can result in elements that are difficult to identify if they become isolated from the main object. Examples of this are the lead filling which can be found in the end of ram's head skillet handles or bronze statuettes, or the metal rods which act as spacers for objects made by the lost wax method – the ends of these are usually sawn off when the object is removed from the mould and are hard to identify out of context (Atkinson 1979).

The analysis of metals provides another tool when discussing artefacts. David Dungworth's analysis of bronze artefacts from the North of England has shown that identifiable metal 'recipes' were in use in the Roman period, some 'dictated by metallurgical necessity, and some by social and economic factors' (Dungworth 1998: 117). In particular, he has observed that brasses with a high zinc content were being used to make military equipment, such as *lorica segmentata* fittings, some coins and some brooches in the early first century AD, as a result of the use of the cementation process in producing the metal, but he has also been able to show that not all military equipment was made from brass, as had been previously thought, but that some items were made from leaded bronze. He has concluded that leaded bronze was used for cast objects whilst brass was preferred for sheet fittings (Dungworth 1997; 1998). The work of Justine Bayley and Sarnia Butcher, in analysing over 3,500 brooches from a range of sites in Roman Britain, has revealed a noticeable correlation of alloy composition with brooch type and that the composition is usually independent of a brooch's findspot (Bayley and Butcher 1995; 2004).

Function

When ascribing a function to an object we have to rely on our own experience, either through observation of ancient artefacts found in particular contexts which provide clues as to the object's use, or through our own knowledge of what we use in day-to-day living. Keys, for example, have changed little since the Roman period and a rod, one end of which has a plate with teeth whilst the other has a loop, will not prove too difficult to identify as a key, although more detailed knowledge will be required to decide what sort of lock would have been opened by that key (see Chapter 7). There is, however, a human propensity to use objects for purposes for which they were not originally intended. The average modern screwdriver, for example, unless owned by a professional or by someone who respects tools, invariably has splashes of paint, owing to its secondary use as a paint can opener (Plate 2). Future statistical analyses of screwdrivers could well lead the archaeologists of the future to misinterpret the purpose of this common tool. In the past people were also inclined to adapt existing objects to meet an immediate need or to recycle the material completely. Glass vessels, which were originally imported into Britain as containers for liquids, were reused as cinerary urns (Plate 53), or ground down to make lids, gaming counters or pendants (Allason-Jones and Miket 1984: no. 4.71), or even remelted to make the glass armlets which are regularly found on the settlement sites of northern England and Scotland (Kilbride-Jones 1938; Stevenson 1957).

Some artefacts found in Roman Britain were dual or multi-purpose. Common finds on both military and civilian sites are bronze knobs, sometimes with iron shanks, which are usually referred to as 'bell-shaped studs'. These have been found attaching lock plates to boxes, as pommels for daggers, as hinges for dolabra sheaths, and as furniture or door studs. Unless found *in situ* or in a matching set, it is rarely possible to attribute an

Pl. 2 Modern screwdriver showing signs of multiple use

individual bell-shaped stud to a specific function, even if it is a simple matter to designate the object as a bell-shaped stud and even give it a type number (Allason-Jones 1985).

Deciding an object's function is not the end of the matter; it may be necessary to consider why there was a need for an object to fulfil that function. The importance of the discovery of a key, for example, is that it indicates that its owner had a lockable box or door and wished to secure something of value in that box or behind that door. The noticeable rise in the use of locks and keys in the Roman period tells us a great deal about life in Roman Britain: the increase in material culture and use of coins resulted in there being more valuable items to steal, whilst the influx of new people, and the continual movement of those people around the province, seems to have led to an increasing sense of insecurity and the wish to lock oneself and one's belongings out of harm's way.

Design

All objects, whether ancient or modern, have been designed for the task they are meant to do; by eliminating those tasks they could not have done it is usually possible to home in on what they were intended for. A case in point

Pl. 3 Pair of chained trumpet brooches

is a bow brooch, a ubiquitous artefact in Roman Britain which not only was decorative but also served the purpose of securing the fabric of dresses or cloaks. Each bow brooch can be stripped down into its constituent parts: the head, the bow, the pin, the spring or hinge that links the pin to the brooch, the headloop and the catchplate (Plate 3). The bow needs to be curved if it is to accommodate much fabric: if a brooch is just intended to be decorative or symbolic there need be little space between the body of the brooch and the pin; if, however, the brooch is to serve a useful function it must provide enough space for a reasonable amount of bunched material to be held. For the brooch to be attached to the fabric there must be a pin and this needs to be sharp enough at its end to pierce the textile without tearing it or making a large unsightly hole. The pin has to be attached to the bow by a method that allows it to be adjusted without breaking, either through a spring made in one with the pin and held within the brooch head, or by way of a hinge, held within the head by a hinge-pin; the head is thus required to hold the spring or hinge and to hide either mechanism. If the brooch pin hangs freely then there is the risk of it falling out and being lost; a catchplate is therefore necessary at the end of the bow in order to hold the end of the pin safely whilst also ensuring that the wearer is not continually pricked by the pin's sharp point.

It is very easy with brooches to become absorbed in the decoration and aesthetic appearance of each individual brooch. The wide variety of types and date ranges of brooches make typological analysis very tempting, but to the wearer a brooch might be an essential element in ensuring that clothing was kept in position. Although brooches are invariably included in the jewellery section of a finds report they rarely appear in parures, or jewellery sets, being seen by their owners as more practical than purely decorative. That said, specific types of brooches, such as those worn by women from Noricum, were often worn by specific groups and can be used to trace ethnic identity (Böhme-Schönberger 1997), while their appearance and decoration may often have conveyed more messages to the contemporary viewer than is evident today (see Chapter 9).

The aesthetic quality of a ballpoint pen may depend on the material it is made from and any additional decoration. Archaeological artefacts can vary from the very beautiful to the exceedingly ugly. Aesthetic judgements as to whether an object is attractive or not will be made by each person who sees it and there will invariably be disagreement as to the conclusions. In the past, people will have also disagreed as to what makes an object attractive but may have based their view on ethnic criteria rather than merely on personal taste. In medieval Sudan finger-rings made from a variety of stones, some very coarse and only roughly decorated, were popular. These to modern eyes look ugly as well as uncomfortable (Allason-Jones 1991: 147, fig. 71, nos. 273–5). The appearance of an accurate copy of a Roman trumpet brooch can often horrify museum visitors as being very garish but some items of Roman-period jewellery appeal to the majority of people today. The Aesica Hoard, for example, includes a silver bracelet with an inset cabuchon garnet, which looks remarkably modern, but also includes a silver brooch which measures 18.5 cm, is highly ornamented and must have been very heavy and cumbersome to wear – this brooch, which to the casual glance resembles a door knocker, is unlikely to appeal to most people today, although they may appreciate the workmanship which went in to making the item (Charlesworth 1973).

Some artefacts are capable of providing much information about the society they derive from if one looks carefully at their decoration. Many ballpoint pens have illustrations on them, particularly those bought as souvenirs. Such a find would be a boon to an archaeologist in a thousand years time, as are similarly decorated ancient artefacts found today. The piece of lead waste lightly incised with a sketch of a fort gateway, found at Newcastle upon Tyne, not only provides an illustration, albeit a rough one, of what a fort gateway looked like in the third century AD but also links us

Pl. 4 Carnelian intaglio showing a legionary's panoply of arms with the body armour supported on a cuirass stand

with the bored soldier who had the time and the artistic ability to doodle the gateway of his fort whilst making some repairs with lead (Allason-Jones 2002b: 219, no. 64, fig. 18.4). The carnelian intaglio from High Rochester which is decorated with a panoply of arms is very stylised but is detailed enough to show the stand on which a soldier's cuirass rested – a wooden artefact which must have been common during the Roman period although none has survived (Plate 4; Allason-Jones 1992). The intaglio also tells us that the population at High Rochester in the third century included at least one person with military connections who was wealthy enough to be able to afford a gold ring with an incised semiprecious stone and whose lifestyle required an intaglio to seal documents.

The decoration on an object may not be immediately obvious or necessarily where it can be seen by a casual glance. Some lignite beads from Ashford in Kent were decorated with small dots of gold leaf but this was only discovered when samples of the material were being studied under the microscope (Allason-Jones 1999a). This somewhat ephemeral decoration had not been noted before and could easily have been cleaned off with the covering dirt during primary conservation. The large silver brooch from the Aesica Hoard, mentioned above, is highly decorated on the back; this decoration would not have been seen whilst the brooch was in position and it is unclear whether these details were requested by the owner, were the result of the maker's pride in his work or were due to the reuse of a decorated strip (Charlesworth 1973: 229).

Almost every ballpoint pen has an inscription, even if it just gives the maker's name. The Roman period in Britain was the first in which the names of individuals are known through the medium of inscriptions. Most of these inscriptions are large stone monuments, tombstones, building inscriptions and altars, and these provide invaluable evidence, particularly for the military and religious life of the province of Roman Britain (see Chapter 6). During the twentieth century archaeologists also began to discover writing tablets, particularly at Vindolanda (Bowman and Thomas 1983; 1994; 2003), and curse tablets (Tomlin 1998; Woodward and Leach 1993), which have provided fascinating details of the daily lives of the military as well as the less wealthy members of society who were not able to afford a large stone inscription.

Small finds can also give us the name of their owner. Many simple cooking pots have the owner's name scratched on the base, particularly those found in a military context where it would be easy for a soldier's belongings to be confused with those of one of his colleagues (Plate 21). This need to identify one's belongings also appears on the impressive bronze shield boss found in the river Tyne, reminding us that even objects which appear to us to be exciting and elaborate may have been commonplace in the Roman period, to the point where one had to use name tags to avoid confusion (Plate 20; Allason-Jones and Miket 1984: no. 3.724). Even unusual objects reveal the names of individuals; at Shakenoak an eight-pipe syrinx was found inscribed with the name Bellica (Wright and Hassall 1973: 332, no. 30), whilst at Corbridge gold finger-rings, made by the *opus interrasile* method, record the names of their owners, Aemilia and Polemios (Johns 1996: 60–1).

Significance

The significance of an object for its original owner may be hard to identify and should not be confused with that object's significance for its finder or for the archaeological world at large. Even a ballpoint pen may have sentimental significance if it reminds its owner of an individual or event important to them. Excavations at Housesteads Roman fort revealed a small gold finger-ring inset with a finely carved garnet intaglio of an actor's mask (Plate 36;

Charlesworth 1969). This was found in the stone drain of the lavatory of the Commanding Officer's House. Clearly it was lost whilst the lavatory was in use; unfortunately for the loser, it would have been impossible to recover the ring without dismantling the whole plumbing system and most of the building. The deep irritation that must have been felt at the loss can still be empathised with all these centuries later. Examination of the ring shows that it has a very small oval hoop, which indicates that it cannot have been worn by an adult hand unless it was placed, as was once the fashion, on the first knuckle – a position which must have led to many similar losses in similar circumstances. The ring would have been expensive and the device of an actor's mask suggests a cultivated cosmopolitan wearer; whether this was the Commanding Officer or a wealthy visitor is now impossible to say but does exercise the imagination. The significance of the ring and its subsequent loss to its owner can only be conjectured, as we do not know whether he or she bought it for themselves or if it was a cherished gift from a friend or family member; nor do we know whether the actor's mask was a family crest or a joke or indicated a real interest in the theatre. The significance of the ring for archaeologists lies in its curious shape and size, which leads us to question how it was worn; its use of gold and garnet, which indicates the status of the owner; and its findspot, which throws some light on the life of the officer class on Hadrian's Wall.

One aspect of significance that is often asked of an artefact is whether its use can be attributed to a man or a woman. This is not always as easy to answer as our predecessors presumed (Allason-Jones 1995). Over the years, for example, many archaeologists have endeavoured to assign particular types of brooches to men or women. These exercises have often revealed more about the background and age of the archaeologists than offered any lasting insight into the use of brooches by people in the past. It is very easy to slip into the error of presuming that gender issues remain constant through the ages. A case in point is the Roman attitude to ear-rings. To the Roman writers no respectable Roman man would ever wear ear-rings, as these were seen to be effeminate or, worse, the decoration of barbarians. If one relies solely on the evidence of the contemporary literature it would be easy to presume that the discovery of ear-rings in a Roman context indicates the presence of women. However, if one looks at the coinage of the eastern rulers from the first century BC to the fifth century AD it is clear that they all wore ear-rings and that in the eastern provinces and amongst Rome's eastern and southern neighbours the wearing of ear-rings by men was an indicator of high rank. The Roman army included many men from the eastern and African provinces and there is no evidence to indicate whether a serving auxiliary was specifically barred from wearing his ethnic ear-rings. It is always important to remember when looking at the material culture of Roman Britain that this was a very cosmopolitan society, with people present from all over the known world, so what was the norm for the city of Rome or for pre-Roman Britain may not have been the norm for all the province's inhabitants.

This cosmopolitan aspect of life in Roman Britain would have altered through time as new people arrived, bringing new ideas and artefacts which can contribute to the evidence dating a site; for example, most of the glass armlets found on native settlements in the north of England provide evidence that those sites are to be dated to the Roman occupation of the area as the glass they are made from was recycled from Roman vessels. Archaeologists can become very obsessed with being able to date artefacts precisely and few objects can help in this quest with the necessary precision. Some objects changed little in appearance over time whilst some types or individual examples may have been in circulation for generations. Objects can be found outside their dated context, either because that context has been contaminated or because the object was already an antique when it was deposited. Objects which are fragile, such as pottery or glass, tend to be discarded when broken and may appear to offer very firm dates, but if these objects were well cared for by their owners or placed in a context where they were less likely to have received rough treatment, they may have been very old when finally discarded or deposited. It is also known that people in the past could have an interest in their ancestors and occasionally collected old items; Cicero, for example, is known to have had a collection of Greek pottery. It may be recalled that few people threw out many or any of their possessions at midnight on 31 January 1999. Everyone today will have objects in their homes that are of twentieth- and twenty-first-century date, many will have nineteenth-century objects, whilst others will have objects dating from the eighteenth century or before; the people of Roman Britain may have had an equally wide date range of artefacts in their houses.

Context

An object may have many contexts between its initial manufacture and its eventual discovery. Its primary context will reflect the use for which it was originally made, whilst its secondary context may indicate its reuse through recycling. For example, a square glass bottle may have been made to transport liquids – this might lead to its being found in a shipwreck or in a domestic setting; that is its primary context. However, once its contents had been used the same glass bottle might be reused as a cinerary urn – its discovery in a burial would find it in its secondary context (Plate 53). The bottle might, however, also be found in a tertiary context, its post-depositional context, where the bottle has been moved with the rest of the burial, for example, to the filling of a ditch. When using context to identify the purpose of an object it is, therefore, essential to consider whether that object has been found in its primary, secondary or post-depositional context.

If an archaeologist in a future excavation found a ballpoint pen lying on a desk by a copy of a daily newspaper with a half-completed crossword, it would not require a great effort of imagination to identify the purpose of that pen. The desk is the pen's primary context and the daily newspaper is an associated artefact; both context and associated artefacts should be considered when objects are being identified. This leads to the tricky question of deposition: how the objects got into the ground in the first place.

In the case of Pompeii or Herculaneum, it is clear that the majority of the artefacts were found *in situ* because in AD 79 Vesuvius erupted, with the result that the inhabitants fled, leaving behind their household goods; the fact that some of those residents were themselves engulfed in the pyroclastic flow or by thick layers of ash indicates that there was little time to select objects to rescue. In Roman Britain such major catastrophes are rarely the reason for objects being found in archaeological contexts, although localised flooding or fire can have a similar result, as at South Shields fort where one of the barrack buildings was subject to a fire at its east end leading to the roof and some of the walls collapsing, sealing the contents (Hodgson 2005).

In 1989 Mike Bishop considered the subject of deposition in regard to military equipment and concluded that there were six reasons why military objects were deposited: concealment, burial rites, dedications, battles, booty and, finally, chance; this discussion is developed in Chapter 5. To Bishop's original list may be added a catastrophic event, as mentioned above, or abandonment because the object is broken or no longer has any value. In the latter case, only objects that cannot be recycled or reused for another purpose are usually thrown on to the rubbish heap and, as Bishop pointed out, 'only items which were susceptible to damage in the first place stood a chance of ending up in the ground' in these circumstances (Bishop 1989: 1); in other words, objects that were not damaged would be handed on or sold and remain in circulation.

Concealment is invariably the reason why coin hoards and hoards of jewellery, such as the Hoxne Hoard or the Snettisham Hoard, were deposited, particularly in the fourth century AD when an increasing sense of insecurity led people to hide away their valuables. Even individual objects may have been secreted away to keep them safe or to hide stolen goods. At Inchtuthil, in Scotland, the systematic stripping of the fort and concealment of fixtures and fittings, particularly bags of nails, when the army left the site may have been intended to deny the enemy anything that might be useful but alternatively may simply be an illustration of military thoroughness (Pitts and St. Joseph 1985).

Equally deliberate is the process of burying objects in graves to provide the deceased with the items needed for their journey to the afterlife or to equip them once they had arrived. Less deliberate may be the deposition of wine containers or cups in the immediate area of the grave – it is not always clear whether these were for the benefit of the deceased or were the remnants of the funerary feast or graveside rituals abandoned on the site at the end of the ceremonies (see Chapter 13).

Dedicating objects to the gods was a practice in Britain before the Roman invasion and continued throughout the pagan periods of the Roman occupation. If these dedications are found within the precincts of a temple or shrine then the reason for the deposition may be clear, but when objects are found in rivers or in wells there can be much debate as to why they are there (Curle 1911; Ross 1968).

Soldiers may have dedicated objects to the deities before a battle in an attempt to engage the gods' support or dedicated items after a battle in gratitude for having survived, but remarkably few objects are found actually on the battlefields themselves. This is largely due to the tendency throughout history for armies (officially) or scavengers (unofficially) to strip the fallen of their valuables before burial, but may also be due to the difficulty in finding battlefields, except by serendipity, with the result that few battlefields have been systematically excavated.

After the battle was won the victorious army would help themselves to the spoils of war. Booty is to be seen piled up on Trajan's Column and it is known that the valuables taken from defeated nations played an important part in the triumphal processions which were so popular with Roman emperors and military leaders. These would have been stored, dedicated to a deity or distributed amongst the favoured after display. Individual soldiers would also have collected trophies to take back home and these may lead to alien artefacts being found within domestic or funerary contexts.

Chance and probability play a part in everyone's life. A soldier picking up an enemy's sword on a battlefield has been subject to chance and probability in being there in the first place; the sword's original owner has been equally a plaything of fate in his loss of the sword. Accidental loss is a factor in deposition, although not always as large an element as is often supposed. It is noticeable that the coins found on road surfaces are usually the smaller denominations. If one drops a large coin one is likely to hear it drop; if one loses a valuable coin one may well retrace one's steps in an effort to find it, and this may be so of any type of artefact. It is, however, remarkably difficult to lose a large object such as a shield. The shield bosses found in the turrets on Hadrian's Wall cannot have been simply misplaced. Presuming that the bosses were still attached to wooden shields, which would have been waist high, it is unlikely that they could have been lost in a building that measured some 14 feet internally (4.7 metres). It is far more convincing that they were deliberately abandoned when the turrets themselves were abandoned or that they were spare bosses which were not attached to shields (Allason-Jones 1988).

There are innumerable reasons why objects find themselves in archaeo-logical deposits, and many will be discussed in the ensuing chapters, but it is important to consider the part that people played in deposition. Any situation that involves human beings can be misinterpreted because each person is different and will act differently in given circumstances. Occasionally objects will have arrived at their final resting place for reasons that are impossible to identify. Some years ago a colleague declared that he had discovered the reason behind the many coin hoards to be found in Roman Britain. His infant daughter had developed a habit of taking coins whenever she found them and posting them down a slit between the floorboards of their living room. When the floorboards were taken up, there were small coin hoards waiting to be discovered. No archaeologist of the future is likely to interpret the deposition processes correctly in such a case.

Conclusions

Context helps to identify objects, although most archaeologists prefer to use the objects to identify the context and this can be very dangerous. When using artefacts to show what a particular building or site was used for, the identification of those objects must be accurate and the analysis of their significance must be as free from bias as possible. All archaeologists bring their own lives and backgrounds with them when studying the past; this is unavoidable, but it is important that everyone studying the past is aware of this and makes due provision.

The people of the past also had opinions, biases, likes and dislikes, and their own ideas of what was appropriate in a given circumstance. During the Roman period Britain was part of an Empire that stretched from North Britain to the Sahara Desert and from Land's End to present-day Iraq. Throughout that Empire there were different peoples with different tastes and expectations, and representatives of all these tribes and ethnic units appeared in Britain in varying numbers. This led to Roman Britain being an extraordinarily cosmopolitan place, and this mixed, even exotic, milieu is reflected in the range of objects to be found in excavations. A high proportion of those people were literate and absorbed new ideas through their reading, or exchanged ideas with people they met, with the result that the assemblage of objects owned by an individual may be confined to the types of objects to be expected of someone from, say, Yorkshire in the third century but might also include a brooch made in the Rhineland, a glass vessel from Alexandria or a coin minted in Trier without necessarily suggesting a close association between that individual and the Rhineland, Alexandria or Trier.

It is important, when dealing with finds, to remember that they are our link with the past and often all that remains after the destructive process of excavation. Every object found was designed for a purpose, either by its owner or by a craftworker answering a market need. The object must have been necessary enough for someone to design it or its prototype, spend time manufacturing it, or money in buying it or the raw materials needed to make it. Every object will have its history of manufacture and use; not every object will have had only one use before being discarded. Every object found by archaeologists also had a reason for its deposition or breakage or loss, in the latter case possibly to the great inconvenience of its owner.

1 | Commerce

R. J. BRICKSTOCK

This chapter is concerned with the artefacts associated with the commercial life of Roman Britain, that is, the sale and purchase of goods and services, normally for profit.

If an exchange was conducted by barter, by which we normally mean a direct exchange of one commodity for another, the objects themselves were the medium for that exchange. If, however, the objects were exchanged by buying and selling in a more sophisticated way (by some form of three-way exchange), the medium of exchange was normally coinage.

Artefacts from Roman Britain that may be associated with commercial activities include:

- any object that could be exchanged for something else, a definition that encompasses both animals (including humans) and inanimate objects;
- the objects used to weigh and/or measure the items exchanged – weights, balances and the like;
- the medium for effecting the exchange of items, which was normally coinage;
- the objects used in the manufacture of coins (and counterfeit coinage).

The first of these categories, the archaeological remains of the various objects traded within Roman Britain, is well covered by the other chapters in this book. This chapter will therefore concentrate on the remaining three categories and on coinage in particular.

What is a coin?

In modern English the words 'money' and 'currency' are almost interchangeable: we all use money; and our currency is made up of coins and bank notes. Virtually any commodity – metal ingots, animals, even sea-shells – can be used as currency, the medium for effecting exchange; what is important is that the objects are of a known and recognised value.

In the ancient world the chosen commodity was frequently a metal: gold, silver or a base-metal alloy, transformed into a lump of bullion produced to a standard weight. A mark of value might be scratched or stamped on the metal by the producer, but even so the receiving party did not necessarily accept the sign at face value because he did not necessarily trust the producer; the transaction was therefore complicated by the need to test the metal received to confirm its bullion content and thus its value.

The next development was a stamp or inscription that could be trusted, a mark placed on the object by the issuing authority (normally the state) to guarantee the value. With the presence (and recognition) of this guarantee the object became a coin.

Today we use an entirely token currency and there is no presumption that a one pound coin contains one pound's worth of metal. This was not so in the ancient world. Coins were normally slightly over-valued, to cover production costs and to allow the issuing authority to accrue a profit, but their face value was almost always very similar to the intrinsic value of the bullion from which they were made.

It should be appreciated, however, that early coins might only function as true coins within the territory of the issuing authority; outside those geographical limits the state guarantee was often not recognised and thus effectively worthless. Coins passing into a neighbour's territory were frequently treated as lumps of bullion (currency) to be melted down and reused. To a degree, therefore, the geographical extent of a nation's political power may be gauged by mapping the area from which its coinage is recovered. The might of the Roman Empire was such that its coins were accepted not only throughout the territory over which it ruled but also for considerable distances beyond its borders, demonstrating the level of Roman influence over neighbouring states.

The invention and spread of coinage

Coinage appears to have been invented in about 600 BC in Lydia in Asia Minor and by the end of the sixth century BC most of the Greek city states, including those of Sicily and southern Italy, were making and using coins.

We do not know why coinage was invented, or indeed why it should have been first produced at that particular time and in that particular location. Some scholars believe that from the outset it was intended to facilitate trading transactions, but at present the most widely favoured theory is that it was conceived as a convenient way of paying foreign (mostly Greek) mercenaries. Such an idea was presumably convenient to both giver and receiver: the state could produce the coins without tremendous effort, and

Table 1 The Augustan coinage system (after Casey 1984)

Aureus (gold)	Denarius (silver)	Sestertius (brass)	Dupondius (brass)	As (copper)	Semis (brass)	Quadrans (copper)
1	25	100	200	400	800	1,600
	1	4	8	16	32	64
		1	2	4	8	16
			1	2	4	8
				1	2	4
					1	2
						1

the mercenaries would find it much easier to return home carrying a small weight of stamped bullion rather than, for example, driving a few head of cattle.

It is probably no accident that the foremost Greek trading nations (Corinth, Aegina and Athens) were also the first to produce their own coins, for the Greeks appear to have used their coins for trading purposes from the start. Even so, for a century or more there were no very small denominations suitable for everyday purchases in the marketplace, so coin use must initially have been confined to fairly major transactions.

The Romans probably first encountered coinage via the city states of southern Italy, but they did not adopt any form of coinage of their own until the third century BC. Their first coins consisted of very heavy bronze weights, which must have proved rather impractical; later in the third century these were superseded by a system of gold, silver and bronze coins on the Greek model.

The basic unit of the Roman coinage system was the silver denarius, introduced in 213 BC. It formed the backbone of an extremely stable currency that endured throughout the remainder of the Roman Republic and the first two centuries of imperial rule. Thus the denarius was a usable and useful denomination until the mid-third century AD, a period of more than 400 years; this is the earliest Roman denomination to appear in Romano-British contexts.

The first Roman Emperor, Augustus (31 BC–AD 14), extended and regularised the Roman coinage system, producing a system suitable for all types of transaction, from international trade right down to the purchase of everyday trifles in the marketplace (see Table 1). This coinage was used throughout the Roman Empire and was also accepted for trading purposes in many areas outside its borders.

The spending power of modern British denominations, introduced in 1971, is being eroded by price inflation, with the result that the ½p coin has been withdrawn altogether and the 1p and 2p coins are now of little practical use. Exactly the same happened to the Roman coinage: during the first and second centuries AD the Augustan system, outlined in Table 1, continued in use, but over time inflation, albeit at very low levels, reduced the buying power of the various denominations. The smallest coins became less and less useful and eventually ceased to circulate.

The result of price inflation, in both ancient and modern contexts, is the abandonment of the smaller denominations and their replacement in the currency pool by coins of greater face value. Since, unlike most modern nations, the Romans did not use a token currency, inflation required ever-increasing quantities of valuable bullion; transactions which were once made using base-metal fractions of the silver denarius came to require the exchange of whole denarii.

In the third century AD various crises, both internal and external, hit the Empire and this had a disastrous effect on the currency. Supplies of fresh bullion for the production of coinage became increasingly hard to obtain and the state responded by debasing the silver currency, a move which eventually precipitated the collapse of the Augustan currency system.

In the late third and fourth centuries there were frequent attempts to re-establish a stable currency system and almost as many failures. The detail of these developments is well covered by a number of modern authors; perhaps the clearest introductions are those of Casey (1984) and Reece (2002).

Roman coinage in Britain

In southern Britain, the late Iron Age tribes produced their own coinage imitating that of Greece and Rome. Iron Age rulers, however, were generally more concerned with their own prestige than with the provision of a useful medium of exchange; accordingly, the range of coin denominations was limited and, as a result, the coinage was of limited use. When the Romans under the Emperor Claudius (AD 41–54) invaded Britain in AD 43 they brought with them their own coinage and this much more versatile system was rapidly adopted throughout the new province of Britannia.

All the Augustan denominations are found on Romano-British sites, though gold coins are largely confined to hoards, quite simply because if you drop something of high value you are likely to spend time hunting for it rather than letting it lie. The two lowest coin denominations are also relatively uncommon in Britain but for an entirely different reason: stable though the currency was, by the time of the invasion inflation had largely driven them out of circulation. This phenomenon is reflected in the pattern of finds recovered on sites throughout the province: coin deposits in first-century levels tend to be dominated by the as and the dupondius; by the mid-second century the sestertius begins to take over; and by the early third century the denarius is more commonly found than any of its fractions.

The debasement of the silver currency in the later second and third centuries is visible in the archaeological record in several ways:

- Very few coins tend to be recovered from early third-century levels because silver was hoarded and base-metal denominations had largely been driven from circulation by inflation.
- The coins that are found in early third-century levels are mostly denarii, a fair percentage of them counterfeit.
- The denarius is replaced by the antoninianus or 'radiate' (probably a 2-denarius piece) as the dominant coin-type of the middle and later third-century levels.
- On virtually all sites there is a sudden explosion in the number of site finds from the AD 260s and 270s. This was not because of a massive increase in economic activity but rather because the silver content of the 'radiate' had been reduced to a ridiculously low level; the coin ceased to be recognised as a silver currency by its users, who thereafter treated it as a copper coin and, since the purchasing power of copper was very low, a lot more coins were suddenly needed to make the same number of transactions.
- Partly as a result of the above, there was a chronic shortage of small change in the AD 270s. Huge numbers of 'radiate copies' were therefore produced in Britain (and various other provinces of the Empire) to alleviate the shortage, and these copies are recovered in large quantities from sites throughout the province.

The instability of the bronze coinage of the late third and fourth centuries, characterized by a lengthy succession of short-lived coin issues, is readily apparent in the numismatic assemblages of Romano-British sites. Relatively large and valuable coins tend to be found in only small numbers; while the smaller, less valuable issues can often be found in superabundance. The number of coins recovered is much more a result of the vagaries of the imperial currency system than a measure of the level of economic activity on a given site at any given time.

Thus, if we plot the coin finds from any site occupied throughout the Romano-British period, the same overall pattern of finds will be observed: variable, but relatively low peaks for the years up to *c.*AD 260 (when the Augustan system collapsed), followed by a series of much more dramatic peaks and troughs. Most of these correspond to economic or numismatic events, but a number of political events (some of wide significance, others relating solely to Britannia) have left their archaeological imprint as well. These also need to be taken into account when interpreting a numismatic assemblage.

All events, whether political, economic or numismatic, will, in one way or another, have had an effect on the pattern of coin deposition – and this in turn will, of course, dictate the range of coinage potentially available for recovery by archaeologists. As a result, it is essential to appreciate the 'normal' pattern of coin deposition (the 'background noise' if you like) before attempting to interpret the finds from an individual site – for what one is trying to do is spot variations from the norm (in mathematical terms, deviations from the mean), variations that might require an archaeological, rather than economic or political, explanation.

What do Roman coins look like?

In theory a coin can be virtually any shape or size so long as it contains the necessary guarantee of value. In practice, coins in the western tradition, including Roman coins, are almost always circular discs. Roman coins, however, are uneven in shape, because of the method of manufacture and anything precisely round or obviously machine-made may be readily dismissed as modern and/or fake.

Roman coins found in Britain vary in diameter from about 35 mm down to about 12 mm and in weight from over 20 g to less than 1 g. Contemporary copies are often very much smaller still, frequently less than 10 mm and occasionally down to 2 mm across and a fraction of a gram in weight. The biggest coins may be 4 or 5 mm thick, the smallest less than 1 mm.

A number of metals were used for coin production – gold, silver and various copper alloys – and soil conditions and the resulting corrosion products can radically alter the colour of the coin as we see it today. Gold coinage is relatively unaffected by its surroundings and normally looks golden when recovered, but silver coinage can range from silver to black or purple, depending on the nature of the surface corrosion products. Silver

Pl. 5 Sestertius of Hadrian, found in the river Tyne at Newcastle. The reverse legend celebrates the 'happiness of the emperor' (FELICITATI AVG). The letters COS III PP imply a mint date of AD 128–38 as Hadrian held the consulship for the third time in AD 119 and accepted the title *Pater Patriae* early in AD 128.

debased with copper or other metals is normally more badly affected and harder to clean than purer silver.

A significant percentage of coinage deposited has undoubtedly been destroyed altogether by corrosion over the centuries and the copper-alloy coinage (called 'bronze' by numismatists) suffers most of all. Even when a coin does survive it can be virtually unrecognisable because of corrosion products on its surfaces. Copper coins that are actively corroding look blue-green or green; the majority, when they come out of the ground, look dark green or dirty brown where once they were polished bronze.

Exceptions to this rule are the sestertii and other coins made of orichalcum (brass), which were originally a bright golden colour. Advantageous soil conditions (e.g. the anaerobic conditions encountered in the lower levels at Vindolanda and Carlisle) may preserve such coins in almost pristine condition and coloration, though they more frequently appear dull reddish-brown or even various shades of greenish-brown when recovered; as a result, brass dupondii may be hard to distinguish from copper asses.

Virtually all Roman coins carried both types and legends, the type being the general design (the picture) and the legend being the inscription (the lettering). On coins of the imperial period, which make up the vast majority of Roman coin finds on British sites, the 'head' side (the obverse) normally carried the ruler's portrait and titles, which can sometimes provide useful dating evidence (Plate 5). The obverse was also normally the side of the

Pl. 6 Silver denarius of Geta, minted AD 210–12, bearing the obverse legend P SEPT GETA PIVS AVG BRIT and reverse legend VICTORIAE BRIT. Septimius Severus and his sons Caracalla and Geta all took the title 'Britannicus' in late 209/10 and coins were struck to celebrate their victories.

coin struck by the lower die: this frequently resulted in a slightly convex appearance, a fact which may sometimes be used to distinguish the obverse from the reverse on a corroded specimen.

The reverse (the 'tails' or 'flip' side of the coin) was, conversely, normally struck with the upper die, which could give it a somewhat concave appearance. A wide variety of types appeared on the reverse of Roman coins, but there was often a strong propaganda element to the designs, which were used by the state to emphasise the benefits of Roman rule, the virtues of the Emperor, his links with the gods, the loyalty of his armies and other such themes, which sometimes represented the hope rather than the reality. Events and regions of the Empire are also commemorated: a whole series of coins were struck, for example, celebrating Claudius' conquest of Britain; the personification of Britannia, familiar to modern British audiences from the 50p coin, appeared first on a coin of Hadrian; and a number of issues carrying legends such as VICT BRIT (or VICTORIAE BRIT) appear to record other military triumphs in Britain (Plate 6).

Viewed as art, Roman coins often leave something to be desired, but they nonetheless offer very useful insights into, for example, imperial dress and hairstyles as they changed over time. It must be remembered, however, that the portraits of the Emperors are almost certainly idealised rather than accurate, as indeed are all the types portrayed; these are the images that the regime wished its subjects to see rather than the unvarnished truth.

Identifying Roman coins

The identification of Roman coinage is beyond the scope of this work – but Roman coin types have been exhaustively catalogued over the last century and good catalogues and guides are readily available:

- The best catalogues are *Roman Republican Coinage* (Crawford 1974), and the ten-volume *Roman Imperial Coinage* (Mattingly and Sydenham 1923–94).
- For simple guidelines for identifying coins, see Reece and James 1986; 2nd edn 2000, and Marsden 2001.
- For brief introductions to coins generally and to the interpretation of coin finds, see Casey 1986, Burnett 1991, and Cooper 1998.
- For the English Heritage guide to *The Production, Analysis and Standard-isation of Romano-British Coin Reports*, see Brickstock 2004.
- For coinage in Roman Britain, see Casey 1984, de Jersey 1996 and, the most up-to-date discussion, Reece 2002.

How were Roman coins made?

Roman coins, like Greek, were struck or hammered. Typically, the metal or metals required to produce the desired alloy were heated together in a clay crucible placed in a furnace. The molten metal that resulted was poured into a series of coin-sized clay moulds. Any impurities floated to the top of the moulds and could be scooped away. The resulting casts could be hammered if necessary to flatten and further shape them to produce the blanks, or flans, from which the coins would be made.

A coin was produced using two dies made of bronze or hardened iron into which the desired design had been cut in negative. The blank was heated (to soften it) and placed on an anvil holding the lower die; the other die was then held over the blank and struck with a heavy hammer to create the coin.

Virtually all regular Roman coins were made in this way. They were mass-produced, in the sense that a large number of coins could be made from a pair of dies in a relatively short space of time, but they were also produced individually and thus show slight variations, both in the shape of the flan and in the way they were struck. We do not know how many coins were made from any given set of dies; there may have been a set number, or the dies may have been used to extinction. We do know that many faulty coins were produced, with the most obvious being 'double-struck', either because the hammer bounced and thereby produced a second image or because the flan was inadvertently used twice; or stuck on one side only because two blanks were mistakenly placed together between the dies and each therefore received only one image.

Copies could be, and generally were, produced in the same way as the regular coinage, and the copying of coins was a common phenomenon in Roman times. There were four main episodes of copying in Roman Britain:

- Claudian copies, produced *c.*AD 44–64;
- 'radiate' copies, produced in the AD 270s and 280s, copying issues of *c.*AD 260–73;
- Constantinian copies, produced *c.*AD 341–46, copying issues of *c.*AD 330–41;
- copies of Constantius II's coinage, produced in the AD 350s.

In all these cases, although the makers were no doubt happy to generate a profit through their industry, the main intention was to generate additional small change. Such copies were almost certainly locally made, perhaps by individuals within the military and/or civilian community that required them.

Sometimes copies were made by reusing old and obsolete coins rather than blank flans, striking a new design over the old. If the re-striking was done imperfectly the old design can still be seen; numismatists call this an 'overstrike'. However, most copies were made using blank flans, though these were often much smaller than those of the regular coinage. Copies were often also very crudely executed, there being no real need to deceive anybody into thinking they were the real thing; as a result, copies could be as small as 2 mm in diameter and bear only a tiny proportion of the original design carried by their prototypes.

Numismatists make a clear distinction between copies and counterfeits. Counterfeits were imitation coins, intended (unlike copies) to be indistinguishable from their prototypes. Their purpose was (presumably) to defraud both the issuing authority and the public and thereby generate a profit for the producers. Counterfeits could be produced by striking: the sixth-century Theodosian Code preserves an edict dated AD 349 (*Codex Theod.* IX.21.6) which specifically forbids mint workers from extracting silver from the alloy before striking coins, making it clear that they must have been striking coins of inferior alloy and pocketing the profit.

Most counterfeits, however, were cast. They were made using pairs of clay moulds into which genuine denarii had been pressed to make impressions in negative. The moulds were then baked to harden them and stacked in line. Molten metal was poured into the moulds via a small pipe and the resulting casts allowed to solidify. The metal alloy used could be debased silver, rather than the purer silver of the prototype; or it could be a copper alloy containing no silver at all. In the latter instance the cast needed to be surface plated in some way, perhaps by dipping in silver alloy, or at least a silver-coloured alloy, to make it look like a silver coin. Counterfeits made in this fashion could be produced by private individuals in almost any location, for the technology required was not very advanced. Baked clay moulds have been found in Britain in a number of places, both major cities, such as York, and minor settlements, such as the *vicus* outside Housesteads fort in Northumberland. Related artefacts include items such as crucibles and scrap metal.

There are a number of ways in which these ancient counterfeits may be detected, though it is possible many of the best may remain unidentified. The method of manufacture often left behind clues, for example:

- an uneven lip on one edge of the coin, formed when metal remaining in the pipe solidified;
- a join-line all around the edge of the coin where the two halves of the mould met;
- file marks around the edge where the counterfeiter attempted to disguise the join-line.

Many counterfeits tarnished over time and thus were soon revealed as forgeries. Nearly two thousand years in the soil can also have an effect; counterfeit coins made by coating a copper core with a more 'silvery' metal are sometimes betrayed to the modern eye by differential corrosion between the various layers of the coin: the copper corrodes more actively than the silver over time and, as result, can 'explode' outwards, forcing the surface plating apart.

Contemporary counterfeiters could also be quite careless about making sure that the two halves of a coin matched correctly; if, for example, the 'head' side of a coin shows the Emperor Septimius Severus (AD 193–211) but the 'tails' side is of a type used not by Severus but by one of his successors, the coin is almost certainly counterfeit. Ancient coins have also been counterfeited in modern times, normally with the aim of producing a unique, and therefore valuable, combination of types. Modern counterfeiters, therefore, do by design what the contemporary forgers seemingly did by accident.

Modern chemical analysis and/or techniques of surface analysis such as X-ray Fluorescence analysis can sometimes be used to detect counterfeits, revealing variations in the alloy and, in particular, the presence or absence of particular metals that should, or should not, be present in the regular alloy.

What were Roman coins for?

Before we move on to the interpretation of coin finds (i.e. the significance of coinage to the archaeologist), it is also important to consider the contemporary significance of these objects: what were they for, and why and in what ways were they important to the Romano-British public?

Roman coins were produced for a specific purpose: to pay people, in particular the army and what we would now call the civil service, the staff of the provincial governors and other officials. This is because the Roman state was primarily interested in the loyalty of its soldiers and officials and hardly interested at all in the workings of its 'monetary economy' (a phrase seemingly foreign to Roman thinking). Coins, quite incidentally, passed into more general circulation and were subsequently used by a much wider cross-section of society for day-to-day trade and (an important element) for the payment of taxes.

Coinage was produced in various mints in the western half of the Empire, from where they were supplied to Britain. Under the early Empire, much of the coinage was produced in Rome itself or in one of a very few other mints, including Lugdunum (Lyons) in Gaul. In the fourth century most of the coinage supplied to Britain was the product of the Gaulish mints, especially Trier but also Lyons and Arles. London's mint, opened in the AD 280s, was closed down in AD 325/6 and produced only bronzes. By the AD 350s the output of Trier was being drastically downgraded for political reasons, and Britain, increasingly, drew its coins from Lyons and Arles, then largely from Arles. In the last years of the fourth century AD, however, the sources of supply were still more remote: Arles, Aquileia and Rome.

The amount of coinage supplied to Britain was directly related to the size of workforce that needed to be paid. Roman imperial salaries, measured in hundreds of denarii in the early imperial period, were paid in silver or (for higher ranks with higher salaries) gold, presumably for the convenience of the state rather than that of the recipients. Thus the imperial authorities ensured that, in their own interests, the supply of precious-metal coin to the provinces was fairly regular both in quantity and in frequency.

This coinage had, of course, to be shipped to Britain from the Continent. Cross-channel sailing was a hazardous business, an undertaking no doubt confined, if at all possible, to the shortest routes and the summer months. Once in the country, the coinage had to be distributed, but distribution of coinage from a point of entry at, say, London or Richborough, would have required lengthy and laborious journeys using carts or pack animals. In order to deliver coins to the northern frontier, therefore, a more attractive option may well have been a coastal voyage to a more northerly port, such as Brough-on-Humber or South Shields. However it was achieved, the distribution of coinage must have been geographically rather uneven, since the vast majority presumably went to the legionary fortresses, the administrative centres and the frontier forts. Once there, however, coins could begin to pass into general circulation.

The amount of coinage involved was huge – millions of denarii per annum – though a percentage may never have reached the forum or fort strongroom, or indeed have been despatched at all; if so, of course, this element would leave no subsequent trace in the archaeological record. Even if the full amount of coinage required to pay the troops actually reached the forts, not all of it reached the troops themselves because, in the early imperial period, various deductions were made at source, to pay for a soldier's food, clothing and equipment. Corn was purchased in bulk by the army, at a fixed rate, from local producers. Some buying may have been done at a very local level or possibly at a regional level but probably not (for purely practical reasons) at a provincial level. If buying took place at a regional level, much of the money due to each unit need never have completed the final leg of its journey.

Payments made by the unit were presumably made in coins of various denominations, which then passed immediately into the civilian economy. The remaining element of an individual soldier's salary could be used at will and would thereby also pass into other hands in exchange for all manner of transactions.

Over time, inflation eroded the value of the military *stipendium*, and, since periodic pay rises failed to keep pace with inflation, essential items eventually came to be provided in addition to the stipendium, as a second, and important, element of a soldier's salary. There is little indication that additional supplies of coin were provided for this purpose: the action of the system known as the *annona militaris* probably involved at least a proportion of local collection of taxation in kind, providing food and equipment direct from producer to supplier without any requirement for coins to change hands.

The final element of the later Roman military income was imperial accession and quinquennial donatives, both of which could be described as blatant but effective bribery to buy the loyalty of the armies. These payments were certainly promised in the form of gold and silver, and we have no reason to doubt that they were supplied in the form of precious-metal coinage, delivered to each fort. However, this is not easily assessed numismatically. Very little gold or silver coinage is recovered in the form of individual site finds and the distribution of precious-metal hoards does not necessarily give an accurate reflection of coin circulation.

The gold and silver coins in which both military and civilian salaries and donatives were paid were high denominations, not really suitable for everyday purchases in the marketplace. Small change was therefore required, but that was not delivered to Britain with anything like the same regularity or reliability.

Imperial control over the base-metal currency was much less rigid; indeed, there were times when it seems to have been deliberately ignored and production reduced almost to zero (e.g. in the period *c.*AD 44–64). The Senate was, at least notionally, allowed to oversee the production of the fractional coinage right the way through to the mid-third century, and SC, for *senatus consultum*, appears on sestertii and smaller fractions throughout their period of production. Thereafter, the imperial authorities exercised direct control over the production of small change: the antoninianus and succeeding denominations were technically silver currencies, albeit of a much debased alloy, and so fell within the imperial ambit.

Local needs were presumably met by moneychangers, changing large denominations into smaller ones, but the mechanism by which they obtained their small change is much less clear. There is little indication that base-metal coinage was produced simply because it was regarded as an essential, or even useful, commodity. It may have been sent to Britain by official consignment or it may have been left to individual entrepreneurs to import and distribute it as they saw fit. Accordingly, one should probably envisage charges at each stage of the process. The moneychanger would be buying at a premium, a premium which he would pass on, with interest, to his customers in the marketplace.

Just how general was the use of coinage, therefore? Coins do seem to have become an everyday commodity, though most people would not have dealt in gold other than for the payment of the ancient equivalent of the poll tax. The pattern of finds suggests that coinage became an essential medium of exchange, used for trade at all levels. Base-metal coinage is found throughout Roman Britain, though in greater quantities in some contexts than in others, and while virtually all sites in the province conform to an overall pattern of site finds, different types of site present variations on the theme and archaeologists are able to recognise the numismatic footprint of a range of different types of sites (military/civilian, religious/secular, urban/rural, etc.).

As a general rule, coins are most commonly recovered from urban contexts, particularly the marketplaces of towns and other areas of obvious commercial activity, e.g. the mills excavated at Ickham in Kent. Considerable quantities are also found in forts and the settlements that grew up outside them and at religious sites, such as the temple of Nodens at Lydney, which attracted offerings in small change in the same way as wishing wells and church collection plates still do today. Various other sites, such as villas and native-style farmsteads, however, tend to produce rather smaller numbers of coins, although this is probably not because the inhabitants were not coin users (for all were, perforce, taxpayers) but because they made the majority of their transactions elsewhere.

In the fourth century in particular, the small change performed another, very significant, function in which the state had an interest: citizens were required by the state to produce their poll tax (1 solidus annually) in gold coin (Jones 1964), but the fractional coinage provided a way of saving up towards that rather substantial sum. This provides a ready explanation for some very large hoards of base-metal coinage of the late third and fourth centuries AD. The state can therefore at this date be expected to have attached some importance to the provision of small change and, as a result, the primary destination of consignments of bronze coinage may have switched from the military to the civilian context. In other words, the Roman state machinery cared little for the everyday convenience of its citizens in their economic activities; coin supply was geared almost entirely to the twin aims of paying out money where it was needed to buy loyalty, and then clawing back as much precious metal as it could. Whether the base metal came back again was probably not of particular concern.

All this goes a long way towards helping us understand the periodic interruptions in base-metal coin supply visible, at certain times, in Roman Britain, and also in various other (equally peripheral) parts of the Empire. The base-metal currency was, in some respects at least, less tightly controlled than the gold and silver, and it might be quite some time before an interruption in supply was corrected because the purpose for supplying coin differed from the desire to alleviate a shortage of small change that might inconvenience users of the marketplaces in settlements such as Wroxeter, Corbridge or Aldborough.

However, it is quite clear, from the pattern of finds recovered from Romano-British sites, that when a shortage of small change arose, somebody – locally – felt the need to do something about it; hence the wholesale copying of contemporary small change already referred to in the AD 50s and 60s; again in the AD 270s and 280s; again in the 340s; and yet again in the 350s. This in turn suggests that the inhabitants of Roman Britain found the possession of small change more or less essential (at least at those times). This makes it all the more curious that when official supplies of Roman coin ceased to enter Britain in *c*.AD 400, nobody saw the need to produce more small change. The answer may be that the cessation of direct imperial control in the early fifth century also spelled the end of tax collection in the usual manner (if not altogether) and thus the removal of what had certainly once been one of the primary functions of the base-metal coinage.

Deposition and recovery

Our knowledge of the supply and distribution of coinage, based largely on the precious-metal coinage, is patchy but fairly extensive and from that knowledge we can speculate fairly intelligently about the subsequent circulation of coinage within the province. From there, however, it is something of a leap to the coinage deposited and a further leap to the coinage recovered from sites, for that (hoards excepted) is almost exclusively made up of small change, the 1p and 2p pieces of the ancient world.

Hundreds, thousands and occasionally tens of thousands of coins have been recovered from Romano-British sites but these represent only a very tiny fraction of the coinage in circulation at the time. Luckily, however, there is a consistency in the pattern of coin finds, both nationally and regionally, that suggests a significant relationship between patterns of circulation, deposition and recovery.

The Introduction to this book suggests that only those items that cannot be recycled or reused are thrown on the rubbish heap. This was certainly true of Roman coinage, for the vast majority of coins were not deposited but were reclaimed by the treasury and reused, either to strike further coins or for other purposes.

The list of possible reasons for the deposition of artefacts given in the Introduction also applies to coinage: chance deposition; deliberate concealment; booty; battles; catastrophic events; burial rites; dedications; abandonment because the object is broken or no longer has any value. However, the majority of coins deposited – and not immediately recovered – suffered that fate for a limited number of reasons:

- They were dropped accidentally.
- They were discarded because they were useless.
- They were deliberately buried.

The first category probably accounts for a large percentage of our site finds. They are mostly coins which are either not worth recovering or which, for some reason, were not found and reclaimed. They are the ancient equivalent of things lost down the back of the sofa: coins that slipped through a hole in a purse or pocket; coins inadvertently dropped down the cracks between the floor boards of a tavern; coins dropped in the market and trodden into the mud; coins dropped in the bath-house and accidentally washed into the drains; and so on.

The second category includes coins rendered worthless by inflation and, as a result, put to one side and never recovered: the Roman equivalent of the collection of 1p coins that most of us have at home in a jar or kitchen drawer. This category also includes coins that were no longer legal tender, coins rendered obsolete by a coin reform and/or coins demonetised because they had been produced by a usurper (such as Carausius or Magnentius). Demonetised coins could sometimes be handed in and reused; other obsolete coinage was reused unofficially; the metal from sestertii, for instance, sometimes seems to have been reused to produce 'radiate copies'. It may have been dangerous to be caught in possession of the coinage of a defeated usurper – and such coins frequently seem to have been dumped, often in considerable quantities.

The third category, deliberate burial, is concerned largely with hoards. Coins could be hoarded for various reasons and a percentage of these hoards were hidden in a safe place and, for some reason, not recovered. Forts had strongrooms in which valuables could be kept and in large settlements it may have been possible to hire a strong box in a secure place (the equivalent of depositing your money in the bank) – but most people probably hid their life savings somewhere in or around their own property. Savings hoards, deposited and for whatever reason not recovered, probably account for the majority of gold and silver hoards subsequently unearthed by archaeologists.

The distribution of savings hoards recovered in Britain is uneven but this is not to say that saving was something practised in parts of Roman Britain and not in others; one needs to bear in mind not only the greater availability of safe storage facilities in forts as opposed to civil settlements but also the manner of recovery of hoards. The majority of hoards have been discovered as a result of ploughing or, latterly, through the use of metal-detectors, from which it follows that the majority of hoards will have been discovered in the modern arable areas, inevitably skewing the finds' distribution in favour of lowland southern England.

Bronze coinage was also hoarded in quantity, sometimes, as has been suggested above, as a way of saving up in order to pay the poll tax, just as, in modern times, one might save up to pay for the car insurance or for a television licence; dozens of bronze hoards from all around the country fall into this category. Such hoards were probably deposited in much the same way as those of gold and silver, perhaps in a storage jar in a safe place, and for some reason never reclaimed by the owner.

Some hoards are almost certainly accidental depositions. 'Purse hoards' seem to be just that – the contents of somebody's purse, either secreted but more probably accidentally mislaid, and often including a mixture of denominations suitable for making a day's purchases in the marketplace. Occasionally traces of a container, perhaps of leather, survive, but more often they do not (Plate 7).

In addition to these general categories there are other, less usual, types of coin deposit:

- Hoards of coins may be found in Roman grave contexts; for example, two small purse hoards, both of mid-fourth-century date, recovered from two separate graves in the Roman cemetery at Scorton, just across the river Swale from the substantial settlement of Catterick (Brickstock forthcoming).
- Coins could be intended to 'pay the ferryman', being placed in graves on the eyes or in the mouth of the corpse.
- Then as now, people threw coins into wishing wells. The classic example is Coventina's Well, a shrine adjacent to the fort of Carrawburgh on Hadrian's Wall, from which were recovered over 16,000 coins and many other votive offerings (Allason-Jones and McKay 1985). See also Plate 12 for a single coin found in a votive context.
- A few 'hoards' represent the dumping of demonetised coin, or the collection of obsolete coin ready for reuse (Plate 8). These can include folded, damaged or defaced coins.

Coins not only were deposited in many different ways and for many different reasons, they also ended up in a wide variety of different places and soil conditions. As a result we must assume that only a small proportion of the coinage deposited is likely to have survived the intervening fifteen or more centuries to be available for recovery and interpretation by modern archaeologists. The manner of excavation will also have a bearing on the quantity and type of coinage recovered: full and careful excavation clearly

Pl. 7   Purse hoard of late Roman small change from Great Whittington.

recovers a greater amount of material than excavation by machine (for example, during gravel extraction); excavation by metal detector clearly cannot reach the lower archaeological strata; and so on. However, the general consistency of the pattern of finds nationwide has already been remarked upon, leading us to hope that the samples recovered enable us to draw sensible conclusions when we come to the process of interpretation.

Interpretation

So what sort of things can coins tell us about Roman Britain – and (equally important) what can they not tell us?

Pl. 8 The Longhorsley Hoard. The discovery of this bronze coin hoard with a sprue (a product of the casting process) suggests that people living north of Hadrian's Wall in the late second/third century AD were interested in coins more as a source of raw material than as currency.

Firstly, and most importantly, they provide powerful dating evidence – though that dating evidence is perhaps not as solid as is generally thought. Most modern coins have their date of issue stamped upon them but ancient coins did not. The legends (inscriptions), however, often contain material which allows a rough (and sometimes a precise) mint-date to be ascribed. Early Emperors, for instance, had themselves elected annually as Tribunes of the People, and recorded that fact on their coins, so that TRP V together with the head of Vespasian gives a precise date of the fifth year of that Emperor's reign. Fourth-century coins used a complicated series of mint-marks which can be arranged in typologies, allowing fairly precise – but not necessarily precisely accurate – dates to be assigned. Many coins, however, contain no such dating pointers, so the coin can only be assigned to a time bracket, normally the reign of the Emperor depicted, e.g. Hadrian, AD 117–38.

An interpretive problem arises, however, because these dates are mint-dates and not the dates of deposition. The mint-date can give us only a *terminus post quem*, a time after which the coin must have been deposited. It is not known how long particular coins remained in circulation and thus coins cannot be used to give precise dates to archaeological levels. Numismatists term this the problem of 'residuality'.

Residuality is an accepted archaeological concept, and coins, like other archaeological material, may be found in residual contexts. Numismatists, however, also use the word to emphasise the sometimes considerable difference between the date of issue of a coin and the date of its deposition (i.e. as a measure of the elapse of time prior to deposition). Various coin types could remain in circulation for long periods – a circumstance betrayed by the degree of wear exhibited – and may thus be regarded as a residual part of an original currency pool circulating alongside later coin issues.

Our problems are greatly compounded by the phenomenal success of the Augustan coinage system, based around the already existing silver denarius. Since that system lasted unreformed until the third century AD, many issues remained legal tender throughout several centuries, and individual coins could remain in circulation for many decades or even centuries. Silver hoards demonstrate this possibility with great clarity. The recently rediscovered Rudchester hoard of 470 denarii and 16 aureii (Brickstock in prep.) contains a range of coins of Nero through to AD 168, in the reign of Marcus Aurelius. The sequence begins with eight legionary denarii of Mark Antony (32/1 BC), all extremely worn and six of them countermarked, presumably as a test of fineness rather than any attempt at re-tariffing. The Rudchester hoard, therefore, contains coins already up to 110 years old when the Romans reached Northumberland, and at least 200 years old when the hoard was completed.

A yet more remarkable example is provided by a small purse hoard discovered during excavations at Vindolanda in 1999 (Brickstock 2000). Four denarii, found corroded together, included two of Mark Antony, one worn completely flat and its obverse twice countermarked. The other two coins, only slightly worn, were issues of Severus (AD 193–211) and Elagabalus (AD 218–22). Thus we see coins demonstrably still in circulation after an elapse of 250 years.

One way of addressing the problem is to make an assessment of how worn the coin might be. When numismatists talk about the condition of a coin they are making an assessment of the amount of circulation wear exhibited by that coin, as opposed to its state of preservation or how corroded it is. It is impossible to say precisely how long it took for a coin to become 'slightly worn' or 'very worn' – but it can give some indication of the passage of time.

It should be understood, therefore, that coin dates are sometimes less than precise and dates derived from coin evidence should be used with extreme care, especially in ascribing absolute dates to particular points in a pottery typology. Nonetheless, they provide one of the most powerful tools in the archaeologist's armoury for the dating of sites and individual levels within those sites.

Coins can also be used in various other ways:

- They allow us to assess the economic development of sites, regions and the province as a whole, through the quantity and value of the coinage recovered and through the medium of comparative statistical analysis.
- They allow us to identify changing uses for particular sites and parts of sites, e.g. the location of markets and other areas of commercial enterprise.
- They can, to a degree, be used as historical documents – though in many cases they give us a greater insight into the propaganda message of the regime than the historical events of the period.

Weights and measures

The majority of the objects discussed in this volume can be taken as evidence that Roman Britain had a vibrant commercial life, with commodities being made and sold, imported and exported. Occasionally artefacts are found which allow insights into how this commercial life was conducted. These include:

- metal ingots of unrefined ore;
- crucibles and moulds used in the manufacture of coins;
- waste material left over from the above;
- material gathered together for reuse in the above;
- scales, balances and steelyards;
- weights, for use in conjunction with the above;
- lead sealings;
- purses.

Since mining and the production and transport of ore were all closely controlled by the imperial authorities it is not surprising that finds of precious-metal bullion are rare and, when found, often fragmentary. Complete examples of silver ingots, in the shape of flat, waisted rectangles, are known from Kent, with another group from Ireland (*RIB* II.11, 2402.1–12). In the last century of Roman occupation, officially stamped ingots were issued to soldiers and bureaucrats instead of coins, and this use, as a coin substitute, may explain the discoveries in Ireland, as well as providing evidence of trade with that country. All the copper ingots found in Britain have been discovered in Wales and can be described as 'bun-shaped'. Where they carry stamps, these are personal names, probably indicating the lessees of the relevant mine (*RIB* II.1, 2403.1–37). Ingots of lead, known as 'pigs', are occasionally found, usually in areas where sources of lead can be found. Unlike the semi-cylindrical pigs from Roman Spain, the British and Gallic examples are usually rectangular in shape, having been cast in trough-shaped moulds, with the Emperor's name impressed on the base. Despite the obvious official supervision of their production, these pigs can vary in weight from 50 to 101 kg, but the average weight is about 74 kg. The practice of including dating evidence in the imperial stamp appears to stop some time in the later second century AD and Frere has suggested that this implies that 'imperial control was in some way relaxed or reorganized in this period' (Frere, Roxan and Tomlin 1990: 38).

Crucibles and moulds are very occasional finds, and it is not always possible to ascertain whether the former were used for counterfeiting coins or for more respectable metalworking purposes. Moulds used in counterfeiting coins have already been mentioned but collections of scrap metal have been found in various contexts (e.g. the small neatly folded parcels of *lorica squamata* found at Piercebridge Roman fort), seemingly brought together in order to be melted down and reused in the counterfeiting process. Sets of moulds used for the production of coin blanks are virtually unknown in British contexts, which is understandable given how little official coinage was produced in Roman Britain.

Lead or copper-alloy weights have been found on quite a number of sites, occasionally inscribed with their weight in Roman pounds and ounces. Frere, in his discussion of Roman weights, draws attention to the difficulties inherent in their study because individual weights rarely conform to each other or to the usually recognized norm, and the assessment of surviving stone weights rarely agrees with the conclusions reached from studying the metrology of the coinage (Frere and Tomlin 1991a: 1–5). There is also the added difficulty that metal weights are often damaged by corrosion or wear.

The Roman pound (*libra*) was smaller than the modern British pound (327.45 g as opposed to 454 g); the Roman ounce (*uncial*) was also slightly smaller than the modern measure (27.288 g as opposed to 28.4 g) and 12 ounces rather than the modern 16 made up a pound. However, it was also common for weights to have numerals without any indication of *unciae* or *librae*. For very fine measurements, such as a jeweller might require, the *uncial* could be subdivided, down to the *siliqua*, which was equal to 1/144th of an *uncial*.

There has been much speculation as to whether there was already a system of weights being used in Britain in the pre-Roman period based on the 'Celtic pound'. This debate hinges on the weights of Celtic coins and the suggested correspondence of the so-called 'currency bars', found in

Table 2 Table of weights used in the Roman Empire

Weight		Mark of value
as	1 *libra* (Roman pound) = 12 *unciae*	I
deunx	11 *unciae*	S = = -
dextans	10 *unciae*	S = =
dodrans	9 *unciae*	S = -
bes	8 *unciae*	S =
septunx	7 *unciae*	S –
semis	½ pound = 6 *unciae*	S Ϛ
quincunx	5 *unciae*	∴∵
triens	4 *unciae*	:: or ....
quandrans	¼ pound = 3 *unciae*	... or ∵
sextans	2 *unciae*	.. or =
uncia	1 ounce	. or 8

the south of Britain in Iron Age contexts, with multiples of the postulated 'Celtic pound'. Frere noted that 'all the surviving inscribed weights seem to be related, however inaccurately, to the Roman *libra*', and suggested that this reflected the long history of trade between British and Mediterranean traders (Frere and Tomlin 1991a: 4). His discussion of the 'Celtic pound' and its Continental neighbour, 'the 'Gallic pound', concludes, 'although there is no need to doubt the existence of Celtic systems of weight in pre-Roman times, we have no accurate knowledge of the values involved', and his synopsis of the difficulties inherent in trying to untangle this problem is a useful cautionary tale for Roman finds specialists (Frere and Tomlin 1991a: 4).

Two different types of weighing machine are known from Roman contexts, the balance (scales with beam arms of equal length) and the steelyard (a scale with beam arms of unequal length). The former, normally suspended from a central lug, could be used just like a modern pair of scales by placing the object to be weighed in one scale pan and balancing weights in the other. Alternatively, since the arm was calibrated at various positions along it by incised dots or lines, the object could be weighed by positioning a counterweight on the arm. Roman scales are rare finds but have now been recovered from several British sites, including Colchester (Crummy 1983: 99; see also Liversidge 1973, fig. 77).

The steelyard worked in a similar way to the balance, but it was suspended from a point close to one end of the arm. A single pan was hung from the arm and counterweights were moved along the calibrated length of the arm to

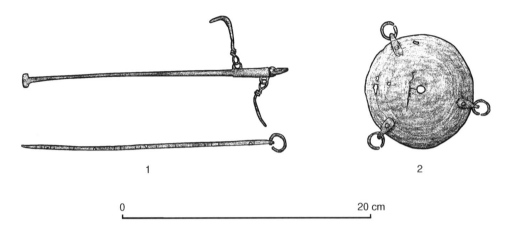

Fig. 1 Steelyard and weighing pan from Colchester

ascertain the weight (Fig. 1). The steelyard was often made more versatile by having two different hanging positions, each with corresponding calibration on the arm. The example found at Colchester (Crummy 1983: 99) could therefore weigh up to 6 *librae* on the one scale and from 6 to 40 *librae* on the other.

Artefacts indicating the measurement of volume are less common than those indicating weight. The Carvoran *modius* with its inscription certifying that it held 17½ *sextarii* is a rare survival and of particular interest as the standard *modius* held 16 *sextarii* (Frere and Tomlin 1991a: 58–9). Berriman (1956) and Mann (1984) have offered, as an explanation of this discrepancy, the idea that this particular *modius* was not used to check the amount of corn being paid as part of the *annona* but to ensure that each soldier received his exact weekly ration of 2½ *sextarii* per day.

Lead sealings, made from an alloy containing between 27 and 30 per cent of tin, are being found in increasing numbers (see also Chapter 6). These roughly circular blobs of metal were used to seal writing tablets, bales, bundles and boxes and often still have an impression of the string that bound them to whatever they were securing. Frere has classified those found in Britain into imperial, provincial, taxation, civic, military and private, the latter impressed with personal *intaglii* (Frere, Roxan and Tomlin 1990: 87). Most sealings are found at their point of arrival, rather than at their point of departure. Unusual numbers of sealings found together can indicate specific activities or events, such as those found at South Shields which, with their impressions of the three Severi, reflect the flurry of activity when South Shields became a base for Severus' campaigns in Scotland.

Commercial activity cannot take place unless the customer is able to get the required payment to the vendor. For day-to-day shopping, unless the customer carried coins in a sleeve tuck, this requires a purse. A few tombstones of women show them carrying a variety of leather or cloth purses, the most common being the equivalent of a 'Dorothy bag' (Allason-Jones 2005: 112–13). Bronze arm purses, with their very distinctive clip, have only been found in the north of Britain so far and are presumed to have been military in nature and only used by soldiers.

Examples of objects such as scales and weights may be found in *RIB* (*The Roman Inscriptions of Britain* II: *Instrumentum Domesticum*) and in various excavation reports: see, for example, Crummy 1983.

Postscript

It is worth remembering that coins (and, indeed, any other artefacts) may not necessarily remain undisturbed until dug up by an archaeologist. Once deposited it is possible for coins to be disturbed, reused, redistributed and perhaps redeposited. Coins move around in any number of ways: through the movement of soil during building activity; through the movement of rivers across flood plains; through the curiosity of ancient and modern holiday-makers bringing back curios; and so on. The Romans sometimes used coins, particularly those showing Christian or other religious symbolism, as jewellery or ornaments, mounting them in brooches or drilling holes in them to make pendants; later peoples, from the Anglo-Saxons onwards, have occasionally done the same.

There is little or no indication of continued coin use in what had been Roman Britain much beyond the first quarter of the fifth century AD. At the time of the construction of the Anglian cemetery at Scorton (a little way north of the Roman burial ground), Roman coins were still available, but were being treated as curios or objects for display: a single grave (of perhaps sixth-century date) yielded six Roman coins, of a variety of second- and third-century types, all pierced and probably originally strung as a necklace around the neck of the corpse. Likewise, Roman coins (sometimes cut into pieces) can appear in Viking booty hoards, but by then they were presumably being treated as bullion. Thus, although Roman coins could be said still to enjoy a limited circulation, their use as currency appears to have ceased.

2 | Travel and transport

NINA CRUMMY

Before the invention of flying machines, there were four ways of moving around: on foot, by boat, by wheeled vehicle or litter, or by riding, and the Romano-Britons would have used whichever was dictated by distance, purpose and social status. Over a short distance, walking would be the usual choice, but the wealthy and the less active might be driven or carried. A farmer going to market might walk, driving his livestock before him or with his produce on a pack animal. He might load up a cart and drive, or, if a navigable waterway flowed between his land and the town, he might go by boat. Over long distances, driving or sailing would be usual, but even then many would walk if they had neither the choice nor the means to exercise it. A merchant tapping into an Empire-wide market would undoubtedly send his goods by cart or ship, and any imports found in island Britain may have been moved long distances along major waterways such as the Saône, Rhône, Rhine, Danube or Nile before ever they crossed the Channel or the North Sea. Trade was a major element of the glue that held the Roman Empire together, and Vitruvius provides a long look and a neat summary of the essential importance of transport to commerce and urban living in general: 'Transport of produce would not have been possible without the invention of wagons and carts on land, and ships on water' (Vitruvius *De arch.* X.1.5).

A question that needs to be briefly addressed here is what, if any, were the major differences between travelling and methods of transport in the late Iron Age and Roman periods? The short answer is that they largely lay in scale and detail rather than in general method. The number of people and goods moving around the country immediately increased after AD 43 as the legions and their supply lines spread throughout the new province and as settlers followed in their wake. A new province with new settlements represents a new market, so merchants and their goods flowed into Britain from other provinces, and then out of Britain as her resources were tapped. The soldiers, sailors, settlers and merchants brought with them new shoes for walking in, new harness and other gear, and new vehicles made with new techniques and new fittings. The basic methods of getting about were the same, but changes in detail introduced a wide range of different object-types to the archaeological record.

The different forms of transport and the wide variety of objects associated with them inevitably result in a considerable overlap, in terms of artefacts, between this chapter and several others. Cavalry harness is military equipment; circus chariots and horse-gear belong to the realm of spectator sports; and transported goods belong to trade. Any overlap serves to remind us that dividing artefacts by function is a useful tool, not a final statement. This is particularly evident when we consider that any journey involved a degree of hazard, so behind transport lies a belief in the power of the gods to protect both travellers and their means of transport, a theme which will recur at various points throughout this chapter, culminating in a section on travel insurance.

Walking

Today we have largely lost the art of walking; for most people even a short stroll in the country has become an event, while walking between towns on metalled roads or country tracks has become the preserve of the serious hiker, the protestor or the antiquarian pilgrim. We have consequently lost sight of the fact that, until very recently, if people wished to get from A to B they walked, and only the wealthy could transport their family and household servants by vehicle whenever they chose. Walkers in the Roman period who were travelling any distance with goods and chattels would use a pack-animal (although human porters were preferred for mountainous routes), and a male mule was considered to be the most suitable beast for a pack-saddle (Columella *Rust.* XXXVII.11). A laden beast is depicted in the House of Julia Felix at Pompeii, with the heavy pack strapped to its back continuing well down its sides (Maiuri 1953: 141).

A man alone is a potential victim for robbers and wild animals, but that was not the only danger facing the walker in antiquity – weather and landscape could also conspire against him. The body of a Roman man found in the upland peat bog on Grewelthorpe Moor, North Yorkshire, in 1850 may have been attacked and his body dumped, or he may have strayed off the road in the mist to be swallowed by the bog. No coins, weapons or other objects were found on the body, but he was supposedly fully clothed in a tunic, a cloak, stockings and well-cut shoes with nailed soles. Unfortunately only the sole of one shoe and some textile fragments now survive, the local policeman having arrived too late to secure the body from his predatory contemporaries, and we can only bewail the loss of so much evidence (Turner, Rhodes and Wild 1991).

The Grewelthorpe body draws attention to the fact that clothing and footwear usually only survive in waterlogged contexts. On most archaeological sites the evidence for walking will, therefore, consist of only the iron hobnails and cleats used on the soles. Hobnails, being small and highly susceptible to wear and breakage, are not always easy to spot. The heads are very distinctive when intact, but a disassociated hobnail shank can often only be identified when found with other hobnails. However, the use of X-radiography has, as with so many iron objects, increased the numbers of hobnails recorded on recently excavated sites; now many more produce a hobnail or two, and the occasional recovery of a group of hobnails in a rural ditch produces the image of an exasperated field-worker finally discarding a shoe or boot that has gone beyond hope of repair (Crummy 2003a: 111, SF 12). Cleats, or boot-plates, are comparatively rare items, but they do occur on sites in central southern Britain, particularly in the late Roman period. Several were found among groups of hobnails in six fourth-century graves in the Lankhills cemetery at Winchester (Clarke 1979: 322, fig. 38), and they are a characteristic feature of late Roman ironwork assemblages at Silchester (Richards 2000: 372–3).

The appearence of hobnails in burials has sometimes led to them being considered as having some particular funerary significance that led to their occasional selection for deposition, perhaps as a symbol of the journey to the afterlife (Henig 1984: 199; Philpott 1991: 173). This contention does not really bear close scrutiny, especially when we consider that unnailed footwear leaves no trace. Contemporary evidence for the early Roman period provides a much simpler reason, that the dead were burned on the pyre fully clothed (Toynbee 1971: 44–50), a fact that can be supported by archaeological evidence. At a mid to late first-century Roman cremation cemetery at Colchester about half the funerary features (pyres and burials) contained hobnails in varying quantities; the absence of hobnails in a grave did not mean an equal absence of footwear on the pyre, but either that the random collection of debris from the cooled ashes had failed to include hobnails or that thonged or stitched sandals had been worn by the dead person (Crummy 2004). The same applied two hundred years later at the opposite end of the country in the third-century Roman cemetery at Brougham, which served both fort and *vicus* (Mould 2004: 392). The apparent rarity of hobnails from cremation cemeteries dug before about 1980 was really a reflection of excavation and post-excavation techniques. Since then, sieving the soil from funerary features has become standard practice, as has the X-raying of even small iron scraps.

Leather footwear may only survive when waterlogged, but in Britain there are many wet contexts close to rivers, in stream beds or bogs, at the bottom of wells or where the water table is naturally high. London, York, Carlisle and Vindolanda have produced large assemblages of footwear, and there are useful groups from many other sites. As with other artefact types, many forms of footwear were in use at any one period and these forms changed in a continuous flow over time, lending themselves readily to classification and close dating, and providing a reflection of contemporary fashions.

The military boots worn by the invading legions in the mid-first century represent the introduction of an entirely new technology to Britain. Instead of the simple one-piece shoes of the late Iron Age (none of which has yet been found in Britain), their insoles and outer soles were separate pieces and the complex lattice-work upper was cut in one with the middle sole, all these sections then being nailed together. This method of construction produced boots that had a tough sole for long marches yet kept the foot cool at the same time. An added advantage was that they could be easily repaired. Boots of this form were made to a standard in the military camps in the first century, but by about AD 100 it would appear that contracts for supplying the army were issued to civilian shoemakers, as by the second century the types of boots worn in military establishments were the same as those used by the rest of the population (van Driel-Murray 1987: 33).

The range of Roman footwear can be broadly defined as boots, outdoor shoes, house shoes, sandals, house slippers and bath slippers, for which there is a range of Latin terms, including *calcei, caligae, perones, socci, crepidulae, carbatinae* and *soleae* (Plate 9). They were worn as appropriate to situation, social status, gender and weather conditions. Composite shoes might be stitched or thonged rather than nailed, and nailing might be used on sandals as well as shoes and boots. The upper could be closed or have elaborate openwork, perhaps to reveal brightly coloured socks, and might be gilded or set with tiny decorative studs (van Driel-Murray 2001a: figs. 1 and 3). Rather more unusual items were wooden overshoes and bath slippers made with cork soles and leather uppers, with the cork, if not the whole slipper, imported from the continent.

Leather made from cattle or goat skin was used in the manufacture of these shoes, and its supply was part of the economic chain that led from farm to finished product via butcher, skinner, tanner and shoemaker. Deer skin was also used, but depended upon a rather less reliable supply from hunters. There has proved to be a complex relationship between the army, tanning technology and leather supply, a link so close that tanning disappeared as the grip of Rome on Britain began to fail in the late fourth century, to be

Pl. 9 Range of shoes from Vindolanda

replaced by the older and simpler technology of curing (van Driel-Murray 2001b: 64–5).

A tremendous amount of work on Roman footwear has been done in recent years, and far more literature exists than can be referenced here. Footwear can now take its place in regional studies on the leather trades, Empire-wide studies of changing fashions, and site studies relating to zones of use and gender-specific styles, while its symbolic potential and use in rites of commencement and termination has also been revealed (van Driel-Murray 1999; 2002).

Carriages, wagons and carts

Roman literature supplies the names of many vehicles, some used only by specific groups of people or on specific occasions. Among the latter was the *pilentum*, a state carriage with four wheels used in religious processions, and the *currus triumphalis* or triumphal chariot, which was also heavily decorated. A range of vehicles was available for the ordinary traveller. The *carpentum* was a covered two-wheeled carriage that was usually pulled by mules. It had a substantial, often gabled, roof, and could be luxuriously furnished to make a comfortable long-distance travelling carriage. The *car-ruca* was a larger four-wheeled travelling carriage, which on long journeys had beds for sleeping in comfort (*carruca dormitoria*). The *reda* was a large four-wheeled carriage of Gaulish origin, usually drawn by two or four horses. The Romans also adopted from the Gauls the *petor(r)itum*, which had no cover and was of rough construction. It was used for conveying the household servants while the master and his family travelled more comfortably and sheltered from the weather in a *reda* or *carpentum*. The Roman *cisium*, a light open gig, was a self-drive hire vehicle kept at post-houses which was usually pulled by one or two mules or horses. The *birota* was a two-wheeled two-passenger two-horse vehicle that could be hired along with a *cursor*, a servant who led, rather than drove, the horses. A *lectica* might also be hired; this was a litter made from a couch fitted with a canopy and curtains. It was carried by either six to eight strong slaves, or a pair of mules could be harnessed between the carrying poles, one in front and one behind.

The *benna* was a wagon of Gaulish origin with curved sides of basketwork, but the principal wagon was the two-wheeled *plaustrum* (or *plostrum*), a larger version of which had four wheels and was distinguished by the term *plaustrum maius*. Both were of simple construction, with a flat platform of boards from which projected a central pole to which oxen, or sometimes mules, were yoked. They were sometimes fitted with low planked sides. 'Lorry' is probably the best translation for *plaustrum maius*, as it would have been used for carrying heavy goods. The *plaustrum*'s wheels were often not spoked but made from three solid boards. They were fastened to the axle, which passed through wooden rings or blocks set beneath the platform, so that as the wheels turned so did the axle, lubricated by oil or fat (Virgil *Georgics* II.444; III.536).

The *essedum* also originated in the north-western provinces. Caesar uses this word for the war-chariot of the British tribes, describing it as having an open front so that the driver could run out along the pole to stand on the yoke (Caesar *Bell. Gall.* IV.33), but it was also used to refer to an open-fronted, self-drive carriage that travellers could hire at inns. *Covin(n)us* was another name for the war-chariot of the Britons, and it too seems to have developed in peacetime into a travelling carriage. Children may also have been taught the principles of driving on small chariots pulled by a goat or small pony (Balsdon 2002: fig. 7b).

The imperial post (*cursus publicus*) relied upon the availability of hire carriages, with or without a driver. At the main stages of the *cursus* were inns known as *mansiones* or *stationes*, set about 25 to 35 miles apart, with smaller establishments or *mutationes* (changing-places) in between. As well as the carriages, draught animals and drivers, and the usual facilities for bathing, eating and sleeping required of any inn, mansios also provided porters, cartwrights, veterinarians and escorts for taking the vehicles and their teams back to the previous station (Casson 1994: 183–6).

The Roman military chariot, the *currus*, is distinctive, but the wagons and carts shown on campaign on, for example, Trajan's Column, differ little, if at all, from those used in civilian life. Ballistas might be mounted on specially adapted carts that could be manoeuvred into battle position, or in mountainous terrain were carried on light mule-carts with large wheels and then set up on tripod bases (Lepper and Frere 1988: 106).

Another chariot also deserves mention: the *currus circensis* or light racing-chariot of the circus, called a *biga* when pulled by two horses and a *quadriga* when pulled by four. This was built for speed and control, and was as light as possible so as not to tire the horses. The frame was of wood, with a springy floor of interwoven straps and a low breastwork probably made of hide. The floor was low and the spoked wheels were smaller than those on other vehicles, in order to keep the centre of gravity close to the ground (Plate 10). Unlike the military *currus* and the *currus triumphalis*, any metal fittings were kept to the bare essentials and there was no unnecessary decoration that would add to the weight. The 'racing'-chariots shown in the 1926 and 1959 *Ben Hur* films could not be further from the real thing. Estimates of the weight of racing-chariots place them at around 25–30 kg, so that, even when the weight of the charioteer was added in, four horses might only be pulling the equivalent of 20–25 kg each. Only one circus is known from Britain, that found at Colchester in winter 2004–5, but there are probably others still to be located at major settlements like York and London (Crummy 2005; see also Chapter 10).

Although there were so many vehicles in use, only a few fragments of the wooden bodies have survived to the present day, and Röring's design for his famous reconstruction of a travelling carriage in the Römisch-Germanisches Museum in Cologne is based on extensive research rather than a single find (Röring 1983). Largely made in order to display a set of vehicle fittings and decorations in the museum's collection, it has all the essentials of the Roman carriage: a pivoted front axle (a Gaulish invention; White 1975: 81) and a body suspended on leather straps or ropes fastened to lateral braces, in turn fastened to the axles. The wheels are spoked and have iron tyres. The decorative fittings are perhaps the most surprising part, as they consist of figurines of deities and animals, which, if found loose on an archaeological site, might not be recognised as part of a vehicle.

Pl. 10 Reconstruction of a racing chariot and its maker, Robert Hurford

If finds of vehicles and vehicle parts are scarce on the Continent compared to the literary references, they are even rarer in Britain. This paucity of material evidence means that it is impossible to define any differences in vehicle technology between the different regions and sites of Roman Britain, or between Britain and the other north-west provinces of the Empire. Rather than matching the broad overviews that can be produced for footwear and the leather trades, the most fruitful lines of study are at present confined to intrinsic studies of metal vehicle fittings.

One type of decorative vehicle fitting that occurs in Britain is a mount on a polygonal base, supposedly used at the top of a pole around which the reins were looped when the carriage or wagon was stationary. The most common form has an eagle head on the top and a waterbird (probably swan or goose) projecting upwards from the base (Fig. 2(a)). The latter probably prevented the reins from slipping down the pole. These objects were first identified as cart fittings by Károly in 1890, and were further studied by von Mercklin and Alföldi in the 1930s. The Continental finds have a very wide range of decorated terminals and basal projections, from simple bell

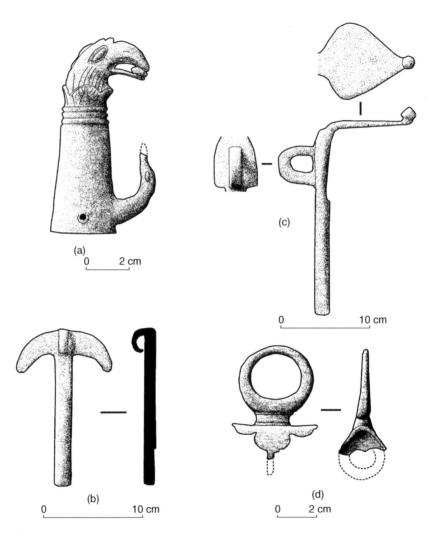

Fig. 2 (a) Bronze eagle cart mount from Water Newton; (b) iron linchpin, after Manning 1985; (c) iron linchpin with spatulate head and toe-step, after Manning 1985; (d) bronze terret from Margidunum

or baluster shapes to fingers, snakes, basilisks or even human heads, but the British examples are usually of the eagle/waterbird type, a first-century form often occurring on military sites (Károly 1890; von Mercklin 1933; Alföldi 1935; Crummy 2000). The early mounts are by no means common, but the only certain later example, being perhaps as late as the third century, comes from Vindolanda and is topped by a full-figure horse (Toynbee and Wilkins 1982). A damaged griffin from Trawscoed, Dyfed, may be another such (Davies 1987).

Iron fittings from spoked wheels are perhaps the most frequently found vehicle parts. The wheels were made up of a central hub or nave, to which turned wooden spokes were fitted, usually six, eight, ten or twelve. A felloe (or felly), made either from one bent piece of wood or from several, was then slotted onto the outer ends of the spokes. The felloe was usually fitted with an iron tyre shrunk on to the outside. The axle was slotted through the centre of the hub and secured by a linchpin. The hub was often strengthened by iron bands, called nave hoops or nave rings. A remarkable find of many cart fragments from Neupotz, Germany, produced wheels with iron rings fitted both around the outside of the nave and inside its hollow centre, and the ends of the axles were also bound with iron (Künzl and Künzl 1993). Similar complete or near complete wheels of Roman date have been found in Britain at Bar Hill, Strathclyde, and Newstead, Borders (Macdonald and Park 1906: 92; Curle 1911: 292–4, pl. 69). Although found on Roman military sites, these wheels are probably of native manufacture. They have hubs of elm, narrow spokes of willow, and one-piece felloes of ash; unusually, the most complete has eleven spokes. A letter sent to Vindolanda records that wagon parts were being sent there, including 34 hubs, 38 axles and 300 spokes (http://vindolanda.csad.ox.ac.uk, Tablet 309; Birley 2002: 93). Newstead produced many iron wheel fittings, including no fewer than twenty-four nave hoops from a single pit. Although nave hoops also occur in some hoards of ironwork, on most excavations vehicles are usually only represented by a linchpin or two. They conjure up an image of a lost pin, a loose wheel, and then – crash! Of course, linchpins have a distinctive form and are easily recognised, but when tyres and nave hoops break up, there is little to distinguish them from all the other iron strip fragments found on archaeological sites.

The typology established by Manning for the iron linchpins in the British Museum identifies La Tène types and divides those of the Romano-British period into two groups, crescentic-headed and spatulate-headed; he then further subdivides them as to whether or not they have a loop on the head, and what form the loop takes (Fig. 2(b); Manning 1985: 71–4). A few examples have large leaf-shaped heads set at right angles to the pin, large enough to provide a toe-step for mounting the vehicle instead of being purely decorative (Fig. 2(c)). Some pins had a copper-alloy head slotted on to an iron shaft and probably came from high-status vehicles, especially as the terminals were usually decorative. Some of these items will be considered below in the section on travel insurance.

The pole running from the body of a wagon or carriage up to the yoke could also have iron fittings known as pole bindings. A few are known, some coming from hoards and others from excavated sites. They served to strengthen the end of the pole where it was weakened by the hole for pegging on the yoke. Newstead has produced not only some pole bindings but also a wooden yoke (Curle 1911: pl. 69, 1; Manning 1985: 74–5). All in all, James Curle's Newstead report of 1911 is a particularly useful work, not only because the waterlogged contexts produced well-preserved iron and wooden objects, but also for its thematic presentation of the finds. Thanks to the Trimontium Trust, the publication can now be found online at www.curlesnewstead.org.uk.

The method of harnessing or yoking traction animals varies considerably on the reliefs, wall-paintings and mosaics that provide our main source of information, as might be expected considering the different animals used, their varying number, the weight of the different vehicles, and the date the image was made. Oxen were used in pairs yoked side by side to a central shaft and then led by reins attached to leather or rope halters. Their breaking and training is detailed by Columella, who advises that they are first broken to the yoke, then to the wagon, and last to the plough (Columella *Rust.* VI). His description smacks of real practice, while Virgil suggests a more delicate process, with the first contact being a wreath of osiers (Virgil *Georgics* III.166–73). A mule might be harnessed between two straight shafts, apparently attached to both a belly-band and a neck-strap, as on the mosaic in the Baths of the Cisiarii at Ostia, with the reins running from a bitted bridle. In some cases the shafts angle upwards at the shoulders and are attached to a head-collar. A second animal could be added to assist with heavy loads, connected to the cart by a trace and kept in the right direction and at the same pace by having its bridle attached to the bridle of the mule between the shafts. Connecting animals at the bridle is a dangerous practice, for if one stumbles and falls it will drag the other with it and inflict serious injury. On other vehicles there is a single pole that rises up between pairs of mules or horses to yoke them at the withers. A trace-horse might again be added to pull level with the pair, or a second pair might be added in front of them, linked by traces running from individual yokes or head-collars to the front of the pole (Casson 1994: 183, fig. 13; Raepsaet 2002: 218–54, 278–9).

On racing-chariots the two central horses of a *quadriga* were attached to the yoke and provided the motive power, while the two unyoked outer horses provided the speed and cornering. The innermost animal was trained to lead the tight turning circle at the posts, while the outermost kept up the speed. Harness was minimal, consisting only of neck-strap, belly-band and bridle. Similar neat harnessing is shown on the horses pulling a cart drawing the sacred images to the Circus Maximus, with the belly-band clearly fastened by a large circular buckle, an analogue for the 'rings with loop-headed spikes' often classified as structural fittings in the archaeological literature for Roman Britain (Manning 1985: 130; Köhne and Ewigleben 2000: fig. 110). If the buckle tongue is missing, the surviving ring is unlikely to be identified as a harness fitting, but such plain iron rings do often occur on rural sites and may come from the harness of plough animals.

Bridles, bits and general harness fittings will be considered below in the section on riding, but here should be mentioned the fitting that crops up most frequently on archaeological sites, and even then not in great numbers – the terret (Fig. 2(d)). This was a guide-ring, usually of copper alloy, set into a yoke, a head-collar or a pad on top of a belly-band to keep the line of the rein, and hence the message, between driver and animal clear. It prevented the reins from slipping down and becoming snagged on the pole or entangled in the hooves or tail. These small objects vary considerably in appearance, but as far as can be ascertained, no one has established a dated typology, or picked up regional variations through classification (see Leeds 1933; Gillam 1958; M. MacGregor 1976).

For readers wishing to pursue the details of harnessing or yoking animals in the Roman period, an excellent source is Raepsaet's *Attelages et techniques de transport dans le monde gréco-romain* (2002), in which details of the ancient sources are given, and replicas are shown, and in some cases put to the test, thanks to Marius the good-tempered ass. More detail of the animals used in antiquity can also be found in various sources, with Clutton-Brock's *Horse Power* (1992) providing a general introduction to the equids.

The goods carried upon farm and commercial wagons obviously varied according to need, but it is informative to note the huge wine casks lain on their sides, presumably secured with wedges, on their way from vineyard to vintner, such as are shown on a relief from Langres, France (Raepsaet 2002: fig. 131). No description of the roads themselves is offered here, but mention should be made of the milestones set up along major routes. They often provide information about who set them up, as well as a dedication to the current Emperor, although distance details are scarce (*RIB* 2219–2314).

Riding

The harness of traction animals was generally plain and of limited type, but the study of Romano-British horse-gear would make a rich field for anyone drawing it all together and tackling it from a chronological or chorological point of view. The enamelled phalerae, pendants and button-and-loop fasteners cry out for a detailed typological study (although see Wild 1970), which might also link on to the designs on seal-boxes and plate brooches, and could valuably be underpinned by metallurgical analysis. Much work on early Roman horse-gear has been done under the umbrella of military equipment studies, but there is a need to try to pick out any differences that may exist between harness found on civilian and military sites. Distinguishing between the two is generally tricky, and a rule of thumb that harness fittings from civilian sites are purely civilian in origin falls down in the face of all the odd pieces of military equipment that crop up on even rural sites, stressing the all-pervasive presence of the Roman army (see Chapter 5). Soldiers moved around the countryside and were in settlements for many reasons, such as requisitioning supplies, keeping the peace and escorting important officials. Many turned to farming on their retirement.

A harness pendant found on the site of the Roman circus at Colchester can serve as a test case. Of the same characteristic size and swivelling two-piece form as the pendants used by the auxiliary cavalry of the second and third centuries, it is nevertheless distinctive in its precise style (Fig. 3(a)). If this was found on a military site, it would unhesitatingly be identified as military itself, but coming from the circus site it is ambiguous. Very few other artefacts were recovered thanks to medieval and later use of the site, and so this piece cannot be set in the context of a larger assemblage and its characteristics. The link of harness pendant and circus ought to declare it as coming from the harness of a circus horse. As the chariot team's harness needed to be kept light, it might, instead, have come from the tack of a horse ridden by a *hortator* or *iubilator*. These men may have provided riding displays between races, but they are usually depicted galloping their mounts ahead of or alongside the teams, perhaps to urge them on, much like modern-day cheer-leaders, or to guide the charioteers around wreckage or signal back information about gaps where a spurt of speed might allow a team to overtake.

So far so civilian, but there are no other known circus harness pendants with which to compare it, and the closest similar pendants are all from military sites. The closest parallel of all comes from the fort at Castleford (Bishop 1990a: fig. 2). Might the story behind the Colchester pendant be more complex than first appears? Although there is no solid evidence for a second- or third-century military presence at Colchester, there is a scatter of auxiliary equipment of that date in the town. Moreover, some of the late Roman burials immediately adjacent to the circus are surrounded by

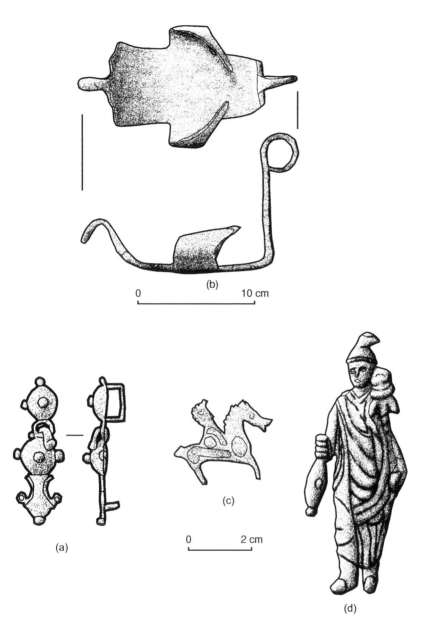

Fig. 3 (a) Harness pendant from Colchester; (b) iron hipposandal, after Manning 1985; (c) enamelled horse-and-rider brooch from Woodyates; (d) bronze figurine of Mercury from Colchester

penannular ring-ditches; this hints at a Germanic (military) origin to part of the population. The town faces the North Sea, and in the early Roman period saw much traffic between its port and the mouth of the Rhine. It is not beyond the bounds of possibility that in the later Roman period troops from the German *limes* landed at Colchester when they transferred to

Britain, and, if not actually garrisoned there, may have rested in a camp outside the town for a few days before moving on to their new postings, exercising their mounts in the secure, yet open, space of the circus.

The above demonstrates how one object can lead to detailed enquiry, and many other items may have a subtext that drives artefact researchers into greater efforts than usual to understand the process by which they reached the soil. If all small finds were treated to the same speculative approach then too much would be written and too little of it would be factual, but it is more than fun to speculate; it reminds us that people and historical events lie behind seemingly insignificant objects (Crummy 2006a: 61–3).

Leaving aside the trappings usually derived from military harness, we are faced with further ambiguity, for there are two catch-all descriptions of function beloved of artefact cataloguers: 'used for ritual purposes' and 'probably from horse harness'. When so many Roman artefacts slot so conveniently into functional categories, the temptation is to make them all do it, whether there is any supporting evidence or not. Many an unknown fitting, especially if it is prettily enamelled, has been described as horse harness, which stresses the need for a serious study of harness fittings from Britain. A classic case is that of the cosmetic sets described in Chapters 9 and 11. At first they were associated with the 'barnacles' forming part of a modern cavesson noseband and were referred to as 'barnacle pendants'. Unconvinced by this argument, the current writer categorised them as amulets – using the alternative catch-all description. Research by Ralph Jackson produced the correct identification and this has led to a major study establishing the unique Britishness of these objects and their use (Smith 1918; Crummy 1983: 145–6, fig. 180; Jackson 1985; forthcoming).

The iron fittings of harness are more forthright. Two-link snaffle-bits of the Roman period are the norm, fitted with side rings for attaching the reins, and a few curb-bits have also been found (Curle 1911, pl. 71; Manning 1985: 66–9). Snaffles are the mildest form of bit, and the Roman ones are little different from those of today. They raise the horse's head and put pressure on the corners of the mouth and on the tongue. The curb, on the other hand, encourages the horse to lower its head and flex its jaw, placing the pressure on the roof of the mouth, the poll and the chin groove. This gives the rider a greater degree of control and today is used by well-trained riders on well-trained horses for events like dressage.

Rope or leather bits and bitless bridles will no doubt also have been in use, as well as halters, but would need to survive intact to be recognised, and, being organic, apart from any buckles or rings on the bridle, have less chance of surviving anyway. A remarkable case, where the leather or rope of a halter was missing but three plain copper-alloy rings pointed to its certain existence, came from the University of Reading's excavations at Pompeii. The skeleton of a donkey lay on its side in a stable, with the three rings on its skull. It had clearly been tethered in its stall, and could not escape the choking ash and fumes. Rings of the same type are common site finds, but could have served a number of purposes and can rarely be allocated with such certainty to transport.

Horseshoes do not occur in convincingly stratified Roman contexts, and any published as Roman should be viewed with the utmost suspicion. They will invariably turn out on closer examination to have come from topsoil. A type of animal shoe that is distinctively Roman is the hipposandal, used on traction animals (Fig. 3(b)). A temporary shoe in the form of a flat plate of iron with side wings, narrowing to a raised hooked front and often a higher raised hooked back, it was tied on to the hoof to prevent animals from slipping in treacherous conditions (Manning 1985: 63–6). The underside of the plate can be ridged or grooved to provide a grip, and one example in the British Museum has a U-shaped strip welded on for the same purpose. This strip has often been cited as a justification for identifying horseshoes as Roman. Hipposandal wing fragments, identifiable by their distinctive shape, occur most often in site assemblages and must have been the parts most prone to wear and breakage. A site providing a good example of hipposandal use has been excavated at Ware, at the point where Ermine Street crosses the river Lea. Seven hipposandal wings were found in a small area, along with a probable fragment of a sole-plate and many other scrap pieces of sheet iron that may also have come from soles. The fragments all came from contexts that were not associated with Ermine Street's construction and main period of use but with its decline, suggesting that the road surface had decayed to the point where hipposandals were needed to help horses or oxen negotiate the slopes down to the river and to cross the ford (Crummy 2006b: 24).

What of the riders themselves? Images from late Iron Age and Roman Britain usually show riders as warriors, no doubt because the reality of a plump merchant ambling along on a mule quenches rather than fires the spirit. A Romano-Celtic rider-god was popular in the province, particularly in the eastern counties. Small plate brooches were made in his image and are found mainly on temple sites, where they were deposited as votive offerings (Fig. 3(c); Ferris 1985; Mackreth 1986; Hattatt 1987: 232–6; Simpson and Blance 1998: 275). On the brooches the rider seems to be weaponless, sometimes carrying only a small baton, but Johns has suggested that this is a debased representation of a sword and sees him as an insular interpretation of Roman Mars (Johns 1996: 104–5). He may alternatively be the sky-god Jupiter, as in Gaul both Mars and Jupiter occur as riders, and a variant brooch from Velzeke, Belgium, shows the rider above the letters IOVIS on an openwork label (Thevenot 1968: 47–50; K. Sas, pers. comm). A fragment of a similar variant brooch, lacking its label, was found at Silchester in the nineteenth century, and a slightly different variant with no label, possibly from Pannonia by its style, was found in Norfolk (Hattatt 1987: 1179–6).

Sailing

Surrounded by the sea, Britain depended upon shipping for much of its trade, and its many long and navigable rivers would also have played a part in the internal flow of goods, as well as providing a source of food. The sea was also a defence, and was feared by many Romans. Caesar's first expedition nearly ended in maritime disaster (Caesar *Bell. Gall.* IV.28–9), Caligula threatened to invade but instead ordered his troops to gather shells which he declared were plunder from the defeat of the sea (Suetonius *Calig.* IV.46), and the Claudian invasion nearly failed when the troops at first refused to take ship to campaign 'beyond the limits of the known world' (Dio Cassius LX.19).

The Roman fleet at the battle of Actium in 31 BC was made up of galleys of many sizes, from the trireme with its three banks of oars up to a great vessel with ten banks of oars that carried the flag. The trireme was the vessel used mainly by the first-century AD fleets based at Misenum and Ravenna, but a fast, light warship, invented by Illyrian pirates and named the Liburnian after them, was also adopted by the Romans. It usually had only one bank of oars but was sometimes adapted to carry two (Casson 1960: 201–14). We can expect triremes, quadriremes and perhaps quinqueremes to have been used in the invasion of Britain, but they were more at home in the Mediterranean than in the rougher waters of the Channel.

The type of sea-going craft used for cross-Channel trade before the conquest is defined by images of ships on coins of Cunobelin, minted *c.*20–43 AD (Muckelroy, Haselgrove and Nash 1978; McGrail 1990a: 43–4). They show a high-sided sailing ship with a rockered keel, one mast set more or less amidships, one (square) sail with stays, a side rudder and a projecting forefoot. A transverse feature on the bow is probably either a cleat for a bowline or a lead for an anchor cable. They had the flat bottom required for sailing close inshore and beaching without damage when necessary, a feature shared with the equally high-sided ships of the Veneti from north-west Gaul (Caesar *Bell. Gall.* III.13–16).

These vessels can broadly be defined as falling within a Romano-Celtic boat-building tradition based on the features of a few excavated craft

(McGrail 1990a: 44–6; 2004: 196). They are an early representation of boats for which the only excavated evidence belongs to the second or third centuries. Deep-hulled, they were built with stout timbers and flush-laid sawn planking caulked with moss, soaked and pounded hazel twigs or fibres. The flooring was also made of heavy timbers, and large iron nails with convex heads were used to fasten planking and framework together, the ends either turned once at a right angle or twice to form a distinctive flat-based hook (Marsden 1990: fig. 7.4; 1994, fig. 5; Rule 1990: fig. 5.3).

In Britain sea-going craft of this type have been found in the Thames at London and in the harbour at St Peter's Port on Guernsey (Plate 11). The mid-second-century Blackfriars Ship 1 is about 18.5 by 6.12 by 2.86 m and St Peter's Port Ship 1 is about 25 by 6 by 3(+) m. The Barlands Farm boat found in the Severn estuary and dated to *c*.AD 300, is smaller, about 11.40 by 3.16 by 0.90 m, and is unlikely to have been used on cross-Channel voyages (Nayling and McGrail 2004). A smaller river-going vessel is represented by a second-century barge found at New Guy's House, London. It had a broad flat bottom and was capable of floating in less than 1m of water, ideal for transporting goods along the Thames (Marsden 1965a).

The wine and oil and ceramics imported into the province were transported in huge numbers in vessels of Mediterranean origin, such as that found at County Hall, London (Marsden 1965b). The smallest craft were capable of carrying 1,500 amphoras, those of the middle range could hold 2,000 to 3,000 and the largest 6,000 or more, about 250 tons (Parker 1992: 26). These pale beside the huge vessels that carried Egypt's grain to feed Rome, some of which reached a capacity of 1,200 tons or more (Casson 1960: 215; Balsdon 2002: 227). However, very large vessels were comparatively rare, and appear not to have been made after the second century AD (McGrail 2004: 155). The trade goods shipped along Britain's coastal waters included building stone. Ragstone from Kent was carried in Blackfriars Ship 1, and this must have been one cargo in thousands from the quarries, as the stone was used in buildings in both London and Colchester, neither of which had local sources of good building stone (Marsden 1994: 19).

The small fishing boats which would have plied the rivers of Britain or served as ferries are more enigmatic. A few logboats dated to the late Iron Age period have been found (Millett and McGrail 1987; McGrail 1990a: 32–6) and craft of the same type probably continued in use well into the Roman period. An intriguing episode has Caesar ordering the construction of boats in a style he had met on his expeditions to Britain, with keels and first ribs of light timber and the rest of the hull made of wattles, the whole being then covered with hide (Caesar *Bell. Civ.* I.54). These are not coracles

Pl. 11 Models of boats in the Museum of London

(or curachs), which have no keels, but a different type of boat entirely, capable of taking to the seas (McGrail 1990a: 36).

If few boats of the Roman period in Britain have yet been found, the situation is not much better with the associated fittings and equipment. Ship nails are rarely identified, apart from when found *in situ*, suggesting that they were made in specific ordered quantities. An anchor and its associated chain of first-century date was found in the river Shelford at Bulbury, Dorset; a lead anchor stock found at Porth Felen on the North Wales coast predates this by perhaps two centuries (Cunliffe 1972: 300–2, fig. 5, pl. 54a;

Boon 1977). The Porth Felen stock came from a Mediterranean vessel, perhaps engaged in the tin trade. There is an oak oar from Newstead, which overlooks the Tweed (Curle 1911: 313, pl. 69, 5), and the port of London has produced the iron terminals of two boat-hooks, but none of the forked terminals from barge-poles found on the Rhine. Had the latter been used in London, the amount of work done along the Thames foreshore by both professional archaeologists and amateur searchers might perhaps have been expected to produce some examples, and Marsden has taken this absence to mean that barges plying the Thames were either punted along or towed from the bank (1994: 17, 19). The lack of much other equipment may instead indicate that it is too soon to draw such a distinction, raising the knotty problem of when to take absence of evidence as evidence of absence.

Small images of boats are rare, but there is a small plate brooch in the form of a merchant vessel from London (Wardle 1998: fig. 18), and the model prow of a copper-alloy warship also found in London was probably made as a votive offering following a successful engagement at sea. It has a stempost in the form of a waterbird, either goose or swan, and a ram with a dog's head terminal, perhaps alluding to the dog's role as the guide of dead souls to the underworld (Jenkins 1957: 65; Merrifield 1987: 46–7, 67; Marsden 1994: fig. 6, d).

The above is by no means an exhaustive list, but it should serve to show how patchy the evidence is when viewed from a purely British perspective. More numerous are the stamped tiles of the British fleet, the *Classis Britannica*, which kept the sea routes free of pirates and transported men and supplies across the Channel. The tiles occur along the south coast and inland from it, and also on the north coast of Gaul. Different fabrics in each province point to different kiln sites (*RIB* II.5, 1–25). Evidence of the fleet occurs even on Hadrian's Wall, where its personnel were co-opted to build a stretch of the Wall lying between Castlesteads and Birdoswald, as well as granaries at Benwell and possibly Halton Chesters, leaving stone inscriptions to commemorate their work (Cleere 1977; Peacock 1977; *RIB* 1944; 1945; *RIB* 1340).

Travel insurance

The dangers of travel were ever present, whether the journey was by land or sea, and the best insurance against robbers, pirates, stormy weather and shipwreck (apart from a strong bodyguard who could swim well) was the protection of the gods. Mercury was the god of travellers, and would have been thanked for successful outcomes and appealed to by those about

Pl. 12   Coin of Fortuna found under the mast step of Blackfriars Ship 1

to undertake a journey, especially if they were traders, of whom he was also patron. Small figurines of the god abound in Britain, and models of his animal companions, the cockerel, the ram and the tortoise, and of his winged herald's staff or *caduceus*, also refer to him (Fig. 3(d)). Several have been found at the rural sanctuary at Uley which lay at the edge of the Cotswolds near the busy Severn estuary as well as the main road south from Gloucester towards Bath and the port of Abona (Woodward and Leach 1993). Another centre for the cult has recently been identified just outside the west gate at Colchester, at the end of the road leading up from London, and it can be no coincidence that the only complete copper-alloy Mercury group was found outside the south-west gate at Verulamium, perhaps originally forming part of the furnishings at another gate-side temple (Green 1976: 58–9; Pitts 1979: pl. 12, 39; Niblett 2001: 120, pl. 14; Crummy 2006c: 57–8).

Mercury was not the only deity appealed to by travellers. Several pipeclay mother goddess figurines were found in a small sanctuary on the rocky island of Nornour in the Scillies, as well as a very large number of brooches, supposed to have been offered there by sailors plying the Severn Estuary or venturing beyond it on longer voyages (Dudley 1968; Butcher 1993). Goddesses presided over road junctions, always uncertain places where footpads might lie in wait. They were known by the number of roads meeting at their particular junction, the Biviae, Triviae or Quadruviae (Zelle 2000: 65; Ricken and Thomas 2005: Taf. 24, 2).

Small protective devices were used in abundance. Military harness pendants often bore the *mano fica*, the fist-and-phallus that combined both male and female sexual imagery, and also the lunula, the crescent moon that symbolised rebirth (Bishop 1988). The linchpins with copper-alloy heads from Britain mentioned above were effectively already protective as they were crescent-shaped, but many of them also had terminals cast in protective forms, such as the heads of waterbirds, dogs and rams, and one example also used a phallus (Bird 1997). A particularly apposite amulet is a coin of Domitian set in the mast step of Blackfriars Ship 1 (Marsden 1994: 49, figs. 44–5). The reverse showed the goddess Fortuna with her rudder, and the coin was placed in the hollow with the reverse uppermost so that it would touch the mast, thereby invoking the protection of the goddess for vessel and crew on all the ship's voyages (Plate 12).

Conclusion

A theme that runs throughout this chapter is the rarity of intact objects associated with transport. Vehicles and boats were made of wood, which rarely survives burial, while their metal fittings, especially those of iron, would usually be unrecognisable when broken and disassociated from the original structure and might often have been harvested for recycling. A more positive picture exists for leather footwear. Although this also requires special conditions for survival, there are now so many well-dated assemblages that information on supply and technology can be used in site reports and inter-site studies as well as providing a picture of changing fashions.

Apart from some groups of iron or military objects, many of the small metal artefacts associated with transport await a champion to set them in the meaningful contexts of date, geographical and social distribution, and regional, provincial or Empire-wide types. This is perhaps because the subject comes partly under the banners of the army, the navy, agriculture, and the *cursus publicus*, as well as of the various animals used for riding or draught, and, viewed from beneath the more general umbrella of 'travel and transport', becomes too tangled a mass of objects to encourage unravelling. The field is certainly huge, and has been only lightly outlined here, but it is ripe for harvest.

3 | Industry

W. H. MANNING

Today the word 'industry' has connotations of large factories with complex machines mass-producing objects, whereas 'craft' involves small-scale production, often by an individual or a small group of workers using relatively simple equipment. In the Roman world this division was less clear-cut and the vast majority of artefacts were produced in relatively small workshops. Where production was on a scale that might justify using the term 'industry' it was achieved by multiplying the number of productive units rather than by using new technology.

A number of 'industries' certainly existed in Roman Britain. Mining was one in which the restricted distribution of the ore deposits inevitably confined the mines, and probably most of the smelters, to limited areas, many of them far removed from the main centres of consumption which were predominantly in the south and east of England. But perhaps the most obvious of all, and the most thoroughly studied, is the pottery industry, which was concentrated in areas where suitable clay was available and from where it was possible to transport the pots to the consumers at an economic rate. Others industries which were of prime importance but which were more widely distributed included metalworking and the production of glass.

Manufacturing

Although the Romans could probably have produced cast iron, they had little use for such a brittle metal and all Roman iron was the more malleable wrought iron which comes from the furnace as a solid rather than as a liquid like copper or lead. A number of iron furnaces are known (Tylecote 1986: 155–65), but most furnaces for smelting other metals will have been near the mines and are probably buried deep below the spoil from later workings. The metals themselves reached the smiths in the form of ingots, such as the iron ingots from the Flavian fort at Newstead (Curle 1911: 288, pl. LXV, 9), or the bun-shaped copper ingots (Tylecote 1986: 24, fig. 10) and the massive lead pigs (Tylecote 1986: 61–73) which have been found in many parts of England and Wales (see also Chapter 1).

Iron remained in its solid form throughout its fabrication, but the other metals were usually reheated and cast in various types of mould, most often the simple two-piece mould, but multi-piece moulds were used for more elaborate items. *Cire perdue*, or lost-wax casting, was mainly used for more elaborate pieces, such as statuary. Gold, silver and copper alloys can also be hammered to produce sheet. It is possible to work these metals while they are cold, but, with the exception of gold, this hardens them and makes them increasingly brittle if they are not periodically annealed, a process which involves reheating the metal and allowing it to cool. The chief archaeological indicators of the working of these metals are the crucibles in which the metals were melted, fragments of the moulds in which the objects were cast and the iron tools which are discussed below. Although the size of many surviving castings suggests that quite large crucibles did exist, those which survive are mainly small, hemispherical, thick-walled pottery bowls (Tylecote 1986: 97, fig. 50, nos. 4–8). Fragments of moulds are not uncommon, almost all being piece moulds, often simple two-piece moulds, used for casting brooches (Bayley, Mackreth and Wallis 2001) or smaller utensils, such as the moulds for flasks and spoons found at Castleford (Cool and Philo 1998: 195–222).

Lead smelted near the mines was transported as massive ingots or 'pigs' which were cast in clay moulds. Small lead objects such as weights might be cast in the normal way, but more commonly lead was used as cast sheets which could be bent or rolled to form troughs and pipes for use in plumbing. When more elaborate forms were required, such as tanks or coffins, one face might be decorated with patterns produced by impressing designs into the flat mould in which the sheets were cast (Tylecote 1986: 61–77). The use of pewter, an alloy of lead and tin which also had to be cast as it could not be cold-worked, was almost entirely confined to late Roman Britain where it was widely used for tablewares, often imitating silver; a surprising number of the stone moulds used to produce these have survived (Tylecote 1986: 49; see also Chapter 7).

Glass was widely used, usually in the form of blown vessels, either free-blown where the form is largely created on the blowing iron, or blown into piece moulds, which was the method used to produce the common square bottles and ribbed bowls (Price and Cottam 1998: 60–1) and the more elaborate beakers decorated with circus and other scenes (Plate 24; Price and Cottam 1998: 63–4). Unfortunately, the moulds themselves have not survived (Price and Cottam 1998: 12). The main tools used in working the glass will have been the blowing iron (a long tube used to inflate the mass of molten glass needed to form the vessel), various bladed or simple shears-like tools, which even today are normally made of wood, and iron shears to cut the vessel from the blowing iron. Although some blowing irons might have been expected to have survived, none has so far been identified, while the shears used by glass blowers cannot be distinguished from those used in other crafts.

The range of tools and equipment available to the Romano-British crafts-man was surprisingly large, and in many cases they are very similar to those still in use until recent times. Almost all of those which have survived were made of iron. Romano-British tools were derived from two traditions: the equipment already in use in late Iron Age Britain and a range of tools used elsewhere in the Roman world, often originating in the Mediterranean area. The latter tended to extend the range of the existing tools rather than intro-duce entirely new types, although this did occur at times, the carpenter's plane being an obvious example (Plate 16). There is little doubt that the Roman army was one of the principal agents by which such tools were introduced into Britain, but it is unlikely to have been the only one.

The key industries or crafts which have left substantial numbers of tools, other than agriculture which is dealt with in Chapter 4 of this volume, are smithing and the related craft of farriery, carpentry, stone working, the building trade, leather working and the processing of cloth. Constraints of space prevent the discussion of all of the artefacts relevant to these crafts, or the citation of more than a limited number of examples, but what has been knowingly omitted is usually either rare or relatively unimportant. Examples from other parts of the Roman world have largely been ignored as in most cases they are similar to those from Britain.

Although the tools discussed in this chapter must have been used through-out the Roman period, they do not occur in equal numbers throughout that period. The reason for this is simple: almost all were made of iron and when scrapped they provided an important source of metal for the production of new tools. It is only when this cycle of use and reuse is broken that an object appears in the archaeological record. Occasionally, as was probably the case with most site finds, broken artefacts were discarded, in some cases possibly as votive offerings, in others perhaps as scrap which was collected but never utilised. The most important collections come from a series of major hoards (Manning 1972a). Some of these were almost certainly votive deposits; others, particularly those associated with the Roman army, were probably scrap, discarded when forts were closed (Manning 2006). These hoards are not evenly spread through the province or through the Roman period but fall into three main groups. There is an early series from the south of England which probably continued a late Iron Age custom of ritual

Fig. 4 Smith's tombstone from the Catacomb of Domatilla

deposition. The second group dates from the late first and early second centuries and can be associated, directly or indirectly, with the Roman army in northern England and southern Scotland. Important examples are the hoards from Blackburn Mill, Brampton, Carlingwark Loch, Loudoun Hill, Eckford and Newstead (see Piggott 1953; Manning 1972a). Finally there is a series of hoards, some of them very large and probably of a ritual origin, of fourth-century date found in the south and east of England, most notably from Great Chesterford and Silchester.

Smiths' tools

Although there is a fundamental difference between the blacksmith who works with a solid metal, albeit at red heat, and the smith who works with copper alloys or precious metals which can be cast and worked cold, the tools used by the two were much the same.

All smiths need a hearth. In the Roman period it was fired with charcoal, with bellows being used to raise the temperature. In the case of the blacksmith, the metal has to be kept almost at red heat as it is worked, while smiths working other metals use their hearth not only to melt the metal prior to casting but to anneal it during working, if the metal is being cold-worked, as sheet metals usually are.

Roman bellows appear in various reliefs or scenes, such as a graffito sketch from the Catacombs of Domatilla in Rome (Fig. 4; Manning 1976: 6, fig. 4), but being made of wood and leather they do not survive. Three other tools were needed to work the hearth: the poker, the rake and the shovel. Unlike the coke used in a modern hearth, charcoal does not form a clinker which has to be removed with a special form of poker, and Roman smiths probably rarely used a poker; when one was needed, any suitable length of iron rod would have sufficed, such as that from Whitton villa, Vale of Glamorgan (Jarrett and Wrathmell 1981: 190, no. 4, fig. 75.4). The rake, which the smith used to manoeuvre the burning fuel, was more useful; the Roman tool has a flattened or slightly dished blade set at right angles to a long stem which often terminates in a socket for a wooden handle (e.g. from the Park Street villa, St Albans: O'Neil 1945: 68, fig. 10.13). The fire shovel is very similar to a modern hearth shovel, the blade having upturned sides, while the long handle is usually twisted, ending in a flattened head which may be pierced for a suspension ring (e.g. Carrawburgh: Manning 1976: 39, no. 149, fig. 23).

Almost all smiths require an anvil, and in the Roman period iron anvils were the norm. They took two basic forms: a large rectangular block with a slightly domed face, and a beaked type which resembles a smaller version of the modern anvil but with a massive tang rather than a solid base. Both types were in use in the final years of the Iron Age, and a block anvil and two small beaked anvils come from the Waltham Abbey hoard (Manning 1985: 3–4). The block anvils found in Britain taper at their base, usually through a distinct step on all four sides, for insertion into a wooden block. Although not particularly large, they represented a major investment of iron on the part of the smith; an example from Sutton Walls, Herefordshire, weighed some 50kg (Kenyon 1954: 64, pl. XVIa; Tylecote 1961: 56ff). The Sutton Walls anvil and another from Stanton Low (Tylecote 1962: 240) have a round punching-hole running from the edge of the face to emerge in the sloping side, which allowed the smith to drive a punch through the metal being worked without damaging the punch itself or the face of the anvil. Other examples of this type of anvil are cited by Manning (1985: 1). Beaked anvils are far less common, but one was found in the fourth-century Silchester 1890 Hoard (Evans 1894: 142, fig. 3). The beak was used to form curved objects, and, as was the case with the Silchester anvil, they could have a punching hole in the flat face. Such anvils were far lighter than the block type; the Silchester one weighs no more than 9 kg.

Small anvils of the type used for delicate work are rare finds. They usually have a block-like head which, on the evidence of examples from London (Merrifield 1965: pl. 125) and the Continent, were mounted in cylindrical wooden blocks bound at their tops with iron collars. An example is known from Usk (Manning, Price and Webster 1995: 246, no. 1, fig. 75).

Tongs were a vital part of the blacksmith's equipment; without them, handling hot iron or crucibles would have been almost impossible. Although a number of small tongs are known, most are large and will have enabled the smith to hold the red-hot metal at a safe distance. Examples of such tongs are known in the late Iron Age (e.g. Llyn Cerrig Bach, Anglesey: Fox 1946: 96, no. 131, pls. VI and XIX). Most of the Roman examples come from hoards, although isolated finds and fragments are not unknown. They are very similar in appearance to modern tongs, often having one handle longer than the other. The commonest and simplest form of jaw is curved or bowed, closing to form an oval with its ends continuing into parallel gripping faces (e.g. five examples from the late Iron Age Waltham Abbey hoard: Manning 1985: 8, A11–A15, pls. 2–4). Others have more elaborate jaws where the gripping faces are set at right angles to the ends of the bow, with the end of one jaw turned through a right angle to form an L-shape while the shorter arm lies immediately above the top of the other jaw. Such an arrangement was designed to prevent the object being worked escaping from the jaws, an obvious danger when handling round-sectioned rods (Plate 13; see Newstead: Curle 1911: 286, pl. LXIII, 2). A rare form from Lanchester has short plate-like jaws, ideal for gripping thin work such as sheet metal (Manning 1976: 23, no. 51, fig. 14). Other jaw forms are known on the Continent and their absence from Britain is probably more apparent than real.

Small tongs are rarer and for some reason are not found in the major Roman hoards. Most are simply smaller versions of the basic form with bowed jaws and short gripping faces (e.g. Kingsholm: Manning 1985: 6, no. A9, pl. 2). A pair from London has short, straight gripping jaws, essentially a small version of the Lanchester type (Guildhall Museum Catalogue 1908: 53, no. 87, pl. XVIII, 5).

The Romano-British blacksmith, like his modern counterpart, had two basic types of hammer, the sledge or striking hammer and the hand-hammer. Within these two basic forms there are a number of variants. The sledgehammers will have been fitted with long hafts, the heaviest of them being the swing-sledge, today weighing between 3.5 and 9 kg, which was used in the initial stages of the work to rough-form the artefact. Roman examples are relatively rare, probably because they were used by smiths who could recycle them if they were damaged. One from Newstead, which is probably early Trajanic in date, is unusual in having a flat striking face balanced by a straight-pane; this is probably too sharp to have been used to spread the hot metal and may have been designed to cut it (Curle 1911: 286, pl. LVII, 6). Others come from the Great Chesterford Hoard (Neville

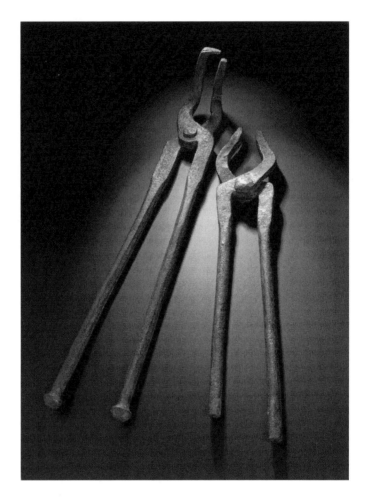

Pl. 13 Iron tongs from Newstead

1856: 6, pl. 1.1) and the Silchester 1900 Hoard (Fox and Hope 1901); both are of fourth-century date.

The lighter sledgehammer, weighing between 2.5 and 3.5 kg, was a hand-sledge used for general heavy work. Again we have examples from Newstead (Curle 1911: 285, pl. LXIII, 1, 11), which are unusual in having blunt cross-panes balancing the normal straight-pane; a similar hammer comes from the fortress at Caerleon (Nash-Williams 1932: 73, fig. 25, 3). Caerleon also produced a sledgehammer with two flat faces (Nash-Williams 1932: 73, fig. 25, 2) and another is known from the fourth-century Great Chesterford Hoard (Neville 1856: 6, pl. 12).

The hand-hammer was a basic tool used in all forms of metalworking and is found in a variety of shapes and sizes; regrettably, assigning any particular example to a specific type of smith is virtually impossible. Almost all are cross-pane hammers which have a rectangular face with rounded edges on one side of the haft and a blunt, chisel edge, which follows the line of the handle, on the other. The cross-pane was used to spread the metal length-wise whereas the straight-pane spread it in both directions. A smith would have had a set of these hammers varying in weight. The Silchester 1890 and 1900 Hoards (Evans 1894: 145, fig. 8, 9; Fox and Hope 1901) contained twelve of them ranging in weight from 1.1 kg down to 0.23 kg, and five came from the Great Chesterford hoard (Neville 1856: 6, pl. 1, 3–7). Most have a diamond-shaped expansion around the small circular eyes, both characteristics of Roman hammer-heads.

The small hammers which must have been used for delicate work are very rare, although a few are known from the London Walbrook (Museum of London).

Although the hammer usually strikes the metal being worked, it can also be used to strike another tool which itself impacts on the metal. Tools of this type include the rare set-hammer, hot and cold chisels, and sets, punches and drifts. Set-hammers are placed on the metal being worked, steadied by an assistant holding the handle and then struck with a sledge hammer. They allow the force to be applied at a precise spot and impact directly rather than at a slight angle as is the case with a sledge hammer. Such hammers are extremely rare, but an excellent example comes from the late Flavian fort at Newstead (Curle 1911: 285, pl. LXIII, 6).

Sets and chisels are used to cut metal, the set being struck with a sledge-hammer, the chisel with a hand-hammer. Both can be divided into two groups depending on whether they are used on cold or hot metal; when used on hot metal they usually had a handle to prevent the smith burning his hand. Today a handle of some form is often used with the cold set to reduce the danger of the smith being injured by the sledgehammer.

In some cases the nature of these tools is clear; hot chisels which have an integral iron handle and a wedge-shaped blade are unmistakable (e.g. from Caistor-by-Norwich (Norwich Museum) and London (Museum of London)), but differentiating between a short, stout cold chisel and a cold set, or even a wedge used to split wood, is less easy. Examples of such tools come from the Silchester 1900 Hoard (Fox and Hope 1901: 248). The basic form of a hot chisel has to be long enough to keep the hand away from the hot metal, but such tools are so similar to mason's chisels that certain identification is impossible. However, one form, with a rounded stem, a slightly expanded head and a convex edge can certainly be identified as a hot set which was probably held in place with either a withy or a wire handle (Coldhams Common, Cambridge: Manning 1985: 9, no. A20, pl. 5). Another, of slightly less characteristic form, comes from Kingsholm (Manning 1985: 9, A18, pl. 5 and others cited there).

The Roman cold chisel, like its modern descendant, was a short tool with a relatively sharp edge and a thick stem just long enough to have been held in a clenched hand. A probable example comes from Hod Hill, Dorset (Manning 1985: 9, no. A22, pl. 5).

Punches are used on hot metal, and their stems usually have a round or square cross-section. The fact that they are used with hot metal means that they have to be reasonably long or have to be held by some form of handle; most Roman punches are relatively short, suggesting that they were probably used with a detachable handle. Some, but by no means all, have a distinct head, and once again there is a problem in differentiating between small chisels and punches, although it is possible that some served both functions in the Roman period (see a group from Hod Hill: Manning 1985: 10, A23–A26, pl. 5 and others cited there). Examples without distinct heads are usually no more than lengths of relatively stout rod with a point at one end (e.g. Verulamium: Manning 1972b: 164, no. 4, fig. 60). Others have a distinct chisel edge (Newstead: Curle 1911: 285, pl. LXIII, 7), or a square-sectioned stem which would have produced a square hole (Newstead: Curle 1911: 288, pl. LXVI, 20).

Similar tools such as tracers, which are struck with a hammer, and gravers, which rely on the pressure of the hand, were used on fine metalwork and cannot be differentiated from punches when the tip is corroded. A probable tracer with a long stem and slightly rounded chisel edge from London is in the British Museum (Manning 1985: 11, A33, pl. 6), and the same collection contains two tools, also from London, which may be either graving tools or punches (Manning 1985: 11, A34, A35, pl. 6).

Drifts are tools used to enlarge holes made with a punch. They are usually shorter and stouter than the punch and taper to their head as well as to the tip which enables them to be driven right through the work. Such tools are rare, but examples are known from Silchester (Reading Museum), and Roman smiths may have used chisels which lacked distinct heads, such as those from Newstead, as a combined form of punch and drift (Curle 1911: 285, pl. LXIII, 7).

The file is essentially a metalworker's tool. Several forms were used in the Roman period – the flat file, the square file and the knife file; all were tanged. Unfortunately the teeth are easily destroyed or concealed by corrosion, although they may be visible on X-ray photographs. The blade of the flat file is normally rectangular in cross-section, often tapering to a point, with teeth on both faces (e.g. London: Wheeler 1930, 77, pl. XXXIII, 4, and Newstead: Curle 1911: 281, pl. LIX, 5). The square file is similar to the flat file but has a square cross-section with teeth on all four faces (e.g. London: Manning 1985: 11, A38, pl. 6 and others cited there). The rare knife file has a knife-like blade with teeth on the two faces but not on the narrow back. In addition to the usual tang there is a small spike on the back at the front of the blade which probably held a wooden handle enabling the file to be held at both ends, an obvious asset when precise work was involved. All of the examples from Silchester have a notch in the blade between the tang and the teeth, a device used to twist or set saw teeth, confirming that these files were used to sharpen saws (Evans 1894: 150, fig. 17).

Before the introduction of specialised machines, nails were made with nail-heading tools which took the form of an iron bar with a tapering hole or holes through it. Such tools are relatively rare finds, but examples with a stout central bar with flattened, discoidal ends pierced by a nail-hole are known from the Silchester 1900 Hoard and Usk (Manning *et al.* 1995, 249, no. 14, fig. 75, 16).

Carpenters' tools

The Romano-British carpenter had a wide selection of tools, many of which were inherited from his Iron Age predecessors, but a few, most notably the plane, were Roman introductions. Today the axe would scarcely be regarded as a carpenter's tool, but in the Roman period it was of prime importance for rough-shaping wooden artefacts. The Romans lacked the variety of axes found in the medieval period and most are of the basic form which, in longitudinal section, tapers from a rectangular butt or poll to a slightly convex cutting edge. The front and back are usually, although not invariably, curved, the curvature of the back often being greater than the front, producing a relatively long edge. The eye is oval and the sides often swell out on either side of it; in some examples small rectangular lugs may flank the socket to increase the security of the handle, a feature favoured by the Roman army in the first and second centuries but rare after that (e.g. the Brampton Hoard: Manning 1966a: 11, no. 6). The basic type can be divided into four groups, depending on the curvature of the blade (Fig. 5; Manning 1985, 15 where examples are cited).

After the axe the adze must have been one of the tools most often used by the Roman carpenter. Few show any degree of specialisation, although quite often the adze blade is balanced by a hammer-head or an axe blade.

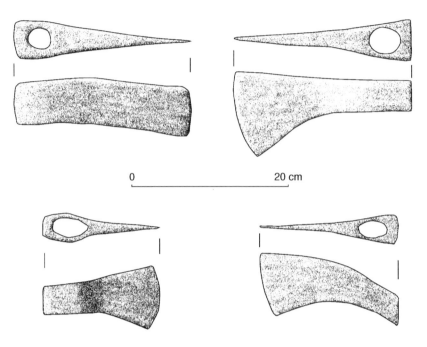

0   20 cm

Fig. 5 Types of axes, taken from Manning 1985

Unfortunately it is almost impossible to differentiate the simplest form of adze, with a narrow neck and angled blade, from a hoe (see Hod Hill: Manning 1985: 16–17, B7–B10, pl. 8, where other examples are cited). Tools which have an adze or hoe blade on one side and an axe blade on the other were probably general tools for clearance, allied to the larger military dolabrae. More specialised forms of adzes are rare, but one with a gouge-like blade in the Silchester 1890 Hoard (Evans 1894: 148, fig. 14), which may be a cooper's adze, shows that they existed.

The adze-hammer was a widely used carpenter's tool, and one which may have been introduced into Britain by the Roman army. In its most basic form the hammer-head is little more than a rectangular butt (Richborough: Bushe-Fox 1949: 154, pl. LXI, 339), but more elaborate examples exist where the eye is surrounded by a long collar and the hammer-head is well formed with a slightly widened face (e.g. Kingsholm: Manning 1985: 17, B14, pl. 8). A particularly fine example, probably of late first-century date, from London has a rectangular collar and hammer-head (Manning 1985: 18, B16, pl. 9).

The Roman carpenter had a variety of chisels which reflect the modern division into paring, firmer and mortise chisels, although, inevitably, it can be difficult to assign individual tools to a particular group. Although most chisels were probably used by carpenters, some of the stronger examples, particularly those with solid handles, could have been masons' tools. A classification which subdivides the main forms has been devised by Manning (1985: 21, fig. 4). The paring chisel is a finishing tool with a thin, flexible blade often with a splayed edge; it is not struck with a mallet as are the other types, but is pushed with the hand or by shoulder pressure. Paring chisels may have integral iron handles or be tanged, unlike the heavier forms which are usually socketed (e.g. London: Manning 1985: 21, B25, pl. 10).

The firmer chisel is used for general woodworking and has a blade which thins fairly evenly to the edge, while the sides of the blade often splay out as they approach the edge. Almost all are socketed (e.g. London: Manning 1985: 22, B31, pl. 10), although two undated examples from Silchester are tanged (Reading Museum). Examples with solid iron handles are also known from Silchester (Evans 1894: 149, fig. 15) and Sandy (Manning 1985: 22, B32, pl. 10).

The mortise chisel has a strong blade and is used for chopping-out mortises and other heavy work. The edge, which is usually the same width as the stem, is formed by a bevel on one face. Most mortise chisels are socketed (e.g. Hod Hill: Manning 1985: 23, B36–B42, pl. 10 and others cited there).

Gouges were widely used in the Roman period (Plate 14). Most were socketed, although some have solid handles and their shanks almost always have a circular cross-section. The curvature of the edge can vary, but the bevel forming the edge is always on the outside of the blade; in modern parlance, they are firmer gouges (e.g. Kingsholm: Manning 1985: 24, B46, pl. 11 and others cited there).

Bits and augers are tools used for boring holes in wood, the difference between them being that the bit was turned in a drill, which in the Roman period was usually a bow or strap drill, while the auger, which was capable of boring larger holes, was turned with a wooden cross-handle. The tips and the heads have a variety of forms on both bits and augers. The majority of heads are either an elongated pyramid (e.g. London: Manning 1985: 26, B51, p. 11) or lanceolate, essentially a flattened form of the pyramid (e.g. London: Manning 1985: 26, B55, fig.12), although this is more common on augers. The commonest type of tip is spoon-shaped, sharpened at its end and edges (e.g. London: Manning 1985: 26, B51, pl. 11 and others cited there); the rarest form has a twisted tip (e.g. Silchester: Reading Museum).

Essentially the auger is a bit which is too large to be turned by a drill. Their heads are almost always lanceolate and the blades are usually spoon-shaped (e.g. Brampton: Manning 1966a: 15, no. 11 and examples cited there).

Pl. 14 Socketed gouge from the 1890 Silchester Hoard

Most Roman saws took one of two forms, either with a simple wooden handle at one end of the blade, or with the blade mounted in a bow or frame which held it at both ends. Assigning fragments to the two forms is made easier by the fact that the back and edge of bowsaw blades are parallel, while handsaws tend to taper from the handle to the tip. The teeth of most saws have a regular triangular form, but some handsaws have teeth which slope towards the handle, a feature which means that they cut as the blade is pulled towards the user. This is contrary to modern practice, but reflects the fact that Roman saw blades were narrow and made of relatively soft iron; by making them cut on the back-stroke the smith ensured that they were under tension when cutting and so unlikely to bend. In modern practice saw teeth are almost always set, a process which involves twisting the teeth, usually in alternate directions, so that they project slightly and produce a cut, or kerf, which is wider than the blade and reduces the tendency of the blade to bind in the cut. Roman handsaws do not show this feature, but some framesaw blades do. An example of a handsaw with a triangular blade comes from Verulamium (Manning 1972b: 166, no. 12, fig. 61) and fragments are known from many other sites (Plate 15).

The bowsaw, which uses a one-piece, curved wooden frame to tension the blade, and the framesaw, which has an H-shaped frame, the tension being maintained by twisting a cord between the tops of the arms, the blade being at the bottom, were probably both in use in Roman Britain, although their blades are identical. A large fragment with set teeth comes from Silchester

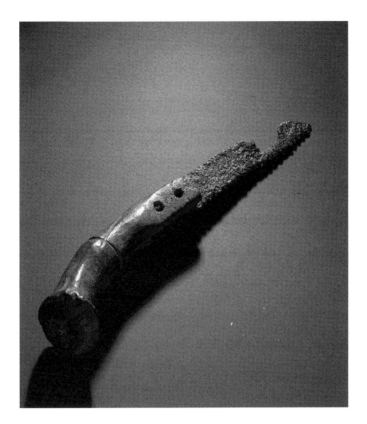

Pl. 15 Iron saw set in an antler handle from Newstead

(Reading Museum), and other fragments, usually without set teeth, are not uncommon (e.g. Hod Hill: Manning 1985: 21, B22, pl. 9). The number of teeth to the centimetre varies with the type of work for which the saw was designed.

The draw knife is another tool used for the shaping of wooden artefacts. It has a strong blade, which may be straight, as on an example from Wilsford Down (Cunnington and Goddard 1934: 235, no. 4, pl. LXXIX, 4), but more often was curved, with the handles set at an angle at its ends as at Hod Hill (Manning 1985: 18, B18, pl. 9).

The float is a very coarse form of file which was used for levelling or enlarging large mortises and the like. Identical tools, known as rasps, were used by farriers and one cannot differentiate between the two types (see Hod Hill: Manning 1985: 28, B79, pl. 12 and others cited there). They may have teeth on one or both faces, while one from Hod Hill has a D-shaped cross-section with teeth on both sides (Manning 1985: 29, B80, pl. 12).

Pl. 16 Iron plane from the 1890 Silchester Hoard

The plane, the carpenter's tool par excellence, was a Roman invention. It is extremely probable that the majority of planes used in the Roman world had wooden bodies (stocks) and that the only metal element was the iron, the chisel-like blade which cuts the wood. Fortunately for archaeologists, a number have been found with additional iron fittings which have made their identification and reconstruction possible, even though the stock is made from wood. The wooden stock had a backward sloping mouth for the iron, which was held firm by a wedge inserted between the iron and an iron cross-bar running through the stock from one side to the other. If other iron fittings are present they usually consist of a sole, turned slightly up at its ends, held in place by large rivets running through the stock in front and behind the mouth. Iron sides could be added to the sole to encase the stock still further and strengthen the cross-bar which held the plane iron in position. An iron sole is known from Verulamium (Manning 1972b: 166, no. 14, fig. 61), while planes with side plates come from Caerwent (Newport Museum) and Silchester (Plate 16; Evans 1894: 151, fig. 18). Most of the planes known from Britain are quite large, ranging in length from 34 to 44 cm. This would equate them with the modern jack-plane, a tool intended for comparatively rough work, and their iron soles may reflect this. Medium-sized planes certainly existed; two from Pompeii are no more than 21 cm long and were probably intended for less strenuous work (Gaitzsch 1980: 113, Nr. 1, 2, Taf. 26, 135). Until recently small planes were unknown in Britain, but a grave at Turners Hall Farm, Hertfordshire (West 2005: 273) has produced a number of planes, around 10 cm in length, which are essentially miniature versions of the larger ones, with iron sole-plates and vertical rivets; in several cases, they still retain their plane irons. They will have been used for delicate work where a larger plane would have been too bulky.

A number of plane irons have been found. Most have straight edges (e.g. Usk: Manning *et al.* 1995: 249, no. 15, fig. 75), but one from Newstead (Curle 1911: 281, pl. LIX, 15) came from a moulding plane and has a shaped edge designed to produce wooden mouldings.

Although carpenters clearly used nails in very large numbers, there is no form of hammer which is unequivocally a carpenter's tool; the claw-hammer intended both to drive nails and to extract them is probably medieval in origin. The claw, however, was known in the Roman period. The cleft end is usually set at a slight angle to the long stem to allow the maximum leverage to be exerted when the nail was being extracted. Long examples could, of course, have been used more generally, for opening packing cases, for example (e.g. Caerwent in Newport Museum). Smaller ones are more likely to have been used to remove nails; one from Usk has a claw at each end (Manning *et al.* 1995: 251, no. 20, fig. 76).

The wedge was used to split wood or stone, but examples can be disconcertingly similar to the smith's set, particularly in a corroded condition. Before the advent of power tools, wedges were widely used to split wood when precise control of the product was unnecessary (e.g. Newstead: Curle 1911: 284, pl. LXI, 6).

Dividers will certainly have been used by carpenters, but also by smiths and masons. The majority have a pair of legs which taper from a flattened, rounded head pierced at its centre to receive the rivet which held them together. Either the rivet can be short with domed heads on each side (e.g. Rushall Down: Cunnington and Goddard 1934: 233, no. 1, pl. LXXVIII) or it can be longer, with a head at one end and a slot in the stem near the other end through which a wedge is pushed (e.g. Colchester: Manning 1985: A39, 11, pl. 6).

Quarrying tools

Tools used in quarrying and to split stone are rare, or at least rarely identifiable, although, of course, quarrymen will have used many of the tools associated with other crafts. Wedges, similar to those used for splitting wood, which were discussed above, were probably used in quarrying; two which can certainly be identified as masons' or quarrymen's tools were found in the core of Hadrian's Wall at Brunton Bank (Manning 1976: 25, nos. 61–2, fig. 15). They differ from the normal wedge in having 'feathers' or nicks cut on opposing edges which would have acted as barbs and prevented the wedge from recoiling when struck with a sledge hammer.

The crowbar will have been used by a variety of crafts for raising heavy objects, but it is not inappropriate to include it here. In fact crowbars are exceedingly rare, although a fine example is known from London with the characteristic straight shaft and chisel edge (Manning 1985: 32, C19, pl. 14).

Masons', plasterers' and allied tools

In the case of chisels there are considerable problems in assigning specific examples to the mason rather than the carpenter. The typical mason's chisel has a solid iron handle made in one piece with the blade, which often shows signs of heavy hammering. The blade usually has a bevel on each face and can be slightly wider than the stem, as is seen on examples from Housesteads (Manning 1976: 26, nos. 68–70, fig. 16).

The small pick was a widely used tool and takes three basic forms, all of which could have been used by masons or quarrymen. They are discussed by Manning (1976: 26).

The trowel is the tool which characterises the mason, although examples will also have been used equally often by plasterers and bricklayers. The Roman ones are virtually identical with their modern descendants, although a number of identifiable types are discussed by Manning (1976: 26).

Various forms of modelling tools will have been used not only by plasterers but also by sculptors working in clay and, upon occasion, probably by potters. The commonest form has paired blades which widen to straight edges, with a central stem which is often barrel-shaped and decorated with concentric grooves. The finest examples come from London (Manning 1985: 32, C13–C18, pl. 13).

Tools used in processing wool and cloth

There is little doubt that spinning wool and weaving were mostly domestic occupations – the widespread occurrence of spindle whorls and loom weights on Romano-British domestic sites is proof enough. A number of tools exist which suggest that at least in some areas the processing of wool and production of cloth may have been organised on a larger scale, and the

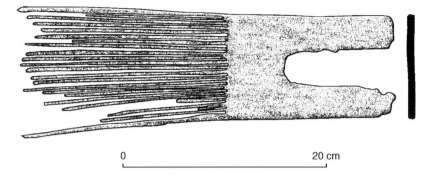

0   20 cm

Fig. 6 Wool comb from Caistor-by-Norwich

fourth-century Notitia Dignitatum refers to a *gynaecium* or weaving centre in Britain at Venta (either Caistor-by-Norwich, Winchester or Caerwent), which indicates that there was some larger-scale production under state control at that time (Manning 1966b).

U-shaped spring shears were widely used in the ancient world for a variety of tasks. They can be divided into three groups by size, although there is no sharp division between the small and medium types. Small shears with blades less than 15 cm long could have had many uses, but cutting thread and the like will have been among them (Verulamium: Manning 1972b: 176, no. 44, fig. 65). Larger shears are the most common type and will certainly have been used for shearing sheep, although that was not their only use (e.g. Barton Hill, near Tarrant Hinton: Manning 1985: 34, D4, pl. 14). Cropping shears, which are more than 120 cm long, are exceedingly rare and only one example is known from Britain, that from the Great Chesterford hoard (Neville 1856: 10, pl. 3, fig. 30). Their manner of use is seen in a relief from Sens in France (Espérandieu 1966: IV, 12) which shows that they were designed to cut the nap on cloth to an even length, being held against the worker's body with the blades parallel to the cloth being cropped.

Before wool can be spun it must be combed or carded to align the strands; in the Roman period, when this was being done on a reasonably large scale, iron combs were used. Most of the British ones have teeth only at one end, the other end being a plate with a deep rectangular recess cut into it which probably enabled it to be slotted into a vertical post when in use (Fig. 6; Caistor-by-Norwich: Manning 1972c: 334). The alternative form, which is common on the Continent, has teeth at both ends (e.g. Great Chesterford: Manning 1985: 34, D3, pl. 14).

At least three types of needles were used in Roman Britain and it is convenient to consider them here, although they differ considerably in their appearance and use. Iron sewing needles were probably common objects but are rare archaeological finds, almost certainly as a result of their destruction by corrosion, although the exceptional conditions of the London Walbrook have produced large numbers (Manning 1985: 35, D14–D32, pl. 15). Bone and copper-alloy examples are found on most sites but it is impossible to differentiate between those used in domestic and industrial contexts.

The baling needle differs from the normal form not only in being much longer, but in being mounted in a handle with the eye in the tip of the needle. It was used to push thread through material in order to sew-up bales; an example is known from London (Museum of London).

Netting needles are not true needles but formers or spacers around which a net is knotted to produce a mesh of constant size. They have a straight stem with a V- or U-shaped fork at each end (e.g. Hod Hill: Manning 1985: 37, D38, pl. 15 and others cited there).

A bag hook is a strong double hook (with both hooks turned in the same direction) with a cross-bar between them which may, or may not, have a tang at its mid-point. It was used to lift bags or bales by catching the binding in the hooks. They were probably used to load and unload large wagons and ships. Examples are rare but they are known from London (Museum of London) and Newstead (National Museums of Scotland, Edinburgh).

A baling fork is a related tool which takes the form of a strong, socketed pitch-fork with a small U-shaped spike set halfway along each of the main tines. It had a similar function to the baling hook, with the main tines being pushed under the binding of a bale which was then caught by the smaller hooks allowing the bale to be lifted (see Great Chesterford: Manning1985: 60, F67, pl. 25).

Leather-working tools

Although the leather-worker used a number of knives, only one is limited to his craft. This is the lunette knife with a semicircular blade and a tang or handle set at the centre of the back (e.g. Kingsholm: Manning 1985: 39, E3, pl. 15). They should not be confused with lunate turf-cutters, which are usually larger and have crescentic rather than semicircular blades.

The Roman cobbler's last is very similar to its modern successor. It has a strong tang, which may simply be the end of the stem, which fitted into a wooden bench, a long stem and a foot-shaped head which rarely follows the shape of the human foot very closely (Fig. 7; Sandy: Manning 1985: 42, E35, pl. 17).

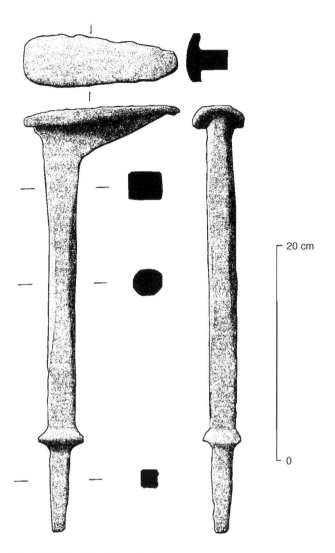

Fig. 7 Cobbler's last from Sandy

Awls are used to pierce the leather to enable it to be sewn. They have thin, sharp points and were normally mounted in a wooden handle. They can be divided into four types which are discussed by Manning (1985: 39).

Punches were used both to create decorative patterns and to make holes for sewing the leather. Some of those used to make patterns are blunt and were not intended to pierce the leather (e.g. London: Manning 1985: 41, E29, pl. 6). Punches used to pierce the leather usually have a gouge-like edge, often forming over two-thirds of a circle, which would have cut discs from the leather (see Water Newton: Manning 1985: E33, pl. 16 and others cited there).

Farriers' tools

The similarity of the carpenter's float and the farrier's rasp has already been noted and the examples cited under the discussion of the floats could equally well have been farriers' rasps.

The farrier's butteris is used to pare horses' hooves, in particular when the hoof is being prepared for shoeing (see Chapter 2). Two types appear to have existed: the first has a blade with a V-shaped section; the second has a flattened U section, the blade itself being straight and curving up into a U at its back-end. The handle of the second type is welded to the top of the U and runs back to form a butt, not unlike that of an antique pistol; halfway along the handle a second bar is welded, rising up and then running back parallel with the handle for a short way (see Sandy: Manning 1985: 61, G1, pl. 26).

Curry combs are used to groom horses. A number of artefacts are known which may be parts of such tools but have lost the thin blade which took the form of a flat plate turned down and serrated at its front. They have three arms and a tang, with the remains of rivets through the flattened ends of the arms (e.g. Sandy: Manning 1985: 61, G2, pl. 26 and others cited there).

Conclusions

As this chapter has made clear, the artefactual evidence for industries and crafts in Roman Britain is largely limited to the metal, usually iron, tools associated with them, and where an industry used few metal tools it usually leaves correspondingly few traces in the archaeological record. In some cases there is other evidence – potters' kilns or the furnaces of some of the metallurgical industries, for example – but in others we must rely almost entirely on the artefacts which they produced. Despite these limitations we have excellent evidence for many of the industries and crafts of Roman Britain, and while we may not have a full range of tools and equipment even for those crafts where many tools survive, we have enough to allow us to discuss a number of trades and their products in considerable detail. One needs only to look at the sparse material which survives from the Iron Age or immediate post-Roman period to appreciate how fortunate the student of Roman industry is in this respect and what a hive of industry Britain was during the Roman period.

4 | Agriculture

SÎAN REES

The Roman army, marching into Britain as an invading force, was not entering an unknown land, or one devoid of any established farming tradition. Indeed it would have been unwise to do any such thing. An army marches on its stomach, we are told, and the ability to use harvesting tools for foraging was an essential component of the soldier's skills. Roman writers knew well not only that Britain was able to feed itself, but that it produced a trading surplus of grain, meat and skins; Strabo (*Geog.* IV.199) mentions British grain exports and Caesar (*Bell. Gall.* V.12) refers to the cereal production of Kent, likening it to that of the Gallic people. This writing, along with countless archaeological excavations of pre-Roman Iron Age sites, gives evidence of an efficient, established agricultural system in tune with topography, climate and soils, using tools made from iron, wood, stone and basketry, to produce food sufficient for immediate demand and for surplus. It had the capacity both to feed non-agricultural consumers such as the aristocracy, specialist craftsmen and merchants in Britain, and for export and trade with that very Roman Empire that now sought to invade.

The agricultural system that the Roman invaders found and inherited would, of course, provide the basis for continuation and development throughout the next four centuries. The implements that archaeologists find on pre-Roman Iron Age sites continue to appear within the first decades of the Roman occupation almost without change. Indeed it is suggested that the initial impact of the invasion would have been an adverse one on an agricultural system that relied upon safe production and storage of seed corn and breeding stock. The ravages of war and the heavy demands of an army that required two years' supply of grain as a safe storage resulted in the need for the importation of grain, perhaps for the first time (Straker 1987: 151–3; Fulford 1989: 179–80). Nevertheless, by the final years of the Roman occupation, different agricultural systems had certainly appeared, evidenced by, among other things, new tool types such as the scythe, heavy plough shares and coulters, and more sophisticated querns and millstones. These improvements were the result of a combination of factors – a greater availability of iron, greater efficiency of tools especially with regard to labour-saving technology, and perhaps greater potential production due to increased exploitation of heavier soils and more productive varieties of crops. How much of this undoubted development can be attributed to the effect of Roman occupation, with the increased demand for food resulting from the tendency towards urbanisation, specialisation and trade, and how much was a consequence of an ongoing continuum is an interesting question, but perhaps beyond the scope of this chapter.

Agricultural tools have their place among the sources of evidence available to the excavator trying to understand site type, the lifestyle of a site's inhabitants or the nature of a regional economy. However, the weakness of a dependence upon tool type as a sole source of evidence has long been recognised (Rees 1981: 66). While some tools, such as late Roman plough coulters, have their function firmly ascribed, many simple tool types may have had a multitude of functions and to reconstruct an agricultural system on a single find of a tool such as the so-called ox goad, for instance, would be dangerous indeed. The broader the base of available evidence, the better the attribution of agricultural system. If that collection of evidence includes the remains of crops or animals themselves (environmental data incorporating, for example, cereal grains, especially if they include remains from different stages of food processing (Hillman 1981), macro-environmental remains from pulses, pollen from weed types known to invade particular crops, food processing features such as corn drying kilns or granaries, and butchered bones from domesticated stock), the agricultural system of a site can be more safely attributed than by using agricultural implements alone. The soil type and topography of a site, giving an inherent probability of a particular agricultural system being employed there, must be examined alongside the available implements (Rees 1981: 83). Given these caveats, the study of agricultural implements has its uses and their descriptions below will attempt to give an idea of the degree of reliance with which function may be ascribed to individual tool types.

Soil cultivation

Small socketed iron tools usually considered to be plough tips or the iron sheaths for light ploughs otherwise made of wood are a common find on pre-Roman Iron Age and Romano-British sites. While in principle the tools could have been used for different functions, such as creating furrows for seed, weeding or cleaning tools, their shape, distribution and the pattern of wear on their pointed ends would suggest a reasonable reliability for their identification as plough tips. Throughout the Iron Age and Roman period, there is an apparent general chronological development as tools gradually tend towards a greater lengthening of the iron tip, presumably as the use of iron became more affordable, which would lengthen the life and durability of the plough. The sheathing in iron of the business end of wooden tools, such as spades, spuds and rakes, which would otherwise suffer a disproportionate amount of wear, was quite common, and the lengthening of the iron part does not, of course, imply any substantive development of the tool type itself. Wooden shares without iron sheathing would also have continued to be used in the Roman period, however, as the second-century wooden share from Usk Roman fort attests (Rees 1979: 45; Manning *et al.* 1995: 238–9). An alternative to iron sheathing could be fire hardening, as on the first-century BC example from Walesland Rath, Pembrokeshire (Fig. 8(d) Wainwright 1971: 94; Rees 1979: 45). A fragment of a wooden arrow-shaped share or perhaps ard-head of the third century from Ashville, Oxfordshire (Fowler 1978; Rees 1979: 46) may have been shod with an iron tip, though the evidence remains tentative, as must be the case with such fragmentary wooden tools that sadly survive only too infrequently.

The iron ard tips, however, are common enough finds. They vary considerably in size, ranging from short tips such as the first-century AD examples from Coygan Camp, Carmarthenshire, to longer, more massive examples such as those from the hoard at Bigbury hillfort, Kent (Fig. 8(c)). It is generally considered that they functioned as protective sheaths to the pointed ends of long wooden foreshares known to have been used in ards such as the Donnerupland ard from Denmark (Glob 1951). That such wooden ards – light soil cultivating tools with no mouldboard capable of physically turning a cut sod – were used in Britain is certain. The ard beam from Lochmaben, dated to 80 BC just before the Roman invasion, is of the bow ard type known from more complete Danish examples from bogs (Rees 1979: 44b). These complete ards show how the composite iron and wooden foreshare would have worked, seated either on an arrow-shaped foreshare supported by the stilt and ard-head (Donnerupland) or on the simple one-piece ard-head and stilt as on the ards from Dostrup (Fig 8(a)), and Hendriksmose (Steensberg 1936: fig. 2; Hansen 1969: fig 1:12). The foreshare, protruding beyond the ard-head as the main working part of the ard, would have been subjected to hard wear, and an iron sheath, covering the upper and front part of the share to protect the wood from the direction of passage through the soil, would have prolonged the life of the share considerably. Though many iron sheaths of this type are known from Roman Britain, their findspots are often in hoards; this does not help particularly in understanding the distribution

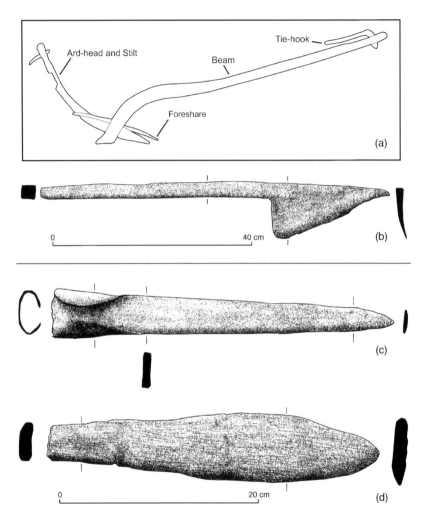

Fig. 8 (a) A bow ard, after Steensberg 1936, fig. 2; (b) iron coulter from Great Whitcombe; (c) iron plough share from Bigbury; (d) wooden ard share from Walesland Rath

of this type of ard in Roman Britain. The twenty or so examples known from Romano-British sites (Rees 1979: figs. 51–8) tend to date from the earlier years of the Roman period and to be indistinguishable from those from the pre-Roman Iron Age. As noted above, their form changes little other than by the amount of iron used in their manufacture, and this difference may be more to do with availability of iron or iron working than with the tool type or its development.

The wooden ards that these iron sheaths served were probably pulled by teams of two oxen, yoked by a horn, or, more likely, a withers yoke (Rees

1979: 72–5). The Lochmaben beam has two holes, one for the ard-head and share and one a small perforation at the yoke end, showing just one position for the fastening of the yoke. The Danish Hendriksmose beam had notches allowing two positions for the yoke, thus allowing adjustment of the depth of soil penetration. Light ards were probably held tilted in the ground to help create furrows, as the asymmetric wear on such tools attests, but the practice of cross ploughing, so that the field was ploughed first in one direction and then in the other to pulverise the soil as completely as possible, is known to have been the norm, both through classical agronomists' writings (Varro *Rust.* I.29.3) and through the excavation of cross ploughmarks in British excavations (Rees 1979: 79–87). Cross ploughing has been found on a variety of soil types, suggesting that the ard could be employed on reasonably heavy soils.

Towards the end of the Roman period in Britain the final logical conclusion of the development of the iron foreshare resulted in the whole share being made of iron. A series of such long shares has been found, the most famous being those from Silchester (Evans 1894: 141; Manning 1964: 60, fig. 5a) and Great Chesterford (Neville 1856: 4, 12, 17). Their interpretation as foreshares, made plausible by their length, shape and wear patterns, is strengthened by the presence of large coulters in the same hoards at Great Chesterford and Silchester. The type of foreshare implies the continued use of a tillage implement of the bow ard type, with share and coulter housed within by a heavy beam; it is difficult to imagine their use in a more horizontal soil entry implement like a crook ard. Nonetheless, the plough by this period must have developed a far greater weight and sophistication and it is unfortunate that we still await finds of wooden parts of working sections of later Roman ploughs.

Finds of coulters from these fourth-century hoards and elsewhere (Fig. 8(b); Rees 1979: 59–61; Manning 1985: 44, pl. 18) are not uncommon from fourth-century contexts and they appear to be a relatively late introduction into Britain. No definite examples are earlier than this, though this may be because the amount of reusable iron they contained resulted in their being gathered into the hoards which are commonly found in late Roman contexts. The implements, used for cutting the sod vertically in advance of the share which cuts horizontally, are similar in shape, with a large triangular blade and long shaft which can be octagonal or rectilinear in cross-section. The coulter is used in any heavy plough for this purpose, but the fact that many are found in the same hoards as iron bar foreshares suggests, as noted above, that they were used in ploughs where the share and coulter pass through the beam. However, one coulter, that from

Frindsbury (Rees 1979: 60, figs. 67d, 63), may have been associated with an open-flanged, symmetrical share of a different type.

Whatever type of plough share they are associated with, coulters certainly imply a more sophisticated, expensive and heavy implement which would have been perfectly capable of tilling heavy soils over large fields. This suggestion is made more plausible by the appearance of other types of heavy shares: symmetric and asymmetric (or winged) shares. These short modern-looking shares would not have been fitted on to bow ard types of ploughs and this, in turn, implies the existence of at least one other type of cultivation implement within the Roman period, probably a heavier plough with a horizontal working part into which the beam is itself fitted. The symmetric shares can date from early in the Roman period, and can be either rounded to cover the wooden share point, such as the Blackburn Mill or Swordale examples, or flanged in the way of modern shares, as on the first-century Bucklersbury House, London example (Rees 1979: figs. 60–2). The asymmetric shares from Folkestone, Chester, Brading and Dinorben are probably late Roman and are especially interesting (Rees 1979: figs. 64, 65). The fact that they cut in one direction only does suggest that the plough used was a one-directional one, and thus may well have had a fixed mouldboard used for turning the soil. This is an important development that, along with the extra weight and durability of these later ploughs, suggests a level of sophistication in agricultural development sufficient to allow effective cultivation of any soil type. The creation of rig and furrow, suggested from excavations on clay soils at the Roman forts of Rudchester and Carrawburgh (Gillam, Harrison and Newman 1973: 84–5; Breeze 1974: 189), and one-way plough marks at early and late Roman contexts at Latimer and Shearplace Hill respectively (Branigan 1971: fig. 14; Rahtz and ApSimon 1962) show that cross ploughing was by no means the only practice in Roman Britain, as heavier ploughs rendered it unnecessary, and, indeed, the ability to create a rig does again provide tentative evidence for the mouldboard plough.

Ploughs certainly were equipped with additions to increase their versatility, as we know from two interesting models of ploughs. The famous bronze Piercebridge plough model in the British Museum (Plate 17; Manning 1971) has projections apparently attached to the beam, which may have functioned as earthboards to cover broadcast seed or to cut drainage ditches or for clod breaking after sowing – the Roman agronomists Varro and Pliny describe such features and their functions. The difficulty, apart from the size of the piece (6.9 cm), and the fact that it apparently shows a religious and therefore perhaps atypical scene, is that we do not know where it was made and, therefore, whether it has any relevance to Romano-British

Pl. 17 The Piercebridge plough group

cultivation tools. The model's beam has a hole presumably for a detachable coulter, which might ascribe a later date in the Roman period than
the second- or third-century date suggested by Toynbee (1962: 149). The
small bronze model of a plough from Sussex (Manning 1966c), dated by
association to the later Roman period, is also equipped with boards perhaps used for covering seed after sowing. Both models have been described
as bow ards, though their schematic detailing and small size make certain
identification impossible.

The identification of plough or ard shares, then, can be made with a
reasonable degree of reliability and their recovery from sites (rather than
hoards) does suggest cultivation nearby. However, tillage requires, or can
utilise, a variety of other implements, though not all are so reliable as
an exclusive indicator of cultivation. Hoes and mattocks (see below) would
often be required to break up clods during ploughing, though these could be

used alone to cultivate smaller plots or for horticultural rather than larger-scale cultivation. Most dubious of all, however, must be the 'ox goads', small iron points first identified as cultivation tools for controlling oxen by Pitt-Rivers (1887–98) and endorsed by Payne (1947: 99); Roman agronomists speak of their use, usually disparagingly (Columella *Rust.* VI.2.11), so we know goads were used. Unfortunately, a pointed stick can be perfectly effective for such a purpose and whether or not the small twisted iron spikes archaeologists are wont to call 'ox goads' are to be reliably ascribed that function is far from clear. Indeed, many other functions have been suggested, including nibs for writing implements (see Chapter 6), and to place any reliance on the identification of a specific agricultural regime from their finding would be most unwise. Their almost universal appearance on Roman sites makes this lack of certainty all the more frustrating. Several different types are found (Rees 1979: 75–9 and figs. 73–4) in iron, bronze and bone.

There is little doubt that Roman ard and plough shares and coulters were generally utilitarian items found either in agricultural settlements or in hoards. Their distribution in Britain, as usual, is slanted towards the south-east, though this may reflect the number of excavations and availability of iron rather than the distribution of the practice of cultivation. Ploughing does, however, occasionally have a religious connotation, as the Piercebridge plough group and the Sussex model show, though the finding of plough shares on a site is a reasonably reliable indicator of soil cultivation; the converse, of course, is not true – the absence of iron plough tips certainly should not be taken as evidence of lack of an agricultural regime involving soil cultivation.

Care of the crop

Alongside (or, on smaller plots, instead of) the plough, manual tools would be needed both to break up clods and to make the seed bed ready for sowing. Sowing, in the pre-industrial age, was done broadcast, a skilful operation requiring experience to obtain an even cover, spreading the seed from leather slings or baskets. Evidence of sowing is virtually non-existent in the archaeological record, though Roman mosaics and wall-illustrations show the process often enough. Covering the broadcast seed with fine soil may well have been done by reploughing using boards on either side of the plough, such as those shown on the Sussex model. It is possible that the iron prongs usually interpreted as the teeth of harvesting rakes and described more thoroughly below could also have been components of

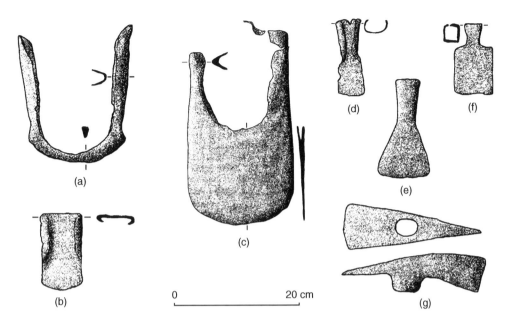

Fig. 9 (a) Iron spade shoe from Tiddington; (b) iron spade from Silchester; (c) iron spade shoe from Frocester Court; (d) iron spud from London; (e) iron spud from Sibson; (f) iron spud from London; (g) mattock from Lakenheath

harrows used for soil preparation or seed covering. The Newstead Roman fort rake, comprising seven teeth in a straight wooden head, is almost certainly part of a harvesting rake, found, as it was, along with scythes. However, classical writers do describe a harrow comprising a wooden frame with iron teeth (*crates dentatae* or *irpex*). Varro's description (*Rust* V.136) of the *irpex* as a straight piece of wood with numerous teeth would, in fact, be not dissimilar from a larger version of the Newstead tool, while, despite Pliny's lack of detail (*Nat. Hist.* XVIII.186), White interprets his *crates dentatae* as an implement consisting of 'a triangular or rectangular frame fitted with several rows of teeth' (1967: 150). If he is right, this could explain why sixteen or seventeen 'rake-prongs' were found together at Walbrook, London, this number being surely excessive for a single straight-headed rake. The so-called rake-prongs do vary considerably in length – from 7 to 17 cm long – and in their degree of curve. It is possible, therefore, that these iron prongs in fact functioned on a number of different types of tools.

Hoes and mattocks of iron required for seed bed preparation and subsequent care of the crop are reasonably common artefacts from Roman sites. 'Mattock' is a term generally used for a multi-purpose iron digging and cutting tool, with one blade with the cutting edge parallel to the handle and one cutting blade at right angles to the handle (Fig. 9(g)), while 'hoe' is generally used for a more purely agricultural tool, with only the latter oriented blade with or without supplementary tines. Few such tools appear in the pre-Roman Iron Age and three of the four Roman hoe types known appear to have been introduced in the Roman period. A small number of two-tined implements of antler have been found from Roman contexts and may also have served as hoes.

Entrenching tools are generally assigned the military function of ditch digging for the defences of forts, owing to their military distribution and their known use as part of the Roman soldier's kit. However, with their broad spade-shaped blade on one side and straight-sided blunt-ended pick blade on the other, they might easily have been used for general earth moving, drainage or ground clearance duties, and their appearance at Chedworth Roman villa and Bucklersbury House, London, suggests that they may have had a more general function than often realised. Double-bladed mattocks, similarly, are non-specific tools which may be used for cultivation and are commonly found on a variety of Roman sites. They are occasionally found in Iron Age contexts (as at Bigbury hillfort; Rees 1979: 313) but become common on Roman sites.

White (1967: 63) attempts to distinguish between dolabrae used for forestry (those with an upturned blade used for rolling logs) and those used for other purposes, military, mining and agricultural, but it is only to be expected that their function was general, including the ground clearance and soil preparation described in Mediterranean contexts by Palladius and Columella (*Op. Agric.* II.3 and *De Agric.* X.2). Single-bladed hoes, on the other hand, are more certainly ascribed an agricultural or woodworking function and their distribution on civilian sites, especially towns, strengthens this interpretation. Some could have been adzes, a tool type that certainly appears in the Iron Age, and Manning has suggested that the narrower-bladed tools with back protuberances could have been adzes while wider-bladed tools could have been hoes (Manning 1970: 19). However, similar narrow-bladed tools have been used for soil cultivation relatively recently (Manning 1970: 19) and such tools could have been general purpose; only when worn blades have demonstrably been kept sharp and pristine can a woodworking function confidently be ascribed. Wider-bladed tools such as those from Castle Hill in Nottingham, Lydney, Chesters and Brampton must have functioned as cultivation tools, with blades 12 cm wide or more (Rees 1979: figs. 82–3), and these stout tools take the development of the tool far beyond those found at Iron Age sites.

A commonly found group of smaller single-bladed and double-tined tools appear to have been an early Roman introduction to Britain. White (1967: 66) suggests these were the *ascia-rastrum* hoes mentioned by classical writers as being used to aerate the soil, remove weeds and tend young plants on a more delicate scale. It is interesting that they are found largely on highly Romanised sites, but towns, forts and small settlements rather than villas. The single blade may be spade-shaped, splayed, or mattock- or diamond-shaped, and the blade and tines are usually set at a slight angle to the haft. Their appearance in both early and late Roman contexts, as for example at Blackburn Mill and Bucklersbury House through to fourth-century contexts at Richborough fort (Rees 1979: 309–10, figs. 84–7), shows that this was a tool type used throughout the period. A much heavier double-tined hoe, which may have been the classical writers' *bidens* (Columella *Rust.* IV.5.1; IV.10.1; V.9.12 and Pliny *Nat. Hist.* XVII.54; XVIII.46), was evidently used for soil breaking and aeration. This is a rare tool type of which only seven examples are known in Britain, with a rather eccentric distribution on Roman civil sites in southern England and Wales and with no examples found on villas. Heavy, effective tools, they have a variety of methods of hafting, being normally socketed (London), or less normally hafted through an eye in the main cross-piece (Coygan Camp), or somewhat eccentrically supplied with tang and rivet (Rushall Down) (Rees 1979: 311–12, figs. 88–90). They are, nonetheless, found in early and late Roman contexts and, like the *ascia-rastrum*, appear to be an early Roman introduction.

Ground cultivation, manual digging of smaller plots and a multiplicity of tasks, such as soil removal, carting of manure and fencing, required spades and shovels, then as now. Again, these are essential tools for the farm and the horticultural plot, but have non-agricultural as well as farming uses and a number have been discovered in Roman mines and industrial sites. Wooden spades are unsophisticated implements which would have been around as long as agriculture, but in the Roman period wooden spades were shod with iron to increase their durability and effectiveness (Gailey and Fenton 1970). Finds of such iron shoes are quite common from Roman sites, and have a wide distribution, broken fragments being surprisingly frequently mis-identified by those unfamiliar with their characteristic cross-section. They come in a variety of shapes and sizes throughout the Roman period but the selection of round-bottomed or square-bottomed shape appears to have no relevance in chronological development or distribution. It would be unwise to attribute any regional significance to the pattern of distribution of different types that we have, given the small sample size of different styles.

A typological classification for spade sheaths was first proposed by Corder (1943) and was refined by Manning (1970) based on blade shape and attachment method. They are commonest from Romanised sites such as towns, villas, small settlements and forts, and different types seem to be found indiscriminately on all site types, in all areas and at all dates throughout the

Roman period. Unshod wooden spades undoubtedly continued in use, and a worn example from Chester may be Roman, while two wooden spades from Silchester, one round-bottomed and one rectangular, show the characteristic marks left by the iron sheath (Rees 1979: fig. 107). The shoes may be round- or square-bottomed, and the sheath may extend all round the sides and cutting edge to the same depth or just have a thin iron strip along the sides. The iron would normally be shrunk on to the wooden spade, but some more sophisticated examples have a variety of lugs or strips with rivets to fasten them, some strips continuing along the upper surface. The amount of iron can vary considerably, some such as those from Colchester and Frocester Court (Fig. 9(c)) being considerably more generous than others, such as an example from Silchester, which just has a narrow iron band along the cutting edge (Fig. 9(b); Rees 1979: figs. 119b, 120 and 115). Some sheaths are splayed, thereby significantly widening the cutting edge. The shodding of spades in iron was probably an Iron Age idea, though none save possibly the example from Keltic Cavern comes from a context earlier than Romano-British. These remain a tool type associated with Romanisation – few purely native agricultural settlements have produced them, and in Wales and Scotland they are known only from forts.

Smaller specialised iron blades generally interpreted as peat cutting spades or spades associated with lazy-bed cultivation are occasionally encountered on Romano-British sites. Small, square blades with a flat cross-section, they were evidently fitted on to wooden blades but the entire back of the spade would have been covered with the protective iron, the wooden parts acting to lengthen the blade and connect with the handle. One example from the Blackburn Mill Hoard is unique, and almost certainly correctly identified, as it has a foot rest on one side to push the blade into the peat. This led to a convincing reinterpretation of several similar tools (but with no foot rest) as spades, hitherto identified as wide plough shares. The reliability of the interpretation of these tools, especially those with splayed blades from southern Britain, however, remains uncertain. The northern group, with generally parallel-sided blades, from Blackburn Mill and Brampton seem more convincingly spade-like than those splayed-sided tools from Bigbury, Wallingford and Silchester (Fig. 9(b)). More definitely interpreted are the lunate blades called turf-cutters, often found on Roman forts associated with the digging of defences, but found also on civilian sites such as Silchester. Their appearance is not dissimilar to their modern successors, with a tanged or socketed haft on a lunate iron blade. And they were used, just as now and as their name indicates, to cut turf. Despite their being associated with military use, turf cutting is a function of any settlement and they may be

Pl. 18 Iron sickle from Risingham

found in towns, villas and agricultural sites as well as Roman forts (Rees 1979: 435–7).

The latter type of tools may belong more realistically to a disparate group of usually socketed or flanged tools generally given the somewhat catch-all phrase of spuds. These are small weeding tools or tools used to scrape down and clean mud from other working tools like shares or spades. There is an enormous variety of these small iron tools and in reality they may have had a variety of functions. Some, with square or slightly splayed blades such as those from London (Figs. 9(d) and (f)), Sibson (Fig. 9(e)) and Lakenheath (Rees 1979: figs. 130–1) would certainly have functioned as small hoes capable of fine weeding work between crop rows, either in fields or in garden plots or orchards. Their identification in excavation reports is pretty haphazard, the term being used rather indiscriminately to cover many different types of tool. The reliability of interpretation of function of such tools is poor.

The harvest

The balanced iron sickle, an efficient harvesting tool for grain, was used in the pre-Roman Iron Age, and Romano-British sickles, with relatively upright blades, do not at first show any design improvement on their pre-Roman predecessors (Plate 18). Some nine implements that have some

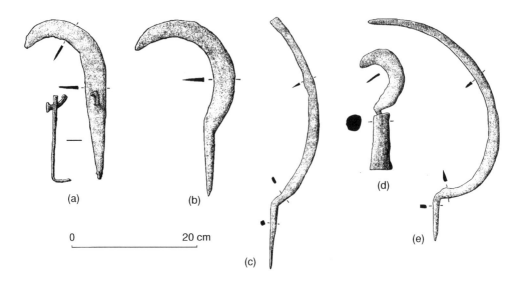

Fig. 10 (a) Reaping hook from Sibson; (b) iron sickle from Llyn Cerrig Bach;
(c) reaping hook from Grassington; (d) sickle from Linton; (e) sickle from Corbridge

claim to be considered balanced – i.e. the blade is set back from the handle
to give a better weight to the harvesting cut and allow grain to be harvested
single-handed at any point on the stalk – are Iron Age, though some small
blades are by no means certainly grain harvesting sickles. The Iron Age
examples from Llyn Cerrig Bach (Fig. 10(b)), Glastonbury, Credenhill and
Croft Ambrey, which are reasonably well developed though generally rather
small tools, are little different from early Roman examples from Walbrook,
Blackburn Mill and Newstead, and the types continue into later Roman
contexts such as Sibson and Great Wakering (Rees 1979: 458). However,
within the Roman period, more sophisticated tools with a greater balance
and slimmer, more elegant blades begin to be found, and it is to these
more developed tools that we can more safely attribute a grain harvesting
function. They remain not especially common tools, and some of those
tentatively listed (Rees 1979: 458–9; Manning 1985: 53, pl. 22, F22) are very
uncertainly dated as Roman. Nonetheless, the fine examples from Ham Hill
and Silchester show the level of sophistication that these tools had achieved
by the fourth century (see also Fig. 10(d) and (e)).

The fact that good balanced sickles are rarely found, yet the supreme
harvesting implement, the scythe, is a relatively common find on Romano-
British sites is one of those oddities of the archaeological record. One has to
remember, of course, that uprooting in the field, using knives to cut off the
ears later at the farm, would need no sickle and has been a common method

of harvesting in many parts of the world until comparatively recently (Rees 1981: 71–2). The absence of curved iron blades on a site certainly should not be used to imply a lack of arable farming.

The numbers of true balanced sickles from the Roman period are insignificant when compared with the great numbers of curving bladed tools often known as reaping hooks (Fig. 10(a) and (c); Rees 1979: 450–61). The variety shown by these hooks is enormous and small curving blades, or fragments of them, are common enough on sites from the pre-Roman Iron Age. There are, as we have already seen with other tool types, more Roman examples found, presumably as iron became more readily available. The problems associated with attributing function to the huge variety of curving cutting tools, some with a slight backward setting of the blade inclining towards a balance, some with more upright blades and some with blades at right angles to the handle, some with short and some with longer cutting edges (Rees 1979: fig. 158), are legion. As well as the suspect attributions given to such tools in the archaeological literature, a different hafting of a blade can result in a tool totally altered in shape from what one expected. The analysis of more recent tools, where the function is actually known, has led us to appreciate how unwise it is to use identification of such tools to reconstruct an arable agriculture regime for an archaeological site (Rees 1981: fig. 2). It could be that the number and variety of such tools suggest specialist functions – harvesting legumes or fruit, or cutting gorse, reeds and leaves for bedding or fodder, roofing and flooring – or, on the contrary, it is possible that small curving blades could each be used for a variety of different functions. Any trip to a rural life museum will reveal a number of curving tools ascribed, presumably from documentary or photographic evidence, specific functions (see, for example, the gorse cutting knife in Rees 1981, fig. 3). That such small, non-balanced tools were used also for cutting grain is graphically shown by the Trajan Column portrayal of the soldier foraging for corn (Webster 1969: pl. XXXI), illustrating the required, two-handed technique. The soldier, leaning forward, grasps a head of corn in his left hand and cuts it with his right with a non-balanced, strongly curving hook, very similar to the example from Newstead (Rees 1979: fig. 181b). Interestingly, it is a soldier, not a farmer, who is shown cutting corn in this way, foraging rather than harvesting his own crop, and this perhaps reinforces the view that these small hooks may have functioned as multi-purpose tools.

From the perspective of the excavator, the one essential of these tools is that the cutting blade is curved and on the concave, inner edge. Other than that, there is much variety, from those where the cutting edge is largely at right angles to the haft (Castleford: Cool and Philo 1998: fig. 46:19) or more evenly curving, and those with long or shorter cutting edges. Most are tanged, with or without supplementary nail fastenings, and the socketed or flanged tools, more commonly found in the Iron Age (such as those from Hod Hill, Manning 1985: pls. 22–3, F26–F33), become infrequent.

The scythe, a tool of consummate design, was certainly a Roman intro-duction into Britain, at least in the form that we know it today. A series of shorter-bladed tools with tangs set at an obtuse angle to the blade have been found in pre-Roman contexts outside Britain, such as those from La Tène, Switzerland (Déchelette 1914: 613.1/8; Rees 1979: fig. 248) and Illemose, Denmark (Steensberg 1942: fig. 38), and it could be that a num-ber of smaller though incomplete implements, such as those from Sibson and Wilderspool and the curious pair from Rushall Down, may best be regarded as short-handled scythes or slashing tools for hay cutting. The familiar long-handled type, normally with a blade 84–120 cm long, makes its appearance quite early on at Roman forts such as Newstead, Irchester, Brampton and Bar Hill (Rees 1979: figs. 236–42) and is generally assumed to be a military introduction for cutting fodder for horses. The famous long scythe blades 130 to 160 cm, from Great Chesterford, Abington Piggotts, Barnsley Park, Hardwick and Farmoor are impressive implements, designed probably for hay harvesting rather than grain and all dating from the fourth century. Experiments carried out by Anstee with a modern reconstruction using various different types of haft found that they functioned perfectly adequately for harvesting grain or hay (Anstee 1967; White 1972) but their findspot at Farmoor (Rees in Lambrick and Robinson 1979: 61–5), an agri-cultural settlement where little evidence existed for arable agriculture while abounding in evidence for grassland, strengthens the hypothesis that they were generally tools for the hay harvest. Certainly the classical agronomists only describe the scythe in connection with hay cutting (Pliny *Nat. Hist.* XVIII.261; Varro *Rust.* I.49.1).

Scythe blades of the longer or shorter type, or even fragments of them, are generally reasonably easily identified because of their conspicuous rolled thickened back edge, straight sides and flat or slightly curving cross-section. Some (Great Chesterford) have additional ribs, while the Farmoor tool has a groove on the upper part of the blade; of the shorter, early type, the Newstead tools have additional ribs at the tang end to strengthen the elbow. Some (e.g. Abington Piggotts, Farmoor and two of the Newstead tools) have a distinct heel between blade and tang, while on most the blade emerges smoothly from the tang. The longer examples usually have a distinct downward point at the end of the blade, a useful feature for gathering the cut crop and depositing it in a swathe well out of the operator's way. Despite their size and weight, these scythes were used by experienced mowers in Anstee's experiments with little bother – using either a full swing with a wide cut while moving forward or short chopping strokes moving sideways. They would have been a labour-saving tool, and interestingly have a southern Britain distribution on large estate farms like Great Chesterford or specialised pastoral farms like Farmoor. One assumes that shortage of labour may have been the momentum behind their development. They were evidently prized implements as one would expect of such large tools, and complete ones will often exhibit repairs – the riveted patches on the Hardwick and Farmoor, several of the Great Chesterford and one of the smaller Newstead scythes show episodes of repair before being discarded.

The ultimate pre-industrial harvesting machine, the vallus, is known only from descriptions by classical agronomists (Pliny *Nat. Hist.* XVIII.296; Palladius *Op. Agric.* VII.2.2–4) and tantalising fragments of stone relief sculptures from Buzenol, Trier, Rheims and Arlon. The machine would mainly have been made of wood, perhaps with iron-shod teeth for cutting the heads of grain. Pushed by oxen, the machine would move forward and the cut grain would fall into the hopper. Experiments with a reconstruction undertaken by the Musée Gaumais at Virton, south Belgium, in 1960 showed the machine to be effective, though how much wastage occurred is not reported. They were used in the *latifundia* of Gaul, within the same soil range and agricultural regime, one might think, as that found in southern Britain, but are, unfortunately, not known to have been used in this country. A forked piece of iron found at Wroxeter (Ellis 2000: 118, fig. 4.17), suggested as a possible tooth from a vallus, is an intriguing discovery but inconclusive. To find or interpret firmly fragments from the first discovered vallus from Britain (or anywhere else for that matter) would have to represent the pinnacle of an agricultural historian's career.

Associated with scythes are the characteristic mowers' anvils used for sharpening the blades in the field (Fig. 11(b); Rees 1979: 480–2, figs. 249–50). They are small wedge-shaped tools with a pointed end and one or two pairs of iron spirals twisted from a bar passing through the body of the anvil. They have a large working head which often displays evidence of hammering. Very similar tools were still in use in the nineteenth and early twentieth century when Curle, describing the example from Newstead, illustrated their use thus: 'The mower sits on the ground, and laying the scythe across his knees, hammers out the edges on the anvil planted between his legs before giving the edge a final polish with a hone' (Curle 1911: 284). Evans (1894: 143–4), describing those from Silchester, adds that stones or other supports were placed under the brackets to prevent their sinking into

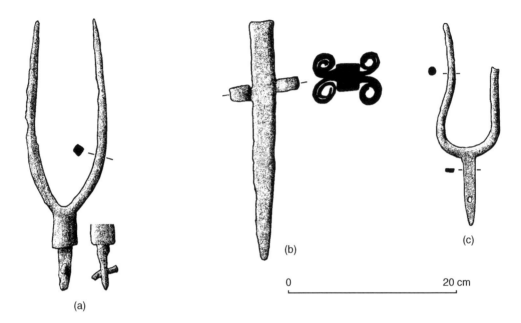

(b)

(c)

0 _____ 20 cm

(a)

Fig. 11 (a) Iron pitchfork from the Bank of England, London; (b) mower's anvil from Silchester; (c) iron pitchfork from Newstead

the ground. They are characteristically found in hoards, Great Chesterford and Silchester having several, or on Roman civil settlement sites throughout Britain. They are clearly a Roman introduction, the first-century example from Newstead being the earliest, but continue to be found throughout the Roman period with no discernible development, though it may be more than coincidental that the fourth-century examples from Silchester and Great Chesterford are larger than the earlier tool from Newstead. Also, the only examples with two pairs of spiral supports are the later tools from Silchester. In view of Curle's description of their use, it is interesting to note the presence of a whetstone in the hoard from Silchester which contained the scythes.

Another almost indispensable tool of the harvest is the pitchfork, used to spread, stack and lift the cut hay or corn. Wooden forks survive from prehistory and indeed were the norm until recent times. However, some all-iron forks do survive from Romanised sites, both military (Newstead (Fig. 11(c)) and Chesters) and civilian (London (Fig. 11(a)), Lydney, Silchester and Baldock (Rees 1979: figs. 251–4)). There are a number of different forms, from straight-sided to curving- and round-bottomed with forked ends, but, given the wide distribution of a small number of tools over a long period, there is almost inevitably no discernible development or preference for one type over another at any type of site. Almost all are tanged, though three socketed tools from Bucklersbury House have supporting projections on the tines to help with gathering loose material.

Along with the pitchfork, the rake is an essential tool of the harvest. Generally even in nineteenth-century Britain harvest rakes were of wood and doubtless this would have been the case in Roman Britain. However, a remarkable survival of a heavy rake with wooden head but seven curving iron rake prongs from Newstead confirms the function of these small iron pointed pieces, which are frequently mis-identified as nails. They have been found on military and civil sites from all dates in the Roman period, and may have also functioned as parts of harrows (see above).

Care of the growing crop, pruning of orchard and fruit crops, as well as tree surgery and collection of leaves and branches for winter fodder and bedding require a range of different tools, generally given the generic term 'hooks' or 'pruning hooks' or pruning saws. Again nomenclature bedevils rather than clarifies, as the numerous small curved blades which are found so frequently on Iron Age and Roman sites could have had a multiplicity of tasks. The billhook, however, is found in the Iron Age (e.g. Glastonbury) in a form that is instantly recognisable to modern farmers. The well-nigh perfect design of this tool means that it has survived intrinsically unchanged for centuries, but this very conservatism of design has resulted in regional differences evolving so that the cognoscenti can distinguish a bill from Suffolk, shall we say, from one made for use in the Midlands. This offers us the possibility of an evolution of regional styles from the beginning. Inevitably the sample from the archaeological record is too small to make any statistically significant conclusions, but there are certainly various blade shapes: the standard two-directional cutting edge set at right angles to one another (e.g. Shakenoak and Hod Hill: Rees 1979: fig. 208); long and mostly upright with just a beak at the top (e.g. Caerwent: Rees 1979: fig. 217a); and straight, upright blades, sometimes with an added projection at the back of the blade, useful for reaching for and securing branches in position prior to cutting (e.g. Colchester, Lakenheath, Thealby Mine: Rees 1979: figs. 221–2). Interestingly, the first of these, the standard shape often associated with the bill now, is one of the few tool types to be more commonly found in the Iron Age, thanks to numerous examples found at the Somerset Lake Villages of Glastonbury and Meare, some of which retain their wooden handles (Rees 1979: figs. 215–16, 218–19). The other blade shapes are commoner in the Roman period, during which time other more axe-shaped blades are introduced, some of which could have been used as bills or for more general woodworking, hedging, forestry or even ceremonial use (Rees 1979: figs. 224–31). Socketed and tanged implements are found, though the Iron Age tools seem generally to be socketed with transverse or front to back nails. The larger Roman bills also prefer a socketed attachment for the handle, though some of the smaller perhaps more multi-purpose tools which gradually slide into the category known as pruning hooks are tanged (e.g. Colchester and Milbourne St Andrew: Rees 1979: figs. 214, 213).

The introduction of the billhook certainly implies the cutting of shrubby growth, but this, of course, can be for a variety of purposes. The modern bill is generally considered a hedging tool, and its use in the establishment and maintenance of field boundaries, separating stock from crop and animals from one another and marking one farm's fields from neighbouring land, coincides with the establishment of a widespread enclosure of field systems which then continued into the Roman period, spreading further afield on to heavier soils. The provision of winter fodder for animals before we have evidence for the establishment of specific hay fields may have depended to a greater extent on late autumn branches. Bills were important tools for cutting and pruning orchard fruit trees, but also for less specifically agricultural tasks such as cutting branches for wattle-and-daub panel infill for house wall construction.

Finer pruning of crops and fruit trees, and harvesting of non-cereal crops such as legumes, fruits and plot vegetables, required a variety of knives and saws. The archaeologist is faced with a bewildering variety of curved blades, angled blades and curving saws which could have been used for these purposes but frankly could have been used for many other purposes as well. There are large numbers of these tools in the Iron Age and Roman assemblages and the attribution of function to any of them is extremely hazardous. They have been given the generic title 'pruning hooks' and some undoubtedly are just that. They can be socketed with or without trans-verse or front to back nails, flanged with tangs or simply tanged (Rees 1979: figs. 193–200). They can have acutely curved blades, short straight blades set at an angle (Rees 1979: fig. 201) and miniature bills. One example from Walbrook retains its short wooden handle, and is similar to a knife the author has used in a nursery to take pelargonium cuttings. Interest-ingly, their distribution is more strongly concentrated in the south-east of England and far more so than that of reaping hooks (Rees 1979: maps 12 and 13), so it is possible that their traditional identification as tools associated with horticulture and fruit growing is not entirely spurious. Continental tools usually associated with viticulture are uncommon in Roman Britain though some of these smaller bill-like tools with back projections have been found – e.g. Shakenoak (Brodribb, Hands and Walker 2005: fig. 4:57, no. 386).

Inevitably, during any attempt to categorise curving blades into types for attribution of function, there are tools which do not fit comfortably into any tool type. Another term, that of 'slashing tools', has grown up, which may not be too far from the truth, as they seem an appropriate size for vegetation and scrub clearance. Two heavy curving-bladed tools from Bigbury and Wroxeter (Rees 1979: fig. 232) and, more probably, a series of fine wide-bladed tools from Bigbury, one of which has a scythe-like rolled rib on the back (Rees 1979: figs. 244–7), may represent an intermediate tool between hook and scythe.

Animal husbandry

Tools employed within animal husbandry include those used for the cutting of crops for animal fodder, such as the scythes and billhooks already described. Others, such as the farrier's butteris used in the care of horse hooves and curry combs used for grooming, are found on both civilian town and villa sites – Caerwent, Gadebridge Park villa, Sandy – and in the fourth-century hoards from Silchester and Great Chesterford (Manning 1985: 61). Horses, mules and donkeys did not play a great part in Romano-British agriculture as far as we can see, though the classical agronomists and classical illustrations occasionally show them used in Mediterranean contexts for threshing, drawing the plough and drawing light vehicles (Applebaum 1987: 511–13).

More important to the Romano-British farmer were sheep and goats, cattle and pigs, poultry and geese, though few tools directly associated with their care have been identified. The obvious exception is, of course, sheep shears, the double-bladed scissor-like tools allowing flexibility for cutting, familiar to modern visitors to traditional sheep shearing contests. Reasonably common a find on Romano-British sites and easily identifiable, at least when intact, their function is beyond dispute, though they may have been used for other tasks within woollen or textile preparation. Their discovery can give the excavator a reasonably reliable indication of the practice of sheep shearing; though, as ever, a fair number of our examples come from hoards and are thus devoid of immediate context. Leather-working tools and those associated with weaving do, of course, imply the use of animal products, but the leather and textile industrial sites are by no means necessarily in areas adjacent to the agricultural settlements which produced the raw materials and they cannot be regarded as agricultural tools.

Other animal products such as dung for fertiliser, milk, meat, bone for tool making, horns for handles and glue, and fat for tallow were probably processed more immediately on the farm. Few of these products have tools or equipment which can be proved to be associated, though a little might be said concerning milk and cheese production. While cheese production certainly does not require any specific tool or pottery type, trays or bowls with perforations to allow the easy separation of whey during the pressing of the curds can be useful. Large perforated ceramic trays and vessels perforated with holes in the base have long been considered to be the Roman vessels used in cheese making, and are fairly common finds on Romano-British sites, both civilian and military. Alcock (2001: 60–2) mentions cheese presses from Silchester, Colchester, Lower Halstow and Leicester, including large flat strainers with big perforations of such a size as to imply production on a fairly large scale. Commoner on Roman military sites, such as Usk, Corbridge, Holt and Bainbridge, are smaller simple bowls with perforated bases suggesting small-scale production by individual soldiers. The vessel from Lower Halstrow has concentric rings on the base interpreted as assisting in retaining the cheese during pressing, while another from Templeborough Roman fort could have been for cheese making or used for separating honey from combs. Alcock makes the interesting suggestion that the ubiquitous mortarium could have been used to make cheese, the spout facilitating the removal of whey from the curds; the grit, rather than for pounding, could have been incorporated to retain bacteria from the last batch of cheese to help with the commencement of the new.

The sweetener used in Roman cookery was, of course, honey and we know that bees and beehives were kept for honey production. Bee-hives were presumably made of some perishable substance such as woven straw or wood, the traditional materials even now. However, ceramic beehives have been mooted, such as the large perforated vessels found in the Alice Holt, Farnham pottery assemblage (Clark and Nicholas 1960: 57; Lyne and Jefferies 1979: 51). The small ventilation holes are too small for bees to pass through, the roughening of the interior may have been intended as keying for the attachment of the combs and the cable rim decoration may give a hint as to the original material for hives from which the ceramic hives had derived. This suggestion, made originally by Frere, would provide a convenient explanation for these large vessels which would have to have been used rim downward on a support to allow access. Both these theories for bee keeping and cheese making are fairly speculative and cannot be used as incontrovertible proof of any such activity on a settlement.

Food processing

The presence of a quern (Plate 28) on an archaeological site certainly does not imply that any specific type of agricultural regime was undertaken there, and merely suggests, as Barbara Noddle (pers. comm.) was wont to remark, that the inhabitants ate. Grain can be imported to a settlement, and in towns, forts and industrial establishments including, fairly obviously, larger corn mills themselves it undoubtedly was. As specialist farms, such as Farmoor, grew up with perhaps no arable regimes on site, grain would have to be imported, while, of course, the majority of farms would process grain retained for home consumption rather than the surplus used for export. Querns found in large numbers near sources of stone suggest that querns were probably manufactured rather than used there, and on some larger mills, where large-sized millstones clearly were the industrial-scale milling tool, hand querns continue to be found, suggesting that they sometimes had an ancillary role (Spain 1993: 55).

Curwen's original studies of quern types from Iron Age and Roman Britain (1937; 1941) have proved remarkably robust, later specialists retaining much of his typological analysis (e.g. Welfare 1995; Watts 1996; Shaffrey 2006). The simple saddle querns and the somewhat cumbersome beehive querns found in the Iron Age develop into sophisticated rotary querns, many different forms of which are found throughout the Roman period. Querns are found made from a variety of stones, and King (1986) suggests that the typology of quern shapes tends to relate to the stone most suitable for a particular type of fashioned grinding surface. The most highly prized were evidently the fine-grained but light Niedermendig lava stone, imported from the Rhine. These have characteristic grooving on the grinding surfaces designed to take the ground flour in grooves from the centre to the outside of the stone. These grooves, easier to cut in lava than in coarser stone, tend to be a characteristic of the fine imports, though locally quarried and fashioned stones of old red sandstone and millstone grit are occasionally found with similar grooving in imitation (as at Usk, see Welfare 1995). Grinding surfaces need to be rough, obviously, to work on the grain, and the appropriate surface can be achieved by different forms of pecking, segmented-radial grooves, partial groove around outer edge only, cross-concentric grooving and a mixture of pecking and grooves (Shaffrey 2006: fig. 4.11). As well as different dressing styles, different upper and lower stone shapes are found and Shaffrey provides useful illustrations of the different types found – flat-topped, disc, rimmed and beehive upper stones, and cake, disc, lozenge, pyramid and beehive lower stones (Shaffrey 2006: figs. 4.11, 4.13–4.22). The different styles do not apparently imply very much in the way of date, though features such as full perforation of the lower stone and disc and pyramid shapes tend to be later, while most of the simpler, bulkier beehive style are early – first and second century. Over 50 per cent of the old red sandstone querns studied by Shaffrey are 350–450 mm in diameter and some 70 mm thick. Writers ascribe a gradual increase in size from the first century AD throughout the period, and the large fourth-century stones of 560 mm diameter or more are thought to imply mechanisation, these being too large to be turned conveniently by hand (King 1986).

The general increase in the size of querns and the eventual logical appearance of millstones certainly suggests an increased industrialisation of the supply of grain and its processing into flour, presumably to supply the increasing number of urban and industrial centres or even specialised non-arable farms and estates. The donkey mill from Clyro Roman fort, for example, is a serious piece of equipment capable of producing a large amount of flour, perhaps from imported grain or perhaps implying a locally produced surplus trading in flour (DCMS 2002: 31). Its appearance at a fort, manufactured from a local stone rather than the imported lava from which the London example was made (Wheeler 1930: fig. 34), suggests larger-scale processing at the fort, either for immediate consumption or for supply elsewhere, though the grain production may have been gathered from the wider surrounding area. Other writers suggest that the flour itself may have been exported. Branigan (1977), for example, mentions that Gatcombe Roman villa may have produced surplus flour for export to Caerleon. Spain (1993) cites probable examples of watermills at several forts on Hadrian's Wall, including Carvoran, Vindolanda, Housesteads, High Rochester and Newstead, and suggests that this would have been commonplace, given the positioning of the forts at streams with a suitable flow for mills. He also interprets a wooden structure on the Fleet estuary, in London, as a possible tidal mill, while watermills are increasingly being discovered in other areas, such as at Ickham in Kent (Spain 1984).

Conclusion

There is an assumption that querns ground grain for flour; reasonable enough, though it would be interesting to know if different types of querns might imply a different type of grain for which their design had an increased efficiency. Also, little is known about the processing of so many of the crops which the archaeo-botanical record tells us were produced on Romano-British farms. How were legumes processed, how were fodder crops cut and chopped, and what of fruit and the production of beverages from apples and pears, for instance? The important lesson we must bear in mind when reviewing agricultural tools is that they tell us only part of a complex story. The greater the amount of evidence from palaeo-environmental sampling of seeds and pollens, faunal remains from domesticated animals, and the soil types, topography and traces of field systems at or near the settlement, the more reliable and comprehensive will be the analysis of the agricultural system at that site.

5 | Weaponry and military equipment

M. C. BISHOP

> There are known knowns; there are things we know we know. We also
> know there are known unknowns; that is to say we know there are some
> things we do not know. But there are also unknown unknowns – the
> ones we don't know we don't know. And each year we discover a few
> more of those unknown unknowns.
>
> Donald Rumsfeld, 12 February 02

Like most classes of artefact from the Roman period, it is impossible to study
military equipment from Britain without placing it in its wider imperial (in
the geographical sense) context. This serves both to inform and to temper
our conclusions about the mechanisms involved in, and the information
that can duly be deduced from, the artefactual record; but it also provides
a much needed sense of perspective. Such a study is not dependent only
upon archaeology, however, for the representational, literary and subliterary
sources (as in all areas of Roman military studies) help to enhance the overall
picture (Bishop and Coulston 2006: 1–22, 39–47).

At any one time, there were vast quantities of arms and armour in use in
the Roman world. In Britain alone, there would have been (and this is a crude
approximation by way of illustration) some 20,000 legionaries in the first
century AD, requiring the appropriate number of helmets, swords, shields,
and so on. A roughly equivalent number of auxiliaries would obviously
have doubled these figures (see also Cheesman 1914: 53–6). Nevertheless,
this body of matériel should not be seen as a recurring drain on Roman
resources, since it represented a 'universal stock' of military equipment
which was replaced and recycled in the normal course of events, with only
a comparatively small amount of 'new' equipment – in the sense of items
manufactured from newly acquired resources – to balance that which was
lost for any reason. Thus the arms and equipment of the third-century army
in Britain, although completely different from those of their first-century
predecessors, were probably made out of much the same material, give or
take the odd vexillation leaving the province or coming in. Carl Sagan once
summarised the recycling of matter in the universe as 'we are all stardust',
and the same is inevitably true of the raw material of the universal stock of

military equipment, with only small flecks of detritus occasionally inveigling their way into the archaeological record.

There indeed is the rub: how can we be sure that the sample of weaponry and equipment we recover is representative in every way of the original population of artefacts? In order to understand what Roman military equipment can tell us, we need to feel comfortable about its taphonomy: in other words, how did it get into the archaeological record and what happened to it before, during and after that event? Once we begin to comprehend the strengths and limitations of the artefactual evidence, then we can begin to assess it and (ever mindful of Rumsfeld's whimsical – yet useful – three-tiered pantological model) what it can tell us about the past.

Whilst 'weaponry' is fairly unambiguous as a class of artefact (although not completely so because of the existence of weapons designed specifically for hunting), there is always a measure of fuzziness in the definition of the term 'military equipment'. Objects that were uniquely military, insofar as they were only used by the army, are not problematical, providing that we are able to define which items they happen to be (and, even then, not all specialists agree on such definitions, it has to be said). More complex are those things used in both civil and military society – cart fittings are a good example – for whilst they can quite reasonably be called 'military equipment' when found on a military site, their presence in the archaeological record at a site that is not clearly of this nature does not in and of itself proclaim a military presence. Thus we may distinguish three subsets of military artefact: those that were truly military, those that were not, and those that may or may not have been, depending upon context. Moreover, within the soldier's panoply there were bound to be those items that were essential to his task (primarily weapons and armour) and those which were not or were merely incidental to it (clothing, decorative objects and the like).

Deposition

With the scope of the investigation laid out, it is time to examine the mechanisms of deposition, so far as we understand them, in order to attempt to discern any inherent biases in the artefactual evidence.

'Casual loss' is frequently cited as a reason for an item of military equipment entering the archaeological record by writers who, one suspects, have perhaps not given the matter sufficient thought. It is a very specific mechanism that operates in a particular way on only certain classes (and, especially, sizes) of object and should never be seen as a catch-all explanation for deposition.

It is, for example, easy to lose a small-denomination coin such as a 1p – 20.3 mm in diameter and 3.56 g in weight (Royal Mint 2006) – but much harder to lose a Churchill tank – 7.47 m long and 39 tonnes (Vanderveen 1969: 191; cf. *ATB* 1973: 34; 1976: 26–7, 48–53). Both find their way into the archaeological record, so it is clear that more than one loss mechanism is in operation here: caution should always be exercised before claiming 'casual' or 'accidental' loss as the reason for the presence of a military artefact in the ground.

There is no doubt that Roman military equipment could be 'lost' (without any hint of casuality): the *decurio* Docilis writes to his prefect Augurinus at Carlisle relating how some of his troopers did not possess ('deessent') certain items of equipment (Tomlin 1998: 57). However, the objects he lists (including javelins and swords) are scarcely the sort of things a cavalry-man would carelessly drop without noticing (Bishop and Coulston 2006: 24). Other reasons must be sought for Docilis' logistical shortcomings (see below).

Ultimately, the smaller and less functionally significant an item might be, the more likely it is that it could be lost accidentally. A simple test of criticality needs to be applied to an artefact before this becomes plausible, however. Thus an apron stud, small and largely non-functional (Bishop 1992: 100–1), could indeed suffer casual loss, as could just one of the ten rivets attaching a lobate hinge to *lorica segmentata*. A lobate hinge itself, on the other hand, was critically functional and its loss would definitely be noticed quite quickly (Bishop 2002: 32–3) – which was presumably why it was held on with ten rivets in the first place; likewise a helmet was essential and, one suspects, actually very difficult to lose accidentally.

There were other ways in which accidental loss could occur. Shipwreck has been suggested as one possible reason why a *legio VIII Augusta* shield boss ended up in the river Tyne (Bidwell 2001: 9), but given that we have epigraphic evidence for the dedication of a shield from Tongres (see below) this is by no means an open-and-shut case of 'casual loss'. Nevertheless, military equipment has been recovered from maritime contexts elsewhere in the Empire (Feugère 2002: 208). What is interesting here is that loss at sea is scarcely casual. A helmet from Bosham harbour may have been deposited as a result of shipwreck, but it may equally have been a votive offering (see below; Plate 19).

Accidental and casual losses were never, therefore, major mechanisms for military equipment entering the archaeological record, but they are

Pl. 19 Helmet found in Bosham harbour

important for they demonstrate artefacts that are in everyday use which
have not been pre-selected for deposition (although, as was hinted above,
those suffering casual loss will only have been those more prone to do so in
the first place).

   If the military equipment in the archaeological record only represents a
tiny proportion of the original stock, then we must not only question just
how representative such a sample can be, but also consider the nature of
'normal' deposition of arms and armour. We have established that this was
not by means of casual or accidental loss, although they have their part to
play. The simplest explanation is that the bulk of the military equipment we
find was deliberately deposited in some way, albeit with a range of motives
that could still potentially bias any assemblage.

   It is accepted orthodoxy (particularly relating to the earlier imperial
period) that Roman soldiers were not normally buried with their military
equipment. Indeed, there is documentary evidence showing how a deceased
soldier's heirs received the value of his equipment in cash (Gilliam 1967).
Nevertheless, some soldiers were buried with arms and armour and these
are generally held to be the exceptions that prove the rule; precisely how
exceptional they were, however, is unclear. Two soldiers were interred, one
on top of the other, at Canterbury, each with his own sword (Fig. 12). There
was thought to be circumstantial evidence of a hurried or even secretive
burial (Bennett, Frere and Stow 1982: 185–90), and it may well be that foul

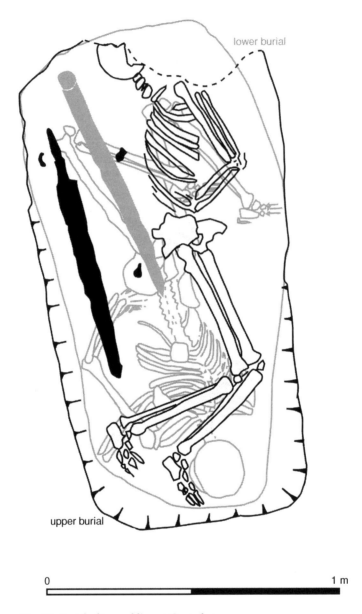

lower burial

upper burial

0   1 m

Fig. 12 Burial of two soldiers at Canterbury

play lay behind this unusual interment, as has been suggested was the case for the body of a soldier in a well at Velsen in the Netherlands (Morel and Bosman 1989). In the later Roman period it became far more common for equipment to be buried with its owner, perhaps as a result of new cultural influences from contact with (and even recruitment amongst) Germanic and trans-Danubian peoples (Bishop and Coulston 2006: 270–2). It is even found buried outwith a specifically Roman context, whether it be in graves in areas or contexts traditionally thought of as non-Roman (Breeze, Close-Brooks and Ritchie 1976), or even as curios in later periods (Böhme 1986). Some of the dead, it seems, were reluctant to be parted from their arms and armour; thus its very significance to them must inevitably colour our interpretation of it.

For many years, items of Roman military equipment from rivers have been interpreted as the victims of accidental loss, those recovered in (what is thought to have been) the vicinity of the Rhine ferry at Mainz being one of the most frequently cited cases for deposition (e.g. Robinson 1975: 68). Placed in a context of prehistoric and early medieval riverine deposition, however, this appears a rather unlikely explanation.

The deposition of artefacts in watery environments was well established in Britain, as for much of mainland Europe, long before the Romans arrived (Bradley 1998). Indeed, patterns of deposition in large European waterways, such as the Rhine, show that the tradition continued from prehistory right through into the Roman period and beyond (Torbrügge 1972), so it is clear that Roman arms and armour found in similar circumstances may well have been subjected to the same sort of ritual practices. The Fulham sword or helmets from Bosham harbour and London may be examples of this practice, not least because they mirror finds from Continental Europe, although these may well be a self-selecting group precisely because they retain their post-depositional integrity better than, say, body or limb armour or sets of belt plates. The catapult washer found at Bath amongst a wide variety of votive artefacts is clear evidence of this mechanism in operation (Cunliffe 1984: 81). Moreover, the votive deposition of military equipment is explicitly mentioned in Continental inscriptions (Bishop and Coulston 2006: 30–1).

What we cannot know, of course, is how such offerings were selected. Logically they ought to have been especially prized possessions and so, once again, not necessarily typical of the general population of artefacts, but there is no way of being certain of such an assertion. A comment by Florus – about how the Augustan general Vinnius deposited captured weaponry in water rather than burn it – suggests that the offering of captured equipment *en masse* was the exception, rather than the rule (*Epitome* II.24).

The archaeology of battlefields and conflict landscapes is a burgeoning area of archaeological study (Coulston 2001; 2005), but there are few Roman-period sites in Britain that definitely fall within this category. The precise locations of most of the major battle sites remain unidentified: the Medway (Webster 1980: 98–9) during the invasion, or the defeat of Boudica

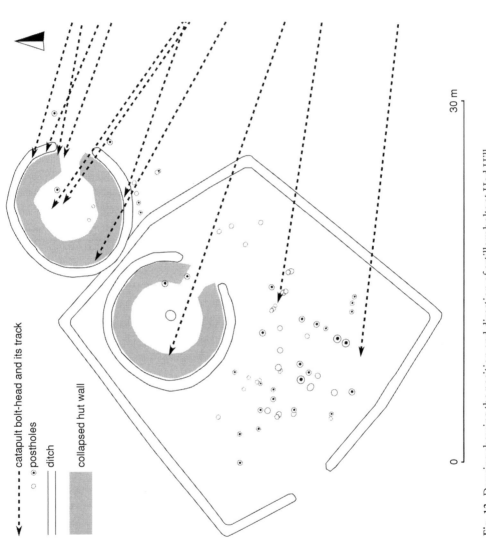

- - - - - catapult bolt-head and its track
⊙ postholes
═══ ditch
▨ collapsed hut wall

0 ⊢──────────────────────────┤ 30 m

Fig. 13 Drawing showing the position and direction of artillery bolts at Hod Hill

slightly later (Webster 1980: 96–101), or even Mons Graupius (Maxwell 1990) – all long-sought but still eluding us. Finds of first-century AD catapult bolts surrounding a hut within the hillfort at Hod Hill (Fig. 13; Richmond 1968: 32–3, fig. 14) or second-century slingshot and artillery projectiles from Burnswark (Jobey 1978: 89–91) have been argued as either the results of training exercises or genuine traces of combat and thus are unhelpfully ambiguous. Sites from elsewhere in the Empire show how even the most apparently straightforward examples, such as the battlefield at Kalkriese (Schlüter 1993; 1999; Carnap-Bornheim 1999), Krefeld-Gellep (Pirling 1971; 1977; 1986) or the mine at Dura-Europos (James 2005), all show signs of complex post-combat pre-deposition – in other words, stratinomic – processes in operation which imply that 'loss on the battlefield' is by no means cut-and-dried as an explanation for deposition. Indeed, the likelihood that armies (and indeed looters) will have ransacked conflict zones in order to remove useful items means that the material that does survive to be found is, in and of itself, a special category (those items which could not for some reason be recovered by those 'processing' the combat space in the aftermath). That same oblique comment by Florus mentioned above implies that it was normal to burn surplus captured weaponry.

Unfortunately, the circumstances of the deposition of the catapult bolts from Hod Hill must be counted amongst 'known unknowns', because whilst we have the ones that were excavated, we cannot know whether any (and, if so, how many) may have been recovered after the original event, whether it be loss in combat or in training, and so were not available to be excavated.

Thus battlefields are no more promising in terms of the quality of evidence they reveal about any weaponry and military equipment that may be recovered from them. In the first place, that evidence is a scarce resource, but in the second, even if it is found, it is not clear how it is to be interpreted and what sort of sample it presents of the original corpus.

Soldiers have always captured trophies from their enemies and in the classical world such acts were formalised into *tropaea* and displays in triumphal processions like those of Aemilius Paullus (Plutarch *Aemilius Paullus* 32–4) or Titus (Josephus *Bell. Iud.* VII.3–6). These items might be valued in a tokenistic way (symbolising defeat of the enemy) or as bullion, or even as both.

There are no major deposits from Britain that can be interpreted as booty on quite the same scale as the Danish bog hoards (Jørgensen, Storgaard and Gebauer Thomsen 2003) or the riverine finds of cavalry equipment that may derive from the Batavian revolt (Holwerda 1931; Jenkins 1985) or the

Alemannic invasions (Keim and Klumbach 1951; Fischer 1991). There are, however, occasional deposits of equipment which may derive from plunder or the trade in it, and a fragmentary piece of cavalry harness from Gallanach on the west coast of Scotland may be an example of a Roman military item being subjected to down-the-line trade after capture (Ritchie 1974: fig. 2, 8). Roman artefacts from lochs in Scotland may conceivably be booty that has acquired a dual role as votive offerings (Piggott 1953), as could a hoard of material (mainly cavalry equipment) found at Fremington Hagg (Webster 1971). The latter could equally well be an itinerant metalworker's stock hoard of scrap, however, and there is no helpful context to suggest the most likely interpretation. Equally, a Roman cavalry helmet from an Iron Age context in Leicestershire may be the spoils of war or a diplomatic gift (Faulkner 2006: 547).

Since there clearly was a demand for (and trade in) plundered items amongst those peoples opposing the Romans (although by no means prominent in the archaeological record in Britain), it is not surprising that there appears to be a considerable body of evidence for the Roman army going out of its way to limit access to its 'war surplus' (Manning 1972a: 243–6). Not only would it form valuable trophies for an enemy, but it represented a significant resource in terms of raw material if recycled (or even, in the case of weapon heads, just reused). This is one of the reasons why, upon withdrawing from a site, unwanted arms and armour (particularly damaged and scrapped items) generally seem to have been buried. The disposal of 10 tonnes of nails in this fashion in the legionary base at Inchtuthil when it was abandoned is often seen as a classic case of such a resource denial strategy (Pitts and St Joseph 1985: 109–13). Another famous instance of this practice is possibly the Corbridge Hoard, an iron-bound leather-covered wooden chest containing armour, weapons, and sundry other fixtures and fittings, which was buried at Corbridge – probably at the time the phase II fort was abandoned (Allason-Jones and Bishop 1988). This interpretation of the circumstances of its deposition is by no means clear-cut, however: it has even been suggested that it was specifically buried in order to accumulate rust and verdigris for medicinal use (Davies 1970) – a hypothesis which may seem unlikely now, but was not unreasonable at the time it was suggested.

Beyond its curiosity value, what is interesting about the Hoard is what is not there: more 'known unknowns'. Just as the question with the Inchtuthil nails will always be 'if they left that many behind, how many did they take with them?' (and it is by no means clear what proportion of the nails used at the site these represent: Shirley 2001: 144–5), so the assemblage of material in the Corbridge chest invariably invites speculation about what did not get left behind.

More commonly, odd items are placed into pits and ditch terminals along with all the other rubbish cleared away (Bishop 1986: 722). The pits and wells around the fort at Newstead may be another good example of this process, although in recent years a ritual or votive interpretation of such deposition has come back into fashion amongst some (Ross and Feacham 1976; Clarke and Jones 1994) but by no means all scholars (Manning reported in Anon. 2006: 3). Nevertheless, it is evident that there was an efficient recycling regime in operation within the Roman army that meant that, when an object was damaged, it would find its way back from its owner to the workshops where it could be either repaired or recycled. Thus odd pieces of equipment can be found either around accommodation (after it has been damaged, but before the owner has sent it to the workshops, which was probably the case at Longthorpe: Bishop 1986: 721–2) or in the workshops themselves, as at Carlisle (McCarthy, Bishop and Richardson 2001) or Exeter (Bidwell 1980: 31–5).

Deliberate concealment often led to equipment, like other rubbish, finding its way into pits and ditch terminals when sites were cleared upon abandonment, although this was by no means the only way it could be put beyond use. Outside the northern defences of the legionary base of Vindonissa at Windisch (Switzerland), a long linear midden built up during the first century AD and this consisted not only of vast amounts of stable sweepings but all manner of artefactual waste, including large amounts of scrap military equipment – the whole is now estimated at some 50,000 cubic metres (Hartmann 1986: 92–4). The chemical environment produced by the animal waste ensured excellent survival, even for organic materials. Such middens were once thought to have been rare, and Vindonissa as the exception rather than the rule, but other examples are now coming to light, as at Inveresk in East Lothian (Bishop 2004: 9–15, 183–5) and perhaps London (Wilmott 1991: 67, 176–8), both of which were truncated before they could develop on the scale of Vindonissa. The possibility that they were more common than originally believed must now be entertained.

Paradoxically, we lack the most important component of the 'universal stock' – those items which survived, or if lost were then found, or if damaged then repaired or recycled. These too are 'known unknowns', insofar as we know they existed, but lack the physical evidence to enable us to study them. As an example, consider the three principal types of body armour: mail, scale and segmental. In order of prominence in the archaeological record for the first century AD, it might be observed that first comes segmental as the most common, then scale, then finally mail. But we have to ask to what extent this situation reflects the use of such armour, rather than its vulnerability to attrition and its resultant propensity for premature entrance into the archaeological record. The integrity of a mail shirt in everyday use is close to perfect when not subjected to blows in combat, whereas segmental armour was (as modern reconstructions have shown) prone to loss, even in peacetime (see Bishop 1989: 1–2). If the depositional record is indeed skewed in this way, then we are presented with a false impression with no way of knowing that it is indeed misleading. In this instance, experimental archaeology, in the form of repeated use by re-enactors, acts as a useful indicator but can, of course, provide no definite indisputable answers.

Thus the objects that survived and did not enter the archaeological record remain as hypotheticals and we can only hope that those items that did eventually get deposited are, to some degree, representative of that 'universal stock'.

Production, repair and distribution

Archaeology has much to tell us about the techniques of production of Roman military equipment, and the artefacts themselves are one of the most important sources of information. The most useful pieces are those that are unfinished, a common reason being failed castings amongst copper-alloy objects or splitting in organic materials like wood or bone.

Ferrous objects, like most weapon heads, had to be forged into shape from billets of iron (Sim and Ridge 2002: 73–115), although some plate armour shows signs of having been through some sort of mechanical rolling process to form the sheet (Fulford et al. 2005: Table 1; D. Sim, pers. comm.). All production was labour-intensive and much of the assembly work on complex items shows only the minimum of competence necessary for the task.

Copper alloys always began in a molten form, some items being cast into shape, others formed from sheet produced from ingots. The Romans used a wide variety of such alloys, ranging from nearly pure copper, through brass (alloying with zinc), to bronze (alloying with tin), usually adding a proportion of lead when casting artefacts (leaded gunmetals). A particular type of brass, orichalcum, the same alloy as was used in some early imperial coinage, was favoured by the army from the first century AD onwards, possibly because its golden colour made it as attractive as it was functional. The increased use of the two-part mould during the second century AD (as opposed to the one-off lost-wax method found before) meant that it became easier to copy existing pieces of equipment (see Bishop and Coulston 2006: 243).

The fourth-century writer Vegetius – probably using a first-century AD source – tells us that the legions produced all the weaponry and equipment they needed (*De Re Militari* II.11) and this is largely borne out by the archaeological evidence until the later Empire, when Empire-wide state-controlled factories took over most – but by no means all – equipment production (Bishop and Coulston 2006: 233–40). A papyrus from Egypt records the material produced in a legionary workshop over two particular days (Bruckner and Marichal 1979: no. 409), but to judge from the condition of most military finds and, indeed, the very existence in the archaeological record, it is likely that the bulk of the time of such workshops was spent in repairing, rather than manufacturing, equipment.

There are hints amongst the artefacts for a degree of individuality creeping into what is usually viewed as a homogenised body of material. Such trends are difficult to track, however, owing to the movement of units around the Empire when circumstances demanded (as, for example, during the Dacian Wars, when substantial detachments from the army of Britain seem to have participated in the campaigns).

Just as it is apparent that most arms and armour recovered from the archaeological record have suffered in some way prior to deposition, it is frequently manifest that there has been earlier damage that has been repaired, and this is only to be expected if a care-and-maintenance type of system such as that outlined above was in operation. If the quality of manufacture is variable, that of repairs is frequently abysmal, strongly suggesting that the ordinary soldiery carried out most of their own day-to-day maintenance as and when it was needed. Attrition-prone items like the *lorica segmentata* all too often show signs of repeated repairs, usually of a make-do-and-mend nature. Thus plates that should be hinged together are riveted fast, or missing hinges are replaced by crudely cut-out imitations of the original. Missing hinged spindles have bent and crimped pieces of wire substituted, and the original elegant domed rivets are replaced by ugly malformed lumps designed more for function than for appearance.

Arms and armour, whilst suspect as a source of information about most aspects of their primary use, paradoxically constitute an extremely informative body of data about manufacture and repair during the Roman period once they have adopted a secondary role as components in the stock of scrap or items retained for cannibalisation. They become slightly more enigmatic upon assuming their tertiary function – as discards – since the reasoning

Pl. 20 Replica of the shield boss found in the river Tyne. The name of the owner has been applied along one edge using a series of incised dots.

behind their disposal is, as we have already considered, opaque to say the least.

The army thus produced the bulk of its weaponry and equipment (in the earlier imperial period at least) and distributed it by selling it at a fixed notional cost to the soldiery. It then became the property of the soldier and he might choose to mark this by inscribing his name(s) upon it, usually in the form of 'X in the centuria/turma of Y', either by scratching the information on to the item or, more commonly, by punching small holes to make up the letters, the so-called *punctim* technique (Plate 20). Such information not only conveys something about the status and ethnic origin of the owner, but can also demonstrate multiple ownership of some long-lived items, like helmets. The Coolus-type helmet from London has four names inscribed on its neckguard (Robinson 1975: pl. 54), covering a period of up to a hundred years, assuming all individuals owned the item for the full duration of their service. In reality, of course, the situation is likely to have been far more complex but, caveats notwithstanding, it is clear that some items of equipment could be extremely long-lived. In the later Empire, manufacture of some items became centralised, but it is likely that this was by no means the case for all matériel and evidence for local production and repair continues to be found on later sites.

Rust in peace

Once artefacts were buried, that was by no means an end to their woes. Despite the discovery of copious amounts of Roman cavalry equipment (Bishop 1988) and an ever-growing body of well-preserved leather (van Driel-Murray 1989b; Winterbottom 1989; Connolly and van Driel-Murray 1991), finds of the actual straps from horse harness are exceedingly rare, and then usually only in the form of mineral-preserved organics (e.g. Jenkins 1985: 148, pl. X, B). This may seem curious, until it is realised that more than one method of treating leather was available in the Roman period. Whilst tanned leather survives well in the right conditions, oiled hide is seldom found except as mineral-preserved organics, so the likely explanation for the shortage of straps must be that a method such as oiling was used to prepare horse harness.

Thus the imbalance between the survival of organic and inorganic components of the soldier's panoply is further complicated by differential persistency within those subgroups and this phenomenon is by no means confined to organic materials.

One of the reasons segmental body armour was so vulnerable was its combination of ferrous plate and copper-alloy fittings, inevitably inviting bimetallic electrolytic corrosion. Paradoxically, once in the ground there is evidence that the proximity of copper alloy actually retards the corrosion of iron or steel past a certain point, one possible reason why fittings are normally only found attached to small pieces of ferrous plate (Bishop 2002: 80–1). In comparison with helmets or swords, plate armour is seldom found in watery contexts on the Continent, so it is unsurprising that a similar absence is observable in Britain.

Using the evidence

As with all archaeological evidence, the taphonomic processes that governed the deposition of Roman weaponry and military equipment in the archaeological record effectively prescribe the uses to which the artefactual data can be put. However, as long as this is understood to be the case, there is much to be gleaned from the study of finds of arms and armour, since they comprise a rich source of information about an important component of society in the Roman period. Not only does military equipment bear witness to the technical and technological achievements of the day, but it is also redolent with implicit metadata, defining as it did the soldier's place within the contemporary social hierarchies.

The habit of deliberate deposition, whether it be by burial, as votive offering or as part of the site abandonment process, means that the army tends to have a high artefactual profile in the archaeological record. Whilst finds of arms and armour are rare from temporary camps (and this is indeed true of most other classes of artefact), any sort of protracted occupation seems to have led to deposition of material and this fact has its corollary in the observation that the presence of Roman military equipment on a site almost invariably points to the presence of the army. Some writers are unhappy with this notion and 'casual loss' tends to be invoked in circumstances where military items are found but the army is thought unlikely to have been present. However, the more equipment found at any given site, the more likely it becomes that a military presence must be acknowledged.

Vegetius (probably drawing on the writing of Iulius Frontinus, governor of Britain in AD 74–8: Schenk 1930: 88), describing a somewhat idealised model for garrisoning policy, observed that the army should be based in towns in order to oversee the passage of supply convoys and that, if towns as such did not exist, then forts were to be constructed for this purpose (*De Re Militari* III.8). As towns began to develop in Roman Britain, it is hardly surprising then that we find military equipment in them dating to the second to fourth centuries. Whereas finds of early arms and armour are usually a sign of an underlying military base, this later manifestation is something quite different and it may well be that we are witnessing dispersed garrisoning or civil billeting by the military. Thus the concept of a 'military zone', once favoured by historians, may need to be rethought, as the army appears to have been everywhere within the province, much as it seems to have been elsewhere in the Empire (Bishop 1991; 1999).

Military equipment is therefore, perhaps unsurprisingly, a prime indicator of the presence of the army. Residuality, whereby earlier artefacts work their way into later contexts through the mechanism of disturbance, can complicate the picture but is unlikely to obscure it completely. Thus the comparatively large quantities of arms and armour found around the banks of the Walbrook in London still indicate the presence of an early military base in the vicinity, although post-military landscaping has served to relocate the material, perhaps by flattening a midden (see above).

We have no idea what a Roman soldier's expectation of involvement in combat might have been at any given time whilst serving in Britain. It is, however, fairly obvious that this would be the time at which the greatest strain was placed upon items of arms and armour and this is the most likely reason for damage occurring to artefacts. So it is that, apart from the damaged armour, the Corbridge Hoard included bundles of spearheads with broken shafts, presumably awaiting rehafting, and a broken scabbard (Allason-Jones and Bishop 1988: 103–5). The armguards found at Carlisle were all in need of repair at the time of deposition, and examination shows them all to have been repaired several times before, some of them being 'cut 'n' shuts' (made up from several cannibalised donor pieces; pers. obs.).

How did spearshafts get broken and how did armguards get repeatedly damaged? The answer may seem obvious, but our earlier observations on the possible causes of attrition to segmental armour should serve to counsel caution. If repeated repairs were necessitated for segmental armguards simply by wearing them, one might suspect that some sort of redesign, or possibly even abandonment of this type of defence altogether, might have resulted. Those are complex items, however, whereas spearshafts are not and damage to these is strongly suggestive of use in combat (whether it be practice or in earnest). Moreover, both the Corbridge Hoard and the Carlisle finds belong to the first half of the second century and it is tempting to see them as linked in some way and possibly associated with otherwise unattested (but nevertheless sometimes assumed) conflict on the northern frontier in the Hadrianic period. Moreover, Docilis' admission about missing items of equipment (above) may also be as a result of loss or damage in action (the latter more likely than the first, as we have seen), rather than 'casual loss'.

Practical design elements in arms and armour inevitably reflect the style of fighting and how that evolved diachronically. The curved body shield associated with legionary troops was ideally suited to the sort of close-order fighting employed by heavy infantry (and finds its modern descendant in the riot shields used by many police forces). Early helmets with a flat neckguard, like the Coolus type found at London, may reflect a more hunched style of fighting which was precluded by later helmets with deeper neckguards – there are no complete examples from Britain but component parts have been found at many sites, including Corbridge (Robinson 1975: figs. 113–14) and Chester (Anon. n.d.: 3, no. 2) – which required a more upright stance. This may reflect a change from the use of the short *gladius Hispaniensis*-type sword, used primarily for stabbing, to the longer *spatha*, suitable for both swinging and stabbing (Connolly 1991; Coulston 2007b).

The design of Roman body armour, with its heavy emphasis on shoulder protection, as well as the form of infantry helmets – intended to deflect blows outwards and downwards – makes it apparent that the likely opponents' style of fighting was also being anticipated. That there may have been concerns about the amount of protection afforded by first-century AD armour is suggested by the evolution in design that occurs in the second century. There was an increased emphasis on protecting exposed limbs, through the use of greaves and articulated armguards (both of which occur in the Carlisle finds), as well as further enhancement of the helmet bowl by the introduction of crosspiece reinforces. Such radical developments are first witnessed in Trajan's wars in Dacia and rapidly spread to Britain, helped no doubt by the use of British detachments during those wars and their returning with these innovations.

Status, display, taste and prowess

As warriors, Roman soldiers clearly took some delight in their appearance. Equipment was always decorated to some degree beyond its mere functionality, whether it be the elegant lobate hinges of first-century *lorica segmentata* or the more vulgar embossed decoration of second- and third-century cavalry 'sports' armour (Garbsch 1978). There was a well-defined military aesthetic which changed with time, but is always recognisable. Indeed, such was the quality of the ornamentation to modern eyes that nineteenth- and twentieth-century scholars were often misled into viewing military artefacts such as the elaborately embossed Fulham sword scabbard in purely art-historical terms, invariably imbuing them with a high status which more modern research suggests they seldom deserved (cf. Bishop and Coulston 2006: 34). Nevertheless, the temptation to attribute fine items to 'officers' equipment' is one that has proved difficult to resist and must be reviewed critically and objectively whenever it is encountered in the literature.

Appearance not only was important to the individual and his peer group, but also served to define his place in society, a fact that is made apparent by the images on figural military tombstones, where key symbolic components in the iconography – the sword and belt, the length of tunic, the military cloak or cape, the horse if a cavalryman – made the illiterate viewer immediately aware of the status of the deceased. Such symbols were as important in life as they were in death and the soldier marked his place in peacetime society with their help (Coulston 1988b; 2004; 2007a).

Completely impractical elements of equipment, such as helmet crest and plume fittings or decorated saddle plates, served to introduce an element of showmanship and display into Roman military life, although they may have served a role in unit identification on the battlefield (Bishop 1990b). Military artefacts are also key to understanding how tastes amongst the soldiery changed over time. Thus military equipment from Britain in the mid-first century AD, with its delicate classical motifs and niello inlay (Grew and Griffiths 1991: fig. 4), differs very little from that from, say, the Rhineland or the Danube (Unz and Deschler-Erb 1997: tables 38–40), but is instantly recognisable against comparable items from the third century, where a taste for openwork decoration and a more plastic style of ornamentation are found (Oldenstein 1976). The fourth century saw a preponderance of chip-carved belt fittings, once thought to be a sign of the presence of Germanic troops, often characterised as *laeti*, but nowadays thought more likely to be the current Roman fashion (Plate 38). This process of evolution in taste (to call it 'barbarisation' as some have done is to load it with a subjective and questionable value judgement) went on throughout the history of the Roman army (Bishop and Coulston 2006: 270–2), so that even the soldier of the first-century invasion army of Britain used equipment derived from encounters with foreign foes in Rome's past (helmet and mail armour originating in Gaul, sword and dagger in Spain, and so on). Such a process is observable in armies of all periods, and the fact that the Roman army changed quite radically in appearance over the three and a half centuries of its presence in Britain should occasion no surprise.

The use of military equipment as an aid to identifying troop types has proved a contentious issue. Trajan's Column played a large part in suggesting to scholars that legionaries and auxiliaries could be differentiated by their equipment: on the Column, citizen troops (legionaries and praetorians) wear segmental armour, carry curved rectangular shields and wear tunics over bare legs. Auxiliary soldiers (non-citizen troops) have mail shirts (often mistaken by scholars for leather, since the detailing of the mail is too fine to show on many photographs: Coulston 1989: 33), carry oval shields and wear leggings that reach just below the knee. Irregular troops are bare-chested and wear trousers. This is clearly a visual shorthand that presumably deliberately oversimplified reality for the sake of clarity. Nevertheless, it must be founded in fact – there must have been some degree of differentiation between troop types – in order for it to work as a device. The ubiquity of finds of segmental armour from the Roman world subsequently led some twentieth-century scholars to question this hypothesis and propose a much more homogenised view of the army (Maxfield 1986). Whilst this view found some limited acceptance (Sauer 2000: 22–8; 2005: 122), it also brought forward more reasoned arguments examining the basis for both the new and old hypotheses (Coulston 1988b; Bishop and Coulston 2006: 254–9). In truth, the circumstantial evidence still seems to confirm the crude overall picture given by Trajan's Column – that legionary and auxiliary equipment differed – but indicates that a far more complex set of distinctions was in operation, not only between troop types, but between units, and even within units. Moreover, that situation changed with time.

Conclusion

For all their many uses as a diagnostic tool for the study of a particular segment of ancient society, Roman weaponry and military equipment were primarily designed for a specific purpose – achieving a successful outcome in combat (so-called high-intensity threats). A secondary aim sprang from their use in the maintenance of law and order (or low-intensity threats). Paradoxically, neither of these functions was prominent in securing the survival of artefacts in the archaeological record and it is the unusual or heterodox circumstances attached to all of the instances examined above that mean this class of evidence has to be treated very carefully before attempting to make any generalisations.

Each piece of weaponry or military equipment has a story to tell. It might be about its manufacture (was it cast, forged or cut from sheet?), its manufacturer (was he competent or incompetent, and what were his aesthetic choices in forming the object?), its owner(s) (had it been treated with care, and was it personalised in some way?), or its life history (had it been repaired one or more times, was it demonstrably damaged at the time of deposition, and are the circumstances of its loss apparent?) as if these were implicit or explicit metadata attached to the artefact. One thing is certain in all this: each military artefact that has survived is special, simply by virtue of its having done so – it had the good fortune to become a known known and, fortunately, each year we also discover a few more of those.

6 | Writing and communication

R. S. O. TOMLIN

We know the date to the day when literacy arrived in Britain, but for all the lip-service paid to 'education, education, education', the anniversary has never been celebrated. The day was 25 September 54 BC, when Julius Caesar and Quintus Cicero, the orator's younger brother, wrote to him 'from the nearest shores of Britain' as the invading army prepared to leave the island. Cicero in Rome received their letters (or joint-letter) on 24 October (Cicero *ad Atticum* IV.18.5). For the next century or so, there is little evidence of literacy; only a few very brief British coin-legends and graffiti on imported Roman pottery, and a few writing *stili* like those found at Braughing (Greep 1983; 2003; Öllerer 1998). The important skills of reading and writing returned with the Roman army in AD 43, and multiplied its technological superiority over the natives: 'the need to record and tabulate unit strengths, movements of troops, acquisition and dispensation of supplies, is part of the logic of an organisation which depended, for its efficiency and effectiveness, on economy of numbers' (Bowman 1994: 96). These skills spread from the army and the administration to civilians who found a use for them, for example the businessmen whose letters and accounts have been found at Vindolanda, but in fact the lives of all the inhabitants of the province were ruled by written records. A striking instance is a waxed writing-tablet found in the London Walbrook (Tomlin 1996b). Dated 14 March 118, it is the first page of the record of an inquiry into the ownership of five acres of Kentish woodland, 'the property in question, the wood Verlucionium, fifteen *arepennia* more or less, which is in the canton of the Cantiaci in Dibussu[...] parish, neighboured by the heirs [of...] and the heirs of Caesennius Vitalis and the vicinal road'. A Roman citizen called Lucius Julius Bellicus claims to have bought it from another, Titus Valerius Silvinus, 'for forty denarii, as is contained in the deed of purchase'. This unique fragment implies the existence not only of Roman law (for purchase by *mancipatio*), but also of written records, exact if somewhat out-of-date, detailing the ownership of land, farm by farm, throughout the province. Keeping these records was not a public service, of course, but necessary for collecting the tax on land. Directly or indirectly, they would affect the agrarian population, whether it was literate or not.

Pl. 21 Grey ware dish on which the name of the owner has been scratched to distinguish it from other similar dishes

Literacy in Roman Britain – in crude terms, the proportion of the population who could read and write – cannot be quantified. We can only study it impressionistically, by looking at written documents of all kinds, and wondering who wrote them, and why, and who was likely to read them or be affected by them. Even the concept is difficult to define: reading is not the same as writing, and the 'literate' ranged widely in competence, from the owners of bowls, cups and plates who could scratch their name in a few laboured capital letters (Plate 21), to the clerks of the army and the administration, to businessmen and lawyers, to the provincial landowners who could read Virgil and compose Latin verse (see Liversidge 1968: 294–322; Barrett 1978). The largest samples of Roman handwriting found in Britain, the Vindolanda wooden ink-tablets and the Bath lead tablets, both indicate a spectrum of skills which ranged from sophisticated letters of recommendation or consolation to an illiterate 'curse' with angular scratches intended to look like writing (Tomlin 1988: 84–94). Some of the Uley lead tablets are even blank: mute evidence of a spoken spell, perhaps, or inked texts which have leached away (Tomlin 1993:113; for ink on lead, see Reuter and Scholz 2004: 15, figs. 16 and 17).

The question is quite complex, therefore, but the evidence is extensive and has been well studied (Hanson and Conolly 2002; Pearce 2004). An influential inquiry into ancient literacy has noted 'the remarkable care with which the most inconsequential-seeming pieces of writing from Britannia have been recorded' (Harris 1989: 269). This is not altogether a compliment to the province – the author warns that 'patriotic optimism' may exaggerate its literacy – but it recognises that Romano-British inscriptions have been collected ever since the late sixteenth century, and that fortunately (or unfortunately) the number of discoveries year by year is small enough for them to be assembled by one or two editors. Thus every year since 1921 an account has been published annually, at first in the *Journal of Roman Studies*, and since 1970 in *Britannia*. *The Roman Inscriptions of Britain* (*RIB*) consolidates the record by collecting 2,262 'monumental' inscriptions on stone found before 1955, as well as fifty-two on other materials, mostly silver, bronze and lead (Birley 1966: 226). In the succeeding fifty years, another 527 stone inscriptions were found, and have been collected in *RIB* III. Meanwhile the inscribed objects of personal ownership and use found before 1987, which epigraphists quaintly call 'instrumentum domesticum', have been collected by *RIB* II. This however excludes hundreds of writing-tablets of lead and wood found since 1973, which have been published elsewhere and will be consolidated in *RIB* IV.

The written evidence for writing and communication in Roman Britain can thus be divided into 'monumental' inscriptions on stone and 'instrumentum domesticum' (including writing-tablets) of other materials. The division is not absolute, since metal and even wood were sometimes used for 'monumental' inscriptions, although in Britain this is very rare, and a few 'personal' objects were made of stone. It is also uncertain whether metal or ceramic 'votives' given to the gods should be regarded as 'monumental' like altars, or as the personal property of the donor. Another distinction to bear in mind is that made in studying the history of writing-materials, between 'hard' (stone, etc.) and 'soft' (paper, etc.), or between texts 'which are *incised* and, on the other hand, those which are *written* (whether with a brush or pen)' (Bowman and Thomas 1983: 32). Implicit also is a distinction between the tools of writing, and the materials on which they wrote (Wheeler 1946: 56–8; Liversidge 1968: 175, fig. 76; Božič and Feugère 2004; Feugère and Lambert 2004: 173–92). So the division between 'monumental' stones and 'instrumentum domesticum' is not the only one possible, but it is conventional among epigraphists.

Stone inscriptions

Stone inscriptions are divided by *RIB* I and III into altars and other religious dedications, building inscriptions, and tombstones, which in their different ways fulfil the human need of a permanent record, however inferior it may be to the 'monument more lasting than bronze' claimed by the poet Horace. *RIB* 311 (Caerwent) is the only British example of the inscribed statue bases of grandees found in other provinces, but there are many funerary epitaphs of soldiers, businessmen, craftsmen and other incomers, and the members of their families. Inscribed stones and slabs attributed the buildings of which they formed part, notably Hadrian's Wall itself, with inscriptions over many a gate, and hundreds of 'centurial stones' incorporated into the wall-curtain. Altars marked a contract with the gods, implied by the closing V S L M formula: the dedicator 'fulfilled his vow willingly, deservedly'. This ceremony is best depicted on the Bridgeness 'distance slab' marking the eastern end of the Antonine Wall, which the legate of *legio II Augusta* inaugurates by sacrificing a bull, a pig and a sheep (Plate 55; *RIB* 2139). It is touchingly implied by a metrical slab from the western end of Hadrian's Wall, on which Antonianus promises the mother goddesses to gild the lettering if they prosper his undertaking: there is no trace of gilding (*RIB* 2059). These altars reveal the range of deities in Roman Britain, from those of the Roman pantheon – notably Jupiter 'Best and Greatest', honoured by garrisons every New Year – to local Celtic gods who found themselves literate for the first time, and exotics from Germany and the East (Birley 1986). Mithras is one of the latter, but not the Christian god, the most successful of them all, no doubt because stone inscriptions are scarce after about AD 260. The Celtic gods are often 'identified' with familiar Roman gods, for example Sulis Minerva at Bath, but this is not necessarily a mark of sophistication. Compare two altars from the remote moorland shrine of Vinotonus south of Bowes: *RIB* 732, dedicated by a centurion of the local garrison, identifies him with the Italian god Silvanus; but *RIB* 733, dedicated by his commanding officer, an aristocrat from Parma in northern Italy, does not.

'Monumental' inscriptions range widely in quality and size. A few, for example the funerary altar of Nero's *procurator* Julius Classicianus, the Hadrianic forum inscription at Wroxeter, and the Antonine list of legionaries from Southwark, in their layout and quality of lettering match any Roman inscription cut anywhere at the time (*RIB* 12, see Grasby and Tomlin 2002; *RIB* 288; *RIB* III, 3016). But many are no more than workmanlike, if not amateur – itself an index of literacy – with their irregular letters and crowded layout (Plate 22): this is typical of many altars and tombstones, and of almost all the 'centurial stones' and quarry-face graffiti. In size, some are very large, for example the Wroxeter inscription already mentioned, at 3.70 m wide, and the gate-inscriptions at Verulamium, 4.30 m wide, and at York, 2.48 m wide (*RIB* 288; *RIB* III, 3123; *RIB* 665). Somewhat later, but even larger, the

Pl. 22 Building inscription of the Cohort of Lingones. Although an official inscription, it suggests a limited level of literacy.

five butting slabs of *RIB* 1235 at Risingham were originally 5.72 m wide. The ubiquitous 'centurial' stones, however, are only dressed rubble facing-stones inscribed with the name or number of a legionary sub-unit, and many once-substantial inscriptions have been reduced to the merest fragments. Two-thirds of one letter, an excellent 'A' once some 255 mm high, is all that survives of the inscriptions of the Temple of Claudius at Colchester, a city which has produced another rare survival, a well-shaped gilt-bronze letter 'V' 190 mm high (*RIB* III, 3128; *RIB* 198). Two conjoining fragments at Winchester carry the letters [. . .]NTO[. . .], obviously 'Antonine', which are the tallest ever found in Britain, no less than 0.29 m high (*RIB* III, 3034).

The choice of stone was largely dictated by geology: masons chose a local building-stone, if there was one. For example, slate was used at Chester and Hardknott, magnesian limestone at York, limestone at Bath and Gloucester, but most inscriptions from the military zone are sandstone. This is invariably the case with Hadrian's Wall, as with its facing-stones: 'buff' sandstone in the east, red sandstone to the west of the Red Rock Fault in Wall Mile 53. Sandstone tends to be coarse-grained, but it was the medium for the Wroxeter forum inscription, masterfully drawn and cut on two thin butting slabs of 'white' Grinshill stone, a fine-grained local grey sandstone which was later used for mouldings in medieval building-work. In the south-east, at Silchester, Verulamium and London for example, where freestone was not available, imported limestones or marble were used. At Colchester, the very early tombstone of the centurion Favonius Facilis was cut on Lothringer freestone, the Gallic limestone which his legion had just been using at Neuss. But the contemporary tombstone of the trooper Longinus was made of British oolitic limestone probably from Bath (*RIB* 200; 201; Hayward 2006). In London and Canterbury, white Italian(?) marble might be used for dedications and funerary plaques; at Caerleon it was actually preferred to the local red sandstone for an important Trajanic building-inscription (*RIB* 330). At Bath, despite the excellent local limestone, there is an enigmatic marble fragment which reads [. . .]IB ♦ CL ♦ T[. . .]. This is the abbreviated name of a Roman citizen, Tiberius Claudius [. . .], and since the lettering is first-century in date, and of the highest quality, it is tempting to identify him as the 'Great King' Tiberius Claudius Togidubnus, who might have merited this exotic medium (*RIB* III, 3050). In the south-east, a frequent choice was Purbeck 'marble' from south-eastern Dorset, a dense fossiliferous limestone sawn into small thin slabs, highly decorative when polished, but brittle and liable to break out when chiselled. Its use points to an epigraphic paradox. South Dorset is the source of excellent stone – its Portland clads modern London – but the county has hardly produced an inscription: just two tombstones, and an early altar dedicated by a legionary centurion (*RIB* 188; *RIB* III, 3047; *RIB* III, 3046).

Epigraphists tend to study the written text, first reading the letters and 'restoring' what is lost, and then elucidating the allusions and historical context. Epigraphic conventions and abbreviations are more familiar than the mason's tools and working methods. Thus the drawings in *RIB*, careful and objective as they are, ignore the scratched setting-out lines and other evidence of preparation. One of the distinctive group from Birrens, for example, still shows the marks left by the dividers used to draw its letters. This was spotted by Richard Grasby from R. P. Wright's squeeze of *RIB* 2110, while he was studying constructed capitals in the inscriptions of Roman Britain. Letter-forms may also reflect the brush-strokes that preceded them, as on the altar of Aulus Cluentius Habitus in the Carrawburgh Mithraeum (*RIB* 1545). This inscription, incidentally, is Roman Britain's peak of literary snobbery: the man reduced his place of origin to the single letter 'L', since he expected his fellow-worshippers to know that his namesake and remote ancestor, famous for being Cicero's client, came from the small Italian town of Larinum (Birley 1951).

Careful measurement is needed to elucidate the geometry of important inscriptions, but some lapses are easily spotted. Thus the symmetry of the Caerleon marble slab was spoilt by inserting an extra numeral after Trajan's consul-year, COS III instead of COS II, presumably because its preparation spanned two years. Such a hiatus between preparation and inscribing is apparent on the gate inscription at Great Chesters, where Hadrian's name and titles are crammed into the bottom two-fifths; the rest is blank, without any reference to the builders (*RIB* 1736). At Housesteads, a carved monumental panel was not inscribed at all, obviously because it had broken in half (Wilson 1969: 204, pl. XV.1). Blank 'centurial' stones have also been found – the panel indicated by a scratched outline or recessed ansate panel – because they were not used, or perhaps were only painted. A wooden ansate panel, not incised but presumably once painted with an inscription, has been found at Carlisle – the only wooden 'monumental' inscription from Britain, except for *RIB* 1935 (Caruana 1987). 'Centurial' stones, like quarry-face graffiti and the crude altars dedicated to 'Veteres' and other obscure gods, were cut by soldiers with the picks or mason's points used for dressing stone, but the precise, formal lettering of the Caerleon marble slab, for example, would have required a craftsman using a mason's carving chisel; it is difficult to distinguish between this and a carpenter's, but we would expect a heavy-duty all-iron tool with a knob one end and a double-bevelled chisel-point the other. One such has been found at Housesteads (Manning 1976: fig. 16, no. 70; see also the Italian tombstone of a *lapicida* in Susini 1973: pl. 2).

The role of public inscriptions in the life of Roman Britain is a matter for surmise. Were they largely decorative – and soon ignored? Were they only a primer for people like the fictional businessman who taught himself to read 'the letters on stones'? (Petronius *Satyricon* 58: 'lapidarias litteras scio'). Were they even *meant* to be read? Consider the Bainbridge slab, with its maze of ligatures and delightfully visual borders: it owes its impact to a capricorn, a wingless Victory, an eagle, a military torque, a draped Genius and a bull (*RIB* III, 3215). A few inscriptions have been found standing *in situ*, like the altar of Marcius Memor in the precinct at Bath, or the altars dedicated to the nymphs of springs at Carrawburgh, Chester and Risingham (Bath: *RIB* III, 3049; Carrawburgh: *RIB* 1526; 1527; Chester: *RIB* 460; Risingham: *RIB* 1228). Some tombstones were still associated with the ashes of the dead when found, or with a tomb (for example, *RIB* 156; 200 and 365; 400). Tombstones which arrogantly assert military conquest, the two already mentioned at Colchester and the horseback head-hunter at Lancaster, survive paradoxically because they were flat on their faces when found, fallen, probably pushed (*RIB* 200; 201; *RIB* III, 3185). But the Romans themselves recycled their stones. A famous photograph shows the excavators of Birdoswald in 1929 conducting a mock-sacrifice in the barrack-block they have uncovered. Unknown to them, their altar stands on one inscription and the future editor of *RIB* stands on another, both stones having been reused as paving in the fourth century (*RIB* 1912 and 1909 respectively; Wilmott 1997: 6, fig. 4). The Romans also cannibalised tombstones for town-walls, for example Classicianus' altar in the east wall of London and an early veteran's tombstone in the west gate of Alchester; at Cirencester three tombstones were found stacked ready for use in the wall, but never used (*RIB* 12; *RIB* III, 3121; *RIB* III, 3060; 3061; 3062). Legionary tombstones were defaced and used wholesale to rebuild the north wall at Chester, in this case perhaps a deliberate insult to a disbanded legion (Clay 2004). This *damnatio memoriae* is inferred, but we know that the names of Geta and other fallen emperors were still read after their deaths, because they were systematically removed from their monuments; however, the Unconquered Sun suffered the same fate at Corbridge, apparently because the meaning of the original dedication had been lost, and sixty years later it was thought to be dedicated to Elagabalus (*RIB* 1137).

We have some two centuries of stone inscriptions, which implies that they continued to fill a need, but they are incomplete as evidence and carry a built-in bias. The earliest, for example the epitaphs of Julius Classicianus and Favonius Facilis, belong to the mid-first century; but after two centuries, from the 260s or so, they become quite rare. This means that the fourth century is hardly represented in stone (hence the dearth of Christian evidence), and also that fewer than 3,000 inscriptions 'represent' a population of 2 or 3 million at a time, a total say of 20 million people during these two 'epigraphic' centuries. Moreover, the distribution is not uniform: it largely reflects the dispositions of the army and its dependants; more than two-fifths of the total, some 1,130 stone inscriptions out of 2,800, come from the Hadrian's Wall frontier alone (see Jones and Mattingly 1990: Map 5.10). Even towns like Gloucester, Bath and London, which do produce stone inscriptions, owe many of them to a military presence of some kind, like the Dorset altar already mentioned. Stone inscriptions, a truism but worth emphasis, were cut by people with 'the epigraphic habit' (MacMullen 1982). Many of them belonged to the Roman army and administration, which had the necessary time, skills and money, and, like modern governments, justified their existence by self-advertisement. It was natural for the legate of *legio VI Victrix* to erect an altar 'because of successful achievements beyond the Wall' (*RIB* 2034), or for a cavalry prefect to erect one to Silvanus, the god of hunting, 'on fulfilment of his vow ... for taking a wild boar of remarkable fineness which many of his predecessors had been unable to bag' (Plate 23; *RIB* 1041). Even common soldiers, besides erecting altars

Pl. 23 Altar to Silvanus from Bollihope Common, now in Stanhope Church

and tombstones, cut their names on unfired bricks and quarry-faces as they worked.

It is exciting, but not really a surprise, to find the same man 'represented' more than once in our limited sample. The centurion Cocceius Firmus, for example, erected five altars at Auchendavy (*RIB* 2174; 2175; 2176; 2177; 2178; and see Birley 1936), and the prefect Silvius Auspex three at Birrens (*RIB* 2100; 2104; 2108). Birrens is one of the forts – Maryport and Birdoswald are others – where the accident of survival due to remoteness or local interest has yielded a long sequence of altars dedicated to Jupiter by commanding officers. The same man is even 'represented' by inscriptions from two unrelated contexts, for example the centurion Maximius Gaetulicus with his two altars on Hadrian's Wall and at Newstead (*RIB* 1725; 2120); years later, he dedicated a third at Novae on the lower Danube, when he had risen to be *primus pilus* after fifty-seven years' service (*AE* 1985: 735). Centurions like Ferronius Vegetus of the Twentieth Legion are represented both on Hadrian's Wall and at base; Sollius Iulianus of the Sixth, for example, is named on a building-stone at Hare Hill and on a scrap of leather at York (*RIB* 1769; 1867; 468; *RIB* III, 3454; *RIB* II.4, 2445.16). In the lower ranks, the *vexillarius* Barates of Palmyra, who commemorated his British wife Regina at South Shields with a sumptuous tombstone in the Palmyrene style (Plate 54), is likely to be the [Ba]rathes of Palmyra obscurely buried at Corbridge; and Cassius Severus, the legionary of the Twentieth who borrowed money at Carlisle on 7 November 83, the veteran of that name buried at Chester (*RIB* 1065; 1171; Tomlin 1992 and *RIB* 526). These intriguing coincidences remind us that stone inscriptions do not tell us about the whole population, but about 'people who used stone inscriptions' (Mann 1985: 206).

Instrumentum domesticum

'Instrumentum domesticum' is perhaps a better test of literacy, since the evidence is more widespread and the military bias is less, but many 'graffiti' are no more than personal names, and real 'manuscripts' are most unusual. It is easy to treat quite rare documents as typical, but 'typical' documents are actually very rare. One example is the military 'pay sheet'. A soldier was paid three times a year, with deductions, which made a written record necessary. A papyrologist has reckoned that in the three centuries from Augustus to Diocletian there were in theory 'at the very least 225,000,000' such records. Some ten or so have actually survived. The British contribution would have been more than 20,000,000 – of which nothing survives but the entry in a Vindolanda document which notes that men were sent 'to York, to collect pay' (Fink 1971: 242; *Tab. Vindol.* I no. 154; Bowman and Thomas 2003: 155). These records would be ephemeral, of course; but think of another document, the last will and testament of a Roman citizen. It was his (or her) privilege to write one, and there was a social obligation to do so. Citizens formed a provincial elite, and we can only guess their number in Britain: what with legionary soldiers and auxiliary veterans, administrators, businessmen and other immigrants, and then their descendants, the number might have grown from (say) 25,000 to 100,000, before the *constitutio Antoniniana* made the distinction obsolete in AD 212. But wills continued to be written, on 'tablets' of any material, whether wood, paper or parchment (*Digest* 37.1.1 (Ulpian)). Thus, during the centuries of Roman Britain, their number must have exceeded half a million, if not a million or more, but all that survives is a single tablet, the first page of the 'wooden book' found by Welsh peat-cutters in the hills above Trawsfynydd (Tomlin 2004).

Wills and pay sheets are examples of 'manuscripts', but first we should consider 'instrumentum domesticum' proper, those objects of daily use which happen to be inscribed for one reason or another (Feugère 2004b; Reuter and Scholz 2004). Many such inscriptions were part of the manufacturing process, whether they were cut or moulded for the manufacturer's own convenience, or to attract and inform the consumer. The latter added others in the course of use, usually to mark his ownership. When the army made lead water-pipes for its new fortress at Chester, it incorporated an elaborate moulded text dating them by emperor and governor, even though they would soon be buried (*RIB* II.3, 2434). Likewise it stamped a proportion of its bricks and tiles before using them in baths, barrack-blocks and other buildings. Lessees of lead mines cast their ingots in moulds which dated them by the Emperor, and stated origin and ownership. Also required by the manufacturing process were the names cut on hides to identify them in the tanning-tank, the numerals cut by coopers into barrel staves as an aid to assembly, the batch-totals on unfired tiles. More immediate in their appeal are inconsequential graffiti scratched by common workmen, such as their autographs or *jeux d'esprit*: 'Every day for thirteen days Austalis has been wandering by himself', for example, and 'Enough' (*RIB* II.5, 2491.147 and 159; Tomlin 1979). These were not required by the manufacturing process, and are gratuitous evidence of literacy.

It is easy to smile at the military stamping its tiles and bricks to forestall pilfering civilians, like the British Army whitewashing its coal dumps, but civilian manufacturers also incorporated their names in the product.

Examples are iron tools, bronze vessels and brooches, shoes, tiles, samian ware and mortaria, the moulded bases of glass bottles, clay figurines, the little stone dies known as 'oculists' stamps' which were used for marking cakes of eye-salve (*collyrium*) with the prescription and its author's name (Fig. 20(d)). The distribution of the latter interestingly reflects the Roman road-network (Jackson 1996: 179, fig. 21.1). This indeed was a key factor in the spread of literacy, as has been stated by John Wilkes (2005). All these names were rather like a modern trademark, a guarantee of origin and quality, an encouragement to brand-loyalty. But inscriptions might also inform. Weights were useless without numerals; captions were added to wall-paintings and mosaics, to the barbotine ware and moulded glass souvenirs of gladiators and charioteers (Plate 24); painted labels in particular specified the contents of amphoras, for example 'Lucius Tettius Africanus' finest fish sauce from Antibes; (product) of Africanus' (*RIB* II.6, 2492.24). This all implies consumers who could read, who would buy jewellery and hardware with appealing but non-utilitarian inscriptions, for example the bronze baldric fittings with integral lettering invoking Jupiter's protection, the 'motto beakers' painted with jolly slogans in white slip, the enamelled brooches, metal strap ends, rings and other personal items inscribed VTERE FELIX, 'Use (this) and be happy.' Special objects might be personalised before use, for example in the Hoxne Treasure silver spoons professionally inscribed with the owner's name, and Lady Juliane's gold bracelet with its openwork VTERE FELIX DOMINA IVLIANE (Hassall and Tomlin 1994: 306–8). Auxiliary veterans could acquire a bronze military diploma, their very own certified copy of the law at Rome which guaranteed their status, and they even seem to have commissioned 'souvenirs' of Hadrian's Wall, enamelled bronze bowls naming forts (Tomlin and Hassall 2004: 344, no. 24).

These are special items, but informal ownership-inscriptions are very common, especially names scratched on reused amphoras and the samian and coarseware vessels liable to be confused or 'borrowed' in a crowded social context. Even illiterates marked their property with 'crosses' and other symbols. This all implies the promiscuity of military life in barracks, just as military equipment was marked by means of dot-punched letters (Plate 20) or labelled with inscribed metal tags, but similar graffiti are found in towns and even villas and other rural sites (Evans 1987; see also Frere in *RIB* II.7, 13 (samian) and *RIB* II.8, 29 (coarseware)). Other evidence of use is numerals denoting capacity, scratched on amphoras, jugs and cooking-jars. Vindolanda has produced the unique graffito CORS MDCCCLXXXIIII,

Pl. 24 Moulded glass vessel showing a chariot scene and giving the names of the participants, from West Cemetery, Colchester

taking stock apparently of *cor(iandri) s(emina)*, '1,884 seeds of coriander' (*RIB* II.8, 2503.1).

These ownership-inscriptions are 'domestic', but those on votive objects are akin to 'monumental': the dedicator publicly transfers his ownership to the god, often (like an altar) with the formula V S L M. The most striking instance is the temple treasure found near Baldock comprising seven gold plaques (the largest number ever found outside Egypt) and twelve silver, embossed with images of a Minerva-like goddess standing in her temple (Tomlin and Hassall 2005: 489, no. 30; noted there as 'found near Baldock', but which can now be described as the 'Ashwell temple treasure'). This is Senuna, the subject of a silver statuette dedicated by Flavia Cunoris; compare the bronze statue of Mars from the Foss Dike, which cost Bruccius and Caratius 100 sesterces (*RIB* 274). This idea of votive plaques persisted into Christian thought, with the Chi-Rho silver 'leaves' in the Water Newton Treasure (*RIB* II.3, 2431.1, 4–11). The name of Senuna, hitherto unknown, has now been recognised on a silver ring, which like other rings inscribed with the name of a deity was probably regarded as the god's property, who thus had an interest in protecting the wearer (*RIB* II.3, 2422.3). After all, British gods could now read. This is taken for granted by many of the 'curse tablets', especially those at Bath and Uley, which are petitions to Sulis Minerva and Mercury carefully incised on lead (see below and Tomlin 2002).

Votive objects are hardly utilitarian, but the inscription is secondary. Some engaging inscriptions have no ulterior purpose at all, for example 'writing practice' like the Virgilian tags found on tiles and wall-plaster and in the Vindolanda tablets; and alphabets on stone and pottery, and the signatures not of ownership scratched on tiles, wall-plaster, building-stones and quarry-faces, which attest literacy in quite humble persons concerned only to display or develop it. Then there are objects of no intrinsic value like the metal tags and 'curse tablets' already mentioned, where the message is everything, for example the incised lead labels or lead/tin alloy sealings attached to packages. They are comparable with the enamelled seal-boxes once attached to writing-tablets, which are themselves not inscribed, but bear witness to documents and letters now lost (Holmes 1995; Tongue 2004; cf. Derks and Roymans 2002).

Writing-tablets

No book actually survives from Roman Britain, whether in the form of a papyrus roll (*volumen*) or of the *codex* of parchment or papyrus leaves bound together, but there is ample evidence that they existed (Tomlin forthcoming). Papyrus, the 'paper' made in Egypt by hammering together strips cut from the stem of a local water-plant, and exported all over the Empire, has not yet been found in Britain, except as a few mineralised scraps in the Corbridge Hoard of metalware (Allason-Jones and Bishop 1988: 86, no. 298, 2 with 87, fig. 103). But Britain is special for being the first to furnish examples of the papyrus substitute already well known from literary sources, the wooden leaf tablets used for writing in ink known as *philyra* or *tilia* (see Bowman and Thomas 1983: 41–2; *Digest* 32, 52, *CIL* ii.4125; Augustan History *Antoninus Pius* XIII.1; Herodian I.17.1; Dio Cassius 72 (73).8.4)). *Tilia* means 'limewood', but in Britain alder was mostly used.

They were first recognised at Vindolanda in 1973, and have made the fort famous; others have been found at Carlisle, a fragment at Caerleon, and some scraps of later date in a rural context near Lechlade (Bowman and Thomas 1983: 34–6; Tomlin 1998). How they were made has not really been studied, but essentially they were shavings of wood, cut (it would seem) with a plane or drawknife. They were then trimmed into rectangular 'pages', and sized perhaps with beeswax, so as to take ink (Bowman and Thomas 2003:13; for a discussion of the use of veneers, see Pliny *Nat. Hist.* XVI.84, 231–3).

This ink has not been analysed, but it would have resembled modern Indian ink. Its manufacture is described by Roman writers: resin was burnt in a reducing atmosphere to make lampblack, which was then collected and mixed with gum arabic as a bonding-agent (Vitruvius *De arch.* VII.10.2; Pliny *Nat. Hist.* XXXV.25, 41–2). In practice, domestic soot may also have been used, just as for colouring the wax of *stilus* tablets. This black, carbon-based ink could have been stored in powder form; after water had been added, it would need to be stirred or shaken before use. It was used in ink-wells, which in Britain are mostly made of South-Gaulish samian; their distribution implies ink-writing in forts, town centres and the port of London, at least until the reign of Trajan (Willis 2005). A few examples have been found in other wares, bronze and glass, including one from London which carries the neatly incised inscription IVCVNDI, '(property) of Jucundus', which implies an office where it was one of several (*RIB* II.8, 2503.287). Outside Britain there is evidence of ink-wells in pairs, for black and red ink, the latter used for 'rubrics' (headings), and also leather carrying-cases for ink-well and pens (or *stili*) (von Boeslager 1989; Öllerer 1998: 41–3).

The pen itself is something of a problem. The Latin word is *calamus*, a reed, which would resemble the pen artists and calligraphers devise by cutting one end of a bamboo cane at a diagonal, and making the point into a nib by squaring it off and piercing lengthwise. A few such *calami* have been found in Egypt, but none yet in Britain, although certain small knives have been plausibly identified as 'pen-knives' (Božič 2001b; Feugère 2004a; see also *RIB* II.3, 2428.8 and 14). Whether the Romans also used feather quills, like those of medieval and modern times, is uncertain. None has yet been found, not even at Vindolanda with its extraordinary wealth of tablets and organic material of all kinds. The Latin words for 'feather' – *plumus* and *penna* – have given modern languages their word for 'pen', but the first literary evidence of use is seventh-century (Isidorus *Orig.* VI.14). Metal pens, however, consisting of a tapered bronze tube with an integral split-nib at one end, like a modern 'dip' pen, have occasionally been found

(Božič 2001b). Six are known from London, and others from Verulamium, Baldock and South Shields (see Jackson in Stead and Rigby 1986: 139–40, fig. 61, no. 393; Frere 1972: 144, no. 167, fig. 51; Allason-Jones and Miket 1984: 220, no. 3.749). Vindolanda and some other sites, notably Strageath, have also produced a strange implement, consisting of an iron point with a spiral end for attachment to a wooden handle. This was first identified as an 'ox-goad', but the finer examples could certainly be used as dip-pens (Birley 2002: 35; Dieudonné-Glad 2002; see also Chapter 4). The difficulty is that the Vindolanda tablets were evidently written with a split nib (Bowman and Thomas 2003: 13). So the identification is uncertain, and this spike may even be a crude *stilus*. Another possible writing-instrument is a rectangular bone strip with one end rounded and pierced, examples of which have been found at Castleford (Greep 1998: 283–4). They resemble a long, narrow label, but there is no sign that they were ever inscribed, and they have been variously identified as 'paper-knives', although these were not needed with a papyrus roll, or as parchment-smoothers, even as children's 'pen-knives'; more plausible identifications are as 'rulers' or as an alternative to the metal wax spatula (Božič 2002: 34–6).

There is a wealth of ink texts from Carlisle and Vindolanda, two forts on the Stanegate 'frontier' linked by a letter sent to the prefect at Vindolanda asking him for a recommendation to the 'district officer' (*centurio regionarius*) at Carlisle (*Tab. Vindol.* 250; Bowman and Thomas 1994; 2003; Tomlin 1998; see also Bowman 1994; Tomlin 1996a; Birley 2002; Pearce 2004). Fragments of letters have been found at Carlisle, but the most notable finds are returns of the wheat and barley consumed by the *ala I Sebosiana* for three-day periods, and an official report of missing cavalry weapons. The many military documents found at Vindolanda include the strength-report of the First Cohort of Tungrians on 18 May in a year unknown, formulaic statements of readiness ('All who should be are at duty stations, as is the baggage'), stereotyped requests for leave and a contemptuous note of British cavalry tactics. An officer also reports from an outpost: 'My fellow-soldiers have no beer. Please order some to be sent.' Building-materials are organised, including lead, lime, stone and clay. Fragments of household accounts range from wheat and barley to oysters, olives, wine and beer, including a long schedule of the poultry consumed by the prefect's household day by day during the years 102, 103 and 104. All sorts of things are itemised, from bowls to curtains, from condiments to dog-collars, hunting-nets and boot-nails. The commanding officer, a Batavian noble from the Rhine estuary, drafts a letter in good Latin to his patron, apparently a senator resident in Rome, hoping that 'thanks to you, I may be able to enjoy a pleasant period of military service'. His wife receives a delightful letter from another prefect's wife, its signature incidentally the earliest manuscript of a woman from Britain, which invites her to a birthday-party on 11 September, 'to make the day more enjoyable for me by your arrival'. Other letters make tantalising allusions to the writer's state of health: 'I am suffering very severely from a headache', and 'When I was writing this I was making the bed warm', perhaps an allusion to fever. A lady gives thanks for the letter of comfort which has been sent her by another 'just as a mother would do'; perhaps she has suffered a miscarriage or the death of a child.

The alternative medium to ink was waxed wooden tablets (*cerae*), regularly used for note-taking and memoranda since they were reusable, but whose sturdiness made them ideal for correspondence and legal documents (see Lalou 1992 for illustrations). They were rectangular sheets of wood in various sizes according to format, the regular wood being silver fir (*abies alba*) which was not native to Roman Britain, so the tablets must have been imported, whether finished or in block. Other woods are known, and elsewhere even ivory, but silver fir with its regular grain would split easily into sheets, just as it was riven into barrel staves. Alternatively tablets may have been sawn, like an unfinished block of willow tablets found in Egypt (Sharpe 1992: fig. 35). One or both faces were then recessed, leaving a margin, and coated with beeswax coloured with lampblack or soot; there is also literary reference to red wax. It was applied by means of a heated iron spatula with triangular blade, terminating in a knob or even a bust of Minerva, appropriately the goddess of learning. Twenty of these Minervas have now been found in Britain, mostly at rural sites (Feugère 1995: Type A5; Božič 2002: 33–4; Crummy 2003b). Spatulas could also be used to delete a whole text before reuse, or to add more wax to a worn tablet. The surface was then inscribed with a *stilus*, a bodkin-like instrument usually made of iron, although bronze and bone were also used (Manning 1985: 85; Major 2002). One end was sharpened into the writing-point, the other splayed into a square tab or spatulate 'fish-tail' used as an eraser before re-writing, so that 'turning the *stilus*' meant to make a correction. Many must have now corroded into unrecognizable 'nails', but they have often been found in forts and towns, notably some 200 at Vindolanda, where they are almost as common as waxed tablets, and more than 150 at Silchester, as against only one tablet (Birley 2002: 35; Boon 1974: 62–4). But careful survey has also disclosed that they are widespread in the countryside, being found at many villas and other rural sites, where stone inscriptions are almost unknown, and other evidence of writing (including tablets) is uncommon (Hanson and Conolly 2002).

Incised waxed tablets were the negative of ink-written pages in appearance, since the *stilus* made letters by exposing the pale wood underneath the black wax. The surface was protected by hinging tablets together by cords passed through holes bored in the margins, either in pairs (diptychs) used for letters, or in threes (triptychs) used for legal texts written in duplicate, or in multiples (polyptychs), appropriately called a *codex*. This meant a 'block of wood', and by extension the wad of bound pages, wooden but later made of parchment or paper, which is the ancestor of the medieval and modern book. The Trawsfynydd tablet, for example, was the first of 'some 10 or 12 leaves . . . joined together with a wire which was *entirely corroded* when it was first found', the whole being described by an eye-witness as a 'wooden book' (Tomlin 2004: 145). 'Pages' could be readily erased and rewritten, which of course made forgery easy, which is why legal documents were written in duplicate, the inner text remaining sealed until it was needed to confirm the outer, visible text. This format was fossilised in metal by veterans' military diplomas, where in time, since the inner text was never needed, it came to be inscribed more and more perfunctorily. Wax is less durable than metal, and it survives best in dry conditions, for example in Egypt and a Transylvanian gold-mine, and at Pompeii and Herculaneum, but hardly ever in Britain, where the context is always waterlogged. In spite of this, a diptych found in London Walbrook retains its wax, but unfortunately the letter it contained is almost illegible (Tomlin and Hassall 2003: 374, no. 23). The Trawsfynydd tablet, despite being taken from Wales to London when found, and then spending 150 years in various cupboards without benefit of conservation, retains a black surface-stain with paler traces of writing. This ghostly text is formulaic, so it is possible to read that a man whose name is now lost, a veteran auxiliary soldier perhaps, designates a woman as sole heir to his estate. The rest of his will followed, on the tablets which have now been lost (Tomlin 2004).

The waxed surface has usually disappeared altogether, but quite often the *stilus* bruised or cut the wood underneath, and some of the text can be reconstructed if the tablet was used only once. A Vindolanda tablet which retained its wax was routinely photographed before conservation, but the wax then floated off, leaving a palimpsest of illegible scratches. But it can still be read from the photograph as a letter relating to the transport of commodities (*vectura*) (Birley, Birley and Birley 1993: pl. XIX). *Stilus* marks in the wood are more visible when a tablet is wet, but there is visual 'noise' because of the wood grain and surface damage, which can be reduced by image enhancement (Bowman, Brady and Tomlin 1997; Bowman and Tomlin 2005). British tablets, like those already cited, are usually correspondence or legal documents. Another Walbrook tablet has turned out to be a deed of sale, but a special one: 'Vegetus, assistant slave of Montanus the slave of the August Emperor and sometime assistant slave of Secundus, has bought and received by *mancipium* the girl Fortunata, or by whatever name she is known, by nationality a Diablintian, from Albicianus [...] for six hundred *denarii*.' The purchaser was an imperial slave, quite an important official in the Treasury, to use an anachronistic term, and 'the girl in question' came from what is now northern France; her vendor warranted that she was in good health and not 'liable to wander or run away', and promised to reimburse the purchaser if anyone else established their title to her in whole or in part (Tomlin 2003). These clauses are formulaic in deeds of purchase by *mancipatio*, the archaic procedure by which Roman citizens bought real estate, slaves and animals. The bloodless detachment of the language recalls a piece of business correspondence which has also been found in the Walbrook: Rufus greets Epillicus and his colleagues, and tells him to liquidate a slave, in his own words to 'see that you do everything carefully to turn that girl into cash' (*RIB* II.4, 2443.7; Tomlin and Hassall 2006: 488). But it should also be remembered that Regina was the slave of Barates before he married her, while at Bath the 75-year-old priest of Sulis was handsomely buried by Trifosa his 'freedwoman and wife' (*RIB* 1065; 155).

London is the main source of *stilus* tablets in southern Britain, but they have been found elsewhere; at the Chew Stoke villa, one was even used for an ink text relating to *mancipatio* (*RIB* II.4, 2443.13). The great majority are northern, however, with at least fifty from Carlisle and more than 250 from Vindolanda. Many of these have not been read, and are likely to remain illegible, but at Carlisle for example there is one which was broken in half for reuse as a 'diptych' addressed to 'Marcus Julius Martialis, at Newstead or Carlisle' (*RIB* II.4, 2443.10; Padley and Tomlin 1991: no. 813). This implies the fast-changing Flavian order of battle in the north, which also emerges from a fragmentary Carlisle loan-note dated 7 November 83. Quintus Cassius Secundus of the Twentieth Legion acknowledges a debt of 100 denarii to Gaius Geminius Mansuetus of the same legion which he will repay with interest (Tomlin 1992: 146–50). The date is only weeks after Agricola's victory in the far north at Mons Graupius: evidently his legions in winter-quarters were already beating their swords into bank shares.

The *stilus* was adaptable too – less than ten years after Cicero received that letter from Britain, his correspondent was fighting for his life with a *stilus* against the daggers of his assassins on the Ides of March – and it could be used for informal graffiti on bronze and silver vessels, on samian ware and wall-plaster. Whole 'manuscripts' might be incised on metal, for example gold amulets and leaden 'curse tablets'. Minute lettering was possible on gold with its wax-smooth surface: the Billingford amulet carries no fewer than ten lines of tiny magical symbols, legible Greek and Latin cursive, in the space of only 30 mm (Tomlin and Hassall 2006: 481, no. 51). Lead could be inscribed almost as easily, the silvery letters scratched by the *stilus* somewhat resembling those of a waxed tablet against their dark background. Excavation of a Roman town-house in Leicester has lately produced a thick rectangle of sheet lead with a twenty-six-line text beautifully inscribed in a strong, legible 'cursive', listing twenty persons suspected of stealing a cloak (Tomlin 2008), and at Bath there is an interesting group of tablets made from eutectic 'pewter' alloys of lead and tin cast under pressure into thin, flexible sheets which provided a surface as smooth as paper. It is no coincidence that one Bath tablet, like another from Uley, calls itself a 'page' (*carta*) (Tomlin 1988: 118, no. 8; Hassall and Tomlin 1996: 439, no. 1). Still, many are quite rough, and the lead is often an irregular molten lump hammered out flat. The expertise of the lettering also ranges very widely, suggesting that one was expected to write one's own tablet, but experienced scribes could write with great freedom; they write the letter 'O', for example, in a single rotation without lifting the *stilus* point, rather than the two strokes habitual on waxed tablets. Two of the Bath tablets are positively calligraphic: the Rustic Capitals of Docilianus' plea to the most holy goddess Sulis that she inflict 'the greatest death' upon the unknown thief of his hooded cloak, and allow him no sleep or children until he returns it to her temple; and the list of names in most elegant cursive on a round pewter plate, headed by Severianus son of Brigomalla, which was then folded into four and thrown into the sacred spring (Tomlin 1988: 122, no. 10; 146, no. 30). These Bath tablets, none of which is explicitly written by a Roman citizen, let alone a Roman soldier, are precious documents of a small-town society outraged by the theft of clothes and petty sums of money (Tomlin 1988). Much the same is true of Uley, in the countryside far from town or fort (Tomlin 1993; 2002). Both collections leave an impression of articulate resentment, if not angry literacy, among quite humble civilians including countryfolk, 'whether pagan or Christian, whether man or woman, whether boy or girl, whether slave or free' (Tomlin 1988: 232, no. 98).

| Domestic life

QUITA MOULD

In this chapter, the contribution finds can make to our understanding of domestic life in Roman Britain will be discussed. By analysing the finds, is it possible to differentiate domestic buildings from other building types? Is it possible to identify the use to which individual rooms were put? Is it possible to work out who lived within those rooms? One major domestic concern, the raising of children, is purposely avoided. Children are usually poorly represented in the archaeological record; despite this, or maybe because of this, children and the experience of childhood throughout the ages is currently an area of much research (Wiseman 2005). Some artefacts associated with childhood, such as toys, are discussed in other chapters (see Chapter 10) but it should be remembered that in the past there was often little distinction between objects used by adults and those used by children.

It is in domestic contexts that the widest range of finds may be discovered, and, as family living is inextricably linked to most areas of human endeavour, many of these objects are also mentioned in the other chapters of this volume. Not all categories of domestic artefacts receive the same level of attention in publications. Domestic pottery has a very high survival rate and the sheer quantity recovered from excavations on Romano-British sites has ensured that the potential of this category of artefact is generally appreciated and it often dominates the average excavation report. Other types of domestic objects may receive less consideration for a combination of reasons: they are usually found in secondary contexts, they are frequently found incomplete, they are generally unprepossessing and, the worst sin of all, rarely can they provide an independent date.

It is difficult for us, who have been brought up and totally immersed in a materialistic, consumer society, not to make assumptions about the quality of life as reflected by possessions. When comparing the quantity and variety of artefacts recovered from the excavation of a Romano-British urban settlement or a villa complex with that from a 'native settlement' in the west or north of the country, for example, the contrast is marked and it is difficult to overcome preconceived ideas that a lack of Roman finds equates to a lack of resources and a poorer or less sophisticated lifestyle. While the occurrence of Roman objects must reflect a degree of Roman influence and an acceptance of that influence, the lack of Roman finds may not necessarily reflect a lack of opportunity to attain them or the disposable income to buy them. The acquisition of Roman 'trappings' may have been positively rejected in favour of other expressions of wealth and influence. Recent research indicates the deliberate selection of particular aspects of Roman material culture by some native communities (Cool 2004b) and suggests that many items may have been put to alternative uses.

Context

Domestic objects are rarely recovered from the spot where they were used but are principally recovered from secondary contexts. Just as today, most Roman households were kept clean, with floors regularly swept and rubbish removed for disposal elsewhere. Unless the item was small and easily lost or accidentally dropped in a location from which it was difficult to reclaim it, such as between floorboards or in an enclosed drain, domestic objects are rarely found within buildings. For the most part, evidence of day-to-day lives is found amongst refuse dumped in pits and ditches, as back-filling for disused wells, or incorporated into general demolition debris or spreads of material used to level ground surfaces prior to building. Only occasionally are domestic objects found in the locations in which they were used, preserved *in situ* as a result of exceptional circumstances. Perhaps the best-known 'exceptional circumstance' is the eruption of Mount Vesuvius in AD 79, though the Boudican destruction of Colchester, Verulamium and London also resulted in similar *in situ* deposits. The disaster that befell those living around the Bay of Naples in August AD 79 gave little time for the organised removal of household goods, and the abandoned houses and their contents now provide a remarkable glimpse of domestic life in first-century Italy. The internal layouts of rooms were preserved and a variety of furniture, fittings, utensils, fine tableware and everyday crockery was found still in the locations where they were originally used or stored. Nothing is quite as simple as it seems, however, and the pitfalls that await the unwary when attempting to interpret domestic artefacts are described in an important study of the finds assemblages from individual rooms within thirty Pompeian atrium houses (Allison 2004).

Sometimes domestic items are recovered from contexts in which they have been deliberately placed but not where they were originally used; instead they were put there as an act of 'considered deposition' rather than simply rubbish disposal (see Chapter 12). Household items, particularly storage and cooking vessels, could be deliberately placed as a votive offering in a significant location, or as part of a ritual to mark the beginning of the construction of a building or well or, alternatively, to mark the end of its use. The concept of such 'structured deposition', not only in a Roman context but also in more recent times, was brought to the attention of a wider archaeological audience by Ralph Merrifield (1987). Domestic pottery and glass used for the storage or serving of food and drink were often placed as grave goods accompanying a burial or cremation or were used to contain the cremated remains (see Chapter 13 and Plate 53). There is also the phenomenon of hoards containing highly decorative tablewares being deposited by the very wealthy at the end of the fourth century, principally in East Anglia. The recovery of spectacular objects or groups of objects is exceptional, and their significance is easy to spot; it may be more difficult to recognise the significance of a mundane item. If an object is complete when found the possibility that it may have been deliberately deposited, rather than lost or discarded as part of general domestic rubbish, should be considered. In a society where little could be wasted, few serviceable objects would be thrown away.

Buildings

Whilst the excavation of a building forms the *raison d'être* for most Romano-British excavations, it is not always easy to identify the purpose of each building through its finds assemblage. Over the years, archaeological research has created a vicious circle wherein a building's use is identified by its finds based on the presumptions of the excavation team at the time of discovery; this finds assemblage becomes the 'typical' assemblage for that type of building from then on. When a building with a similar layout is found, even if it has no finds assemblage or a different finds assemblage, it is also presumed to have had the same purpose as the first building. An example of this is the identification of fort hospitals, which was originally based on the excavation of a building at Novaesium, a site which produced a large assemblage of medical instruments; all buildings of this type when excavated in a fort are now presumed to be hospitals, even if they produce no medical equipment (Allason-Jones 1999b). In the case of the turrets on Hadrian's Wall, their identification as military installations is obvious, given their attachment to a physical frontier; the finds, however, reflect the domestic and leisure pursuits of the soldiers occupying these buildings rather than their purely military activities (Allason-Jones 1988).

In the case of the structural artefacts, all buildings had doors and most had windows; rarely can those from domestic, military or religious buildings be differentiated. Wooden doors were hung on drop hinges, smaller examples of which were used on shutters and cupboard doors. Heavy doors might be pivoted at the top and bottom with the pivot hole having a metal lining of iron or copper alloy. Door handles and latches were of wood, except in the grandest of households. Amongst the few to survive and be recognised is a latch bracket of alder wood from Castleford (Morris 1998: 343, no. 25, fig. 154).

While many of the windows were shuttered, examples of iron window grilles are occasionally found in Britain; that from the villa at Hinton St Mary in Dorset is exceptionally well preserved (Manning 1985: 128, R17), but pieces of broken grille are more difficult to recognise. The 'crosses' placed at the junctions where the vertical and horizontal bars or straps meet are more frequently recognised than the bars themselves. Window glass, except in military contexts, was usually confined to the more affluent households and was not necessarily used in every window. Most window glass of the period was translucent and the pale green of 'uncoloured glass'; as a result a glazed window would let in light but would obscure rather than frame the view. In the fourth century, window glass was blown, producing thinner panes which were more transparent. Blue window glass matching the wall-plaster of the bath suite at Gorhambury indicates that an element of design had gone into this building (Neal, Wardle and Hunn 1990).

A range of structural ironwork may be expected amongst any Romano-British finds assemblage and is rarely an indicator of a domestic dwelling as opposed to any other building. Numerically, most ironwork assemblages are dominated by the remains of iron nails (Manning 1985: 134–7). These vary in size according to timber thickness. The characteristics of obviously differing types are worth noting as they may provide information on a building's structure that might otherwise go unrecorded. The presence of extremely large nails may suggest the reuse of boat timbers, as may clench-bolts or rove nails which were used in boat construction and also in domestic woodwork of plank and ledge construction, such as doors, shutters and hatches. Joiners' dogs, shanks bent upward into a spiked arm at each end, were used to join wooden boards, and T-staples, or T-clamps, resembling large T-headed nails, secured hollow box-flue tiles that channelled hot air from hypocaust systems through heated rooms. Examples found with the arms of the head bent over indicate that they were also used for other purposes. Often found broken in demolition debris, T-staples may be confused with nails but can be distinguished by their longer and thicker shanks. Wallhooks, with pointed shanks to be driven into the wall, and L-shaped or U-shaped terminals, are common finds and were used to hang items around the home. The storage of goods in bags suspended above floor level and away from vermin must have been a useful asset in every household but would be equally essential in military, industrial and religious buildings.

Rooms

Conspicuous aspects of the interior decoration of the wealthier homes have been the subject of detailed study; for example, mosaics (Neal and Cosh 2002; www.ASPROM.org), ornamental stone used to decorate walls and floors (Pritchard 1986) and painted wall-plaster (Davy and Ling 1982). The interior fittings of modest dwellings have been, unavoidably, less well studied. It would seem that in many of the rural settlements in the north and west of the country items of free-standing furniture were scarce; built-in platforms in recesses were used for sleeping and dining; shelves and smaller recesses, some equipped with cupboard doors, stored household goods. Other household and personal belongings were stored in wooden boxes of varying size. Instead of the highly decorated tessellated floors and painted plaster walls that graced the reception rooms of the wealthier households, the majority of homes had very plain interiors and people walked on floors of *opus signinum*, timber boards or simply beaten earth. The floors of the timber buildings of the successive early forts at Vindolanda (AD 90–140), for example, were covered with layers of dried bracken mixed with straw and mosses; these survived because of the exceptional conditions which favoured the preservation of organic remains at the site (Seaward 1993: 93–9, 116). This has been interpreted as a form of 'carpeting' to protect against the cold and damp prevalent on the northern frontier (Pugsley 2003: 5). If this was the case, and the buildings were not later used for stock and the material was not simply animal bedding, it is likely that similar measures would be taken elsewhere to keep floors warm and dry under foot.

It would also be dangerous to presume that a room within a building continued to be used for its primary purpose throughout its existence. The fortunes of its inhabitants may have changed from generation to generation. Many villas, for example, show evidence of their family's improving circumstances as extra wings were added, bath-suites installed and mosaic floors laid; in some villas a less happy trend may be discernible as the bath-suite of one generation became the corn-dryer of the next.

Several archaeologists have attempted to attribute rooms on the basis of the finds found within them. This is not always possible, as a well-run household would have kept its rooms clean and tidy, particularly its public rooms, thus leaving little evidence on which to base any identification. The main reception rooms of a villa or a townhouse are usually identified more by their layout than by their finds. A *triclinium*, or summer dining room, for example, often had an arrangement of three sofas on a raised dais whose foundations leave obvious traces. Bedrooms, nurseries and the more private living rooms are unlikely to be easily identified, either by layout or by assemblage. The use of these spaces may have depended on the ethnic origins of the family as well as their financial standing; certainly, whether the rooms were used by both men and women, by old and young, by family or servants would be difficult to ascertain on our current level of understanding.

Furniture

Attributing a specific item of furniture to a particular room has to take into consideration whether the house was large enough to warrant rooms being used for specific purposes. Much of what we know about furniture of Roman date comes from depictions on funerary monuments, invariably with military connections, and wall-paintings, and may reflect artistic tradition. The recovery of complete items of furniture from Roman Britain is extremely rare, though small furniture fittings are commonly found. It is a measure of the rarity of the survival of recognisable pieces of furniture that Joan Liversidge's splendid book devoted to the subject (Liversidge 1955), although written more than fifty years ago, has only recently been updated and the topic revisited by Croom (2007).

It is usually presumed that the funerary reliefs from military sites in the north of Britain depict the range of furniture that might be expected in the living rooms of a wealthy provincial household (Tufi 1983: nos. 40, 42, 43). How much these reflect the furniture owned by the deceased during their lifetime, however, is debatable. The tombstone of Victor from South Shields, for example, shows a typical funerary banquet scene, with Victor reclining on an elaborate couch with inlaid decoration, and at first sight suggests a wealthy young man; but the inscription informs us that Victor was the Moroccan freedman of an ordinary cavalryman (Plate 25). The implication is that the type of furniture depicted was part of the repertoire of the stone carver and considered by him to be suitable for a tombstone, rather than

Pl. 25 Tombstone of Victor from South Shields showing a couch decorated with inlay

reflecting Victor's own furniture. Occasionally, however, elements of such items are recovered during excavation; the burnt remains of a wooden bed or couch, believed to have caught fire during the Boudican revolt, were found at Lion Walk, Colchester (Crummy 1984: 42). Two rectangular mattresses were found, lying one above the other, in the corner of the room. The upper mattress had the remains of two further fabrics lying on top, thought to be blankets or possibly the loose covers of a couch, while the position of carbonised wood found alongside suggests it may have come from the frame. The burnt remains of an oak-framed bed, along with charred feathers and wool from the mattress, have been found at the Roman cemetery at Beckfoot, Cumbria (Bellhouse 1954: 51).

The recovery of items of wooden furniture preserved by damp burial conditions is less remarkable but still remains something of a rarity. A small rectangular tabletop, or possibly seat, of ash wood (*Fraxinus* sp.) was found at Castleford (Morris 1998: 338, 18, fig. 154, pl. 43) and decorative furniture finials and furniture legs of turned wood have been found in waterlogged contexts elsewhere (see Chapman 1980: fig. 73, no. 670; Liversidge 1977: fig. 87, nos. 1–4; Padley 2000: 107, fig. 70). When broken beyond repair, wooden furniture, indeed any household object made of wood, was likely to have been burnt on the domestic hearth.

Tables with carved legs ending in feet that take the form of an animal paw or hoof were the height of fashion and are depicted on tombstones with other household furnishings (Tufi 1983: no. 42). While many of these tables were probably of wood, fragments of circular tabletops and carved table legs of shale survive in Britain, principally from sites in the south and west, close to the source at Kimmeridge, in Dorset. The thick table tops have concentric bands of decoration on the upper face, while the lower has a wide, flat rim around the edge into which the legs were fixed with a mortise and tenon joint and held with glue or by a dowel (Lawson 1975: fig. 13). These tables serve to remind us that housework was an essential domestic task as shale tables need to be kept oiled if they are not to dry and split; as these were expensive items, it is likely that a proud householder would wish to display them to visitors and would have to decide whether to risk using the tables in rooms with heated floors.

Wooden chairs and basket chairs of wickerwork are also shown on tombstones (Tufi 1983: no. 42), with the latter always, in Britain, confined to the tombstones of women (Plate 54). As these are also depicted on the pipeclay figurines of seated mother goddesses, it is possible that they were used by nursing mothers (Allason-Jones 2005: pl. 55). The iron frames of folding stools with decorative copper-alloy finials, which opened in a similar manner to a modern deck chair, on the other hand, are usually associated with male burials and are thought to have military links. A frame, with chaff possibly from a seat cushion, had been burnt on a funeral pyre and then placed in a pit at the west end of a burial at Holborough, near Snodland in Kent (Jessop 1954: 22–33, fig. 12). Another, said to have leather from the seat adhering to the seat bars, was found in a barrow at Bartlow Hills at the beginning of the nineteenth century (Jessop 1954: pl. X11; Liversidge 1955: 28–31). Iron bars ornamented with a series of collars, thought to come from the stretcher bars of a stool with an X-shaped frame, were found at Newstead (Liversidge 1955: 33) and in the Corbridge Hoard (Allason-Jones and Bishop 1988).

Many furniture fittings are difficult to identify with certainty. A wooden dining couch found in the House of Menander at Pompeii (Civali 2003: 139, SAP 4270A) presents a range of copper-alloy fittings that would defy all but the most imaginative to identify correctly if disassociated from their original frame. They include both plain and inlaid (*intarsia*) sheet strips, moulded feet and figures cast 'in the round' that embellished the sides of the headboard. While differential preservation may account for the lack of wooden knob handles, furniture handles of metal are also comparatively rare. Small copper-alloy drop handles are invariably identified as the carrying handles from helmets. Iron handles, unless complete, can easily slip detection and disappear into the 'miscellaneous' category of a finds report. Rings of copper alloy or of iron were commonly used as simple furniture handles, being secured to a wooden furniture frame by a split-spiked loop, but they do have other possible uses. Similarly, copper-alloy studs, circular, often dome-headed nails, with short shanks, suitable for upholstery and often used to secure the edges of upholstered furniture today, are versatile fittings. They were used on a number of objects, including domestic items, horse equipment and military fittings.

Small strips of bone inlay are found on occupation sites and in cemeteries. The inlay decorated wooden boxes, and other items of furniture such as beds, couches and biers on which the deceased was transported to the place of burial or cremation (see Chapter 13 and Plate 25; Philipps 1977: no. 248). Recently, part of the frame of a wooden cupboard carved to take bone inlay has been found in a well at Burnby Lane, Hayton in East Yorkshire (Hartley *et al.* 2006: no. 138). Some of the bone strips had been attached to the wooden furniture carcass by small nails; others have no visible method of attachment, and must have been glued into place. Usually the inlay is cut in geometric shapes, rectangles, squares and triangles, but occasionally other shapes, such as a horse's head, are depicted. The inlay has simple incised decoration, with patterns comprising parallel grooves, lattices and ring-and-dot motifs being popular. Small bone finials may be handles or possibly feet from boxes with bone inlay decoration.

Food

Artefacts associated with the storage, preparation, cooking and serving of food are dominated by vessels of pottery, both numerically and by weight (see Tyers 1996). Glass vessels also make up a significant proportion of the domestic items associated with storage and dining that are recovered by excavation. Though light in weight, vessels of glass tend to end up in a larger number of smaller pieces than pottery and methods have been devised to estimate the number of individual vessels represented so that the numbers of vessels of each material can be compared. Complete, or near complete, metal vessels are not commonly found on occupation sites but do occur as highly prized dining and drinking services in burials or in hoards of late Roman date. Elsewhere it is usual for only very small fragments of these metal vessels to be recovered because when broken, or no longer fashionable, the metal could be melted down and recast. This difference in survival can influence conclusions as to the status of a site's occupants. Wealthy households are often presumed by the quantity of samian ware found, when a really wealthy household is more likely to have used gold, silver or pewter tableware, which is unlikely to have been left for an archaeologist to find.

Lids, handles and handle mounts, easily detached from the body of the vessel and subsequently lost, may redress the balance. Jug lids and handles, patera handles and handle mounts from buckets, basins and bowls are also easy to recognise (den Boesterd 1956). Folded rivets used to fill small splits in sheet metal vessels and, together with sheet patches, to mend larger areas are occasionally found in Roman contexts, as at the villa at Dalton Parlours (Wrathmell and Nicholson 1990: fig. 72, nos. 51–7). They are comparable with others from later periods (Egan 1998: 176–7, nos. 488–94) but their use is seldom recognised. Metal vessels, being often intrinsically beautiful objects in their own right, have been studied from an art-historical perspective in the past and some confusion in the nomenclature and functions ascribed to some of the types has resulted. Flatwares, that is, platters, dishes, shallow bowls and similar forms, in pewter, copper alloy and precious metals, were used to serve food but are also found in ritual contexts. Copper-alloy buckets, more steeply sided basins, dippers, strainers, cups and jugs were used for the mixing and serving of wine. Recently, the function

Pl. 26 Bronze patera found on the Herd Sands, South Shields

of metal vessel forms has been reconsidered. Limescale deposits, observed on the interior of jugs with trefoil-shaped mouths and hinged lids, suggest that they were used to heat water (Koster 1997: 30).

The patera, a long-handled bowl similar to a small modern saucepan, had a number of uses (see also Chapter 12 and Plate 26). Essentially similar vessels of copper alloy, differing slightly in size, profile and ornamentation of the handle, are often grouped under the term 'paterae' in the British literature, though they may be called saucepans, skillets, *trullea, casseruola* or *tegame* elsewhere. Traditionally the patera has been considered a vessel used to heat food, probably because it so closely resembles the saucepan in use today. None of the hundreds of examples recovered from Pompeii showed any traces of fire blackening that might indicate that they had been used to heat food (Allison 2004: 56 quoting Tassinari 1993: I, 232) and only three of those whose exact findspot is known came from kitchen areas. Context is clearly important when identifying the use of each patera; for example, there can be little doubt that many of the undecorated examples with thickly ringed bases found in military contexts were used for cooking. They were part of the standard kit of the first-century AD Roman soldier, probably serving as 'mess tins', the food being both heated in and eaten directly from them (Bishop and Coulston 2006: 119). The heavily repaired condition of many paterae, such as those found with cauldrons in a similar state in the Prestwick Carr Hoard (Hodgkin 1892), shows that they had been subject to a long culinary life before being finally deposited. Patera handles, often found separately, may bear a manufacturer's stamp, while occasional examples name the unit that issued the kit (Bennett and Young 1981; Bishop and Coulston 2006: 119). The style of the handle terminal can reflect dating, those with the distinctive pierced disc handle being of Flavian date (Bennett and Young 1981: 42). The style of the handles may also indicate use. It has been suggested that the larger and shallower vessels with animal head handles were used to wash the hands before dining (Allison 2004: 58). The smaller, highly decorated examples of enamelled copper alloy and of silver also seem more likely to have been used as serving vessels, and are more probably to be associated with liquid than food. This is borne out by the nature of the other wine-related vessels with which paterae are frequently associated when found deposited as grave goods (see Chapter 13) and when depicted on altars (see Chapter 12).

Pewter vessels are relatively uncommon finds in domestic contexts, being more often discovered in ritual deposits (Beagrie 1989). That is not to say that they were uncommon in the homes of the late Roman period, but they are likely to be under-represented in the archaeological record of such sites. Pewter, being chiefly composed of lead, is easily melted down and recycled; in addition, it is particularly susceptible to deterioration when buried. A cache of pewter vessel fragments that included plates, bowls, flagons and small drinking vessels, collected for melting down and recasting, was found at the site of a succession of water mills at Ickham, Kent (Mould 2010a: 241–3). Stone moulds in which pewter 'flatwares' were cast have been found, the most northerly to date coming from Catterick (Blagg 2002: 302, fig. 372, nos. 57–60).

Some of the largest groups of shale tableware have been found at Silchester (Lawson 1975) and Dorchester (Woodwood, Davies and Graham 1993: figs. 78–80) and include fragments of flat circular platters, and shallow and straight-sided bowls, along with decorated and shaped vessel handles. Flat serving trays or cutting boards of shale, which are rectangular or circular in shape with a decorative border around the edge, date to the late first and early second century (Crummy 1983: 69). There are rare examples in stone; one of micaceous schist came from the Southern Lanes, Carlisle (Padley 2000: 105).

Whilst one might imagine that the poorer sections of the community habitually ate off wooden plates and bowls, as was the case in later centuries, little evidence for this could be found in a recent study of Roman domestic woodwork (Pugsley 2003). Even when taking into account the problems of differential survival and preservation of wooden artefacts, only a very small number of wooden plates and bowls survive or appear to have been used (Pugsley 2005: 3, fig. 1.2). It appears that the highly organised pottery industry was able to supply the needs of most households, supplemented by vessels of metal and of glass in the homes of all but the poorest inhabitants. Those wooden tablewares, including cups, plates, bowls and serving implements, that have been found come principally from London, Carlisle and Vindolanda, where burial environments favour the preservation of organic materials. Occasionally examples have been recovered from wells at villas, such as Dalton Parlours (Morris 1990: 224), and other rural occupation sites. The cruder forms had been carved and appear to continue the pre-Roman traditions. Others, however, often from later Roman contexts, were lathe-turned and show a high degree of skill in their making, indicating that they were expensive, highly prized items. Indeed, Pugsley has suggested that certain wooden vessels, notably from London and Fishbourne, imitate contemporary metal and glass forms and were intended to be purely decorative (Pugsley 2003: 108, fig. 5.14–15). Drinking sets of turned boxwood, comprising a hemispherical drinking cup and a serving ladle with a long handle, have been found at London, York, Carlisle and Vindolanda (Pugsley 2003: 102, 108–10). They are thought to have been imported from the Continent, possibly with the army.

Small spoons used to eat delicacies at table appear to be a Roman introduction to Britain, whilst the range of larger spoons, ladles, spatulas and scoops used in the home when preparing and serving food may have already been in use in the Iron Age (Plate 27). Very small spoons with long handles, often with their bowls reduced to a flat disc-shaped end, were used to extract expensive cosmetics or unguents from long-necked vessels. Spoons were made in bone and wood, copper alloy and occasionally pewter or silver, those of copper alloy frequently being tinned to give the appearance of silver. Spoons appear to have been subject to changes of fashion: those with circular bowls, sometimes referred to as *cochlearia*, date to the first and second centuries; examples with a raised moulding around the inside of the bowl date to the second century. Copper-alloy spoons with pear-shaped bowls were in use from the second century, and those with bowls that constrict into a 'waisted' neck close to the handle, variously described as mandolin, lute, purse or bag-shaped, appear to date to the later third and fourth centuries. Clay moulds for casting copper-alloy spoons with 'purse'-shaped bowls have been recovered from Castleford in a pit containing third- to fourth-century pottery (Bayley and Budd 1998: 195–203). While the handles of spoons with circular bowls are straight, spoons of other bowl shapes are often offset with a small shoulder close to the bowl; some are

Pl. 27 Selection of spoons from South Shields Roman fort

pivoted, allowing them to be folded, indicating the survival of a Roman habit of taking one's own spoon to dinner parties.

Spoons made of precious metals frequently form a component of late Roman treasure hoards. It has been suggested that, in the context of late fourth/early fifth-century hoards, it was the weight of the metal that was pertinent and the spoons may represent nothing more than a convenient unit of monetary exchange (Hobbs 2005: 206–7). The Hoxne Treasure contains the largest group of spoons yet found (Bland and Johns 1993); the silver spoons are gilded and engraved or inscribed, and some have coiled handles with bird head terminals. With the other precious-metal tableware this group represents ceremonial feasting of the elite, probably the 'family silver' of a very wealthy family.

Bone spoons, usually made from the long bones of cattle or horses, represent the other end of the spectrum. These have been used throughout history and may be difficult to date independently. A range of bowl shapes is known (MacGregor 2001: 181–2), some with decorative knobs at the end of their handles. Those with a perforated bowl, possibly used to stir and blend ingredients or used as a game, date to the first and second centuries and have a distribution restricted to northern Britain (Greep 1998:

275). One example from late Roman occupation in Castleford (Greep 1998: fig. 120, no. 137) has a long oval bowl and handle and looks much like a more recent marrow or mustard spoon. Spoons of moulded cattle horn did not become common until the early post-medieval period.

Kitchens

Kitchens may be identified by the items used for food preparation which were discussed above as well as by their built-in fittings, such as the two tiled hearths found at Folkestone. This particular kitchen had not been used by a tidy family as animal bones and potsherds were found scattered all over the floor and there was even a rubbish pit behind one of the hearths.

Wealthier homes had a raised cooking hearth, but burnt patches on floors suggest that the majority cooked on a central open fire. Much food was cooked in pottery jars placed directly in the hot ashes or balanced over the embers on an iron tripod, grille or gridiron. Study of food residues and the presence of burning, sooting and limescale on pottery is providing interesting insights into Roman cooking practices (Cool 2006) while the shapes of the pots and cooking methods employed may reflect the cultural traditions and origins of those using them (Swan 1992). Meat might also be cooked on a gridiron, a frame of iron bars on short legs (Manning 1985: 100). Shallow pans of iron with folding handles, or less commonly of copper alloy, are sufficiently similar in shape to modern frying pans to suggest they may have had a similar function. The surviving examples are often heavily patched and apparently well used; however, being found predominantly in hoards of late Roman metal vessels, it is uncertain whether they were everyday cooking utensils.

Large and elaborate chains, swivels and suspension loops of Roman date, used to hang heavy cauldrons, and the flesh hooks and large ladles used to handle and serve the contents, are illustrated and discussed by Manning (1985: 100–2, 104–5). Associated with 'down-hearth' cooking over an open fire in the native tradition, the large-scale, more elaborate items of ironwork are suggestive of mass catering, feasting and communal celebration rather than domestic cookery. Cool (2006: 48–54) has pointed out, however, that whilst these may appear to hark back to Iron Age cooking methods, caul-drons and cauldron chains are more often found in the Roman period 'as containers for votive hoards and were deliberately deposited in lakes and pools'. Similarly, a range of hearth tools, shovels, rakes and pokers, often with spirally twisted stem handles and scrolled handles, have been found that might be associated with the tending of a sacred fire, large central fire or blacksmith's forge rather than the management of a domestic hearth.

Knives are amongst the most commonly found domestic items of iron, being recovered from nearly every Romano-British excavation, though often represented by broken blade fragments only. Complete or near complete knives are easily recognisable while broken blades have a distinctive triangular cross-section. This stalwart of domestic ironwork has over a hundred entries in the British Museum catalogue (Manning 1985: 108–23) where Romano-British knives have been classified into twenty-four types, some of which are further subdivided, according to the type and position of the handle and the shape of the back. The majority of knives have a tang, or spike, that was driven into a cylindrical handle of wood, bone or horn. Others have strap handles to which bone handle plates were riveted, or have a solid handle, often with a ring terminal by which they were suspended. Knife handles and handle plates of bone and antler, often ornamented with a range of simple incised decoration, are described by MacGregor (2001: 167–9, fig. 88). Handle fragments can be distinguished from inlay by their semicircular cross section. Handles of wood or horn may survive as minerally preserved remains present on the iron tang or scale handle. Occasionally, knives bear an inscription running along the back of the blade. A knife stamped with 'VICTOR V F' (Victor of Vienne made (this)) was found at Catterick (Mould 2002: fig. 277, no. 237); another with a 'VICTOR' stamp came from Ickham (Mould 2010b: 225, no. 630).

Knives were used by a variety of trades as well as in the home. The shape of the edge, which varies according to the extent that a blade was resharpened, and the thickness of the back may suggest that a blade was used for a craft function. Narrow blades with solid handles and folding knives are most likely to have been used as razors or surgical instruments. Clasp knives, or folding knives, have pivoting iron blades and decorative openwork handles; a hound chasing a hare is a popular motif used on handles both of cast copper alloy and of carved bone. Whetstones are common finds, being necessary to sharpen all edged blades. Made principally from varieties of local sandstone, of roughly rectangular shape with rectangular or oval section, they have their faces distinctly dished by the repeated sharpening of the blade edge.

Knives were used for cutting, slicing and paring, while large-bladed heavy knives, known as cleavers, were designed for chopping and used in butchery. Many have socketed handles or thick, solid handles. The use of cleavers, and the type of butchery they represent, was a Roman introduction. Evidence from the cleavers themselves and cleaver marks on the upper limb bones

Pl. 28 Facsimile of a rotary quern

of cattle may suggest that their use increased through time on military and urban sites, although they are rarely found on rural, non-villa settlements (but see Cool 2006: 89).

Grain was ground between the upper and lower stones of a quern (Plate 28). Three types of quern may be found on Romano-British excavations: the saddle quern, the beehive quern and the flat disc or 'rotary' quern. The simplest form, the saddle quern, essentially belongs to the pre-Roman era but is occasionally found on later sites. Beehive querns, which also started as a native type used in pre-conquest Britain, gradually replaced the saddle quern and continued in use throughout much of the Roman period, particularly in the north of the country. Flat disc-shaped rotary querns were brought in with the Roman army and were soon copied in local British stones, particularly sandstones and gritstones, and widely employed.

Beehive querns show a number of distinct regional forms which are defined by several criteria, including size, profile, the number of handles, the provision and position of the handle hole, and the diameter of the feed pipe down which the corn was poured. This classification has been refined over the years and is well summarised by Wright (2002: 267). Beehive querns are very commonly found in military forts and their *vici* and are one of the few items of material culture found on native rural settlements in northern Britain between the first and fourth centuries. In the south of the country, however, they were soon replaced by the 'new technology' of the flat disc-shaped quern which the Roman army brought with them. These were made from volcanic lava, predominantly from the Mayen quarry in the Eifel area of west Germany. The upper and lower stones have grooved grinding surfaces, radially grooved or divided into sectors, called harps, and cut at an angle. Lava querns are common in the south-east of the country and found on military and villa sites further north in the first and second centuries (Buckley and Major 1998: 245). Querns of millstone grit, quarried in the north, were traded to the southern counties in quantity during the third and fourth centuries. Study of the querns from Silchester, and the types of stone from which they were made, shows clearly the wide trading network that the town enjoyed with the south and west of the country compared with other towns in the region (Shaffrey 2003). As research continues, characteristics of flat querns are being identified that apparently relate to dating; for example, partially perforated spindle holes occur on the earlier querns while fully perforated spindle holes, flanged hoppers and rectangular feed pipes are seen on examples of later date (Shaffrey 2003: 161). Quern stones tend to become larger and thinner as the Roman period progresses.

The action of the beehive quern crushed and tore the grain, producing a coarse flour or meal. The flat disc quern sheared and ground the grains and it was possible to adjust the position of the stones allowing the grain to be more finely ground, producing finer flour. Sites where both quern types were in use at the same time may suggest differing types of grain processing were being undertaken. Wear visible on some beehive and flat disc querns suggests that the upper stone was not fully rotated but rather moved from side to side when in use. The lower stones were set into the ground or placed on a collar of clay for stability. The lower stones of four beehive querns were found set into the floor of Structure X at the villa of Dalton Parlours (Buckley and Major 1990: 106). This evidence, together with related finds, has suggested that the building was part of a milling and baking complex rather than a domestic kitchen. At Silchester a rare survival of a complete flat disc quern has been found, both the upper and lower stones being present, set into a floor, and abandoned when the building was destroyed by fire (Shaffrey 2003: 164).

Quern stones remained of value when broken, often being reused as whetstones, grinders and rubbers, or incorporated into the structure of a building in its hearth floor, as a doorstep or built into the fabric of the walls. The frequency of broken querns in pits and wells on Romano-British settlements in the north has prompted the suggestion that their deposition

Pl. 29 Mortarium from Housesteads

might be linked to a ritual act of closure rather than simple rubbish disposal (Allason-Jones 2009).

Heavy stone bowls are traditionally associated with food preparation and appear to have served a similar function to the more commonly found ceramic mortaria. Those with pouring lips in their rims are known as stone mortars. While the name mortar implies that foodstuffs and spices might be pounded or ground within, the pouring lip suggests that they could also be used for liquids. Recently the 'received wisdom' concerning the use of ceramic mortaria, and by implication stone mortars, has been called into question (Cool 2004b) and a number of other possible suggestions put forward, such as the preparation of pigments, that may only be confirmed or denied by further research (Plate 29). Stone bowls, along with mortaria and querns, may be found on native sites where other aspects of the material culture are limited, although it should be noted that stone bowls and mortars, with a few exceptions, tend to be a phenomenon confined to the south-west of the country (Cool 2005: 55). Stone bowls made of Purbeck 'marble' with curved profiles are thought to date to the late first and second centuries; those with straighter sides (and consequently wider bases) appear to be of fourth-century date (Holbrook and Bidwell 1991: 279). Stone mortars of Cornish elvan stone, and later large 'Trethurgy bowls' with square-shaped carved lug handles, dating to the fourth to sixth centuries are found in the west country; both have wear patterns that suggest they were used for grinding rather than pounding (Quinnell 2004: 138).

Iron fittings from wooden coopered buckets are commonly found; these buckets were made of a series of vertical staves grooved at the bottom to provide a seating for the circular base. The iron fittings comprise hoops, handles and handle mounts. The wooden staves were bound together with two or more hoops (circular welded bands of thin-sectioned iron strap) that were hammered on when hot and shrank to fit on cooling. The paired handle mounts, placed between the side of the bucket and the encircling band, have looped or ring terminals to hold the hooked ends of the curved handles. Those buckets built entirely of wood, with hoops made of twisted withy bindings and rope handles, may leave no trace. Buckets made of leather are known from the late medieval period onward but have yet to be recognised from Roman contexts. While it is unusual to find domestic items in the location in which they had been originally used, buckets are an exception. Waterlogged deposits within a well at Dalton Parlours contained the remains of five near-complete stave-built buckets and their iron fittings, and parts of at least sixteen others (Morris 1990; Scott 1990). Well buckets have a loop in the centre of the handle to prevent the rope or hook from slipping as it is being hauled to the surface and the contents from spilling. The buckets in the well at Dalton Parlours were household buckets intended to be carried by hand, as their handles lacked suspension loops, which might account for the large number of losses (Morris 1990: 221).

Rectangular wooden troughs have been found in London, Carlisle and Vindolanda (Pugsley 2003: 114–15). They are comparable with troughs of more recent date that served as containers in which kneaded bread was left to rise prior to baking, and it has been suggested that the Roman examples are also likely to be associated with bread making. Not all food was home cooked: in the town, 'fast food' was available from stalls and street vendors and bread could be bought from large-scale bakeries. Iron bakers' peels, used to move bread in and out of hot ovens, have been recognised at Housesteads and Catterick (Manning 1976: 39, no. 150 and fig. 23; Mould 2002: 90, no. 108, fig. 274).

Scapula scoops, made from the shoulder blades of sheep or cattle, may well have been used in the Roman home to scoop flour or other dry goods (MacGregor 2001: 179–80). Carved, long-handled scoops and ladles and dippers of wood were used for the same purpose as today. One wooden implement, a spatula with a long, shallow bowl and a notched handle with a pierced terminal, appears to be a specifically Roman utensil for stirring and tasting food. An example of boxwood found in London (Pugsley 2003: 117, fig. 5.28) is notable in having a decorative terminal carved into a bearded African head.

Storage

Chests, boxes and caskets were used to store a wide range of items in the home. While individual fittings from boxes are commonly found, the recovery of associated fittings provides an opportunity to gather information about the original container. Ideally, the associated items should be lifted in a block or their positions recorded in sufficient detail to allow the dimensions of the container to be estimated. If the position, depth and orientation of the nails and other metalwork are noted, the box may be reconstructed. Any minerally preserved remains of wood present on the metalwork will allow the species of wood to be identified. Analysis of the position and direction of the grain will indicate its thickness and the joints used in the box's construction. The dove-tailed construction of the leather-covered, alder wood chest used to contain the Corbridge Hoard, deposited between AD 122 and 138, was reconstructed in this way (Allason-Jones and Bishop 1988: 94–6, fig. 107), as was the box deposited in a fourth-century burial at Butt Road, Colchester (Crummy 1983: 85–8, figs. 90–1). The remains of the box in the Colchester burial were comprised principally of iron nails and iron loop hinges with copper-alloy angle bindings, decorative corner plates and studs. A lock plate of gilt copper alloy had part of the iron locking mechanism adhering to the back and a finger-ring key of copper alloy still protruded from the keyhole. Close scrutiny of box fittings found in a pyre or *bustum*, again at Colchester, revealed that an area of rawhide from the box cover had been preserved by close proximity to the copper-alloy lock plate; the wet rawhide stretched over the wooden frame of the box had shrunk upon drying to form a hard, protective covering that also helped to hold the construction together.

The lids of large chests had loop hinges comprising a pair of nailed straps with articulating ring terminals. A pair of split-spiked loops, also known as double-spiked loops or split pins, could have served the same function. Strap hinges, with a pair of arms articulating around a central pin, are also known from the Roman period. Iron hinges occur on many Romano-British occupation sites and are described and illustrated by Manning (1985: 126–7). Copper-alloy hinges and even examples of silver from decorative caskets are also known. Hinges of bone were used on cupboard doors, and possibly the lids of chests, and the individual cylindrical components are sometimes recovered. These hinges comprised a series of bone cylinders, usually made from the long bones of cattle, threaded on to a central wooden spindle; the cylinders were attached to the door and frame by a wooden dowel or turned bone peg that fitted into a drilled hole. Components without a peg hole were used as spacers between the pivoting parts. These are fully described by MacGregor (2001: 203–5, fig. 110).

Small personal items, cosmetics and ointments were stored in cylindrical lidded vessels (*pyxides*) of turned wood (Plate 30). Some of these boxes are so small that it is doubtful whether they ever served a practical use but may have been prized for their own sake. Many were of boxwood but examples of beech, willow, hazel and maple have been found in Britain. A *pyxis* made of shale, a material that could also be turned on a lathe, was part of the Thetford Treasure (Johns and Potter 1983: no. 83). Highly decorative needle cases of turned wood have been recovered from contexts dating from the AD 70s to the early second century, two still with their needles safely inside. Though only four examples have been recovered from this country, one each from London and Carlisle and two from Vindolanda, it is likely that they would have been found in many households as textile production was a domestic activity.

In addition to vessels of pottery and glass, wooden containers were used for the storage of drink and foodstuffs and baskets were used to store and transport dry goods and fruit. Bentwood containers are known but are extremely rare, being easily broken and crushed and consequently difficult to recognise. The highly fragmentary remains of a single example, with an oak base and a wall of ash with iron clip mounts at the rim, have been found at Harlow in Essex (Pugsley 2003: 96–7, fig. 4.51). Pugsley has suggested that these were used for the storage of papyrus rolls (2003: 95), though they could have been usefully employed to contain a range of dry goods. The recovery of basketry is also rare. A solid turned wooden base of oak from a basketry container, identified by the ring of holes encircling the base, was found at Vindolanda (Pugsley 2003: 142, fig. 7.4). A pit in the floor of a building at Old Grapes Lane, Carlisle, contained the remains of an object made of 'woven' rushes using the basketry technique of twining (Padley 2000: 106). The excavators thought it to be the remains of a basket used to store animal feed. A fragment of basket made of woven strips of split willow was recovered from Exeter (Earwood 1991: 278, no. 6, fig. 132) but could not be conserved. Such items must be vastly under-represented in the archaeological record and it is only in relatively recent years that conservation treatments have been developed that allow their long-term preservation, study and display.

Pl. 30 Turned wooden box from Carlisle

Amphoras were used to transport and store wine, oil and other delicacies and several studies have improved our knowledge of their contents
and the origins of those contents (Cool 2006). Casks, stave-built wooden
vessels also used to store and transport goods, are often called barrels
though strictly speaking a barrel is a specific size of cask with a capacity of
36 gallons (Earwood 1993: 68). Perhaps surprisingly, no evidence of the use
of casks has been found in Britain before the Roman period but they are
very commonly found on Romano-British sites reused to line wells. Many

are made of silver fir or larch, trees not native to Britain, providing evidence that they were imported, though examples of oak are also found. The use of these imported woods for buckets suggests that they were made from wood derived from knocked-down casks. Casks are large in size, about 2 m high, but other, smaller, stave-built vessels are also known. These smaller vessels were provided with holes to take a simple rope carrying handle and a bung-hole through which the contents could be decanted.

Narrow-necked vessels containing liquid were stoppered by a wooden bung; dry goods may have been prevented from spoiling by the protection of a flat lid. The larger flat discs of stone commonly found, of a size that would appear unnecessarily large for a simple gaming counter, are likely to have been used as simple lids for storage vessels. A comparable disc of charred oak wood came from the Southern Lanes in Carlisle (Padley 2000: 106, K17), where wooden bungs have also been found. One example had branded letters, presumably representing the name of the shipper of the goods rather than the contents (Padley 2000: 109, fig. 71, K13).

Security

It is noticeable through the finds from domestic sites that security for one's possessions became an important aspect of life in the Roman period. While metal locks and keys, as well as simple latch-lifters, are known from pre-conquest Britain, there is no doubt that there was a dramatic increase in their use during the Roman period on house doors, cupboard doors and chests. This increased interest in security may be interpreted in different ways: it may point to the population becoming more affluent, so a householder had more material possessions to protect, or that people were becoming more nervous about their personal security. One result of the rapid expansion of urban living and the increasingly transient population may have been an increasing lack of trust in one's immediate neighbours and fellow townsfolk.

There are two basic types of Roman lock: mounted locks that were fixed in place and used on doors and furniture, and padlocks that were movable and used in conjunction with a staple and hasp or a chain to secure a range of items, including slaves. The mounted locking mechanisms used in the majority of households are likely to have been of wood, though they rarely survive. An example dating to AD 105–20 has been found at Vindolanda (Birley 1997: 41, fig. 16), cut from a block of wood with internal channels containing 'tumblers' that could be raised by a simple key.

Keys of bone and wood, with a row of simple projecting teeth to work such mechanisms, have also been found at Vindolanda (Birley 1997: 22–5, fig. 10), and bone examples have been occasionally found elsewhere (e.g. South Shields: Allason-Jones and Miket 1984: no. 2.22).

Metal keys are common finds and easily recognisable. Manning (1985: 88–97, pls. 37–43) provides comprehensive descriptions of the types found in Roman Britain (Plate 31). Latch-lifters, to raise a single bolt or tumbler, were in use from the Iron Age and throughout the Roman period. Examples of Anglo-Saxon date are usually of much smaller size, with an angular rather than a curved stem. Tumbler locks were operated by either lift keys, that lifted the tumblers to free the passage of the bolt, or slide keys, that both lifted the tumblers and moved the bolt. T-shaped lift keys have a simple bit with a single upstanding tooth, sometimes two, to each side. L-shaped lift keys, the most common Roman key type found, usually have two or more teeth to one side. Slide keys are of a more robust form with a thick, shouldered strap handle with a pierced ring bow, some with decorative mouldings, and a toothed bit. Lift keys are usually made of iron; slide keys may be of copper alloy or iron. Occasionally keys with copper-alloy handles and iron bits are found, though differential corrosion frequently results in only one component surviving well.

Lever locks, like the simple locks currently in use, have been used from the Roman period onward. Those of medieval date are known as rotary locks. Lever locks are usually made of iron, though two small silver padlocks of this type were part of the Hoxne Hoard (Bland and Johns 1993: 12). Their keys have the slots cut in the key bit in the manner of modern keys. The key stem either ends in a pin projecting beyond the key bit or has a piped (hollow) stem to fit over a pin in the lock, centred in the middle of the keyhole. The keys with a projecting stem are large and, being capable of opening a lock from either side, were principally door keys. The small keys with piped stems were used to lock caskets or small boxes. An unusual version takes the form of a 'key-ring' with the bow of the key orientated so that it could be worn on the owner's finger, providing extra security. Examples of both copper alloy and iron have been found occurring in burials, either worn on the body or still remaining in the keyhole of the lock plate of the box it secured (Crummy 1983: 85–8).

Barb-spring or barrel padlocks comprise a cylindrical or angular metal case into which a single or double spring bolt is inserted through a hole in one end. The bolts are often found and are distinctive, having a single 'fin' or pair of 'fins', known as the leaves or springs, projecting from the side. The lock is opened by a key inserted in a hole at the opposite end of the case. The

Pl. 31 Selection of keys from South Shields

barb-spring padlock key has a strap handle with a rolled loop or a pierced ring terminal at one end, the other end being bent at right angles to form a simple bit pierced by an angular hole or holes. The holes fit over the springs or leaves of the padlock bolt and by compressing them allow the bolt to be withdrawn. When found, these keys often have the bit snapped off and may only be distinguished from the handle of a different utensil if the beginning of the right-angled bit remains. Barb-spring padlocks and their keys were used in the post-Roman period and care must be taken in dating examples from multi-period sites.

Conclusions

Though the unusual or spectacular finds grab our attention, to appreciate the range of Roman domestic artefacts we must look at the more humdrum items that better reflect the everyday lives of the majority of the population. A glance at the 'finds' section of any excavation report gives some measure of just how unprepossessing much of the excavated material associated with domestic activities really is. However, what also emerges is the size of a domestic assemblage and how much more is to be found in excavating a dwelling occupied after the Roman invasion when compared to an Iron Age site. The trade links on which the Roman Empire was built resulted in people of each province having access to the goods of all the other provinces. The introduction of coinage provided a convenient means of exchanging these goods. Someone living in a British house could, potentially, now buy material from all over the world, and many did. Some of these imported objects reflected their owner's origins but some simply reflect an individual's taste.

In analysing this material it is also only too easy to fall into the trap of presuming that the furniture and fittings of the individual rooms in a twenty-first-century western house would be similarly distributed in a Romano-British dwelling and that an object of a certain type has continued to be used in the same way for two thousand years. The population of Britain, however, was very diverse, with people bringing their ways of life from every province of the Empire. Consequently, the domestic arrangements of the folk of Roman Britain varied as greatly as those of the inhabitants of the country today and there is no single 'Roman domestic life' waiting to be uncovered by the archaeologist. Invariably, rich and poor lived side by side and, in the case of owner and servant or slave, often within the same dwelling; in these cases, the material remains of the one group may swamp, and indeed obliterate, the few traces of the other. The contrast between rich and poor, military and civilian, or urban and rural might initially appear to be extreme but may still reveal similar assemblages during excavation. Outside their professional roles, the life of a soldier or a priest would require artefacts of a domestic nature, as would the life of a farmer or an urban artisan, so differences in their material culture may not always be immediately observable (Allason-Jones 2001).

According to Martial, in Rome a poor man had a toga, hearth, bug-ridden bed, rush mat, lock and key, and cup (quoted in Alcock 1966: 71). If we ignore the toga, a poor man in Roman Britain may have been similarly equipped. Given the right depositional conditions we stand a chance of finding them all, though rarely together, admittedly. Whether we would recognise them for what they were and attribute them to the belongings of a poor man is another matter.

Light and heat are fundamental human needs, and public perception still strongly associates the concept of bright and warm rooms decorated with wall-paintings and mosaics with the Roman period, projecting a sense of comfort and civilised living back into the past. But what is the artefactual evidence in Roman Britain for artificial light and heating and how does it compare to Roman Italy and other parts of the Roman Empire?

Heating

One of the best-known structural elements of Roman houses is the hypocaust (or underfloor heating system). This consisted of the floor of a room being supported by pillars and heated by the hot gasses of a fire passing underneath it (see Degbomont 1984; Yegül 1992: 356–82; Nielsen 1993: 14–22). The furnace (*praefurnium*) could be stoked from the outside and the hot air circulated underneath the floor and up the walls through hollow box flue tiles. Roman furnaces did not have metal grates but the fire was made directly on the floor of the furnace. The main fuel used was wood and several recent studies have attempted to assess a hypocaust's technical requirements and heat output (e.g. DeLaine 1988: 22–5; Manderscheid 2004: 22). Experimental and theoretical studies (Rook 1978; Hüser 1979; Grassmann 1994) have calculated heat input, fuel consumption and conditions within the heated room. This research has demonstrated the effects of the radiant heat generated by wall tubes and also illustrated the uneven distribution of heat across floors and walls. A hypocaust system could be run with relative ease (DeLaine 1988: 24) but questions remain about the length of time required to reach comfortable temperatures when firing a hypocaust up 'from scratch' (Hüser 1979: 27). The amount of fuel consumed can be calculated, and this has obvious cost and environmental implications. Thus Blyth (1999) argues that fuel costs for public baths would have been easily covered by the entrance fees but it remains uncertain whether smaller hypocausts in private houses and baths were continually (or even regularly) fired. In Britain, hypocausts are attested in bath buildings (Rook 1992) and in the dining and reception rooms of relatively grand urban houses and villas.

Even in the absence of structural evidence, the location of a hypocaust may be indicated by the presence of box-tiles (Brodribb 1987: 70–83). These were set vertically into the walls and transmitted heat from the underfloor cavity into the room. The faces of box-tiles are usually treated (by scoring, combing or roller-made relief patterns) to give the superimposed plaster a better grip. The relief-patterned designs in particular have been used to establish production centres and chronological frameworks (Betts, Black and Gower 1994).

A less easily identifiable element of the hypocaust which may crop up among ceramic small finds is the so-called space bobbin (Brodribb 1987: 67–9). These bobbin-shaped objects were used to form a space between the wall and vertically mounted wall tiles and were held in position by iron cramps. Wall cavities created in this way may have formed an alternative, and possibly earlier, solution than box-flue tiles to the problem of conducting hot air and preventing damp wall plaster, but spacer bobbins remain rare finds in Roman Britain.

The majority of the population probably relied on hearth fires for heat as well as cooking, particularly in traditional round houses. This contin-ued an Iron Age tradition in which all domestic life was structured around the hearth fire. As in the recent past, people would have been skilled at banking the fire so it would smoulder overnight, thus avoiding the poten-tially difficult process of having to light a new fire. It can be assumed that strike-a-lights (such as flints and iron bars) were used to light fires (and indeed lamps) but these are rarely identified among domestic assemblages. Hearth fires probably also functioned as the main source of artificial light in the home, especially as in Britain neither the Iron Age nor indeed the later Anglo-Saxon population used lamps.

In addition to hearth fires and hypocausts, there were also more mobile heat sources in Roman houses. These included braziers and water heaters. Water heaters are complex bronze objects that are frequently depicted as part of dining scenes (Dunabin 1993; 2003). Braziers are probably best documented at Pompeii, where both elaborate bronze (Dell'Orto 1992: 173, no. 58; de Caro 1996: 222) and ceramic (Ward-Perkins and Clar-idge 1976: no. 156) examples are preserved. Braziers appear to have been used both for heating and (if they have an open top) for food preparation (barbeque-style cooking and reheating). They may have been especially important in houses that lacked hearths and kitchens (Salza Prina Ricotti 1978/80: 239–40, fig. 2; Dell'Orto 1992: 187). Penelope Allison (2004: 89–92,

102, 126) has examined the location of braziers in Pompeiian houses and found that many examples came from the gardens, corridors and smaller rooms but it is unclear whether this reflects active use or temporary storage.

No complete examples of either braziers or water heaters are known from Roman Britain but it is possible that zoomorphic supports and other elaborate bronze fragments originally derived from them, or from candelabra and other stands (Henig 1970; Bailey 1996: 83–106).

Lighting

Lighting equipment represents a completely new form of material culture that was introduced after the Roman conquest in AD 43. This chapter will briefly review the evidence for Romano-British lamps and candlesticks in terms of their typology, chronology and production but the focus will be on the social and economic significance of the adoption of these objects. The use of artificial light represented a significant economic investment as the use of oil or fat as fuel effectively involved the burning of foodstuffs, even if the lamps and candlesticks themselves were relatively cheap. The availability of artificial light would have had an impact on daily life, extending the working day but also affecting activities such as reading and writing and Roman-style dining. It could also be argued that much of the significance of lamps lay in the overt adoption of a very urban and 'Roman' form of material culture (see below). This chapter is based on the author's recent work on lighting equipment which discusses all these issues in much greater detail (Eckardt 2002a). There are few other regional surveys (see Leibundgut 1977) but for questions of typology, chronology and iconography there are a large number of excellent museum catalogues, in particular those discussing the collections of the British Museum (Bailey 1980; 1988; 1996).

Roman lamps with a single wick (Plate 32; Fig. 14) would have provided as much light as a modern candle and, given the limited number of lamps in Britain, most homes must still have been very gloomy by modern standards. Compared to alternative light sources such as fires, the presence of lamps must nevertheless have had a significant impact on the perception of rooms in terms of colour (e.g. wall-paintings) and space (Ellis 1994).

Lamps would have been quite awkward to handle – the oil had to be filled into a small central opening, probably using small spouted pottery vessels, which are also sometimes identified as feeding bottles (see

Pl. 32 Bronze single-nozzle lamp from South Shields

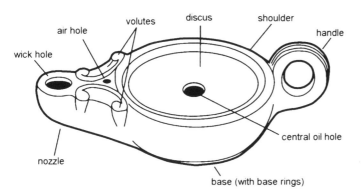

Fig. 14 Drawing of a single-nozzle oil lamp

Chapter 11). Maintaining lamps (i.e. trimming the wick and refilling with oil) must thus have been a labour-intensive task. How long a lamp burned depended not just on the volume of the container but also on the width of the wick and on the permeability of the lamp body, presumably giving bronze lamps a distinct advantage. A number of the metal and some of the ceramic lamps have multiple nozzles (Plate 33). This would have increased the amount of light provided but also required more fuel and presumably caused more sooting. Soot and smoke from lamps is often commented upon by ancient authors (Quint. XI.3.23; Vitruvius *De*

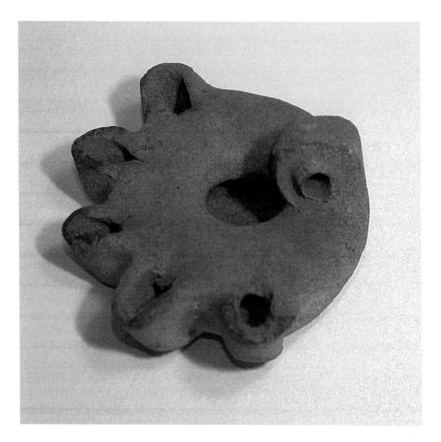

Pl. 33 Five-nozzle ceramic lamp from South Shields

*Arch.*VII.3.4; Juvenal VII.225). Lamps and candlesticks probably also represented a significant fire hazard, and it is possible that localised fires in domestic contexts may have been started by accidents involving lighting equipment.

Roman lamps occur in two main forms: open (tallow) lamps and closed (oil) lamps. Ceramic Roman closed (oil) lamps in Britain can be further divided into three main categories: picture-lamps, factory-lamps and circular lamps, with the first two being by far the more common. Picture-lamps are so called because the discus is usually decorated while the name 'factory-lamp' was originally applied to describe the simpler and less decorated lamps of the later first and second centuries which often bear a maker's stamp. This chapter will briefly review only those types that occur commonly in Britain, using the basic typological system first suggested by Loeschcke (1919), which, despite some refinements and additions, has largely stood the test of time.

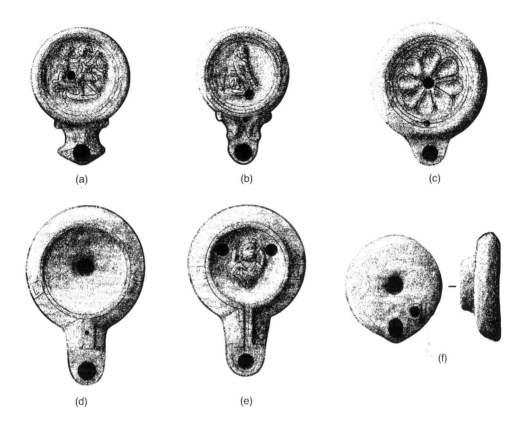

Fig. 15 (a) Picture-lamp (Loeschecke 1919, Type I); (b) picture-lamp (Loeschecke 1919, Type IV); (c) picture-lamp (Loeschecke 1919, Type VIII); (d) picture-lamp (Loeschecke 1919, Type IX); (e) picture-lamp (Loeschecke 1919, Type X); (f) wheel-thrown circular lamp

The three most common types of picture-lamp in Britain (Fig. 15; Loeschcke 1919, Types I, IV and VIII) are distinguished by the shape of the nozzle and the presence or absence of volutes. Type I has volutes and an angular tip to the nozzle. The width of the angular nozzle (as well as shoulder forms) can be used to distinguish further chronologically signif-icant subtypes. In Britain, the start date of picture lamps is defined by the Roman conquest of AD 43 and the vast majority appear to date to the first century (Bailey 1980: 126–52; Eckardt 2002a: 179–82).

Picture-lamps have been much studied for their decorated tops (known as the discus), which can bear images ranging from deities, chariot racing and animals, to erotic scenes. Lamp iconography thus offers a unique and often playful insight into Roman daily life. There are also some early lamps decorated with motifs such as 'Victory' or an altar flanked by trees, which provide a powerful illustration of the ways in which Augustan propaganda pervaded Roman art (Zanker 1988). It also seems very likely that individual images were imbued with meaning by their owners, for example by selecting the image of a specific deity. Images on lamps found in graves may have an even more explicit link to identity; thus the so-called female gladiator from London (Mackinder 2000: 10–37) was identified as such because she was buried with a lamp depicting a defeated gladiator. However, it is more likely that the significance of this image lies in the symbolism of overcoming death and is completely unrelated to the woman's profession or lifestyle. While it is difficult to identify selection and the reasons for it in individual burials, it is even harder to demonstrate consistent links between the overall contexts of lamps and the images with which they are decorated; in other words, selection of, for example, religious images for deposition in temples or a province-wide preference for certain motifs has yet to be demonstrated (Eckardt 2002a: 117–33).

Factory-lamps, if decorated at all, usually have a face mask on the discus (Fig. 15(e)). Compared to picture-lamps, this type has a more elongated nozzle and a wide sloping shoulder. Some examples have shoulder lugs, which can be pierced and which probably reflect the suspension lugs of metal lamps. Factory-lamps occur with and without handles and these can be applied or made in the mould; handles appear to be rare in picture-lamps, where they tend to be applied. The presence or absence of handles clearly has implications for portability – it appears that other forms of lighting equipment such as torches and lanterns were used to provide light outside the home and 'on the move'. Two main types of factory-lamp (Types IX and X) were distinguished by Loeschcke (1919) based on the design of the nozzle and in particular the shape of a 'channel' between the discus and the wick hole. Factory-lamps are usually dated from the Flavian period (but probably beginning as early as AD 60) into the second century, with Type X first occurring around AD 100. Many factory-lamps have a maker's or workshop's stamp in relief on their base. The name usually occurs in the genitive and is occasionally followed by the letter 'F' (for fecit: 'made by'). Among the Romano-British lamps there are some unusual examples, which appear to be derived from factory-lamps but vary in shape; these derived factory-lamps are especially common in London (Eckardt 2002a: 193–9).

All the lamps discussed so far were made from two-piece moulds; as air bubbles in the moulds are often still visible on the finished lamp, it is clear that plaster moulds were commonly used although these rarely survive (Bailey 1976; Cerulli Irelli 1977). Ceramic moulds were, however, also employed and examples of such picture-lamp moulds are even known from Roman Britain (Eckardt 2002b). While lamp usage always appears to have been lower in Britain than in many other provinces (see below), demand appears to have been sufficient to trigger some local production. This is concentrated in or near the urban and military centres, in particular Colchester (workshop with moulds), London (on the basis of fabric identification, in particular mica-dusted lamps) and Verulamium (again on the basis of fabric only). Makers' stamps, especially on factory-lamps, have been used to identify and track specific producers and their output but it is now clear that the same name (e.g. that of the prolific Fortis) can appear on lamps of very different fabrics. In some cases we may be dealing with authorised branch workshops but, given that new moulds could simply be taken from existing lamps, copying was clearly widespread (Harris 1980).

In addition to mould-made ceramic lamps, there is one other type of closed lamp that commonly occurs in Britain, in particular from the second century AD onwards (Goethert-Polaschek 1985). These are wheel-thrown circular lamps with a simple stub handle and round nozzle (Fig. 15(f)). Circular lamps occur across the province, but with a particular emphasis on the south and with multiple examples known from Caerleon, Baldock, London and Colchester (Eckardt 2002a: 206–9).

Closed oil lamps were also produced in bronze. A wide range of forms is known, including examples with volutes and of factory-lamp shape, but the impact of recycling means that relatively few such lamps survive in the Romano-British archaeological record. Lamp stands (candelabra) of metal or stone are equally rare in this province but must have represented a significant investment and thus are invariably found in the context of formal dining or ritual such as burials and temples (Bailey 1996; see also Chapters 12 and 13).

Especially in the later Roman period in Britain, lamps are increasingly replaced by candlesticks. Candles were produced by dipping the wick into molten tallow or wax, which in Italy appears to have been a rural holiday activity (Columella *Lib.* II.c.21, 3). Beeswax was expensive and probably rarely used in domestic contexts in Roman Britain. Indeed, residue analysis of a candlestick from Cologne identified cattle fat as the fuel (Goethert 1997: 28). Candlesticks come in a wide range of forms and appear to have been made mainly of clay or iron although there are also bronze and lead examples (Fig. 16; Eckardt 2002a). On some of the iron examples the candle would have been placed on a spike but socketed candleholders, often with a wide drip guard, are the most common type.

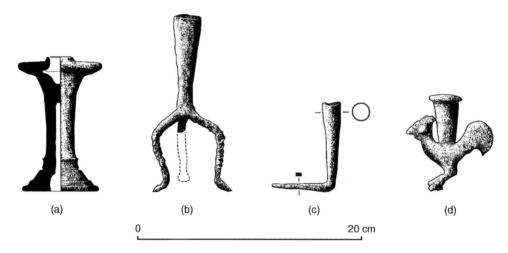

(a)   (b)   (c)   (d)

0   20 cm

Fig. 16 (a) Candlestick of pottery from the New Forest; (b) iron candlestick from Lydney Park; (c) iron candlestick from Alcester; (d) bronze candlestick in the form of a cockerel, from Lydney Park

While there are some early ceramic candlesticks, the majority can be dated to the third and fourth centuries AD. As they are usually wheel-thrown or handmade, there is a great deal of variation and it is difficult to identify industries or types other than those at York and in the New Forest. York produced mainly squat candlesticks, often in Eboracum ware. The New Forest candlesticks are characterised by a tall, slender and usually plain stem with a wide drip guard which curves upwards. These candlesticks are part of a well-studied late Roman pottery industry (Fulford 1975) and, judging from the fabric and the painted decoration, were made and distributed together with ceramic vessels. It is interesting that other late Roman pottery industries do not appear to have candlesticks among their repertoire, perhaps suggesting a lack of demand for this form of lighting equipment. It is, of course, also possible that wooden candleholders were used instead (see Paulsen 1992: 130–9).

A number of iron candlesticks consisting of a simple socket set on to three legs have been found in sanctuaries (Plate 34) while iron 'spike' candlesticks perhaps occur more commonly as settlement finds. In the latter type the socket is set at right angles to a tang or spike which could have been driven into the wall (Fig. 16(c)). Some of the bronze candlesticks are of the tripod type discussed above but there are also bronze and pewter candlesticks of zoomorphic shape. Birds, and in particular cockerels, appear to be an especially popular motif and, as several examples come from sanctuary sites

Pl. 34 Iron candlestick from Carrawburgh Mithraeum

such as Lydney Park and Nettleton, the selection of a bird associated with
Apollo may not be accidental (Fig. 16(d)).

All the lamps discussed above would have burned oil, although this
need not have been olive oil as is usually assumed. Residue analysis has
demonstrated that other oils (hazelnut or walnut, radish and castor) could
also have been used (Rottländer 1992; Copley *et al.* 2005). By contrast,
so-called 'open lamps' probably burned animal fat and tallow. It has been
suggested that 'open lamps', which commonly have handles, could have
acted as trays or lamp stands but a large proportion of the ceramic examples
have traces of burning, suggesting that they functioned as lamps in their

own right. The majority of ceramic open lamps are of a simple figure-of-eight shape, with an applied or mould-made handle and generally without decoration. An unusual group from Colchester has simple linear decoration on the base (Eckardt 2002b). There are also some wheel-thrown open lamps of very basic circular shape with a small pinched-out nozzle.

While it may be assumed that both the lamp and the fuel were cheaper than the closed and often decorated ceramic lamps, the distribution of ceramic open lamps in Britain is largely limited to the main urban and military centres and thus mimics that of other first-century lamps (see below). By contrast, open lamps made of bronze, iron and lead appear to have been used very differently. Iron open lamps, especially the most common figure-of-eight shaped examples suspended from an iron rod and L-shaped hook, commonly occur in hoards and burials. While they may have acted as high-status objects in life, they are thus specifically selected for ritual contexts and this practice appears to be especially common on rural and villa sites. This pattern of use and deposition is in marked contrast to the urban and military bias that most of the ceramic lamps show and also to that of lead open lamps. These latter lamps are again usually of a figure-of-eight shape, with a horizontal handle. In terms of their social distribution, they once again show a marked military and urban bias and in terms of their spatial distribution they appear to cluster in the west. That lead lamps are more common in the lead-producing areas of Britain may not appear to be a remarkable result, and their military bias could equally be explained simply by the military involvement in the exploitation of lead and silver in the province. What is striking, however, is the fact that lead open lamps come from occupation deposits rather than overtly ritual contexts like the iron open lamps. It is also interesting to note that not all lead lighting equipment occurs close to the production sites. Lead candlesticks in fact cluster in the south-east of the province; in other words the distribution of these two forms of lead lighting equipment is mutually exclusive. What all these patterns appear to demonstrate is that not just the artificial light itself mattered to the user, but that lamps and candlesticks made of different materials were used in very specific and deliberate ways.

Lighting outside the home

Regardless of the material lighting equipment was made of, the symbolism and magic of artificial light also played an important part in

Roman ritual. In Britain, a number of sanctuaries dedicated to 'eastern' deities such as Cybele (The Triangular Temple at Verulamium) and Mithras (Carrawburgh, Caernarfon, Rudchester and London) contained lamps and other lighting equipment, perhaps reflecting the role of light effects in mystery cults (Eckardt 2002a: 96–8, with further references; see also Chapter 12). Lamps also occur in burials, although not as frequently as on many cemetery sites along the Danube and in Gaul and Germany. In some cases multiple lamps are associated with incense burners (tazzas), hinting at the importance of light and purifying smells in funerary rites (Eckardt 2002a: 98–115). There is some evidence that lamps were placed into burials alight, perhaps to light the deceased's path to the underworld symbolically (see Chapter 13).

Apart from ritual contexts, we have so far discussed only the domestic role of lighting equipment but there were also some forms of lighting equipment designed mainly for use outside the home. On the whole, ancient cities did not possess efficient street lighting, making travel at night uncomfortable and dangerous (Suetonius *Caes.* 31.2). Torches and lanterns were used, and for wealthy Romans these were carried by slaves (Juvenal III.285–90). Unsurprisingly, no archaeological evidence for torches survives from Roman Britain.

Lanterns were composite objects made from a bronze frame with an organic material, such as horn or pigs' bladders, shielding the light source (Martial XIV.62; Feugère and Garbsch 1993; Eckardt 2002a: 229, fig. 101). In Britain, only a very few fragmentary remains of lanterns (in particular the small hooks with domed terminals which helped to suspend lanterns from chains) have been recorded, mainly from sites with military associations.

Conclusions

If we examine the use of lighting equipment in Britain across the whole of the Roman period, some remarkable trends emerge. The first pattern is one of changing intensity of use over time. The vast majority of lamps appear to have been used in the first century, in the decades following the Roman conquest but declining sharply after AD 100. The use of lighting equipment recovers slightly in the later Roman period (with candlesticks) but never to the level of first-century lamps. A similar sharp decline in the use of lighting equipment after AD 100 has been observed in Roman Switzerland (Leibundgut 1977), where it has been explained in terms of the demilitarisation of the province. The same argument cannot be made for Britain, where significant garrisons remain in the north and in Wales for the entire Roman period. If we accept that the adoption of lamps is closely related to an urban and essentially Mediterranean lifestyle, it is possible that the recruitment of non-Mediterranean troops in the later Roman period had an impact. Economic factors may have also played a part, although it is difficult to see why finewares, such as samian, continued to be imported but not lamps. The rise and fall of lamp use in Britain also does not correspond closely to the consumption of olive oil (as evidenced by Dressel 20 amphoras). We therefore have to ask whether lamp consumption in Roman Britain could have been about symbolic use and social practice, and not just about availability and trade?

The question can be addressed by examining the contexts of lighting equipment from Roman Britain. It is difficult to construct a meaningful contextual comparison on the level of feature or deposit type. Too rarely is it known whether a lamp comes from an occupation deposit, a pit or a midden; even when that information is present it would not really reveal much about how lamps were perceived and used. Instead, broad site categories such as 'military', 'urban' and 'rural' can be employed and for Britain such an analysis shows that lamp usage is very strongly biased towards large military sites and the major urban centres (Eckardt 2002a). The use of lamps is never really adopted on rural or even villa sites, nor in the smaller settlements across the province. This may partly be a result of the historical development of the province and the particular chronological profile of lamp production and consumption in the north-western provinces. In the first century, when lamp consumption in Britain peaks, the majority of sites in existence (and on which excavation has traditionally focused) are the major urban and military centres. The peak of villa occupation is later, and at a time when lamps are rare in Britain. Arguing for a simple chronological explanation is, however, not satisfactory. If we examine the sites more closely, the restricted character of lamp consumption is underlined. It is really only on a very limited number of sites (Colchester, London, Verulamium, Richborough, Usk, Caerleon and York) that significant numbers of lamps have been found and these are all sites especially closely connected to the Continent, and linked to the military and civil administration of the province.

The initial peak in lamp consumption would thus have been caused by an essentially incoming population which had been used to artificial light and continued to use lamps in Britain. Lamp use never really spread beyond forts and towns, either because there were not enough people who wished to adopt a form of material culture explicitly associated with the Roman conquerors or, perhaps more likely, because in most people's lives there was simply no need for lamps. Most activities carried out on rural sites and in smaller towns could be completed using traditional light sources, such as hearth fires and torches, rather than investing in inconvenient (leaking, sooty) and expensive lamps.

Viewing the use of lamps as a cultural practice has implications as to how we think of the province of Britain in relation to other parts of the Roman Empire. The use of lighting equipment in Britain is very restricted, both in terms of chronology and in terms of the types of sites on which lamps occur. The overall number of items of lighting equipment recorded from Britain is roughly equivalent to that from a single major site in Gaul or Germany (such as Trier) and certainly far inferior to that of Mediterranean areas. The scarcity of lighting equipment in Roman Britain could be seen as a 'failure' or lack of 'Romanisation' but it could also represent an example of active choices made by the native population. Some of the new objects reaching these shores made sense or could be adapted to traditional practice; others remained restricted to incomers or those members of the elite who made a specific effort to follow an explicitly 'Roman' lifestyle.

ELLEN SWIFT

The basic and most common categories of personal ornament in Roman Britain are brooches, bracelets, finger-rings, ear-rings, necklaces, pins and belt sets. Very rare object types include headbands and body chains. Many of these categories of object occur in a wide range of materials, bone and copper alloy being the predominant materials, but glass, iron, jet, shale, ivory, silver and gold were also used. In Roman Britain, it is uncommon to find personal ornaments made from gold and precious stones during the excavation of settlements and cemeteries as these mostly come from hoard finds. The publications of large hoards that include jewellery are therefore essential reading for this type of material (Thetford: Johns and Potter 1983; Hoxne: Bland and Johns 1993; Snettisham: Johns 1997). For a wider overview of precious-metal jewellery in Roman Britain, which also includes some consideration of items made from non-precious materials, Johns's monograph (1996) is invaluable. Site report catalogues are most useful for dress accessories made from non-precious materials; Crummy's Colchester report (1983) is always a useful starting point, and the bibliographies on the web page of Barbican Research Associates are also valuable.

Jewellery

Roman brooches occur in three main categories: bow brooches, which are arched in profile; plate brooches, which are usually flat; and penannular brooches, which are ring-shaped with a break in the ring (Plate 35). Brooches in each category also occur in other periods, but the individual brooch types are so distinctive that this is rarely much of a problem. The standard reference work for brooches has recently been published by Bayley and Butcher (2004). For fourth-century crossbow brooches see Swift's monograph (2000a), which also gives details of the important literature in other languages.

Some brooch types, for example the so-called 'Nauheim' bow brooches and early penannulars, overlap in their period of production from the pre-Roman Iron Age into the early Roman period. Plate brooches often occur

Pl. 35 Selection of brooches from South Shields

in animal form (zoomorphic) or in the shape of objects, such as sandal soles, flasks, miniature weapons, etc. (skeuomorphic); most of these are enamelled, though some have glass or stone settings rather than enamel.

Bow brooches occur in a bewildering range of types, many of them at first glance very similar to one another. The key to the typology established by Hull (see appendix 2 in Bayley and Butcher 2004), which most artefact specialists follow, lies in careful attention to the way that the brooch is put together, particularly the fastening mechanism. Though there is not space to cover the details of all the different types here, the terminology used to describe bow brooches and place them within a particular type is initially quite difficult, and is therefore worth explaining in some detail.

The head of the brooch is the area where the pin is attached (though, confusingly, the brooch may be worn the other way up, with the 'head' at the bottom) and the foot is the other end. The bow is the arched section that links head and foot. The pin is found on the back of the brooch; it may be hinged, in which case it is a separate piece of metal attached to the brooch by a simple hinge, or sprung. In the simplest sprung types the whole brooch is made from one piece of wire, coiled at the head of the brooch to create some tension (hence the word 'sprung'), and slotted into a catch at the base of the foot. This kind is called a one-piece brooch. More complex sprung brooches may have a separate spring pin attached to the head of the brooch in various ways. The chord of the spring is the piece of wire that runs down its outside; there may be a hook on the top of the head to hold it, or the chord may be slotted through a projecting knob called a lug. The spring may also be threaded on to a separate bar running through its centre called the axial bar. Easily confused with this, there may be a piece protecting the spring or hinge that runs crossways at the head (the crossbar); or there may be a cylindrical spring cover which performs the same function. Brooches with a separately attached pin can be described as two-piece brooches. All of these features may be important in identifying the particular type of bow brooch and evidence of them must therefore be carefully noted. The types are sometimes named for the appearance of the brooch (e.g. trumpet, knee, headstud) and sometimes after the site where the original type brooch was found (e.g. Polden Hill, Colchester, Langton Down, etc.).

The main types of metal bracelets are solid cast, wire, strip and cable bracelets (made from more than one strand of wire twisted together). Glass bracelets may occur as solid bangles and as bead bracelets. Bone and ivory bracelets are often narrow and flat, sometimes fastened with metal pins or bound together with a small section of sheet metal. Jet, shale and iron are also occasionally used. As with the brooches, the details of the fastening are important for accurate identification of different types; the shape of the cross-section is also a useful diagnostic feature. Hook-and-eye fastenings are easy to identify; hook-and-plate fastenings are similar, but the 'eye' is replaced by a flat plate with a hole in it. There are also expanding bracelets with overlapping sections of wire. In general, early strip bracelets are wide, later ones narrow; most are formed from an unbroken band, though hinged bracelets are not unknown (e.g. nos. 82 and 83 in Allason-Jones 1996: 32). Both early and late bracelets may be decorated with a range of patterns; these are useful further pointers to a possible date, as slightly different patterns were preferred at different times. Cast bracelets in the form of a snake, for example, were popular in the early Roman period; the greater the naturalism of the representation, the earlier they tend to be. A high-status form of late bracelet, in gold, occurs decorated with the openwork technique; sometimes an inscription is included, or the pattern may be purely vegetative. The Hoxne Treasure is a notable late assemblage that includes many gold bracelets (Bland and Johns 1993). Crummy (1983) and Clarke (1979) are most useful for typology; see also Swift (2000a) for a consideration of late types. Kilbride-Jones (1938) is useful for glass bracelets but Price (1988; 1995a) has provided updates,

confirming that, since Kilbride-Jones's publication, the distribution of
finds of glass bracelets has widened considerably. Bracelets became more
uncommon in successive periods, such as the Anglo-Saxon and medieval
periods.

Necklaces are usually composed of glass beads, though other materials,
such as amber or jet, may also be seen. The commonest bead shapes are
spherical, cylindrical, square cylindrical, diamond-faceted (a square with
the corners cut off), hexagonal cylindrical and biconical (two cones with
the bases pressed together). All of these occur most often as one-colour
translucent glass; blue and green are the most popular colours whilst hexagonal green cylinder beads mimic the natural crystal shape of emerald. In
the late Roman period opaque annular beads decorated with coloured trails
of glass can be found; these are similar to pre- and post-Roman beads and
may therefore cause some confusion in identification. Guido's monograph
(1978) is the standard reference work and includes the pre-Roman types;
her volume on Anglo-Saxon beads (1999), edited by Martin Welch, may also
be useful for separating out Roman-period beads from those of other periods. See also Swift (2000a) for distributions and types found more widely
in the Roman provinces. Beads in materials other than glass tend to be of
more unusual shapes; jet beads are sometimes flat and ribbed and invariably
come from bracelets (Allason-Jones 1996); amber beads are often large and
may be carved into different shapes. A particularly distinctive type of early
Roman bead is the melon bead, ribbed vertically, in blue or blue-green
faience. It has been suggested that these may have sometimes been used
to decorate animal harnesses (Price 1995b: 107) and this was confirmed
by a find of a melon bead necklace associated with a horse in a burial at
Krefeld-Gellep in the Rhineland (Pirling 1997: grave 3960).

It can be difficult to ascertain how beads were arranged on necklaces as
they have not always been excavated carefully enough. There are, however,
a few examples in which the arrangement of the beads has been preserved,
for example necklaces strung on wire, which suggest that an alternation
of colours and shapes was usual, mimicking jewellery made from precious
stones (see Swift 2003).

Bead necklaces might include a pendant, or a pendant might be worn
separately on a chain. Pendants on glass bead necklaces are usually made
from copper alloy or, sometimes, silver, but may occur as part of high-status
jewellery also, made in gold. Lunula pendants, the shape of the crescent
moon, were associated with women in the Roman period (the goddess
Luna is often shown with a crescent behind her head). They are found as
part of female jewellery, and also seem to have been used to decorate animal

harnesses (Massart 2003). Phallus pendants are also known; for example, a series of large bone phallic pendants, with a fist at one end and a phallus at the other, have been found in Roman Britain, principally at military sites (see Crummy 1983: 139; see also Chapter 12). Antler pendants decorated with a phallus also have an association with military sites in Britain and along the Rhine and Danube (Greep 1994: 87).

Finger-rings of glass and other materials such as rock crystal are known, but the most common are made of metal, usually copper alloy, silver or gold. Some are made of simple pieces of wire, and some are cast in particular shapes (snake rings, for example, are very similar to the snake bracelets described above), but most have a central decorative feature (the bezel) sometimes with a glass or semiprecious gem setting, or with a flat engraved field. The bezel tends to be the most important part for identifying the type, especially the details of how a setting is cut and inserted into the ring. Henig (1978) has published the most-used English reference work; Guirard's work (1989), however, has clear drawings and is worth referring to. Finger-rings are often set with an intaglio, an oval of semiprecious stone with carved decoration, which can be used as a seal (Plates 4, 36 and 43). A vast number of different designs are known (see Henig 1978) and glass imitations of intaglios, with moulded designs, are fairly common. Marriage rings are known from the Roman period, often with a representation of clasped hands, or, in the late Roman period, a portrait of the happy couple, sometimes with an inscription or symbol that associates them with Christian marriage.

Roman ear-rings are invariably designed for insertion into pierced ears. The more elaborate types, set with glass beads or semiprecious stones, are easy to recognise, with a hook to go through the ear and sometimes pendant drops. The simpler types are easily missed, such as broken rings with slightly pointed ends. Allason-Jones (1989) is the standard reference for Romano-British material.

Hair pins are usually made from copper alloy or bone, though other materials such as glass, jet or ivory are sometimes used. The head is at the top of the pin, and is an important feature for classification. The pointed section that sticks into the hair is called the shaft. Conical, spherical and bead-and-reel head shapes are popular; faceted heads are often found in jet. Figurative designs, especially busts, are also found; these tend to predominate in more high-status materials like silver or ivory, though they also occur in bone (Plate 37). Crummy (1979) covers the types of bone pins in more detail; Cool (1991) does the same for metal pins. Handmade pins, e.g. those made from bone, tend to be quite similar in different periods, so caution is needed here.

Pl. 36 Garnet intaglio with an actor's mask, set in a gold finger-ring, from
Housesteads

Pl. 37   Figurative hair pins

Belt sets

A wide range of belt set types is known; the occasional gold or silver example exists, but most are of copper alloy. They are often, but not always, associated with military sites and they have a tendency to crop up in very late contexts (edging into the fifth century AD) on villa sites. The belt set

Pl. 38 Chip-carved strap end from Wall, Staffordshire

usually consists of two pieces, the buckle and the plate, hinged together, though one-piece items are also known. There may also be a strap end, which would originally have been attached at the other end of the belt; it would protect the end of the leather as well as having a decorative purpose. The central pin, which fastens the belt buckle by slotting through a hole, is called the tongue. For classification, the shape of the buckle and belt plate, and the way that they link together, are important features. The decoration can be very varied and early belt sets may be embossed, enamelled, or cast in openwork (pierced) designs. A common design in the second half of the first century AD is a simple raised circular boss surrounded by a couple of concentric rings. Second- and third-century designs are often based on the pelta motif. Later belt sets may have stamped or chip-carved decoration in geometric or vegetative patterns (Plate 38). The best-known type of belt set is the late Roman chip-carved set of many pieces, produced in large-scale manufacturing centres on the Continent. This type of belt set sometimes includes strap guides, suspension loops and extra plates, such as propeller-shaped fittings, to strengthen the belt and stop the leather curling. Not many chip-carved belt sets have been found in Roman Britain; they are predominantly associated with sites on the Rhine–Danube frontier. Late Roman buckles are usually decorated with animals (zoomorphic), often two animal heads facing one another (confronted). A specifically British type of belt found in the very late Roman period is the buckle loop decorated with two horse heads, this time facing away from each other (addorsed); the buckle plate is a long, narrow strip of metal. For more detail on Roman belt sets see Bishop and Coulston (2006) and Chapter 5. For the fourth century, Swift (2000a) provides an introduction and further references to the Continental literature, which is important in this period. Since many buckle types originated on the Continent it is more useful to use the typologies put together by Böhme (1974) or Sommer (1984) for late material, rather than those suggested by British specialists (Hawkes and Dunning 1961; Simpson 1976) though there are some variants not found on the Continent. Post-Roman belt sets continue to develop from the Roman Continental series, but are comparatively infrequent finds in Britain and fairly distinctive in appearance.

Accessories

More rarely, one may come across other items relating to dress. Headbands were known in the Roman period; there is, for example, one from a grave at the Lankhills cemetery in Winchester (Clarke 1979) which was made from leather, of which only traces remain, decorated with gilt bronze settings, some in the form of scallop shells, and yellow glass pieces; a further example has recently been found in the new excavations at Winchester (N. Cooke, pers. comm.). A single example of a body chain, which would have been worn cross-wise across the body, has been recovered as part of the late Roman Hoxne Treasure (Bland and Johns 1993). This was a very high status item in gold and it is unlikely that examples were ever made in other materials. A range of metal fittings are associated with the military, which include fittings from body armour (*lorica segmentata*) and apron or baldric (sword belt) mounts (see Chapter 5). Button-and-loop fasteners are found frequently, though not exclusively, on military sites, and Wild (1970) suggests they were used on military horse harnesses rather than as part of dress (see Allison *et al.* 2004: 8.2.2a for a more recent discussion of possible functions).

Reconstructing dress assemblages

How were personal items worn in Roman Britain? There are several ways of approaching this question, but none is without problems. We can examine art-historical representations from the Roman period of persons wearing jewellery, particularly on funerary monuments, but it is difficult to know how far these represent the reality of everyday life in a province like Britain, especially as the principal collections of material, such as the mummy portraits of Roman Egypt (e.g. Doxiadis 1995) and the grave reliefs from Palmyra in Roman Syria (Mackay 1949), are not from Britain or even from the western provinces (for a possible exception see Plate 54). Representation at death may also show an ideal rather than actual version of typical dress. They are still the best art-historical evidence available, however, as other representations on relief sculpture that include jewellery, e.g. barbarians wearing torques to signify their barbarian status, are often archetypes which are probably even more unreliable as evidence of everyday life.

Turning to the archaeological evidence, the most obvious way to examine jewellery which may have been worn as an assemblage is to look at grave contexts, though here too we cannot be certain that adornment at death approximated to the number and combination of items that would have been worn during someone's life on any particular occasion. For the early Roman period, cremation is the dominant burial rite amongst graves which have been recovered by archaeologists, and obviously the evidence for dress items of this period is much more fragmentary as a result. Even in the late Roman period, when inhumation was the norm and jewellery not uncommon as part of a grave assemblage, the jewellery was often deposited in a heap (perhaps once in a bag or box) in the grave rather than being worn (many examples can be seen at the Lankhills cemetery: Clarke 1979). However, we can at least look at the types of jewellery that are combined in a grave assemblage and therefore are likely to have been combined when worn; and there is a growing number of excavated late Roman graves in which the person was buried wearing jewellery, allowing the examination of how exactly the items were worn in death, and, arguably, in life also. In some instances, where deposition of dress accessories does not appear to be a deliberate part of the grave ritual, a stronger case can be made that this is how the items were worn in life. Hair pins, for example, are sometimes the only item relating to personal appearance found in a grave, still in place near the head. In these instances, their inclusion seems more a by-product of the hairstyle, rather than a specific funerary rite, and it can perhaps be suggested to relate to use in life rather than funerary use. Another instance of 'accidental' inclusion of dress items comes from a couple of burial groups found in Canterbury (Johns 1982). In one, bodies had been thrown into a pit, and in another they had been deposited in a gully and had seemingly remained exposed to the air for some time (M. Houliston, pers. comm.). In addition to the unusual circumstances of deposition, the place of deposition, in both cases within the city walls, is also not normal Roman practice. The circumstances of burial suggest that the bodies were disposed of without significant funerary attention to their dress. The presence of multiple bracelets worn at burial in both of these instances, therefore, suggests the manner in which they would have been worn in life. However, because these burials are to some extent 'special cases' it is difficult to extrapolate from them more widely.

Toilet articles

Wooden combs, sometimes of boxwood, such as an example from Shakenoak villa (Brodribb, Hands and Walker 1978), have occasionally been found, often in waterlogged deposits or in grave contexts; but most surviving combs are made of bone, ivory and antler. Galloway (1976) provides some useful notes on terminology. Simple combs consist of a single piece of material, whereas composite combs are fixed together with connecting plates, usually riveted with metal pins. Either type may be double-sided, with two rows of teeth, sometimes of varying size, or single-sided, with one row of teeth.

According to Lloyd-Morgan (1977: 330–1) Roman mirrors can be made from metal (polished silver or bronze) or silvered glass; the most common shapes are rectangular or circular. There may be decoration on the back of the mirror or in a border around its edge on the front face. Metal mirrors often had wooden frames but these rarely survive. Silvered glass mirrors sometimes have lead or wooden frames. Lloyd-Morgan's publications (1977 and 1981) are useful sources of further information.

Toilet sets, consisting of tweezers, nail cleaner and an ear scoop/cosmetic spoon associated together on a metal suspension loop, are known, as are so-called 'chatelaine brooches', in which the tools are suspended from a bar on the brooch (Plate 39). There is much diversity in these object types, particularly the nail cleaners (see Crummy and Eckardt 2003 for discussion of different types). The items also occur individually, in slightly larger versions; there are several types of spoon, for example, with flat circular bowls, concave circular bowls, or concave bowls of long oval shape (Crummy 1983: 59–61). Spoon probes, with a spoon at one end and blunt bud-shaped terminal at the other, could have had multiple purposes, for cosmetic and medical use (Crummy 1983: 60). Iron Age/early Roman cosmetic sets have been identified by Jackson (1985) in south-east Britain; these are crescent-shaped with two constituent parts, a 'pestle', often with pointed ends, and a 'mortar' with a central groove or hollow. They were probably used to grind pigment for make-up (see also Chapter 11 and Fig. 21).

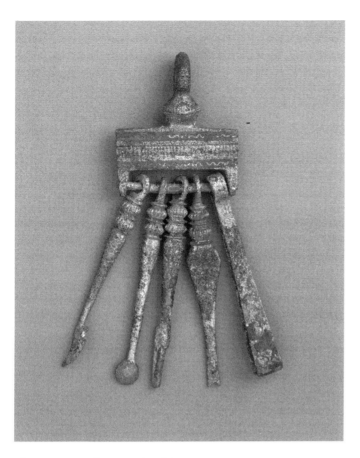

Pl. 39 Bronze toilet set or chatelaine

Cosmetic palettes, flat slabs of stone with bevelled edges, are occasional finds, and may also have been used for mixing medicines (Crummy 1983: 57). Small glass bottles were used as containers for cosmetics, but probably also had many other uses; when identifying such items, assumptions should not be made about usage, though sometimes contextual evidence, such as the (rare) surviving contents of the bottle, or associated finds of other toilet items, can be used to suggest the function. Two glass containers, one globular with a narrow neck and one bird-shaped, from a domestic context at a site in Roman Spain, for example, were found to contain a reddish powder, made from gypsum, calcite, haematite and an organic binding substance; the most likely use of this preparation is for cosmetics (Perez-Arantegui 1996). A notable Romano-British example of a surviving paste in a cylindrical tin box comes from Southwark in London (Evershed *et al.* 2004); on analysis it was found to be composed of tin oxide, animal fat and starch, and again it is thought to have been a cosmetic.

Why and how the objects were used

Toilet articles and dress accessories were obviously used to curate and decorate the body and to make it more attractive within the norms of a particular culture. Yet this was not their only role. The conspicuous display and use of dress and toilet equipment and accessories communicates important social and cultural messages. Dress items and particular ways of presenting the body may be used to construct and display a particular ethnic or cultural identity. Toilet activities are also practices that have particular cultural associations; not all cultures engage in, or attach value to, practices such as shaving or plucking hair, for example. Both toilet practices and objects used for adornment are associated in many cultures (including the ancient and modern western world) with women, and are therefore, inevitably, used as signifiers of gender identity. Dress and toilet are deeply cultural activities, concerned with presenting the body in a particular way, and constructing or communicating a particular image or identity, especially relating to conventional gender roles within a society, but also with respect to other aspects of identity and status.

The wearing of some types of jewellery and personal ornament is clearly primarily a display of elite status. Through elaborate and expensive jewellery, a member of the elite would display the wealth of the family (Stout 2001 gives a summary of this topic in relation to Roman jewellery). Deposition of this material in a grave could be interpreted as an attempt to show that wealth was disposable, or to indicate that the construction of a particular status at death was felt to be worth the expenditure of a large sum of money (see Struck 2000 on further questions relating to status display in Romano-British graves). The presence of precious-metal jewellery in a hoard, meanwhile, indexes its function as a means to store wealth, as, unlike grave goods, it was intended to be recovered (Hinton 2005: 7–38, includes some useful material on jewellery in Roman hoards). Elite status could be constructed for jewellery in various ways, most obviously through the use of valuable and rare materials. Kent notes that silver would have been worth a hundred times the value of copper alloy in the Roman period while five gold solidi would have paid a soldier for a year (Kent 1977: 159–62). This gives us an indication of the relative value of different materials during the period, though values may of course have fluctuated somewhat through time and from one area to another. Other materials with high value in the Roman world were precious and semiprecious stones as well as exotic materials such as ivory. Fine workmanship, for example particularly difficult craft techniques such as openwork or filigree (e.g. the Hoxne bracelets, see Bland and Johns 1993), could also be used alongside valuable materials to construct a luxury product (see Ogden 1982: 41–55 on craft techniques).

Particular types of jewellery appear to be restricted by gender in the Roman period, both in Britain and in the wider Roman world. Necklaces and ear-rings, for example, were normally worn only by women. Items like this, associated with one sex, can therefore be used to construct a particular gender identity. This is usually the same as the biological sex of the individual, but there are examples of dress accessories associated with women being buried with men, and therefore being used to construct a kind of 'third sex' for the individual in question. It is often noted that, in Roman Britain, rings and brooches are more common items of jewellery in the early Roman period, whereas pins, bracelets and necklaces are more common in the late period. This seems to show a gradual decline of, by and large, non-gendered personal ornaments, and a rise in strongly gendered ones, and it may suggest some changes in how jewellery was perceived through the period and what it was used for. The most common brooch type in the late Roman period is also strongly gendered: the crossbow brooch, which is invariably associated with the military and civilian elite. The increase in gendered jewellery also corresponds with the increasing occurrence of representations in the western provinces of women wearing jewellery, perhaps suggesting that it only became an important part of the construction of a western provincial woman's feminine identity in the later Roman period, after a long period of exposure to Roman culture. There may also be some implications for the changing nature of a woman's appropriate role. A further trend relating to jewellery, which can be demonstrated to exist both in Roman Britain (e.g. strongly at the Butt Road cemeteries in Colchester, see Crummy, Crummy and Crossan 1993: 130 and appendix 1) and more widely in the Roman world (e.g. in Italy, see Oliver 2000; Roman mummy portraits from Egypt also seem to follow the trend) is the tendency for young women, as opposed to adult women, to be buried with jewellery, or for them to be buried with greater quantities of jewellery than older women. This is usually interpreted as symbolic of an unmarried status, representing a dowry (Crummy *et al.* 1993: 130; Oliver 2000; Puttock 2002).

The toilet in Roman culture is also fundamentally linked to the construction of a Roman woman's elite identity, signifying both her feminine identity and her membership of the elite. This is evident from a wide range of sources of evidence, including textual sources (see Wyke 1994), tomb-stones, wall-paintings and decoration on silver vessels, examples of which show women engaged in their toilet and attended by servants. The use of commodities such as cosmetics, expensive substances constantly in need of replenishment, would demonstrate the disposable wealth available to a family. The conspicuous consumption of leisure is also important here, as only an elite woman would have the leisured existence that would allow for a complicated and time-consuming routine of toilet and adornment as described in the textual sources (Balsdon 1962: 261). There is some evidence to suggest that a few women and their families in Roman Britain subscribed to these cultural norms. A sandstone tombstone from Chester shows a woman holding a mirror and attended by a servant in a typical exam-ple of a widespread Roman funerary motif (Wright and Richmond 1955: no. 120). In addition, some very Roman toilet items such as mirrors, combs and toilet caskets are archaeologically associated with women through grave contexts (Crummy 1993: 273–4), though these must be distinguished from provincial Roman toilet articles such as tweezers and nail cleaners which seem to have been used by both sexes (Crummy and Eckardt 2003). Along with mirrors, combs and toilet caskets, grave finds of some glass unguent bottles used for cosmetics (see above) have an association with demonstrably wealthy adults and may also be associated with female graves (Cool 2002: 145). All of these items could be interpreted as signifying an elite gendered identity at death constructed through toilet items, though other interpretations of the unguent bottles have been put forward (see Cool 2002). In addition, toilet and dress items themselves sometimes have self-referential decoration emphasising their importance in feminine culture, for example hair pins showing a bust with the elaborate hairstyle that could be created with their use. Items with strongly 'Roman' figurative decora-tion associated with toilet and adornment, like these pins (another example is a silver hair pin from the British Museum showing Venus putting on a sandal: Plate 37), sometimes occur in more prestigious materials, such as ivory or silver; where provenance is known, these examples are largely asso-ciated with major towns (such as London, St Albans and Colchester). The evidence from subject matter, material and provenance combined strongly imply that these decorative pins also emphasise the importance of the toilet in constituting Roman gendered elite identities (Hall and Wardle 2005 take a similar view, and catalogue figurative examples from London; see Swift 2009: 150–4 for a detailed discussion).

It is necessary to make a distinction between Roman toilet items that are gender-associated at burial and found widely across the Empire and others of a more provincial Roman character, and unique to Roman Britain, which may have been used by both sexes and which have different types of distributions. The copper-alloy nail cleaner, for example, is a Romano-British type of artefact without parallel abroad, and its distribution shows a predisposition towards rural sites (Crummy and Eckardt 2003; see below). Cosmetic grinders, too, are a type of object only found in Britain, and of arguably 'Roman' status since they span the divide between Iron Age and Roman periods in Britain and sometimes have 'Celtic' type decoration (Jackson 1985).

Regional and cultural identities

It is less easy to understand the role of artefacts in constructing group or cultural identities than to address their use to communicate status and to display gender difference. However, dress was certainly felt to be an important indication of regional and cultural identities in the Roman world – we only have to look at the art-historical representation in the period of 'other' peoples and cultures distinguished through their stereo-typically foreign dress – and it is likely that personal ornaments and even toilet articles in Roman Britain were used in some instances to construct particular cultural or regional identities. Any single object might have multiple differing uses and meanings; notwithstanding, some personal ornaments and toilet items in Roman Britain can be grouped in categories that seem likely to be useful in examining their use as cultural or regional identifiers. Two that seem to be emerging as a consequence of recent research are, firstly, objects that were not a part of the indigenous culture before the Roman conquest, such as finger-rings and ear-rings, and which were introduced to Britain directly from Rome or from Roman Gaul, and secondly, objects that show continuity in either form or decoration (or both) from the pre-Roman Iron Age (though it must be noted that Roman cultural influence in the later pre-Roman Iron Age also existed, see Hill 1997).

Considering the material which strongly implies Mediterranean Roman culture first (and which also includes the combs, mirrors, caskets and fig-urative hair pins in high-status materials discussed above), these objects tend to be quite uniform, both within Britain and also across the Roman provinces, and often display clearly Roman iconography. Finger-rings are one of the clearest examples. The same typologies for finger-rings can be used on both British and Continental material, a uniformity in culture across the provinces that is suggestive of Roman rather than indigenous influence. Finger-rings also occur in high-status materials such as gold and silver as well as lower-status materials like copper alloy, and many are set with semiprecious intaglios that show a range of Graeco-Roman themes, from mythology to scenes of everyday life (Plates 4, 36 and 43). The possibility of using rings set with intaglios to seal letters also creates an association between these objects and writing and literacy, which was, in the West, clearly a product of exposure to Roman culture (see Cooley 2002), though they could also be used purely as jewellery. Wearing such a ring might be a way of deliberately communicating a familiarity with Roman culture, though it might also be an incidental product of exposure to it, especially with material that dates to a century or more after the Roman conquest; we always have to take into account the four centuries of the Roman occupation, and the likelihood that the cultural significance of the adoption of particular artefacts will 'drift' with time.

The ear-ring is another culturally Roman object (in the provincial Roman West, at least) that reveals the introduction of a new cultural practice, in this case piercing of the ears. Böhme-Schönberger (1997) suggests, for Continental material, that the presence of ear-rings in a grave may indicate a greater degree of 'Romanisation', which we might gloss more carefully as a (partial?) adoption of Roman culture by the occupant. In line with this, examining a sample of fourth-century graves from provincial sites in the western provinces that contain ear-rings, it is noticeable that they tend to contain other items that are strongly Mediterranean in origin and style, such as coral bead necklaces, otherwise not widely found in provincial cemeteries (see Swift 2004). Considering Roman Britain in particular, Allason-Jones (1989: 37, 142–54) shows that ear-rings in general are more likely to be found on military sites or town sites than on rural sites. Several possible explanations can be suggested. If the ear-rings were worn by women, and thus being worn as a part of Mediterranean Roman culture, it is possible that their preponderance towards military sites could be explained by a higher exposure to or adoption of Roman culture on military versus non-military sites. This could be by indigenous Romano-Britons, or by incomers at the site who had a greater familiarity with Roman culture than the local population (see below for a further discussion of foreigners at military sites). It is possible that the wearers of this type of material culture perceived themselves to have, or were trying to communicate, some kind of Roman identity. It is also plausible that 'Roman style' goods were simply more available on military and town sites, and/or were perceived as status goods that could be used in the expression of status irrespective of their Roman connotations. Conversely, if the ear-rings were being worn by men, their presence may be related to the non-Roman practices of provincials who served in the army (Allason-Jones 1989: 17–18). The interpretation hinges, as so often is the case with dress accessories, on who exactly is wearing the items and in what circumstances, often not clear from the contextual details available, though inter-site spatial studies (e.g. that by Allison *et al.* 2004 of the Roman fort at Xanten) could potentially help in the future.

In general, the types of 'Mediterranean Roman' objects discussed above show innovation both in form and in practices related to their use (e.g. Roman-style toilet routines, body modification or writing). They are, there-fore, likely candidates to be chosen as signifiers of 'Roman' culture or what this was understood to represent, though this only remains one possibility among many, and we will never fully understand the intentions of their makers and users (Gosden 2005: 209).

Moving on to examine objects with a more provincial or even 'British' character, object types that have been associated with the pre-Roman indigenous culture include cosmetic grinders and trumpet and dragonesque brooches, particularly those embellished with 'Celtic' decoration, stylised patterns with precursors in the pre-Roman Iron Age. Cosmetic grinders and another provincial-style toilet item, the nail cleaner, appear to be unique to Britain (see above). Some of the brooches of 'Celtic' style are found in pairs; this suggests their use to pin the shoulders of a dress of pre-Roman origin (Plate 3). These kinds of objects tend to have distributions within a particular region of Britain and are also in some cases associated with rural/non-Roman sites. The dragonesque brooch, for example, is regionally distributed in the north of Britain (M. MacGregor 1976); Crummy and Eckardt (2003), meanwhile, have shown that some types of nail cleaners occur in distinct regional groupings, that they are found mostly on rural sites (arguably those with less exposure to Roman culture), and that these correlate with tribal *civitas* areas. Cosmetic grinders occur on sites in south-ern Britain, some from Iron Age contexts, and in Roman-period contexts many findspots are at rural/small town sites (Jackson 1985).

For some object types, then, a case can be made that they are a product of indigenous culture. What does this actually mean for those wearing these objects? 'Celtic' style objects could have been deliberately chosen to display 'resistance' to Roman culture. Dragonesque brooches, for example, have been suggested as representing the conscious expression of non-Roman identities in response to the Roman military presence in the north (Jundi and Hill 1998: 134; see also Webster and Cooper 1996 on the concept of resistance). Any account of this kind that an archaeologist gives is likely to be too reductive. Yet distributions by site type and region, which tend towards particular zones or site types, show that the distinctions in material made by considering the form and decoration are meaningful. Whether this expresses a conscious opposition of non-Roman to Roman, or differing ways of 'being Roman' (Mattingly 2004: 22) or, more pragmatically, differing availability of and exposure to Roman-style goods, is open to debate.

Perhaps another way of looking at the problem is by considering the 'way of seeing' represented by these artefacts. Rotational symmetry, which is strongly associated with Celtic art, is found in much 'Celtic'-style decoration of the Roman period; for example, it is the organising principle of the dragonesque brooch. Washburn (1999) observes that different cultures often have distinctive principles of symmetrical organisation in their art, and to some extent this can be argued to be indicative of a particular way of seeing the world. In support of this, it can be observed that rotational symmetry as a principle of organisation, as well as occurring in 'Celtic' art, is also evident in other aspects of Iron Age culture, such as crouched burials in circular pits, or round houses, both structured on a central point. Using Washburn's idea, therefore, the production of 'Celtic'-style objects in Roman Britain arguably implies the remnants of an Iron Age worldview surviving into the Roman period. Objects that show a fusion of cultures, Roman and 'Celtic' in this case, actually show us the practice of interaction between Roman and indigenous.

Military identities and people travelling

Several types of brooch – the Aucissa and knee, as well as the various cross-bow brooches – are thought to have been associated with the military in the Roman period. Crossbow brooches from the late Roman period have the best-documented military connections, through textual and art-historical sources as well as archaeology, though sometimes the military status conferred was only nominal as military dress was worn by any high-status official in the late Roman period. The archaeological evidence confirms that in Britain crossbow brooches were a military item: the largest number from any site in Britain is from Richborough fort, and most other British finds also come from military forts, e.g. on Hadrian's Wall and along the Saxon shore, though they are occasionally found in other contexts (e.g. grave contexts at Lankhills cemetery outside Winchester). Studying the alloy composition and style of the brooches in combination makes it possible to identify imports into Britain (see Swift 2000a: 81–8) and it seems likely that many of the crossbow brooches found in the province were imported; they are thought to have been produced in state factories. Aucissa and knee brooches are earlier types that have been suggested to have been worn by the military. In the case of the knee brooches, the distribution across different military sites, with high numbers relative to other kinds of brooch at some and very low numbers at others, is apparently sufficiently distinctive to support the previous interpretation, by Cool, that they must be linked not only with the military but with specific contingents of troops coming from Germanic areas (Cool 1983: 30; Eckardt 2005: 156). Clearly, military transfers were one of the principal means by which long-distance travel occurred in the period for men and women, the former as soldiers and both whilst accompanying army personnel. This is the likely explanation for unusual feminine personal ornaments that show a bias to military sites and large towns (which would have had a substantial military presence). A good example is a type of fourth-century bone pin with a known production site at St Denis in Paris (Belarbi and van Ossel 2003: 319), which has a distinctive head with a very rudimentary human face, clearly demonstrating the transformation of material culture over four centuries as it is a bastardised version of the figurative hair pins of the Roman period discussed above, though scarcely distinguishable as anthropomorphic by now. It is found in Britain in very small numbers, and is heavily biased in its distribution in Britain towards large towns and military sites (information from Belarbi and van Ossel 2003: 342, fig. 12). The small quantity and particular distribution (which is wide, though limited by site type) suggests that the examples found on British sites are unlikely to have been copies made by artisans in Britain; the pins are also far too cheap and easily produced to be worth trading over long distances. The most likely mechanism of dispersal would be women travelling with the army. Nor is it the only example. The bias in the distribution of ear-rings discussed above could be attributed to the same cause; there are also other unusual subtypes of personal ornament, e.g. other specific varieties of pins (Cool 1983; 1991) and bracelets (Swift 2000a), which show the same strong bias to military sites and large towns. There are also corresponding instances of bracelet types that can be shown to be British occurring abroad at military sites; for example Swift (2000a: 178–9) and Sas (2004: 364–9) document evidence from the Continental coastal fort of Oudenburg in Belgium and at Krefeld-Gellep in the Rhineland. It is important for scholars to distinguish categories of late Roman material culture that were very unlikely to have been manufactured in more than one place and occur in too small a quantity or were of too low a value to be the product of trade, from the apparently similar yet actually very different debate concerning the Germanic origin of material culture from Anglo-Saxon graves. Doubt has rightly been cast on the assumption that 'Germanic-style' brooches originated in Germany, because it can be shown that in most cases such brooch types were made in Britain, were produced over long periods, and diverge significantly from Continental prototypes. This forms an obvious contrast to the late Roman material studied here.

These patterns encourage us to be cautious about attributing a military symbolism to items purely on the basis of their association with military sites. For those objects for which there is evidence of military use from independent textual or art-historical sources (such as brooches used to pin the military cloak, or belt sets girding the military tunic) a military distribution may confirm this use in practice. Any bias to a 'military' distribution in an unusual subtype of personal ornament, however, particularly a feminine dress accessory, rather than denoting military status perhaps suggests people travelling. Examining the distributions of unusual objects allows the archaeologist to glimpse the cosmopolitan nature of the population inhabiting large towns and military sites, which is also known through other sources of evidence such as inscriptions.

It is arguable to what extent these small divergences in material culture were actively used to signal difference; they may, paradoxically, be more visible to the archaeologist than they were to the wearers and viewers at the time. However, the existence of regional dress accessories, both within one province and across the western provinces more generally (see, for example, Swift 2000a), makes it possible to explore questions of the social performance of cultural identity through dress items, especially where these are found in grave contexts. An example is a group of graves at the Lankhills cemetery in Winchester, originally studied by Clarke (1979). He proposed, on the basis of both the grave ritual and the objects found, that the graves could be associated with one another and linked to Pannonia or Sarmatia, both in modern-day Hungary. The male bodies in the group were buried with military dress accessories, crossbow brooches and belt sets, in a rite unusual in Britain, and the female graves, more particularly only those of young women, contained large numbers of bracelets worn at burial, a practice found in Roman Pannonia and not elsewhere. Guido (1979), in the same publication, suggested independently that the carnelian beads found in some of the graves of the foreign group originated in Sarmatia. Clarke's idea was initially met with scepticism (e.g. Baldwin 1985), and it was pointed out that other graves with worn dress accessories at burial did exist in Roman Britain. Subsequent studies, however, have provided supporting evidence for some elements of his original proposition and introduced more subtlety to the debate by examining the material and physical remains very closely. Swift (2000a), for example, shows that a buckle in grave 234 is regional to Pannonia and Dalmatia and that some of the glass bead types are unusual in Britain but found in the Danube area. It was also noted in this study that the division between young women wearing many bracelets and older women wearing few bracelets was also found in some cemeteries in Pannonia – although the Lankhills bracelets themselves were shown to be British types. Another study of the foreign grave group carried out by Swift (2004) looked at the details of the materials from which the bracelets were made and their association with the left or the right wrist. It was found that, similar to trends in the Danube region, bracelets on the right wrist were copper alloy only, whereas bracelets on the left wrist were made from a wide range of materials. Finger-rings were only found on the left hand, also a trend that can be demonstrated in Danubian material. Comparative material is scarce in Britain, as jewellery was less often worn at burial, but at Butt Road, Colchester, which also revealed a number of graves with worn personal ornaments, finger-rings were apparently being worn on both right and left hands (Crummy *et al.* 1993: 144, table 2.56). Evans, Stoodley and Chenery (2006) brought a new dimension to the debate by using isotope analysis to investigate the possible origin of the group, a technique based on the different physical forms (isotopes) of trace elements in drinking water. By examining the isotope concentrations that build up in tooth enamel, Evans, Stoodley and Chenery were able to show that each of four male graves in Clarke's suggested foreign group, all buried with a military burial rite of crossbow brooch and belt set, had an isotope profile strikingly different from a control group (presumed to be indigenous) from the Lankhills cemetery, and did not spend their childhood in the Winchester area, though among these four males the profiles varied enough to suggest that they did not all originate from the same area. The isotopic analysis of a sample of bones from the female graves in Clarke's 'foreign' group, however, showed only one significant outlier from the control group, perhaps coming from south central Europe, with the remainder having isotope values consistent with a childhood in Britain. Taking all the evidence together, it is clearly the case that some of the graves are of foreigners as Clarke suggested, and that he was right to suggest, from the presence of a conspicuously different burial rite, cultural influences from central/eastern Europe. Yet the analysis by Stoodley, Evans and Chenery also shows that material culture, in this case particularly dress, is being used to construct a similarity between these burials that is belied by their disparate origin. The Roman army is a strong unifying factor here; those responsible for burying these men of widely different geographical origin 'disguise' their origins at death through dress accessories associated with a Roman military identity, which apparently supersedes their differing 'ethnic' affiliations (see also Swift 2006). For some of the female graves, a 'foreign' identity may have been constructed at death irrespective of their actual origin, as they themselves seem from the evidence likely to have been born in Britain, but to have been assigned a foreign burial rite by those responsible for their burial.

Magical, ritual and religious uses

Many of the materials used for dress accessories in the Roman world were believed to be protective or magical, for example amber and jet. Iconography may also be an indicator of magical or religious function. The gods of everyday good fortune, Fortuna and Bonus Eventus, for example, are frequently represented on intaglios (Henig 1978: 99–100), which thereby become lucky talismans. The animals chosen for enamelled zoomorphic brooches may also have had religious associations; while some are typically Roman, such as the eagle (associated with Jupiter and of course also with the army and the Emperor) or the peacock (associated with Juno), Johns (1995) has argued that some animals, such as the hare, can be linked instead with 'Celtic' religion. Given the widespread amuletic use of jewellery in the ancient world (see Sas and Thoen 2003) and also the widespread religious/ritual connotations of images in general in ancient societies, it can perhaps be suggested that the motifs chosen for brooches are very likely to have been perceived to have protective or lucky qualities (see Swift 2009: 179–85), though it can be problematic to assign specific 'religious' connotations to a symbol on the strength of textual sources, which inevitably come from other places and periods and can only be loosely extrapolated to Roman Britain.

In some other instances, archaeological context can be used to suggest a particular magical or apotropaic function. Amber beads in late Roman graves from the western provinces, for example, have a particular, archaeologically documented, association with children; so do opaque beads with decoration of trailed glass; it seems likely that they were both used as protective amulets for children in particular (Swift 2003). This also applies to bells, which have sometimes been found on bracelets in children's graves, though more investigation is needed. Both amber beads and bells are also mentioned in association with children in written texts of the Roman period, though these texts are not from Britain. Examples of all of these objects associated with children's graves can be found at Butt Road, Colchester. Grave G1, of a 10-year-old female (Crummy *et al.* 1993: 143, table 2.55), for example, contained a bracelet adorned with a bell and an opaque trail bead as well as other opaque trail beads and an amber bead (Crummy 1983: cats. 1610, 1501– 4 and 1348 G1). Three other infant or child graves at Butt Road also contained one or more amber beads; conversely, one adult female grave had a single amber bead. Grave 94, also a child burial, contained an iron chain with two copper-alloy bells (Crummy *et al.* 1993: 155). A collection of material, thought to have been deposited in a purse, in grave 278 at the Butt Road cemetery is also particularly notable, comprising as it does two coins with pierced holes plus another one in a silver setting for suspension, a pendant in the shape of a horned phallus, a bell, a carved piece of amber in the form of an African head, and a pierced tooth. Crummy *et al.* (1993: 41) suggest that the assemblage was a group of apotropaic amulets intended to protect a child; though the skeleton does not survive, the coffin was of narrow width, probably indicative of a child's grave.

There are also further examples of correlations between religious decorative motifs and the types of sites where objects are found. Intaglios engraved with a particular god or goddess have been found at temple sites associated with that deity; e.g. an intaglio with a representation of Apollo found at the shrine of Apollo at Nettleton (Henig 1978: 92). Enamel 'horse-and-rider' brooches are found primarily at Romano-Celtic temple sites, at rural locations (Johns 1995; Simpson and Blance 1998) and, it is suggested, may have functioned in a similar way to medieval 'pilgrim' badges, though they were, it seems, deposited at a shrine rather than acquired there (Eckardt 2005). In this instance, the dress item 'represents' in some sense the journey undertaken, as well as, perhaps, the deity at a shrine. Woodward and Leach (1993: 323–33) suggest that temple sites tend to have a particular 'profile' of the types of objects found there, including dress accessories. At Uley, for example, finger-rings predominate, whereas at Lydney bracelets and pins are more prevalent. It is proposed that this is related to the cult at the particular site, and it seems very likely in the case of dress accessories that it relates to differing use by gender of different shrines. Wheeler and Wheeler (1932: 41–2) note the large quantities of female dress items found at Lydney, and suggest that the objects can be understood in the context of a healing shrine for feminine ailments. In this case, female jewellery is being used to represent the female body, and thus the association with a particular deity is linked to the reputation of certain deities for healing feminine ailments.

In the late Roman period, objects with Christian symbolism begin to appear, for example finger-rings decorated with a chi-rho motif, or strap ends with fish, peacock, tree of life or chi-rho motifs (Petts 2003: 109–14). The chi-rho is obviously a Christian symbol. It might be argued that the other figurative motifs here are not necessarily Christian, but all were recognised as Christian symbols at the time, and the association of the themes with one another makes it more likely: an important find is a strap end that combines the chi-rho with the other motifs. Interpreting material like this is difficult, however, since the chi-rho symbol was a symbol both of the state and of the Christian religion (Petts 2003: 110). In addition, most of the objects do not have a secure archaeological context. Petts suggests that finger-rings with a chi-rho motif may have been seal rings to create seals for official documents; some of them have the reversed image necessary for a seal, and the presence of the motif on ingots and coinage perhaps lends support to the idea. The motifs may also, however, have been viewed by their owners as lucky or protective items, drawing upon the power of Christ. Henig (2005: 217) points out that a Christian image on a finger-ring, used to seal a document sent to another Christian, will help to cement the sense of being part of a Christian community, and this may also have been an important role for artefacts decorated with Christian symbols (see Swift 2009: 184–5 for further discussion of Christian iconography on personal ornaments).

Conclusions

A recurring theme in this discussion of personal ornament is that of context. In addition to noting the form, materials and decoration, examining the circumstances of deposition of an artefact – in a grave assemblage, its disposition on the body; its association with other artefacts, its spatial distribution within an archaeological site, its geographical spread, and the site-types on which it occurs – is invaluable in the reconstruction of the possible meanings that such an artefact may have had in the past.

10 | Recreation

LINDSAY ALLASON-JONES

The discovery of artefacts that relate to games and pastimes, whether private or public, indicates a society that has some leisure time to fill. There is a basic human need for entertainment, either through large-scale spectacles that provide social interaction, excitement and a sense of team spirit within a wider community or through games of skill, which allow individuals or small groups of people to while away their quieter hours. The archaeological evidence for the large-scale public spectacles is well known from other parts of the Roman Empire but such vast buildings are difficult to find through the keyhole archaeology of urban excavations in Britain. The sporting activities of small groups or individuals require no special buildings but their necessary equipment can be just as elusive in the archaeological record.

The amphitheatre

Successive Roman Emperors were well aware of the political significance of people's desire for entertainment, and the principle of 'bread and circuses' acknowledged the equal importance of keeping a population entertained as well as fed. Traditionally these public games were provided in the amphitheatre.

It is believed that the earliest gladiatorial contests were Etruscan in origin and developed from funerary rites, but during the period of the Republic such contests became increasingly detached from their religious roots and developed into pure entertainment, albeit somewhat ritualised entertainment. By the time of the early Empire gladiatorial games had become recognised as essential elements of life in the Roman world, with games taking place on set days in the year. Extra events were provided to mark special occasions, such as Claudius' successful invasion of Britain, and citizens often stretched their resources to breaking point in their efforts to show their standing in society by sponsoring games.

In order that as many people as possible would benefit from this munificence admission was free, but it is probable that tickets were used to allocate seats, as at Caerleon where a small lead disc was found, stamped with the letters XIII within a triangle (Wheeler and Wheeler 1928: 168; Zienkiewicz 1986: 26–7). Liversidge (1973: fig. 133a–d) suggested that the discs of pottery and bone found at Great Chesterford, inscribed on one face with letters and numbers, were used as seat tickets for the amphitheatre or theatre, although she acknowledged that they might equally have been used in a board game. Since 1973, discs of lead (*RIB* II.3, 2435), stone (*RIB* II.3, 2438), pottery (*RIB* II.3, 2439) and bone (*RIB* II.3, 2440) have been found throughout Roman Britain, often on sites where there is, as yet, no known theatre or amphitheatre, so this identification needs to be treated with caution.

Not every town in Roman Britain would have been provided with an amphitheatre; so far only nine have produced clear evidence of such a building, although there are also possible examples at York and Leicester (Wacher 1975). Glass and pottery vessels decorated with scenes from the amphitheatre are found throughout Britain, however, and indicate that their owners were familiar with public entertainments. The abundance of such artefacts in the recent excavations at Chester amphitheatre has suggested that objects – such as a Dragendorff 37 vessel covered in gladiatorial motifs, from a very worn mould – were being sold as souvenirs, just as one might buy souvenirs at a modern football match (T. Wilmott, pers. comm.), although their size might suggest they were more suitable for the gladiators' meal (*cena libera*) which was sometimes held before the games (J. Bird, pers. comm.). Joanna Bird has pointed out that the pottery from the London amphitheatre includes a significant proportion decorated with gladiatorial scenes or *venationes* (Bird 2008); on the whole, however, the finds from amphitheatres cover the usual range of objects that can be found wherever large numbers of people have gathered, and artefacts that point clearly to a site being used for entertainment are rare.

It is unlikely that British spectators were often treated to the sight of gladiators in combat with lions, tigers, panthers or rhinoceroses, nor does the *venatio*, or wild beast hunt, appear on British mosaics, which may suggest that it was not to British taste or that there were practical or economic difficulties in producing exotic beasts for popular edification. Bear-baiting and bull fights were a different matter, as there were ready supplies of both animals, bears being a regular export from Scotland to amphitheatres throughout the Empire (Martial *De Spectaculis* 7.3). A fragment of first-century AD South Gaulish samian from the London amphitheatre shows a bull fight in which a man with a very small rectangular shield faces a charging bull whilst three bodies lie lifeless on the ground, possibly (from their dress) prisoners *damnati ad bestias* (Bird 2008). A scene on a beaker from Colchester may show a scene of bear-baiting, although no dogs are shown. So far no assemblage from Roman Britain has revealed either bear or bull bones with evidence of damage by sword or spear but, in the latter case, it might be difficult to discern the difference between sword cuts and butchery marks. A bull skull, however, was found in the drains of the London arena and some bear bones have been found at Colchester. The small figures of bears carved in jet which have been found at Malton, York and Colchester are more likely to have had religious or personal significance for their owners than indicate an interest in bear-baiting (Toynbee 1964: 364).

Hand-to-hand fighting between both male and female gladiators took place in the amphitheatre. Different methods of fighting required different armour and weapons; the *retiarii*, such as can be seen on a relief from Chester (Jackson 1983), fought with little or no armour and faced their opponents with only a net and a trident, whilst the Samnites and *myrmillones* were well protected with visored helmets, oblong shields and short swords. Gladiators who fought in the Thracian tradition had a round shield and a curved sword. Finding archaeological evidence of hand-to-hand combat that is clearly gladiatorial rather than military is bound to be difficult. The most compelling evidence for such combat in Britain is a helmet found at Hawkedon in Suffolk, which has holes for a visor to be attached, in the manner of a Samnite gladiatorial helmet (Wacher 1975: fig. 2), although there is concern that this may be an antiquarian import. Doubt has also been expressed as to the validity of the sherd of Italian redware from Leicester, which refers to 'Lucius a gladiator' (*CIL* VII: 1335, 4).

Various representations on pottery, glass and mosaics showing gladiators in training or in combat should also be treated with some caution as pottery and glass can travel independently of first-hand knowledge of the scenes portrayed, and the images depicted on mosaics could have been chosen from pattern books. There are, however, so many of these items in Britain that it seems unlikely that they would have become popular in the province if their owners did not have an interest in the activities of the amphitheatre. A green glass cup of mid-first-century AD date found at Colchester, for example, depicts eight named gladiators, one of whom holds a victory palm (Hawkes and Hull 1947: 299–300, pl. 86). The same scene is to be found on a less complete vessel from Leicester. These vessels, and other examples that have emerged from Southwark and near Exeter, were made in Gaul and imported in some quantities (Allen 1998: figs. 16, 17).

Colour-coated pottery cups have also been found with gladiatorial motifs. Tyers (1996: 167) refers to Colchester wares of the second to late third century combining appliqué and barbotine techniques to depict gladiatorial

Pl. 40 The Colchester Vase, showing the *retiarius* Valentinus being beaten by the Samnite Memno

and religious scenes. The Colchester Vase, for example, shows the *retiarius* Valentinus being beaten by the Samnite Memno (Plate 40). This vessel is quite detailed and Memno can be seen wearing a crested and visored helmet, an armguard, a belt, a loin-cloth and greaves, and wielding a short sword and a cylindrical shield. Valentinus also wears armguards, belt and loin-cloth, but has lost his trident and net. The vessel is marked *legionis XXX*, which may suggest that the legions had gladiators amongst their ranks, but as the Thirtieth Legion did not serve in Britain this may not be relevant. A cup from Lothbury shows that the products of the Castor potteries also had gladiatorial images (Wheeler 1930: fig. 55.1).

This use of gladiatorial scenes to decorate domestic pottery may have been imported with the games themselves or arrived with consignments of Continental pottery, such as samian ware. Hartley (1954) drew attention to a fragment of second-century wheel-cut samian from York depicting a *retiarius*. Stanfield and Simpson (1958) refer to several examples of *terra sigillata* that have individual gladiators or scenes of gladiatorial combat (see pl. 10, no. 127; pl. 14, no. 17; pl. 15, nos. 181–91) but point out that some of the figure types of Drusus I (a potter sometimes identified as X3) were also used by later potters. This may confirm that gladiatorial scenes were popular with customers, but whether this popularity was solely linked to activities in the local amphitheatre is not clear; it is always possible that gladiatorial combat was seen as an allegory of the battle between life and death. A capital from York, for example, with the roughly cut figure of a *retiarius* on one face, is clearly an indigenous product as it is carved from local sandstone; however, its findspot suggests that it was not a structural element but a grave marker (Tufi 1983: no. 117).

The scene of combat between wild beasts and centaurs on the lid of a silver vessel from Mildenhall may suggest that some gladiatorial scenes related to mythological stories, rather than actual events (Brailsford 1951: pl. VII, no. 13/14). The lid of a bronze jug in the form of a gladiator's helmet, which was found during excavations at Southwark, also came from an import (Grew 1980: 382).

It was not only tablewares that used gladiatorial motifs; the makers of pottery oil lamps also enjoyed decorating their wares with scenes from the arena (see Chapter 8). One lamp from Colchester is modelled in its entirety in the form of a gladiatorial helmet (May 1930: pl. LXXIII.38) but it is more usual for a gladiatorial scene to be depicted on a lamp's discus; for example, a lamp from London is decorated with a helmeted gladiator posed with his sword drawn and a rectangular shield (Wheeler 1930: fig. 15.2), whilst another of Gallic manufacture shows a *myrmillo* (Bailey 1988: Q1490). Some of the pottery lamps found on British sites are known to have been made in Britain, so their use of gladiatorial imagery would appear to indicate a local market with an interest in the arena; an example from The Poultry, London, shows a fallen Samnite (Bailey 1988: Q1530) whilst another, from Bush Lane, London, depicts a *hoplomachus* and a Samnite (Bailey 1988: Q1495).

Bronze statuettes of gladiators have been found in London whilst knife handles of bronze from Corbridge (Worrell 2004: 323–4) and Pidding-ton (Friendship-Taylor and Jackson 2001) and ivory from South Shields

Pl. 41 Ivory knife handle in the form of a gladiator from South Shields

(Allason-Jones and Miket 1984: no. 6.2) are so detailed that, in the case of the South Shields example, the strings holding the quilting on the fighter's shield are visible (Plate 41). Most of these gladiators' defences appear to be of padded leather, and if one considers which materials would survive archaeological processes all that would end up in a finds tray are fragments of iron swords and the bronze edging of the shields, neither of which would be instantly seen as gladiatorial rather than military. The trident of the Chester *retiarius* would, no doubt, be attributed to an agricultural use if found in excavations, the buckles of his leather *manica* and *galerus* would be seen as military or related to harness, and no trace would be found of his net.

The amphitheatre would have been the scene for other sporting activities and entertainments. A pot illustrated by Déchelette (1904: no. 653), for example, shows a discus thrower whilst another shows a juggler juggling three rings (1904: 97, no. 105). A pottery beaker from Water Newton, although somewhat incompetent in execution, indicates that several entertainments could be happening at the same time; as well as a pair of gladiators duelling with differently shaped swords, a female acrobat is to be seen vaulting from a horse on to a panther (Toynbee 1962: 190, no. 156). It is also possible that cockfighting took place in the arena, although the backyards of taverns are the more traditional venues. There are scenes of cockfighting on the work of the potter Ioenalis (potter X-12), examples of which have been found at Nether Denton (Stanfield and Simpson 1958: pl. 39, no. 454). Cock spurs are common finds and, whilst it is possible these are the remains of kitchen waste, some of the bones are larger and more fully developed than is to be expected on an eating fowl (e.g. Meates 1987: 151, fig. 62, nos. 460–1).

Racing

The Celts are known to have been enthusiastic race-goers, and in the Roman Empire racetracks for horse racing and chariot racing were often built in association with amphitheatres. In the larger cities a long track called a circus was laid out with parallel sides and rounded ends, surrounded by tiered seats for the spectators. A *spina* ran down the centre, terminating at each end with a pillar known as a *meta*. The size and basic layout of a circus means that few are found, but evidence for a circus has recently been uncovered in excavations in Colchester (Crummy 2005). For a discussion of racing chariots, see Chapter 2 and Plate 10.

In Rome the charioteers were divided into the red, green, white and blue teams; that this convention was at least known in Britain can be inferred from an inscription from Chedworth that refers to 'the green company' (*RIB* 127). A series of mould-blown glass vessels also shows circuses in some detail; on one from Colchester the winner is recorded as Crescens, whilst his less successful colleagues are Hierax, Olympae and Antiloce (Plate 24; Toynbee 1964: 378, pl. 87). At Leicester, Camcumbus, Spiculus, Columbus and Calamus were recorded on a green glass cup (Haverfield 1918: pl. IV);

however, we cannot presume that any of these champions ever raced in Britain; more likely, they were the racing celebrities of the area, presumably in Gaul, where the beakers were made in the mid first century (Toynbee 1964: 378).

A series of glass vessels from the same mould and decorated with two friezes, the upper showing chariot racing whilst the lower depicts gladiatorial combat, appears to be confined to Britain and may thus be taken not only as evidence of glass vessel production but also as confirmation that the population enjoyed both sports. Examples have been found at Topsham, Hartlip and Southwark (Toynbee 1964: 379) and name Pyramea and Crescesia as the charioteers and Petraites and Hermes as the gladiators. Again, these may have been bought as souvenirs at the circus but may also have been on general sale.

Colour-coated beakers with chariot racing scenes are also found (Toynbee 1964: 414, pl. XCIVa; Brailsford 1951: pl. IV, no. 13) while a mosaic with a racing scene was found at Horkstrow in Lincolnshire (Toynbee 1962: 202, pl. 227). A rare depiction of a young boy driving a chariot is known on a relief from Lincoln. The piece is carved in the local oolite, a fact which led Ian Richmond to suggest 'the scene is almost certainly one of the games organized by the *iuventus* of the *colonia*. As evidence for the activities and organization of the aristocracy of the town, the piece is therefore of prime importance' (Richmond 1947). This may be an interpretation too far, however, as charioteers can also be found in funerary contexts.

The evidence that many of the products of the Nene Valley and Colchester pottery factories show chariot and horse races may reflect a long British tradition of interest in racing, even before the Roman conquest. Neither chariot racing nor horse racing requires a formal circus to be built; both can be carried out on any reasonably level area with sticks pushed into the ground to represent the *metae*. Even if provided with a large grandstand for the spectators, such a structure being almost entirely of wood would leave no trace. It is largely through the material evidence that we can suspect that both sports were common across Britain in military and civilian contexts.

Theatres

Throughout the Empire, theatres were built within towns and outside forts, probably as multi-purpose buildings intended for troop training and ritual activities as well as theatrical performances. Theatres were built in a traditional way, with a curved bank of tiered seats surrounding a circular or semicircular orchestra and facing a raised stage behind which was the fixed scenery with many decorative architectural elements. A wide range of dramatic works were available to the acting troupes of the Roman Empire but it is not known how often these were performed in Britain or if British theatre-goers were familiar with the full repertoire.

Theatres are known at Canterbury, Verulamium, Colchester and Gosbecks Farm, although the latter may have been intended primarily for religious performances. Tacitus also mentions a theatre at Colchester at the time of the Boudican revolt (*Annals* XIV.32), and there is an inscription referring to an aedile, Marcus Ulpius Januarius, presenting a new stage to a theatre at Petuaria (Brough-on-Humber), although the actual structure has yet to be found (*RIB* 707). The only completely exposed theatre in Britain is at Verulamium, first built in the mid first century. It was built in conjunction with a temple and was originally used for religious ceremonies.

In the Roman theatre masks were used by actors to identify their characters; an ivory tragic mask from Caerleon (Toynbee 1964: 359) and pottery masks from Baldock and Catterick may suggest that bands of travelling players brought popular productions to rural or military areas (Wacher 1975: pls. 5, 6). The owners of a house at Leicester may have been theatre buffs, as they chose to decorate a room with a painting of tragic masks (Wacher 1975: 348). Masks can also be seen decorating oil lamps (Bailey 1988: Q1501) and Butrio's samian ware (Stanfield and Simpson 1958), and even a garnet intaglio in a gold ring from Housesteads (Plate 36).

The status of an actor was not high and persons of quality who appeared on the stage did so at the risk of losing their standing in society. In Britain a fragment of pottery graffiti links Verecunda, an actress, with Lucius, a gladiator, both of whom would have been of dubious social status. Unfortunately, pots are transportable and we cannot assume that Verecunda or Lucius ever appeared nightly or 'for a short season only' at Leicester.

Finds from theatres, like those from amphitheatres, are mostly indistinguishable from the assemblages found in other contexts. The discovery of hair pins, ear-rings and bracelets at the Verulamium Theatre, however, goes some way to confirm that women as well as men attended performances (Kenyon 1935).

Boxing and wrestling

The depictions on artefacts also give us clues about some of the sporting activities which would otherwise leave nothing in the archaeological record.

Pl. 42 Silver strip depicting a boxer, found at Vindolanda

Such an object is the scrap-metal silver strip, prepared for melting down, which was recently found at Vindolanda (Plate 42). This shows a boxer with his hands raised in front of his body in the traditional defensive pose. In Rome, boxing was hardly the sport of gentlemen as the hands were first wrapped in hard leather thongs and then covered by gloves which incorporated a knuckleduster of specially hardened leather, often with additional metal spikes (Gardiner 1930). Neither bare-knuckle fighting nor wrestling requires a formalised space, and although scenes on pottery indicate that both were carried out in the arena, it would be just as likely to have been a sport of the army and young civilians, practised in small groups where the spectators could see the various moves at reasonably close quarters.

Pugilist scenes are depicted on imported pottery; for example Déchelette (1904) Number 647 shows two boxers, one naked, the other in a tunic, whilst Number 651 shows both combatants wearing loin-cloths. Boxers are included in a gladiatorial scene on a Form 37 Central Gaulish bowl from York, signed as a product of a mould of Bassus of Lezoux around AD 125–50 (Perrin 1990: 277, no. 887). Third-century bowls in the style of the Rheinzabern potters Julius II and Julianus I show naked boxers; the line on which one of the boxers rests his foot may just be a guideline for placing elements of the decoration but it is tempting to see it as one of the ropes from a boxing ring (Bird 1986: 167; 2002b: 42). Similar scenes have not yet been discovered on the products of the British potteries except for an oil lamp from the Thames, which shows a kneeling boxer (Bailey 1988: Q1532).

Hunting

Hunting was a very popular sport in the Roman period but, again, it rarely leaves much behind as evidence, except in scenes on mosaics. Indeed, one has to remind oneself when dealing with artefacts of all periods that most weapons can be used for hunting as well as in battle; only in the rare cases of blunt-tip arrows, used for knocking birds out of the sky without damaging their flesh, can one confidently ascribe a weapon to hunting. Assemblages of the bones of hunted animals can also be difficult to assign specifically to sport, as opposed to the acquisition of food, as one tends to go hand-in-hand with the other. Even the inedible, such as wolves and foxes, may have been hunted in order to protect livestock from predators or provide furs, whilst the appearance on many sites of boars' tusks may be the result of chance finds, the waste from butchery, objects of religious significance or the trophies of the chase.

An altar from Bollihope Common near Stanhope in Co. Durham (*RIB* 1041) records the gratitude of Gaius Tetius Veturius Micianus, prefect of the Sebosian Cavalry Regiment, to the hunting god Silvanus for his success in 'taking a wild boar of remarkable fineness which many of his predecessors had been unable to bag' (Plate 23). Several intaglios have been found which portray Silvanus, sometimes in his syncretised Romano-Celtic role as Silvanus Cocidius, such as the fine jasper found at South Shields which shows the hunter-god dressed in a beret, a belted tunic and thorn-proof leggings, clutching a lagobolan (hunting stick) in one hand whilst holding his catch, a fine hare, out of the reach of his sniffing hound (Plate 43; Allason-Jones and Miket 1984: no. 10.10). A lagobolan would have been

Pl. 43 Jasper intaglio from South Shields depicting the hunter-god Silvanus Cocidius holding up a hare

made of wood and would leave little trace in the archaeological record, as would the stout sticks needed for ratting and other weapons used in the less formal aspects of hunting.

A barbotine-decorated beaker from Bedford Purlieus shows a hunter wearing a close-fitting tunic and short trousers aiming his spear at a stag, whilst his colleague, holding a whip and a scourge, faces a bear (Toynbee 1964: 412). More exotically, a fragment of a similar ware from Colchester shows hunters attacking a leopard; this is more likely to be intended to depict a scene in an amphitheatre than a local hunting trip (Toynbee 1964: 412).

The need to wear protective clothing whilst hunting seems to have been optional. One naked hunter on a pot from Colchester is relying solely on his long knife, whilst his fellow hunter, facing a bear armed with a whip, is well protected by trousers with metal studs, a belt, braces, armlets and a guard on his left arm. Of the third hunter, only a putteed leg survives. A similar diversity of apparel and weaponry can be seen on the Colchester Vase, which has gladiators and huntsmen on one face, with a hound, a hare and stags arranged in two tiers on the opposing face (Plate 40; Toynbee 1962: no. 158).

An almost complete glass bowl from Wint Hill in Somerset is engraved with a lively scene of hare hunting (Toynbee 1964: 376–7, pl. LXXXVI). The huntsman is mounted on a horse and brandishes a whip in his right hand as he encourages his two collared hounds, which are chasing a hare towards a net. A fragment of a wheel-engraved green glass beaker from Traprain Lawe may also depict a hunting scene, although all that survives is the huntsman's head and that of his horse (Curle 1932: 294).

The Castor potteries clearly saw a market in producing pots with hunting scenes as fragments are commonly found showing hounds chasing hares, stags and boars, with some showing the gorier scene of a hound sinking its teeth in its quarry's hind quarters (Tyers 1996: 173). Once again, the dogs invariably wear collars, the leather strap and buckle of which are indistinguishable from belts in the archaeological record. The collar worn by a hound on a pot from Colchester is heavily studded (Toynbee 1964: 411).

A more contemplative sport, although again one more probably intended as a food-gathering activity, is fishing. Whilst many excavations in Roman Britain produce the bones of both sea and fresh-water fish, remarkably few fish-hooks have been found. Examples found in the Mediterranean are invariably of bronze and resemble a modern fish-hook, albeit much larger. It is possible that the anglers of Britain preferred iron hooks, which would be unlikely to survive, or used nets. An unpublished samian bowl from Canterbury shows a fisherman sitting on a rock with his catch of fish attached to a line, and similar scenes can be seen on pottery vessels from Gaul (Déchelette 1904: 91, nos. 556–61).

Toys and children's games

In the cradle babies would have played with rattles and bells until they were old enough for more sophisticated toys, but the discovery of both types of objects in religious and even military contexts makes their specific identification as toys uncertain. A wooden sword found in Carlisle is equally difficult to assign as a child's toy as it may have been a practice sword; the size of a more recently discovered wooden sword at Vindolanda is more convincing as a plaything.

Dolls would have been popular; a jointed doll of wood found at Hitchin resembles others found elsewhere in the Empire in bone, wood or clay (Liversidge 1973: 344–5; see also Elderkin 1930). Examples from Egyptian tombs of the Roman period demonstrate that even the rag doll has a very respectable lineage, though its traces are unlikely to be found in the damper conditions pertaining in Britain. Other cuddly toys may have been common but have left no trace, unless some of the 'pets' seen on tombstones come into this category.

Miniature objects are regularly found in excavations, particularly tools, such as axes, axe-hammers, knives and tongs, and weapons, such as spears and swords (Green 1978: 32). Many of these have been found in ritual or funerary contexts and may have been intended as offerings to the gods or were items intended to be of use to the deceased in the afterlife; some, however, may have been used as toys. The miniature bronze gladiator's helmet, axe and shields found at Kirmington may have been ritual in intention but would have been very attractive to a child (Leahy 1980). Miniature pottery vessels are even more ambiguous, as most will have been used to transport perfumes or other valuable commodities but could easily have been passed on to a child once the contents had been used up; such small vessels are very popular with children today and would have been equally so with Romano-British children.

Pipeclay figurines of small birds were interpreted by Joan Liversidge as toys (Liversidge 1973: 346), as was the bird on Serapion's tomb at Chester (*RIB* 558), but either could equally be interpreted in a funerary context as indicators of the afterlife. Most pipeclay figurines have clear religious significance; an exception may be the curious set of reclining figures of elderly men found at Colchester. Whilst these may be identified as representing a funerary feast, the diners' expressions make these an amusing sight and it is possible that they were intended as a child's toy (Toynbee 1962: no. 143). The discovery of unguent pots in the form of a doe and a hare in the same grave may support the idea that children played with old perfume containers.

Children can often be kept amused with very basic toys. At the Mercury Theatre site, at Colchester, a set of pottery discs of graded sizes has been identified as a simple stacking game (Crummy 1998: 34). The eighteen discs had been cut from grey ware vessels, including two bases, and resemble the modern plastic stacking toys that are designed to develop children's hand–eye co-ordination.

Wall-paintings from Pompeii and Herculaneum show cupids playing games such as leap-frog, blindman's buff and hide-and-seek, which of course leave no evidence for archaeologists to find. Several Romano-British tomb-stones, such as that of Flavia Augustina at York (Tufi 1983: no. 39) or Ertola at Corbridge (Phillips 1977: no. 71), depict children holding balls, though whether this is to show them as they might have been in life, to make it clear they were children or to suggest entertainment on the way to the Underworld, is open to discussion.

Evidence for adults playing with balls is less obvious in Britain but scenes such as that depicted on a mosaic in the Piazza Armerina, Sicily, where two bikini-clad women throw balls to each other, indicate that ball games were not confined to children (Pace 1955). The indications are that the most common balls were gusseted and stuffed with chicken feathers. However, there is documentary evidence that there were at least six types of ball in the Roman world: the follis or *pila* and the follis *pugillatoris*, which could be bounced, the *trigon*, which was a catching ball, the *pila paganica* and the *harpastum* which were used for field games, and balls made of wool, which were probably used for house games, such as indoor bowls. There is literary evidence for a game similar to tennis being played (Seneca *Ep.* 57), whilst a clay mould from Kettering, which shows a man with a curved rod in one hand and a separate circular object level with his knee, may indicate that a form of hockey was known in Roman Britain (Brailsford 1951: fig. 40, no. 7). The larger balls, most likely made by inflating a pig's bladder and then protected by an outer layer of leather, were also used for a game rather like football, as is known through a court case recorded in Justinian's *Digest* (IX.2.II) which dealt with the death of a man who was killed when a ball was kicked into the barber's shop in which he was being shaved. Football is also mentioned by Cicero as an enthusiasm of youth in his discourse *On Friendship* (3.20). The exact ball games played by Augustus (Suetonius *Aug.* 83) or Pliny's friend Spurinna in an attempt to ward off old age (*Ep.* III.1) are not known, but the references appear to support the notion that there was an active interest in ball games that have left no archaeological evidence.

Board games

Almost every Roman site in Britain produces discs, usually between 17 and 25 mm in diameter and 2 and 5 mm in depth, of stone, pottery, glass, shale or wood. Their possible use as theatre tickets has already been discussed and it is important to be aware that the larger plain discs may also have been intended as lids (see Chapter 7). Frere and Tomlin (1991b: 105) have drawn attention to the use of bone discs for accounting, quoting Pliny (*Ep.* VI.33.9), but have also discussed their possible use as gambling tokens, citing the use of the phrase *remi(ttam) l(ibenter)*, 'I will gladly repay', in association with possible symbols for 5 denarii on two bone roundels from Ewell (Frere and Tomlin 1991b: 105). Frere and Tomlin, following Kenyon (1948) and Greep (1991), have identified three principal types of bone counter: a plain disc with one dished or countersunk face; a disc with concentric rings on one face; and, the earliest, a disc with both faces plain.

The discovery of a single glass bun-shaped 'counter' may indicate an inset from a brooch or necklace rather than a game. The very fine set of twenty-four multicoloured glass counters from Welwyn, however, clearly indicates a board game (Stead 1967), as does the group of black and white counters from Lankhills (Clarke 1979: pl. 1b). A similar set of thirty glass counters from Lullingstone was found on one side of a wooden gaming board on top of the lid of a lead coffin; on the other side were seventeen bone plaques (Cool and Price 1987: 123–5). In the case of the glass counters, the white ones were decorated with red, blue and turquoise spots, whilst the red-brown ones had blue, yellow-tinged turquoise and blue-tinged turquoise spots. The bone plaques are not circular but include three triangles, four squares and nine rhomboids, all with incised decoration. Traces of glue were found on the edges of the pieces, which suggests that they had originally been used as inlay; whether they had been reused as gaming pieces or came from the wooden box which had contained the glass pieces is open to debate.

Less obvious objects may have been used as gaming counters. Even small pebbles could have been used on a board scratched on the ground, but more elegant pieces would have been used by the more leisured classes. At South Shields decorated wedges of jet are likely to have been intended for a game (Allason-Jones and Miket 1984: nos. 7.164–8). Some of these are slightly curved and have a suspension ring carved at one end; possibly these were worn around the neck until required, in which case the game must have only needed one piece per player; alternatively they may have been worn as good luck symbols by keen gamesters, in the same way as gamblers today wear dice or poker chips as cufflinks or tiepins.

Several games which relied on the skilful movement of counters on a board are known (Austen 1934; Bell 1960). *Duodecim scripta* was played on the same principles as backgammon, with two players moving fifteen counters each in opposite directions around a board of twenty-four squares. The moves were controlled by throwing three dice and the object was to move one's own counters to safe squares while knocking off the opposition's isolated pieces. The first player to move their counters around the board won. A pottery board decorated with rows of incised ivy leaves found at Holt is thought to have been a sophisticated *duodecim scripta* board (Liversidge 1973: fig. 134).

A second game, which may simply have been a version of *duodecim scripta*, was played on a board with six six-letter words arranged into columns of three. Unfortunately, although fragments of boards survive we have no clear idea of how the game was played. *Terni lapilli* was the Roman version of noughts and crosses, played on a square board with nine squares, each with incised diagonals. Boards for this game are known from a number of sites.

The best known of the Roman board games is undoubtedly *ludus latrunculorum*, also known as 'soldiers', which was a battle game requiring great skill. The pieces were used like the rook in chess and the player's aim was to capture the counters of their opponent by surrounding an opposing piece with two of their own. This game was extremely popular and boards made of stone, pottery, wood and even marble (at Richborough) have been found, with exotic boards in precious metals referred to in literature. The boards scratched on rough stone slabs from Sewingshields (Haigh and Savage 1984) and other milecastles and turrets on Hadrian's Wall (Allason-Jones 1988) would have been drawn by the soldiers in an attempt to provide themselves with entertainment in their off-duty hours. *Ludus latrunculorum* was exempt from the ban on gambling because the moves depended on the players' skill and foresight, and it may well have been regarded as a spectator sport as well as a private battle.

Dice were required to play *duodecim scripta* and the word game, and no doubt throwing dice was regarded as a game in itself; it may be that the cube found at Southwark, which has incised letters on its faces reading P/VA/EST/ORTI/URBIS/ITALIA, was used in such a game. This item was made from basalt but most dice were made from bone or pottery. Some of the bone dice found at South Shields and Corbridge were loaded, suggesting that cheating was commonplace. As is still the practice today, the numbers on the opposing sides normally add up to seven. The game for the long bone dice found in Iron Age contexts, mostly north of Hadrian's Wall, is puzzling as their shape would seem to preclude normal methods of dice throwing (Clarke 1970). However, their use seems to have continued well into the Roman period. Knuckle bones, stones and nuts were an alternative to formal dice but were also used to play 'knuckles' or 'fives', a game which involves throwing small items into the air and catching them on the back of the hand, an activity which is still to be seen in schoolyards today.

One game that it would be difficult to identify from the archaeological record was *par impar*, or 'odds and evens', as one merely betted on the odd or even number of pebbles hidden in the player's hands. In *inicatio* two players each raised the fingers of the right hand, varying the number raised and calling out the total number of fingers raised by both, until one or other guessed correctly. Again this would not be identifiable in the archaeological record, although it still survives in Italy today as *morra*.

Nine men's morris is commonly regarded as a medieval game but stone boards for nine- and three-men's morris have been found at Corbridge and other sites in Britain in Roman contexts. In three-men's morris the squared board has nine points and each player has four counters which are placed alternately on points. The first player to place three counters in a straight line wins. In six-men's morris each player has six pieces and in nine-men's morris they have nine, with the rules and the board becoming correspondingly more complicated. The boards and counters may have been elaborate in the wealthier households but the games would have been just as exciting played with pebbles on scratched earth.

Music

Remarkably little is known about music in Roman Britain, even though it played an important part in religious and civic ceremonies as well as public and private entertainment. More information survives elsewhere in the Empire, but in Britain we have to rely on occasional finds of instrument fragments and representations in art to gain any impression of the musical life of the inhabitants. Some of the latter are rather fanciful and show deities or nymphs at play: a mosaic at Sherborne, for example, shows Apollo playing a lyre in competition with Marsyas on the double pipes (Toynbee 1964: 212). Orpheus is depicted on several mosaics playing an instrument of the lyre type, perhaps a cithera, which was an instrument like a lyre but with more strings and a broader sound box. The Mildenhall silver plates show several instruments being played by happy revellers: cymbals, tambourines, double pipes and pan-pipes, which were all used in the worship of Bacchus (Toynbee 1962: pls. 115–17).

Religious ritual in general would have involved the use of the larger brass section, such as the *tuba*, the *lituus*, the *cornu* or the carnyx, all of which also had a military role. Mouth-pieces, usually of bronze, have been found on a number of sites, such as Lydney (Wheeler and Wheeler 1932: 81, fig. 16) and Colchester (Webster 1960: 75, no. 43); a carnyx, now lost, was found at Tattershall (Piggott 1959: pl. VI). The sistrum, a rattle with loose discs strung along metal bars within a small frame, was mostly associated with the worship of Isis, a sect that particularly appealed to women, and is occasionally found decorating the heads of hairpins (see also Chapter 12).

Fragments of musical instruments have been found which may indicate that music was also played in the Romano-British home. A pair of bone mounts from the yoke of a lyre was found in a fifth-century context at Abingdon, and a similar piece of antler from Dinorben has raised the possibility that the lyre had been played in Britain from the late Iron Age. A bone tuning peg from a large stringed instrument, perhaps a lute, has lately been found in the City of London (G. Lawson, pers. comm.); both lyres and lutes had their strings attached to such devices. The players touched the strings with one hand and either plucked or strummed with the other, possibly using a plectrum.

A small figurine of a young woman from Silchester holds a tibia, a reed pipe which was played either singly or in pairs (Plate 44). An eight-pipe set of pan-pipes found at Shakenoak, which might be identified as the syrinx of Latin poetry, is inscribed with the name Bellicia, presumably the owner (Wright and Hassall 1973: no. 30). It is possible the graded bone pipes found at Corbridge came from a similar instrument (Forster and Knowles 1915: fig. 6). Small pipes have been found in ivory and bone on several sites in London but, unfortunately, none comes from an unequivocally Roman context (Wheeler 1930: pl. XLVII.B). One has a single note and might be more accurately described as a whistle. Part of a wooden pipe found in a well at Ashton, Northamptonshire, belonged to a much larger instrument, probably similar to the one played by the Silchester figurine, and would have been sounded by means of an inserted reed (G. Lawson, pers. comm.). Another of bone, from London, has bronze sleeves which allow the finger-holes to be opened and closed in different combinations (Lawson and Wardle 1998). Such fine equipment had smaller, rustic equivalents, also reed-voiced; a baked clay pipe found at Lydiard Tregoze in Wiltshire seems to represent this sort of popular, everyday music making (G. Lawson, pers. comm.).

Some of the more elaborate instruments, such as the lute and the harp, have yet to be found in Britain though the presence of some may be indicated by fragments. Their forms may be inferred from Continental evidence and

Pl. 44 Bronze statuette of a girl playing a tibia, from Silchester

literary references. Some exotic instruments that are played by deities in art may not bear much relationship to everyday life, but there is evidence that the *hydraulis* was commonly played in military and theatrical contexts. The *hydraulis* was a form of organ, invented by Ctesibios of Alexandria at the end of the third century BC, in which air was pumped by hand into a chamber containing a bronze bell surrounded by water; notes were played by opening and closing vents by means of a keyboard, which forced air through pipes. In Britain, knowledge of the instrument is attested by its appearance, standing on a pedestal, as decoration on Castor ware vessels made in the Nene Valley, but although the many elements, of various materials, which made up a *hydraulis* have been recovered from sites on the Continent none has yet been identified in Britain.

Many of the performances in the theatres and amphitheatres would have had interludes of singing and dancing by professionals and both would have played their part in religious ceremonies, but little is known of singing and dancing in a domestic context. Some people would have hired professionals to entertain their guests after dinner parties but whether the hosts and their guests joined in is, as yet, unknown. The images of dancers on metalwork or pottery are confined to the followers of Bacchus and other deities.

Gardening

Diodorus Siculus was of the opinion that a garden was 'a useful device for avoiding confusion when crowds are present' (V.40). Much of our knowledge of Roman gardens is based on excavations in Italy, with only a few examples in Britain, such as Fishbourne, having been investigated in any detail. However, we should not presume because of the limited evidence so far available that the people of Roman Britain did not appreciate the leisure potential of a garden. The discovery of bedding trenches, as at Fishbourne, is not the only indication of a garden: an excavation in Italy revealed the use of broken amphoras as seed trays. It should also be remembered that many of the agricultural tools discussed in Chapter 4 could also have been used in a more domestic context.

Plumbing requisites, such as drainpipes, may also indicate the provision of water features in a garden. Evidence elsewhere in the Empire suggests that these features could also be decorated with bronze decorative plaques, which might at first sight suggest furniture decoration; indeed, the existence of garden furniture should not be discounted.

Bathing

Plumbing was also an essential part of a bath-house. Bathing in the Roman period was not simply the answer to a human need for hygiene (see Chapter 11) but offered trading opportunities as well as many of the delights on offer in a modern leisure centre. A bather would see his or her time in the baths as an opportunity to meet friends, catch up on gossip and play games, as well as a chance for philosophical reflection. At the legionary baths at Caerleon the discovery of bone needles and two triangular weaving tablets shows that some of the bathers spent some of the time catching up on their mending or on handicrafts, such as embroidery or tablet weaving (Zienkiewicz 1986). These objects from the excavations at Caerleon also confirm that the use of the baths was not confined to the garrison, but that local residents, men, women and children, were also encouraged to use the facilities. A lead disc with one plain face and one face with the letters L.III contained within a wreath, has been identified as a *tessera balnearis* or entrance ticket (Zienkiewicz 1986: 26–7 following Rostowzew 1903; 1905), which may indicate that civilians had to pay for the pleasure of bathing or suggest a system of regulating when the baths were used and by whom.

Parties

Many leisure pursuits leave little evidence. An obvious example is the art of conversation. The layout of many villa dining rooms arranges the formal couches around a mosaic whose motif is based on the story of a classical myth, the intention being to provide a conversation piece. If the villa occupants invariably had the same guests to dinner, it is likely that the mosaic would have soon lost its usefulness as a conversational gambit, but the motifs do indicate the owner and his family's level of education and suggest that they may have read for pleasure (see Chapter 6).

The presence of formal dining rooms in most British villas indicates that holding dinner parties was regarded as a pleasant way of entertaining friends as well as conducting business. The famous Vindolanda writing-tablet in which Claudia Severa invites her friend or sister Sulpicia Lepidina to a party to celebrate her birthday also reveals that holding events to mark important occasions was common (*Tab. Vindol.* nos. 244, 291–4). Not all these events would have been open to both sexes; indeed, many would have been strictly men-only drinking parties. It is noticeable that most of the glass and pottery vessels that show scenes of hunting, horse and chariot racing, pugilism and gladiatorial combat are drinking cups and it is likely that these were used during male drinking parties. It is also noticeable that most of the pottery drinking cups have very narrow bases, making them difficult to place safely on a table if the drinker had had several drinks.

Pl. 45 Bronze dodecahedron from South Shields

Conclusion

It is possible that we are not recognising all the objects used for leisure pursuits in Roman Britain because they do not equate with the objects we would use today. An example of this may be the ambiguous dodecahedra that have been found on a number of British sites (Plate 45). Various suggestions as to their use have been put forward. In 1922 their resemblance to the polygonal dice of the seventeenth century was noted (Smith 1922). The lack of distinguishing marks on the faces proved a problem until it was suggested that the interior of the dodecahedron was filled with wax (as seen on the example from Feldberg) and numbers or letters inscribed on the wax. An alternative use could be the game known as 'A Voyage around the World', in which each knob represented a place and the player had to wind a thread round each knob only once on his journey 'around the world' (Biggs, Lloyd and Wilson 1976: 31–6). There are, however, many more suggestions, each as likely as the other.

The willingness of archaeologists to consider the idea that bronze dodec-ahedra might have been used for a game indicates an awareness that the people of the Roman world at all levels of society did have leisure time and many ways of spending that time. However, it is also just as easy to presume that a more serious object was used for frivolous pursuits. The suggestion that bone discs must have been used for a game like tiddlywinks, because of the bevels on their reverse faces, is a case in point. A. MacGregor (1976) showed that the bevel was the natural result of using long bones whose wall curvature made it impossible to cut a totally flat disc. As has been discussed, it is even possible that some of the discs were intended not for a board game but for the more prosaic pursuit of accounting.

RALPH JACKSON

In 1996 the cremated remains of a healer were found in excavations at Stanway, close to the major Iron Age centre at Gosbecks, to the west of Colchester (Crummy 1997: 66–70; Crummy *et al.* 2007). The burial, dated *c.*AD 50–60, contained a set of fourteen surgical instruments as well as other objects which may have had healing applications (Jackson 1997a; 2007). This set (Plate 46) is not only the earliest such find from Britain but also one of the earliest surviving *instrumentaria* from anywhere in the ancient world; for, while individual instruments are known from earlier contexts, it is not until the first century AD that securely dated sets of instruments have been found. While the interment of the healer and his *instrumentarium* post-dates AD 43, the manufacture and initial use of the instruments are likely to have ante-dated the conquest. In other words, the instruments are probably native British rather than Roman or Romano-British and the healer may have practised medicine before and after the conquest. Whether he was a native Briton or a newcomer, perhaps a refugee from Gaul in the early first century AD, is uncertain, but his instrumentation suggests he was acquainted with both Iron Age and classical healing systems and he may well have been in contact with Roman as well as Gallo-Roman and native British healing personnel.

The burial provides a vivid snapshot of the nature of medicine and healing at the time and, as such, is unique in Britain. Our knowledge of healing during the Iron Age is limited to a small number of unambiguous medical artefacts and Pliny's references to druids which suggest that herbalism and religious and magical therapies fell within their ambit (Pliny *Nat. Hist.* XXIV.103–4). After the conquest there is a wider range of evidence, but it is scattered and fragmentary. We know the names of a small number of army medical personnel at Chester (*RIB* 461), Maryport (*RIB* 808), Binchester (*RIB* 1028) and Housesteads (Plate 47; *RIB* 1618; Gilson 1978). Hospitals (*valetundinaria*), consisting of a central courtyard surrounded by a range of rooms, have been identified in the legionary fortresses at Inchtuthil, Caerleon and Chester as well as in the auxiliary forts of Hod Hill, Benwell, Housesteads, Wallsend, Pen Llystyn and Fendoch. While the function of these buildings has been the subject of debate (Baker 2002; Künzl 2005),

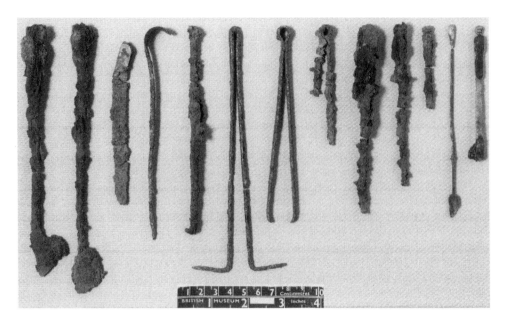

Pl. 46 The set of medical instruments found in the 'Doctor's Grave' at Stanway. Left to right: two scalpels, saw, two hooks, (?) retractor, forceps, tweezers, three handled needles, scoop probe, handle.

largely because of the lack of medical or surgical instruments found within them, it is very likely that most, if not all, were intended as healing centres. It is also clear that Bath was one of the principal Roman spas in the western Empire, as altars and tombstones of soldiers from a wide variety of military units have been found alongside dedications by civilians (*RIB* 139, 143, 144, 146, 147, 152, 156, 157, 158, 159, 160). Spa treatments and baths were recommended for a very wide spectrum of ailments and were undoubtedly among the milder and more positive aspects of medicine in the ancient world (Yegül 1992: 352–5; Jackson 1999; Fagan 2006).

People relied on a range of different strategies to combat disease, including divine intervention, personal hygiene and recourse to healers and doctors. Doctors themselves used a variety of approaches, as can be seen in the preface of Scribonius Largus' work *Compositiones* (*Drug Recipes*) (Sconocchia 1983; Hamilton 1986). Of all the Roman medical writers, Largus (*fl. c.*AD 14–54) is of particular relevance to Roman Britain, as he visited the country as part of Claudius' retinue in AD 43 (Nutton 2004: 172–4; Hanson 2006: 498–9). He advocated a progression from diet to drugs and only then to surgery and cauterisation. The evidence for diet and drugs lies beyond the scope of this volume, but other finds can be used to explore the other remedies available.

Pl. 47 Tombstone of the *medicus* Anicus Ingenuus, from Housesteads

Divine medicine

'Either help or do not harm the patient' was a sound and thoughtful piece of advice given in *Epidemics* III, part of the Hippocratic writings. At a time when a cure for many diseases was elusive and rarely predictable, and 'death . . . was the occupational hazard of being a patient' (Nutton 1986: 36), it was essential to avoid ill-health. As a result, much thought and effort went into the prevention of illness and Greek and Roman medical writers devoted considerable space to discussing preventative measures. Their positive regimen for health included environment, dietetics, exercise, lifestyle, hygiene and body care, but an integral part was played by religious rituals and the power of belief. The gods had the power to inflict or ward off disease and those powers were believed in and accepted by patient and healer alike, as is clear from contemporary texts and imagery.

Many deities had a healing aspect, but some, such as Apollo or Minerva (sometimes with the epithet Medica), had specific healing powers. In particular, there was Aesculapius (Greek Asklepios) and his daughter Salus (Greek Hygieia). No Aesculapian healing sanctuary has been found so far in Britain, but at Lydney (Glos.) a cult-centre of the god Nodens appears to have functioned in a similar way. The complex comprises buildings identified as temple, guest house, baths and – adjacent to the temple – a possible *abaton*, or 'sacred dormitory', where suppliants underwent 'incubation', the 'temple sleep' in which they hoped to receive a divine cure for their malady. This may have come in the form of a mystifying dream prescription; if so, Victorinus, mentioned on a border inscription of the temple mosaic, would have assisted the suppliant towards an understanding, for he was an interpreter of divine-inspired dreams (*RIB* II.4, 2448.3). The end-product of a similar process at Bath may be represented by a fragmentary inscription recording part of a dedication by Novantius in response to a vision (*RIB* 153).

Belief in Aesculapius is evidenced by a modest number of stone altars, dedication-slabs and relief sculptures from military sites in northern Britain. Most of the altars are dedicated to Aesculapius alone or to Aesculapius and Hygieia or Salus, though sometimes with the addition of other deities such as Fortuna or Panakeia. A relief from Risingham (now lost) shows Aesculapius and Hygieia accompanied by Telesphorus, hooded god of convalescence (Phillips 1977: no. 220). A few are in Greek but most of the texts are in Latin while an altar from Lanchester has a parallel text in Latin and Greek, perhaps in the hope of harnessing more divine curative power (*RIB* 1072). A fulsome dedication to Salus (*Salus regina*) on an altar from Caerleon (*RIB* 324) is joined by an intaglio depicting Hygieia found in the fort at Brecon Gaer (Henig 1978: no. 285), but such finds are scarce and the only British example of an intaglio showing Aesculapius and Hygieia together comes from Braintree. Another, equally rare, find from southern Britain is a bronze figurine from near Chichester showing Aesculapius standing in

Pl. 48 Bronze figurine of Aesculapius, found near Chichester, height 6.4 cm

classic pose with the serpent-entwined staff symbolising the support he gave to the sick (Plate 48). Areas rubbed smooth through wear suggest long-term handling by devotees, a vivid reminder of belief in divine power (Jackson 1995b).

Taken together, these finds suggest that the followers of Aesculapius and his 'family' were principally incomers, often from the upper social stratum, some Greek-speaking, many demonstrably or probably medical practitioners, and mostly connected to the Roman army. Others in Roman

Britain probably sought good health by placating and dedicating to a broader pantheon of British and Roman deities and spirits.

Other incomers, although probably from a different social stratum, are evident in magical invocations. Childbirth involved several potential hazards and many women must have died from uterine haemorrhage and puerperal sepsis. There are several examples of a mother buried with a foetus, while a neonatal burial with cut-marks, suggesting embryotomy, has been recognised in the cemetery population at Poundbury, Dorset (Roberts and Cox 2003: 160–1, fig. 3.17). In the hope of protection during pregnancy and childbirth, as well as from uterine disorders, some women had amulets or magical protective texts ('phylacteries'). One, from West Deeping, near Peterborough, is a tightly rolled lead sheet incised with a spell written in fourth-century cursive Latin. It invokes the power of three magical protective deities, derived from Hebrew scriptures, Iao, Sabao(th) and Adonai, to protect Cleuomedes from the pain of a displaced womb and commanding it to stay in its place (Tomlin 1997). Even though Soranus and Galen in the second century AD dismissed the idea of a 'wandering womb', it was linked to a Hippocratic doctrine and had a long tradition that proved very persistent (Jackson 1988: 89–90). Another, an amulet, also of fourth-century date, comes from a Roman building at Dicket Mead, near Welwyn. It is a tiny oval haematite stone engraved on both faces with images which include depictions of a womb. The combination of motifs and words drawn from Greek, Egyptian and Semitic beliefs invested magical power in the amulet, which was probably sewn into clothing or kept in a pouch, if not worn in a finger-ring (Jackson 1988: 106; *RIB* II.3, 2423.1).

Mortal medicine

The third part of the Art of Medicine is that which cures by the hand... It does not omit medicaments and regulated diets, but does most by hand. The effects of this treatment are more obvious than any other kind. (Celsus *De Medicina* VII, prooemium 1)

To Cornelius Celsus, writing in the early first century AD, the effects of surgery were the most readily apparent part of healing. Any change in the patient's condition, whether beneficial or detrimental, was clearly attributable to the hand of the surgeon in both a metaphorical and a literal sense. Similarly, surgical tools are, to us, the most readily recognisable and unequivocal artefacts of Roman medicine. Just as Celsus observed that surgical practitioners of his era did not neglect the use of medicaments and diet, however, we should not neglect to seek in the surviving material remains of Roman Britain the artefacts involved in drug treatments, body care and dietary measures in addition to surgical tools. In fact, despite Celsus' tripartite division, medicine in antiquity had none of the compartmentalisation that characterises healing systems today and the spectrum of healers was very wide. In consequence, a diverse range of artefacts had a potential part to play in treating or preventing disease. Not all were intended exclusively or primarily for healing or health-preserving roles and it is important to differentiate the distinctively medical pieces from those of a quasi-medical nature which cannot be used as unequivocal evidence of medical treatment (Jackson 1990a; 2002; Künzl 1996).

Wounds and injuries have been a part of human suffering since earliest prehistory and treatment was a natural response. The great majority of surgical interventions would have taken place within the soft tissues, which rarely survive, but a few were located in, or penetrated to, underlying bone, and cranial trepanation has been identified in human skeletons at least as far back as the early Neolithic period, although the instruments used for the procedure have not been identified. Even with the upsurge of medical activity in ancient Greece there are surprisingly few surviving surgical tools to accompany the wealth of medical texts. Part of the explanation may be that while some surgical interventions required a specific and purpose-made instrument others did not and could be performed using household, personal or craft implements, such as *stili*, quills, strigils, razors or carpenter's chisels (Jackson 1994: Table 3). Potentially, a considerable part of ancient surgery could be performed without any identifiably 'surgical' instruments and by practitioners who were neither full-time nor formal healers. If, as seems likely, such loan tools were the norm, the surviving identifiable surgical instruments should be regarded as representing only the visible tip of a large iceberg of surgical activity.

By the early years of the first century AD an increasingly large number of distinctive, purpose-made, metal surgical instruments begin to appear in the archaeological record. This coincides not only with the date of Celsus' *De Medicina*, in which many operations and instruments are described, but also with an increase in the evidence for medical personnel (Kudlien 1986; Korpela 1987) and it is conceivable that this proliferation reflects a real increase in professional medical and surgical activity. The contemporary military reforms under Augustus, which probably resulted in improved medical provision for all types of unit, may have ensured the widespread diffusion of Graeco-Roman medical theory and practice and of Roman surgical instrumentation throughout the Empire. From this time on, metal surgical instruments of diagnostic type were made and used throughout the Roman world and their forms remained surprisingly constant.

It is important to recognise that even at this period, when surgical tools in metal become more recognisable, we have only a partial picture of the available instrumentation. Celsus mentions implements and paraphernalia of wood, leather, textile, papyrus, reed and feather (Jackson 1994: Tables 2–4), virtually none of which has been detected in the archaeological record. Rare also are such vulnerable materials as bone and glass, while even some of the metal instruments, notably vessels and containers made from thin bronze sheet and fine iron needles and blades, have often perished or corroded beyond recognition.

The craftsmen who made medical implements and surgical instruments in metal had a good understanding of, and control over, their materials – principally copper and its alloys and wrought iron. If an intricate form or surface treatment was required, copper alloy was the normal medium. Sometimes a specific alloy-type, or a combination of alloy-types, was chosen to enhance the decoration or improve function. For example, the rectangular and tubular drug boxes made from fine copper sheet correspond to the advice given by Dioscorides and others that certain medicaments, especially moist eye-drugs, should be stored in copper vessels (*De Materia Medica* Preface, 9; Jackson 1988: 74). Where robustness of an instrument or component took precedence, as, for example, for bone levers, iron was usually selected as the most appropriate material. It was also favoured, above all, for blades and needles, where a sharp and durable operative edge or point was sought. Some Roman smiths knew and exploited the advantages of steeling by carburisation, which allowed them to combine the qualities of a tough and durable wrought iron blade with a sharp, steeled cutting edge. Galen (II.682K), always adept and assiduous in obtaining top-quality medical materials, knew that he could acquire the best scalpel blades from the Alpine province of Noricum, where the ores of iron yield a natural steel.

Galen practised in elite society in the second century AD and was highly skilled in surgery and in public displays of animal dissection, so probably had no need for ornate instruments, but other practitioners, less well placed, may have found benefit from instrumentation that impressed, by either its novelty, its ingenuity or its decoration. That the second-century satirist Lucian (*Adversus Indoctum* III.29) could assert that he preferred a knowledgeable surgeon with a rusty knife to a charlatan with fancy equipment suggests as much. Many prospective patients quite likely made the assumption that costly instruments represent wealth, which reflects success and, by implication, a skilled operator. Certainly, some Roman instruments display innovative and ingenious design features while others are very ornately decorated or inlaid with costly materials (Fig. 19(d)), including Corinthian bronze (black gold). Others incorporate divine healing imagery such as decorative finials in the form of that most potent of Aesculapian healing attributes, the snake. Belief in the transfer of divine power through the instrument may well have given confidence and benefit to both patient and practitioner.

In addition to the provision of figured, moulded or inlaid decoration on handles, Roman medical implements and surgical instruments display a number of recurrent distinguishing features, notably a careful and effective design, precise, high-quality craftsmanship in manufacture and finish, and dual-purpose or multiple usage. Like the tools of other craftsmen, discussed in other chapters of this volume, optimum instrument design developed in accordance to function, and that design was not altered unless the function changed or new manufacturing materials became available. Since the instruments were adapted to human anatomy and to operations on the human body, their function did not change and some are closely paralleled by their pre-modern or modern counterparts. Careful attention was paid to finish, whether the immaculately smooth surface of those instrument parts intended for insertion into wounds, incisions or the natural body orifices, or the precise interlocking of finely cut teeth on the jaws of the uvula forceps (*staphylagra*) (Fig. 20(a)). Both basic and specialised instruments were designed as multi-purpose tools; a common device was to mount two instruments on one handle, one at either end, and many combinations are known: scalpel with blunt dissector, sharp hook with blunt hook, forceps with sharp hook, needle or probe, lithotomy knife and scoop, double blunt hook, double bone lever, double needle, double probe (see, for example, Figs. 17; 18(c); 19(c); 20(c)).

One very distinctive form of socket, a carefully profiled keyhole-shaped slot, appears to have been used almost exclusively for surgical instruments. It occurs most frequently on scalpel handles with a rectangular grip (Fig. 17(a)) but is also the form of attachment of other composite copper-alloy and iron instruments, including forceps, shears and bone levers, in each case comprising iron operative parts fitted to copper-alloy handles. There were good practical reasons for the manufacture of combination tools. Instrument costs could be reduced, the healer's kit could be kept relatively compact and portable, and an operation could be performed with the minimum number of instruments, saving valuable seconds at a time when speed was of the essence. Thus, design, craftsmanship, ingenuity, decor

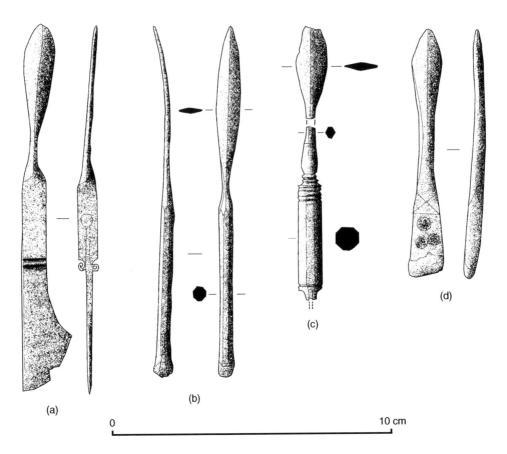

Fig. 17 (a) Scalpel from London, copper-alloy handle, iron blade; (b) copper-alloy scalpel handle from Canterbury; (c) copper-alloy scalpel handle from Gadebridge Park; (d) copper-alloy scalpel handle inlaid with enamel, from Caistor St Edmund

and economy all combined to increase the practitioner's control over the operations that he undertook.

Large comprehensive sets of medical instruments are rare finds in the Roman Empire (Jackson 1995a; 2003). Rather less so are the kits of basic tools, the portable sets that contained the essential instruments of surgery (Künzl 1983). Excepting the Stanway find (Plate 46), Britain has yielded no certain set, large or small. A group of eight instruments, said to have been found at the fort at Cramond, near Edinburgh (Gilson 1983), may well comprise such a set but their provenance is insecure and may not be British. Unconfirmed, also, is the unpublished 'medical box' with instruments reported to have been found in the 1930s 'south of the main east–west road at Corbridge', but lost during the Second World War (Gilson 1981: 5;

Allason-Jones 1999b: 141). Equally tantalising are what may be the remains of a small kit from excavations (1898–1903) at the military site at Wilder-spool, Lancashire – a scalpel, broken forceps, scoop probe and tubular instrument case, illustrated together but with no context information given (May 1904: 79–81, nos. 5, 10, 12, 13).

The most striking aspect of the Stanway kit is the predominant use of iron: there are eight iron instruments, two composite tools of iron and copper alloy, and just four single-piece copper-alloy instruments, only one of which, the scoop probe, is of a distinctive Roman form. This preponderance of iron instruments is at variance with Roman sets in which copper-alloy or composite tools predominate. Single-piece iron instruments are characteristic of the admittedly small number of surviving Celtic medical kits (Künzl 1995), notably those in the La Tène C graves at München-Obermenzing, Batina/Kis Köszeg and Galatii Bistritei, and it is conceivable that the maker of the Stanway instruments was following a distinctive Iron Age tradition. Of the eight iron instruments, six have decorative finials, in three cases with adjacent mouldings. Their similarity suggests manufacture by the same artisan or in the same workshop, probably located in the Colchester region.

While the Stanway instruments are individually idiosyncratic, the range and types of instrument are not, and the composition of the kit – surgical knives, a small saw, sharp and blunt hooks (retractors), forceps, handled needles and a probe – corresponds very closely to examples from the Roman world. In particular it accords with the basic sets of metal instruments which were essential to perform the majority of surgical interventions. It could be argued that such similarity in composition is a product purely of function and that it represents independent invention in response to common needs. More probably it was a result of increased contact between Britain and the Roman world in the decades prior to the invasion.

Further new finds, especially those from burials or 'catastrophe' contexts, as at Rimini in Italy (Jackson 2003; 2009), may transform our picture of healing in Britain. Meanwhile, Roman Britain may be compared to other provinces of the Empire in range, if not in sheer numbers, of medical artefacts. Whether located casually or discovered in excavated contexts, most medical instruments are found individually. They are not numerous but are widely distributed throughout Britain and are not confined to or especially concentrated in the south or in military or civilian spheres, although there is a tendency towards towns. Those from dated contexts span the whole period when Britain was a province of Rome, from forceps in a conquest-period context at Richborough to a specialised form of probe (*dipyrene*) in a later fourth-century deposit at Dorchester, Dorset. The majority of instruments are those types included in the basic sets – scalpels, forceps, sharp and blunt hooks, surgical needles and probes (Figs. 17–19; Jackson 1990a: figs. 1–4).

Commonest is the scalpel, foremost instrument and symbol of surgery (Fig. 17). Virtually all examples are of the distinctive Roman form comprising an iron blade slotted into a copper-alloy grip with a leaf-shaped blunt dissector, but only one (from London) retains the iron blade intact. Most have either a block-like rectangular grip (Type I) or a more slender octagonal-sectioned grip (Type II), with either a simple slot or a keyhole-type blade socket (Jackson 1986: 132–6). There is also a very slender square-sectioned variant with a tiny socket, suggestive of fine and delicate surgery. Inlaid, moulded or incised decoration is occasionally present on all types. The blade was firmly secured, often by solder, and was not readily detachable like its modern counterpart, but it could be replaced by a smith when worn out or broken. The Rimini find demonstrates the potential variety of blade shapes and sizes (Jackson 2003; 2009: Fig. 1). The scalpel was required for the treatment of injuries and wounds, when soft tissue and structures needed cutting, but it was also used to create an incision in elective surgery. It was a combination tool designed to maximise function, economy and ease of use, and its blunt dissector had a wide range of applications from removal of dermoid cysts to surgery of the scrotum. The simplest of all surgical interventions was the incision of a vein for the letting of blood (venesection), a very common expedient in Roman medicine designed to restore the equilibrium of the body by bringing the bodily humours back into harmony (Jackson 1988: 70–3). Venesection could be speeded up by applying a suction cup (*cucurbitula*) to the incision, and many bronze examples have survived throughout the Empire. Curiously, no example has yet been found in Britain, perhaps suggesting the theory took less of a hold in Roman Britain.

The forceps in the basic set was a spring forceps (Fig. 18), usually of copper alloy but occasionally made from iron. Most of the British examples are the general-purpose fixation forceps (Figs. 18(a) and (b)), which has in-turned, smooth, square-ended jaws, and whose uses included dissection and surgical epilation for in-growing eyelashes (*trichiasis*) (Jackson 1996a: 2245–6). Rather less numerous are examples of the toothed fixation forceps, a similarly versatile instrument used to fix, raise and excise skin, tissue or growths. A specialised variant, with broad toothed jaws turned to one side (Fig. 18(d)), was probably used for clamping growths, tumours and blood vessels. An example from Silchester preserves its sliding lock ring, which facilitated sustained clamping, while the forceps from Littleborough has a hooked finial in the form of a stylised Aesculapian snake's head (Jackson and Leahy 1990). The third variety was a pointed-jawed forceps which

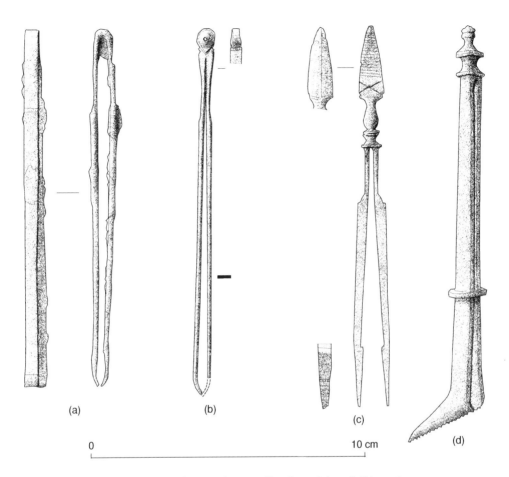

Fig. 18 (a) Smooth-jawed fixation forceps of copper alloy, from Caistor St Edmund; (b) smooth-jawed fixation forceps of copper alloy, from St Albans; (c) pointed-jawed forceps with elevator of copper alloy, from Lancaster; (d) coudée-type toothed fixation forceps of copper alloy, from Silchester

often had fine ridging on the contact face of the jaws to maximise grip and minimise tissue damage. Its use was stipulated in bone surgery but it must also have had many other applications in delicate surgery. A fine example found within the second-century fort at Lancaster (Fig. 18(c); Shotter and White 1990: 37, fig. 6) was combined with a bone lever (elevator) and was probably used principally for skull surgery (Jackson 2005b: 114–15 and fig. 5.2, 4).

Sharp hooks were indispensable in ancient surgery (Fig. 19(a) and (c)). Their principal function was to retract and fix the margins of wounds and incisions or underlying tissue and structure but they also served to seize and raise for excision small structures or tissue, as in the operations for tonsillectomy, *pterygium* (surgery in the angle of the eye) and contraction

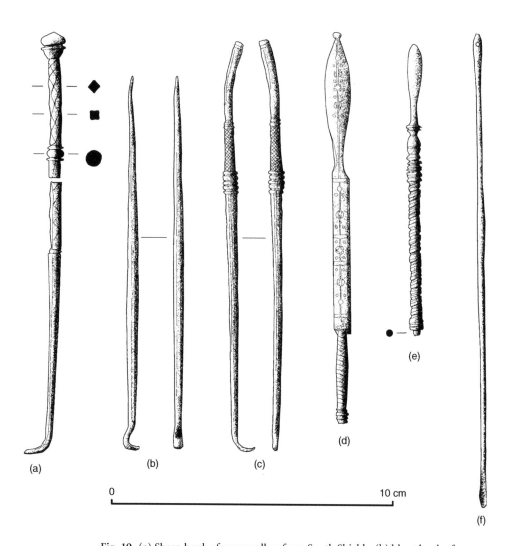

Fig. 19 (a) Sharp hook of copper alloy, from South Shields; (b) blunt hook of copper alloy, from Springhead; (c) needle-holder combined with sharp hook, from London; (d) needle-holder inlaid with silver, from Rochester; (e) broken cataract needle of copper alloy, from Piddington; (f) eyed *dipyrene* of copper alloy, from Colchester

of the vulva (Celsus *De Medicina* VII.7.5; VII.12.2; Paul of Aegina VI.30). To avoid tissue damage and inflammation, the tip was worked to a very fine point, while the distal end of the slender stem is usually decorated with mouldings and facets, surmounted by a knobbed finial, to ensure the operator's fingers did not slip. Excepting the Stanway iron example (Plate 46), British survivors are of copper alloy, as at London, Wroxeter, Silchester, Wanborough and South Shields. A fine example from Housesteads

complements the discovery there of the *medicus* Anicius Ingenuus'
tombstone (Plate 47) and the proposed hospital building (Allason-Jones
1979). The less commonly found blunt hook was used for operations in
which sensitive retraction was involved and puncturing was to be avoided,
above all in the raising of blood vessels, either to isolate them or as a
preliminary to excision. Double-ended instruments combining sharp and
blunt hooks were popular and especially well suited to the operation for
the excision of varicose veins. British examples include those from Stanway
(Plate 46) and Springhead, Kent (Fig. 19(b)), while an instrument from
London combines a blunt hook with a spatula.

The various eyed needles mentioned in the medical texts included a
domestic type for stitching the end of a bandage as well as surgical needles for
suturing, ligaturing and passing a thread. Fine-pointed needles were used for
dissection and cauterisation as well as for perforating pustules, puncturing
skin and haemorrhoids, raising the skin of the eyelid and transfixing small
tumours on the eyeball. Most of these surgical needles would have been tiny
iron instruments and they have not survived, but one variety consisted of
an iron needle point fixed into the socket of a copper-alloy handle, while an
even more distinctive version comprised a slender copper-alloy grip with
an iron needle soldered into a fine socket at one or both ends. Both types
are often found in surgical kits, and British examples include a bone handle
from Southwark and socketed needle holders from London and Rochester
(Fig. 19(c) and (d)), the former combined with a sharp hook, the latter with
an exquisite silver-inlaid design on its handle.

Another distinctive type of needle was a single-piece, copper-alloy instrument with a round-pointed tip, a slender, often decorated, stem and an
olivary terminal. It has been convincingly identified as the instrument recommended for couching cataracts (Künzl 1983: 26–7; Feugère, Künzl and
Weisser 1985: 436–68). The breaking up (couching) of the lens with the tip
of the cataract needle was a delicate, audacious operation – the only ancient
surgery within the eyeball – but one with a reasonable chance of success and
it remained popular up to recent times (Jackson 1988: 121–3; 1996a: 2248–
50). However, it should not be assumed that cataract couching was done
exclusively with this type of needle or that the cataract needle was restricted
to that one operation. Broken examples are difficult to distinguish from
broken scoop probes and no certain cataract needle has survived in Britain,
although there are near-certain examples from Carlisle and Piddington villa
(Fig. 19(e)) and less certain candidates from Caerleon and Alcester. A fragmentary implement identified as a cataract needle at the Brading villa is a
broken scoop probe.

At a time when much internal anatomy was ill-understood, surgical probes had an important role in the exploratory sounding of wounds, incisions and fistulae in advance of surgery. They also had many other surgical and medical uses, from the elevation of cartilage in a broken nose to the application of medication to the eyeball. In consequence, sets of instruments often include several different types, all of which have been found in Britain. The finest exploratory probe was the *dipyrene* 'double olive', a double-ended instrument with an extremely slender stem and a tiny olivary expansion at each terminal, one of which was often provided with an eye so that it could be used with a thread for such operations as the treatment of nasal polyp or anal fistula (Celsus *De Medicina* VII.4.4A–D; Paul of Aegina VI.25). Eyed *dipyrenes* are known from London, Colchester (Fig. 19(f)), Lincoln, Caerwent, Lullingstone and Wanborough and there are solid *dipyrenes* from Richborough, Gloucester and London. Simpler probes, with a pointed tip combined with an olivary terminal, or a plain stem and a pointed tip at each end, as at Corbridge or Lullingstone, could have served as needles in addition to dissecting and exploratory uses. Instrument sets frequently include a scoop probe (*cyathiscomele*) and a spatula probe (*spathomele*) – olivary probes combined respectively with a slender scoop or a spatula – and a *ligula*, a tiny angled disc at the end of a slender pointed probe. Their medical uses, while including surgical applications, were principally pharmaceutical, but above all they were very widely used for toilet and cosmetic purposes and cannot be considered medical unless found with other assuredly medical instruments (see also Chapter 9).

In addition to their principal roles, most of the instruments described above could also have been used as cauteries – vehicles for transferring and applying heat. Though considered an extreme measure, cauterisation was frequently referred to in the medical texts, especially in delicate or small-scale interventions, and it is likely that the beneficial effect of a heated instrument had registered even though there was no knowledge of the need for sterilisation. The main applications were in staunching haemorrhage, destroying unhealthy or mortified tissue (especially ulcerations or carious bone) or removing healthy tissue to gain access to underlying organs or structure. The correspondingly wide variety of size and shape of cautery was available within the existing instrumentation, whether blade, probe or needle (Jackson 1994: 177–9).

A number of more specialised instruments have also been found in Britain (Fig. 20). Those designed for bone surgery include a stout, cross-legged, iron

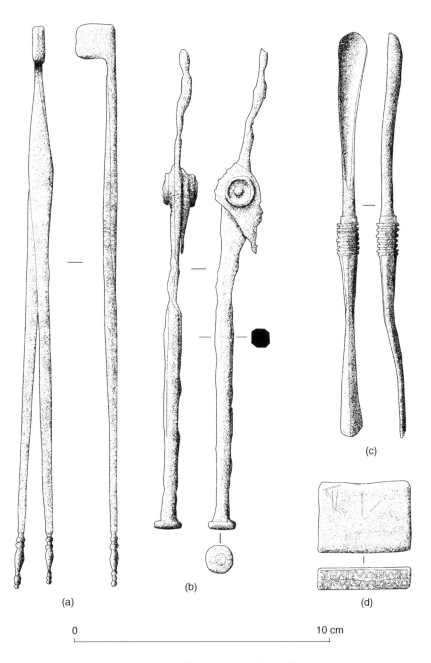

Fig. 20 (a) Uvula forceps of copper alloy, from Dorchester; (b) dental forceps
of iron, from Kirkby Thore; (c) combined curette and elevator of iron, from London;
(d) collyrium-stamp of stone, from Goldenbridge

forceps, which was used for grasping and repositioning fractured bones as well as for removing embedded projectiles; but above all there was a dental forceps, with the tips of its powerful jaws precisely adapted to the extraction of teeth (Jackson 1994: 175–6). A complete dental forceps was found in the cemetery at Littlington, and there are broken examples from the *vicus* of the fort at Castleford and from another fort/*vicus* context at Kirkby Thore (Fig. 20(b)). If tooth extraction proved problematic, bone splinters might require removal with a pointed-jawed forceps, like that from Lancaster (Fig. 18(c)), but the elevator terminal of that instrument also had wider applications in bone surgery. Another, much stouter, elevator is combined with a curette in a finely made single-piece iron instrument from London (Fig. 20(c)). The curette, a scoop with a sharp rim, was a key instrument of bone surgery in which it was used to remove necrotic tissue from chronically diseased bone that had become carious (Jackson 2005b: 102–4, fig. 5.2, 6).

Another cross-legged forceps, but of copper alloy, the *staphylagra*, was designed as a 'pile-crusher' to be used to avoid haemorrhage in the operations to amputate haemorrhoids or to trim an elongated uvula. Examples of the instrument, which has fine, sharp, precisely interlocking teeth set around two edges of the hollow jaws, come from Caerwent, Dorchester (Fig. 20(a)) and Ancaster, a jaw fragment from Leicester and a spring forceps variant from Colchester (Jackson 1992). The Ancaster forceps is significantly different from most other examples and was very likely made in Britain, if not in Ancaster. Further evidence of local manufacture, based on décor and variant form, includes scalpel handles from Caistor St Edmund (Fig. 17(d)), Hockwold, Wenhaston, Cossington and Kimpton, spring forceps from Verulamium (Fig. 18(b)), Richborough and London, a cross-legged forceps from Colchester and a sharp hook from London.

Apart from medical and surgical instrumentation there are a few other distinctive artefacts of medicine. Drug boxes took two principal forms, rectangular and tubular (Bliquez 1994: 66–9, 192–7, 202–3, pls. 18 and 24–6; Künzl 1996: figs. 12, 17–19, 32–4). There are fragmentary tubular copper alloy boxes from Wilderspool, Dover and South Shields. Rectangular drug boxes, made from copper-alloy sheet, bone or wood, have a sliding lid, sometimes ornately decorated with Aesculapian imagery (Künzl 1996: 2634–7), and often with a catch. These have between three and six lidded, rectangular, internal compartments (Jackson 1988: 74–5; Bliquez 1994: 191–2, pls. 24–5). British examples include a broken internal lid from Silchester and the sliding lid of a bone box from Feltwell. Remains and residues of medicaments have been found in both types of copper-alloy box. Other less distinctive drug boxes were also used, as, for example, the round box, of which only the lead lid survived, from Haltern, Germany, inscribed *ex radice britanica* (Fitzpatrick 1991), and the round tin canister of 'moisturising cream' from Tabard Square, London (Evershed *et al.* 2004).

More numerous are the small stone tablets, often called 'oculists' stamps' but more correctly termed collyrium-stamps (*RIB* II.4, 2446; Boon 1983), used for marking eye-ointments (*collyria*) (Fig. 20(d)). The fundamental importance of vision, the vulnerability of eyes to injury and disease, and the relative ease of access to them, resulted in the early development of eye medicine as a speciality (Jackson 1996a). However, in areas of low population density, like Roman Britain, specialisation was rarely feasible and eye treatments were probably administered by *medici* and other 'general practitioners'. It may be significant that the British collyrium-stamps, almost without exception, come from sites located on the main Roman road network, often from towns or their hinterland, places where a 'general practitioner' might access a viable 'market' (Jackson 1996b: 178–9, fig. 21.1; see also Chapter 6). Occasionally, as is clear from literary and papyrus sources, patients treated themselves, for ready-made *collyria* could be purchased in the marketplace (Jackson 1997b). Some were liquid or semi-liquid lotions; others were desiccated sticks, for which the ingredients, generally active and aromatic substances blended with an agglutinant, were mixed to a dough-like consistency, rolled into strips and allowed to dry. In Britain and the north-western provinces of the Empire the sticks were impressed with the edges of collyrium-stamps on which were engraved abbreviated Latin inscriptions, reversed to give a positive impression. These dies usually gave the name of the *collyrium*, the name of its originator or blender, and often an indication for use. The marked *collyria* could be stored together in a box or bag and, after noting the inscription, the user crumbled off the requisite amount and mixed it with water, wine, vinegar, milk or egg-white. Over 300 stamps have survived (Voinot 1999), of which thirty-two have a secure British provenance. Study of the inscriptions has shed light on the relative frequency of different eye diseases (Jackson 1990c; 1996b: 182–4): some thirty ailments are referred to, but in Britain, as elsewhere, almost half of the treatments were focused on just two clearly very prevalent and troublesome conditions – *aspritudo* (trachoma) and *lippitudo* (inflammation, ophthalmia and conjunctivitis) (Jackson 1990c: 282–3). The complicated medical jargon of the dies, as well as the occasional user's name incised on the planar faces of collyrium-stamps, implies that the healers were often literate and it is a reminder that the most important missing part of the material evidence is the medical literature – treatises, manuals and herbals – that some practitioners would doubtless have possessed.

Communal hygiene

Good hygiene is fundamental to good health, and sanitation is perhaps the most essential part of the communal response. The provision of water, the most basic of human needs, has as its counterpart the disposal of waste, both of which become more critical in an urban environment (Morley 2005). To judge from archaeological remains, there existed in Roman Britain at least the possibility of a healthy environment. Many towns and fortresses had baths, latrines and a sewage disposal system, and impressive stone-lined sewers and culverts have been found at York, London, Lincoln and Caerleon, although few of the above-ground structures for the provision of water have survived in recognisable form. In Roman Britain it is apparent that the whole spectrum of water sources would have been utilised (Burgers 2001), but the fetching of water from rivers, probably a major source for the rural poor, leaves little archaeological imprint, just as the above-ground collection of rain-water run-off from roofs, unless collected in stone tanks, is rarely discernible archaeologically. Most frequently encountered are wells, often preserving part of their stone or wooden lining; occasionally the remains of a fallen bucket and chain in the lowest levels survive, but rarely the windlass and well-head structure (see Chapter 7). Composite wood and metal force-pumps have been retrieved from wells in both urban (Silchester) and rural (Tarrant Hinton villa) domestic contexts and serve as a reminder that wells may act as a source for versatile and sophisticated water supplies (Stein 2004). Likewise, the notable discoveries of exceptionally well-preserved bucket-chain systems in two wells at Gresham Street, London – possibly 'the earliest surviving examples of mechanical engineering in Britain' (Blair and Hall 2003: 6) – graphically illustrate the potential for raising considerable quantities of water by such means. With a potential delivery of over 7,000 litres an hour, the eastern well could have supplied fresh water to several outlets – a fort, an amphitheatre and a bath-house were all big consumers in near proximity – and/or a sizeable part of London's population, perhaps through wooden pipes radiating from a distribution tank.

Such pipes, occasionally preserved as lengths of squared oak blocks with central bored holes (Wheeler 1930: 39, pl. XII) but most often evidenced only by the distinctive connecting flanged iron collars (Manning 1985: 128–9), were evidently widespread in Roman Britain, where ceramic and lead pipes, as well as stone- and wood-lined channels, were also used. As distribution systems they may have been connected to a variety of water sources, not exclusively the relatively small number of identifiable aqueducts. The great advantages of ducted supplies were, of course, that they could tap pure, palatable sources and, in theory, ensure a constant flow, though that was an ideal not always achieved. For drinking water, palatability was an important factor, as also the more wholesome nature of certain sources. Although medical writers credited rain water with beneficial effects, both as a medical ingredient and for convalescents, lay writers were less enthusiastic, favouring well water – Pliny noted that it was 'most commendable' and that wells were 'generally used in towns' (Pliny *Nat. Hist.* XXI.23) – but medical and lay writers alike extolled the qualities of fresh spring sources and mineral waters (Jackson 1988: 43–8; 1999).

Baths, like aqueducts, were a Roman introduction to Britain and were the most visible aspect of communal hygiene, as well as being one of the biggest consumers of water. Common and widespread, the baths ranged from the extensive *thermae* at Wroxeter, Leicester and Caerleon to small suites in villas, small forts and minor settlements. They combined a primary hygienic function with a social role and must have varied greatly in the volume and provision of water and level of hygiene: if water had to be raised from wells rather than running through aqueducts, the contents of pools and tanks may have been replenished infrequently. Immersion, however, whether in tanks, pools or sitz baths, was only a part of the Roman bathing process, which usually involved a progress through cold, warm and hot rooms, with access to basins of hot or cold water for washing and refreshing and the use of strigils and unguents for cleansing and deodorising (Yegül 1992: 30–47; Heinz 1996).

The potential benefit to community health of regular visits to baths was in the reduction of frequency of transmission of those epidemic diseases whose vectors thrived on unclean human bodies (Jackson 1988: 49). However, there were negative factors too, and the reality may often have been less salubrious (Scobie 1986; Allason-Jones 1999b: 139; Fagan 1999: 179–88; Roberts and Cox 2003: 130). A frequent, usually integral, facility at baths was the latrine, often of the communal, multi-seater variety. This was a natural adjunct on account of the numbers using the baths but also because baths required an efficient drainage system, part of which could be diverted under the latrine to flush away waste. However, the positive-sounding 'flushing latrine' may

Pl. 49 Bath set from Bayford (copper-alloy handle), London (iron strigil and glass oil flask) and Ribchester (copper-alloy pan)

not always have been what it appeared if, as was invariably the case, the flushing was intermittent rather than continuous and the waste outfall was not very far distant from the facility.

Personal hygiene

For those with the time, resources and inclination, personal hygiene and body care in Roman Britain might take a number of forms. Those considered here are the ones that have left some identifiable artefactual remains. Principal among them are the personal artefacts related to the communal practice of bathing, commonly referred to as 'bath sets' (Plate 49). These comprise a small range of utensils and accoutrements sometimes held on the straight bar of a distinctive D-shaped handle, the curving grip of which could be opened to detach one or more of the objects as they were required on the route through the bath. Surviving handles are of copper alloy or iron, in each instance made from thin strip metal and not easily identified when broken. Secured on the handle were one or more examples of a strigil, a pan and a flask. The strigil, of copper alloy or iron, comprised a slotted solid or open 'box' handle with a curved channelled 'blade', its tip rounded and the edges blunt. Adapted to the curves of the human body, it enabled the user, male or female, to scrape grime and sweat from the skin as part of the cleansing process in the hot room of a baths. Prior to that, and/or subsequently, the bather might detach the pan from the handle in order to take water from a basin for douching or refreshment. The pan, of copper alloy, had a low circular bowl, often with an ornate rim, and a solid flat handle with slotted end (often in the form of a keyhole), for attachment to the handle. The flask, which might be of copper alloy or glass, sometimes highly decorated, and often suspended from the handle by a chain, was used in the final stages of the bathing process for the application of oils or sweet-smelling unguents (Nenova-Merdjanova 1999).

In the Roman world, town baths were the setting for a host of activities linked to personal hygiene and well-being. Haircutting, shaving, depilation and manicure were among the services that might be available. The cutting of hair and trimming of moustache or beard were performed with blade and comb or with the ubiquitous spring shears (true scissors were unknown). Fine shears may also have been used for trimming nails and they had medical and surgical applications, too. Of iron, their form is undifferentiated from domestic, craft and agricultural examples, and specific usage can only be inferred from size and contextual evidence.

More surprisingly, perhaps, the artefacts of shaving have proved somewhat elusive in Britain and there is, for example, no consensus on the identification of razors (Riha 1986; Boon 1991). The blades for facial shaving, whether used singly or in pairs, would have been made from iron, probably with a steeled edge, and their thinness, like that of scalpel blades and surgical needles, made them especially vulnerable to corrosion, so they would be extremely difficult to identify in a rusted and fragmentary state. A case has been made for both narrow-bladed knives and a broad triangular-bladed variety, and diversity is probably to be expected. In the end it was the quality of the cutting edge and the skill of the barber that counted, and in the absence of any lotion other than water these were critical (Carcopino 1941: 157–64).

Tweezers, almost invariably with in-turned smooth jaws, were principally for epilation, though they would evidently have had a number of other body-care applications. Likewise, the so-called 'ear-scoop' would have had a multitude of hygiene uses beyond that of removing wax or foreign bodies from the outer ear. The forked nail-cleaner, too, was probably a general-purpose implement as well as a manicure tool. In addition to, or instead of, cleaning longer nails, it is possible that it was intended for paring the nails, the often sharp internal edges of the groove being guided along the nail by the pair of prongs. Short finger-nails appear from the evidence of Roman statuary to have been customary in elite groups in the Roman world (Boon 1991: 23), though such evidence is hardly conclusive or representative of a wider population. Nails were also pared with fine-bladed knives, with either a fixed or a folding blade, and many of the ornate examples from Roman Britain would have fitted the bill. As *personalia* it is probable that the knives served several other functions, including that of cutting or trimming quill pens.

Whatever the precise use of the individual implements, the popularity of 'toilet sets' in Roman Britain sheds light on attitudes to self-presentation and identity (see also Chapter 9). With large-scale production and removal of 'barriers of privilege', the nail-cleaner, for example, has been shown to have mutated from an elite Iron Age object to an everyday and distinctively Romano-British item, though intriguingly one which still appears to have reflected differences in social meaning (Crummy and Eckardt 2003: 61). Such a process may also be reflected by the British copper-alloy cosmetic sets, rare in an Iron Age context but widespread and ubiquitous in Britain in the Roman period. Significantly, two of the best-contexted complete cosmetic sets, from King Harry Lane, St Albans and from London, were found in association with toilet sets that included nail-cleaners (Stead and Rigby 1989: fig. 126; Jackson 1993: 165–7, fig. 2; 2006: nos. 436 and 319). Two-piece kits, comprising a grooved mortar and a solid, rod-like pestle, they were usually crescent-shaped, with a suspension loop at the centre or end (Fig. 21). Over six hundred examples have been recorded (Jackson 1985 and forthcoming) but only four outside Britain. Evidence of wear is frequently found on the working faces and there is strong circumstantial evidence that they were used for the preparation of powdered mineral cosmetics, most likely colourings for the eyelids and face rather than medicines. There is great variety in size, form and decoration, and the mortar is often elaborated, especially at the terminals, where animal heads, principally bulls (Fig. 21(b)), are a favoured motif. An association with fertility is indicated by the crescent shape, a few overtly phallic mortars and the occasional twinning of male and female animal heads. A frequent device was to model the end loop into the form of a bird's head (Fig. 21(a)). The extreme variability probably represents the customising of a very intimate possession – they were often selected as grave goods – and, perhaps as *personalia* associated with well-being and identity, they were sometimes chosen for temple offerings. In view of the fact that they co-existed in Roman Britain with the more universal Roman paraphernalia of cosmetic preparation – stone palettes, copper-alloy scoop-probes and spatula-probes, and glass, ceramic and metal *unguentaria* – it

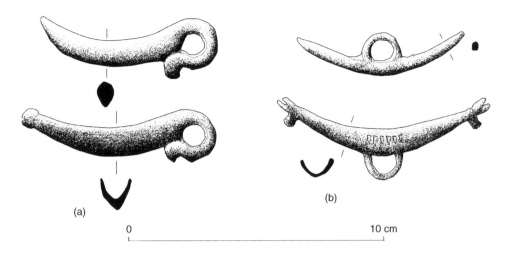

Fig. 21 (a) Cosmetic set of copper alloy, end-looped, from Beckford; (b) cosmetic set of copper alloy, centre-looped, from Chichester

is possible that they were used by those who wished to express or emphasise a British or Romano-British rather than a Roman identity.

Conclusion

From AD 43 until about AD 270 there were perhaps a dozen senatorial and fifty to sixty equestrian military personnel in Britain at any one time. Some of these men would have included a personal physician in their household, as also would the governor, the procurator and those emperors who came to Britain. As yet, no secure archaeological evidence of these healers has come to light, with the possible exception of two altars from Chester. This is hardly surprising. These were mainly brief stays, commissions of perhaps two or three years, and it is the medical personnel of the lower military ranks, the *medici ordinarii* and orderlies, that one might more reasonably expect to have remained in Britain for a longer period of service. At any one time, there may have been several hundred such men serving in the army of the province. Only a very few of them are recorded on stone inscriptions and, even if it is logical to imagine that some of the retiring military medical practitioners might have taken up healing in the civilian sphere, there is no clear evidence for such activity, nor for organised medical treatment centres beyond the forts and healing sanctuaries.

Although medical texts proper are missing from our remains of healing in Roman Britain, one fascinating quasi-textual source has come to light in the form of the Vindolanda writing-tablets. These tablets are a salutary reminder that current absence of evidence is not evidence of absence. Prior to the discovery of the tablets there was virtually no evidence for the practice of medicine amongst the material remains from the Vindolanda forts and *vici*. However, the tablets now provide a sort of case study of healing in a military context in Roman Britain around AD 100. There are a healer, Marcus the *medicus* (*Tab. Vindol.* II, 156), a hospital (*Tab. Vindol.* II, 155) and patients, the latter being listed in a strength report which states that fifteen of them were sick, six wounded and ten suffering from the eye disease *lippitudinis* (*Tab. Vindol.* II, 154). There are remedies, including one for fever, being passed between officers' wives (*Tab. Vindol.* II, 294), a pharmacist, Vitalis the *seplasiarius* (*Tab. Vindol.* III, 586) – recalling another *seplasiarius*, Albanus, in Carlisle (Tomlin 1991: 299–300, no. 24) – and medical supplies, including a very extensive list of commodities geared to the treatment of wounds, ulcers, sores and eye diseases, some of them possibly even the ingredients for a specific wound treatment recorded by Celsus (*De Medicina* V.19.9 and V.26.29), implying that his *De Medicina* or something similar was being used by the medical staff at Vindolanda (*Tab. Vindol.* III, 591). These fragmentary documents and letters allow us, metaphorically, to pull aside the curtain momentarily and glimpse the sort of medical activity that must have taken place, to a greater or lesser degree, throughout Roman Britain.

Few unequivocal medical instruments have been found in fortresses and forts, even in the buildings identified as hospitals, and, with the exception of the Stanway 'Doctor's Grave', virtually no medical instruments have been found in graves. There is, however, a widespread scatter of individual medical artefacts – mainly metal instruments and collyrium-stamps – throughout the province. We do not know who owned them, the exact circumstances or places in which they were used, or according to which medical theories they were employed. Whether they were utilised by men who called themselves *medicus* or *iatros* (or in the case of women, *medica* or *iatrine*), by other practitioners or part-time healers, or by the head of the household, their distribution and dating at least indicate that the practice of classical medicine, undoubtedly tempered by British traditions, became an established part of Romano-British culture. As if to underline that, one of the very few early Christian monuments from Britain to include a mention of the deceased's secular profession is that of Melus, son of Martinus, whose fifth-century AD epitaph, found at Llangian, near Pwllheli, describes him as *medicus* (Nash-Williams 1950: 88–90, no. 92).

12 | Religion

JOANNA BIRD

Religion in Britain, as elsewhere in the Roman world, permeated every aspect of life, endowing natural features of the landscape such as springs, pools and groves with numinous significance. A complex calendar filled the Roman year with religious festivals and observances, and there was a comparable calendar for the Celtic year (Henig 1984: 26–32). The conquest did not mean the overthrow of the native gods, but their integration into a wider pantheon. By a process of syncretism, many deities took on the names and attributes of approximate Roman equivalents, such as Mars Nodens at Lydney in Gloucestershire (Wheeler and Wheeler 1932), and local variations in cult and ritual are only now beginning to be discerned. As well as the classical gods of Rome, the cults of the military were introduced, together with more esoteric religions of oriental origin, such as the worship of Mithras, the Syrian god Jupiter Dolichenus and the Egyptian goddess Isis, and ultimately Christianity. As long as veneration was paid to the official imperial cult – and this was a civic as well as a religious duty – people were generally free to worship other gods as they wished.

Except for Jews and Christians, belief in one deity did not exclude the worship of others, and this is often reflected in the artefacts recovered from shrines. A notable example is the temple of Mithras in London, which housed images of a number of deities, including Minerva and Mercury, the Egyptian god Serapis and the Danubian rider-gods, together with those of Mithras and his helpers (Toynbee 1986; Shepherd 1998). The finds from Romano-Celtic temples regularly show that offerings could be made to more than one deity at the same shrine: the temple of Mercury at Uley has a plaque to 'Jupiter Best and Greatest' (Henig 1993a: fig. 91, 3), a tablet to 'Mars Mercury' and a second tablet where 'Mars Silvanus' has been crossed out in favour of 'Mercury' (Tomlin 1993: figs. 103, 2; 105). The decorated sceptre-binding from the temple at Farley Heath in Surrey combines images associated with the smith-god, the Celtic Jupiter, chthonic deities and perhaps the Celtic Mars (Bird 2007a: figs. 19–20, 78).

Pl. 50 Altar from Benwell. The top has a *focus* for offerings; the side shows a knife and the garland (*vitta*) worn by sacrificial animals.

Statues, reliefs and altars

The most impressive objects in a temple would have been its sculptures and altars (Plate 50). Although inscribed evidence may not survive, these, like the temples themselves and the mosaics and wall-paintings which decorated them, would have been the gifts of relatively wealthy local men or groups such as guilds, who saw this munificence both as part of the responsibilities of public office and as essential to their personal prestige (*RIB* 91; *RIB* II.4,

2448.3; Henig 1984: 141). Statues associated directly with Romano-Celtic temples are uncommon, one exception being the large broken limestone statue of Mercury with his companion ram and cockerel from Uley (Henig 1993a: 88–94). It is possible that some cult statues were made of wood rather than stone or bronze, and have perished: Pliny the Younger mentions that the statue of Ceres from a temple that he was rebuilding on his land was of wood, old and damaged, and in need of replacement (*Ep.* IX.39). Statues may have been portable; the *cellae* of Romano-Celtic temples were small, and the main annual or seasonal festivals probably involved carrying the cult statue in procession. Gregory of Tours records that the statue of Cybele was carried through fields to ensure fertility as late as the sixth century (*Liber in Gloria Confessorum* LXXVI), and a bronze statue of a horse dedicated to the local deity Rudiobus, found at Neuvy-en-Sullias in northern France, stands on a base with stout rings in which carrying poles could be fitted (Green 1992: 181). A similar ring, heavily worn but with traces of silver overlay, was found at the temple site at Wanborough, Surrey, and the same site also produced a substantial copper-alloy pole terminal (Bird 2007b: fig. 34, nos. 60–1).

There is a considerable corpus of religious statuary from Britain. The imported marble heads of Minerva, Mithras and Serapis (Toynbee 1962: pls. 28, 42, 43) from the London Mithraeum have already been noted. A much rarer piece is the gilt bronze head of Minerva from the temple complex at Bath (Toynbee 1962: pl. 20). Local stones were used for the Uley Mercury, and for such statues as the Mars from York, Minerva from the temple at Bruton in Somerset, and Juno Regina, consort of Jupiter Dolichenus, from Chesters (Toynbee 1962: pls. 26, 27, 41). Smaller stone statuettes and groups of figures include the marble Mercury and a Bacchus group, again from the London Mithraeum (Toynbee 1962: pls. 31–4; 1986), and a limestone hunter-god found with other sculptures in a well in Southwark (Merrifield 1996). It should, however, be remembered that a statue alone need not imply the presence of a shrine: statues and statuettes were also displayed in private homes and in public areas, and might be valued as much for their artistic merit as for their religious associations. Often only the heads of statues survive, broken off at the neck; this is the case with the bronze and marble heads mentioned above, and with such stone heads as the Mercury from Cirencester and the native god Antenociticus from Benwell (Toynbee 1962: pl. 29 and frontispiece). While this damage is sometimes ascribed to Christian iconoclasm, Croxford (2003) discusses the possibility that the breaking and preferential retention of statue fragments may have served some ritual or magical purpose.

Stone reliefs also expressed religious belief. Two large relief-decorated monuments come from London, where they were reused in the riverside wall: an arch, perhaps originally the entrance to a religious precinct, and a low screen, both bearing images of classical deities (Blagg 1980). A Corinthian capital found at Cirencester probably comes from a massive votive column, perhaps, like Continental examples, dedicated to Jupiter; it is inhabited by Bacchic figures (Toynbee 1962: pls. 97–100; Henig 1984: fig. 47). Many reliefs depict native deities, including the hunter-god (Merrifield 1996), pairs of gods and goddesses and triple figures or aspects of mother goddesses, water nymphs and hooded *genii cucullati* (Toynbee 1962: pls. 67, 70, 78, 82, 83; 1964, pls. XLIII, a; XLIV, a). Reliefs are also found associated with the eastern cults, and a frieze from Corbridge probably comes from the shrine of Jupiter Dolichenus recorded at the site (Toynbee 1962: pl. 95). Only fragments of the main cult-relief of Mithras slaying the bull survive from British mithraea, but the small stone tauroctony set within a zodiac from the London Mithraeum, dedicated by a veteran of *legio II Augusta*, shows the cosmic range of the cult (Toynbee 1962: pl. 73), while the egg-birth relief from the Housesteads Mithraeum is apparently unique and shows a very personal interpretation of the cult myth (Toynbee 1962: pl. 74).

Stone altars were the primary site of sacrifice and offerings to the gods, and frequently have a round depression or moulding, a *focus*, on the top in which offerings could be placed or burnt (Plates 50, 55). They are normally inscribed with the names of the donors and of the deity to whom the altar was dedicated; many native deities are only known from one or two inscriptions, their nature indicated by the name of their Roman counterparts. Often the donors were acting in some official or public capacity: an altar from Lincoln is dedicated to the Fates and the imperial *Numen* by Gaius Antistius Frontinus, 'guild-treasurer for the third time' (*RIB* 247). The inscriptions would usually have been picked out in red paint, but traces of this are rare; they are generally very formulaic, including such abbreviations as 'V.S.L.L.M.' – *votum soluit libens laetus merito*, 'willingly, joyfully and deservedly paid the vow' – which reflect the Roman concept of a contract between god and donor. Additional elements, such as an image of the deity or cult objects, may be present on the front with the inscription or on the sides of the pedestal. Miniature altars, such as one from York inscribed to the 'Mother Goddesses of the Household' (*RIB* 652), may have been used in the home or workplace, and some of these may have been designed to be portable, such as the altar to Fortuna from the bath-house at Carrawburgh which had an iron ring soldered into the top with lead, perhaps for use with a pole (*RIB* 1537).

Altars could have been sited within a temple, as in the mithraeum at Carrawburgh (Henig 1984: fig. 42), but could also have been placed outside in the temple precinct. A series of altars to Jupiter, found in pits at Maryport in Cumbria, represents a regular official dedication ceremony by the garrison, but it is not known whether each altar was ritually buried when it was replaced, or whether they all originally stood inside a precinct together (*RIB* 817–85). Nor were altars only placed on specifically religious sites; the domestic use of altars in a household or workplace shrine has been mentioned, and altars to Fortuna were often placed in bath-houses to protect the vulnerable (e.g. *RIB* 1210, from Risingham). An altar from Bollihope Common in Co. Durham, dedicated to Silvanus in gratitude for the killing of a particularly fine wild boar, probably stood in the open (Plate 23), while altars dedicated to Neptune and Oceanus marked the site of the Roman bridge across the Tyne at Newcastle (*RIB* 1319; 1320).

Other temple furnishings

Apart from the larger ritual objects discussed above, shrines and ancillary buildings would have required a variety of furnishings. It is probable that some temples operated as treasuries, a function which is well attested in the Roman world. Although coins are discussed more fully in Chapter 1, it should be remembered that they form a considerable portion of the finds at most religious sites, and it has been suggested that the large collection of late Iron Age and early Roman coins at the Wanborough temple may have been the shrine's treasury (Cheesman 1994: 33–4). Boxes and cupboards, as discussed in Chapter 7, would have been needed to hold the coins, as well as priestly regalia, other votive gifts and perhaps the records of vows made at the shrine. The hoard of ritual objects from Willingham Fen was contained in a wooden box (Green 1976: 210); while the wooden part of such items has usually gone, hinges, handles and decorative studs and plaques do survive. Hinges composed of short lengths of pierced bone with a wooden core and pegs were used for both boxes and cupboards (Waugh and Goodburn 1972: 149–50, fig. 53), and are recorded at Wanborough, for example (Bird 2007b: fig. 34, nos. 58–9), while the leaf of a small copper-alloy strap hinge of a type used on boxes was found at Farley Heath (Bird 2007a: fig. 24, no. 98).

Other fittings from boxes may be of copper alloy or iron; they include handles, such as a small enamelled handle and two drop handles from Farley Heath (Bird 2007a: fig. 24, nos. 96–7; fig. 28, no. 15), lock fittings, rings and studs. Bell-shaped, lion-headed and other types of studs were found at Farley Heath (Bird 2007a: fig. 24, nos. 85–90). Boxes were frequently ornamented with bone inlay, or with embossed lids and lock plates of copper-alloy sheet, usually decorated with concentric rings and bosses (see Waugh and Goodburn 1972: figs. 47–8); these are thin and vulnerable, and often only survive as fragments. Part of a copper-alloy box mount from Uley is decorated with biblical scenes (Henig 1993a: figs. 95–6). Other more substantial ornamental plaques and fittings probably came from furniture such as stools and tables (Woodward and Leach 1993: 31; cf. Wheeler and Wheeler 1932: pl. XXIX).

Some cults required the provision of water. Mithraea were designed to imitate the cave where Mithras slew the cosmic bull so, as this had a spring, there were normally arrangements for supplying and holding water in the temples. The London Mithraeum had a well in one corner, the Mithraeum at Housesteads had a spring in a brick basin, and the first phase of the Carrawburgh Mithraeum had a covered spring running through one corner (Shepherd 1998: figs. 87–8; Richmond and Gillam 1951: fig. 2). Stone basins were also found in the Mithraea at London, Rudchester and Carrawburgh (Shepherd 1998: figs. 179 and 212; Gillam and MacIvor 1954: 211; Harris and Harris 1965: 20, 27). Christianity required water for baptism, and there are lead tanks with Christian symbols from several sites, including three from Icklingham in Suffolk (*RIB* II.2, 2416.8–14).

Priestly regalia

Images of priests sacrificing in the traditional cults of Rome show their heads covered with a fold of their toga (e.g. Ferguson 1970: pl. 72), and this is the costume worn by the small copper-alloy statuettes of priests from the temple at Bruton, Somerset, and from Barham, Kent (Toynbee 1962: pls. 53–4) and of a priestess from South Shields (Plate 51; Allason-Jones and Miket 1984: no. 3.392). A variety of head-dresses could also be worn by Roman priests, including the spike of olive-wood worn by the Flamines (Henig 1984: 137); priests of the oriental cults certainly wore head-dresses, the priests of Cybele favouring an elaborate tiara (Ferguson 1970: pl. 5). However, where any connection can be seen, the head-dresses found in Britain seem to be associated with the rites of native religion. Some have been found on

Pl. 51 Bronze figurine of a priestess veiled for sacrifice, from South Shields

Romano-Celtic temple sites, including the probable dedication deposit for the second Wanborough temple (O'Connell and Bird 1994: 16–19, 97–8), others in caches of religious objects deliberately placed in jars or pits, while closely similar items have come from Iron Age contexts, including probable priestly burials (Stead 1995).

All the known head-dresses are made of copper alloy, some with added decoration in other materials, and for such a small number of artefacts there is considerable variety in style and ornamentation which may reflect regional ritual differences. Several show signs of repair, usually to the central finial or to chains; this demonstrates the value attached to sacred objects hallowed by long use, but adds to the difficulty of dating them at all precisely. There are two main types. Crowns were usually composed of chains, more rarely of solid strips, and can be decorated with a variety of finials and linking elements; they normally consist of a band round the brow, two further bands crossing over the head and sometimes a chain hanging on to the breast. Diadems comprise a single taller band sitting on the brow; the band could usually be adjusted to fit, and generally carried additional applied ornament.

The only complete example of a Roman-period crown composed of solid strips comes from Hockwold-cum-Wilton (Stead 1995). Here the finial consists of a disc and a spike, and the four junctions on the circlet carry plaques showing a bearded mask (Toynbee 1962: pl. 139). Probable remains of at least one similar crown come from a hoard of ritual objects placed in a cauldron-like pot after c.AD 260 at Felmingham Hall, Norfolk (Gilbert 1978: fig. 1); they consist of several broken bands, some terminating in hooks, looped fittings showing bearded heads, and small round caps (Gilbert 1978: fig. 4, A–C; fig. 5, A; fig. 9, pl. VII, A). One of the caps has the broken feet of a bird standing on the top and the hoard also included two figures of ravens or crows, each holding a small round object in its beak; it is possible that one of them, now lacking its feet, may have formed the crest of a head-dress (Gilbert 1978: fig. 4, E; pl. VII, A; British Museum 1964: pl. XXIV, 2). Ravens were seen as oracular birds (Green 1992: 174), and such a crest may have been worn by a priest who was also a seer.

The other known crowns are made from chains, and sometimes the only diagnostic elements to survive are the central finial or rings and fragmentary chains. A reconstruction by Matthew Alexander of one of the Wanborough examples showed that a fabric or leather lining would have been needed to hold them in place. Three of the Wanborough crowns carry a wheel, a solar symbol associated with the Celtic Jupiter (Fig. 22); a silver Atrebatic coin from Petersfield shows a horned god or priest wearing a wheel head-dress, with a chain hanging down on to the breast (Bird 1994: pl. 10), and it is possible that such a crown fitted over a cap with horns or antlers attached. These three crowns are all formed from chains of plain links which either simply join or are linked by larger rings (Bird 1994: figs. 24–5, pls. 16–19). A fourth crown is formed of loop-in-loop chains and the finial and junction

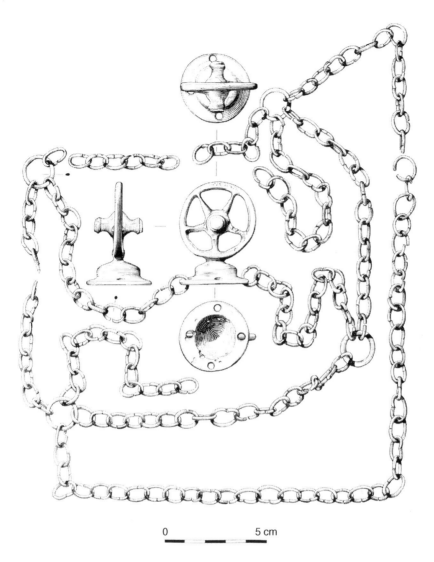

Fig. 22 Head-dress from Wanborough

rings are decorated with hatched ornament; the breast chain carries a vine-leaf pendant, a motif reflected on the local Atrebatic coinage (Bird 1994: fig. 23, pls. 12–15; Cheesman 1994: pl. 6, 264). A similar crown comes from the Farley Heath temple, with plain chains and a knob-like finial; here, however, the only complete length of chain joins a ring with D-shaped loops at the sides, suggesting that a band of metal or leather went round the brow (Bird 1996; 2007a: fig. 18, 76).

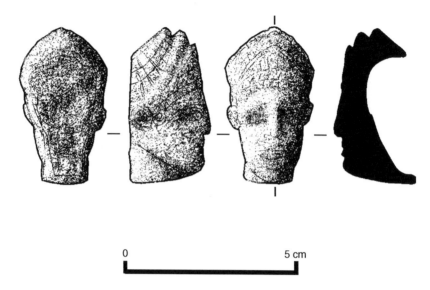

Fig. 23 Small copper-alloy head of a priest wearing a diadem from Ivy Chimneys

Other chain crowns are more elaborate. One found in an urn with other religious objects at Stony Stratford, in 1789, has chains of S-shaped links and discs at the top and junctions; the discs originally carried applied silver roundels decorated with rosettes in relief, and two of them have borders of twisted silver, brass and copper wire (Lysons 1817: pl. XXXV, 2 and 4; Layard 1925: fig. 2). The crown from Cavenham Heath, Suffolk, is similar but the original applied decoration on the discs is now lost; the chains are of S-shaped links, with no apparent hanging chain (Layard 1925: fig. 1). A more fragmentary crown from the Stony Stratford hoard is apparently a variation on this type: the surviving elements are four discs with applied silver ornaments, including triangles decorated with rosettes, nine narrow rectangular silver plates, and chains of S-shaped links. The plates have a hole at each end and are decorated on the long edges with diagonal lines, giving a stylised resemblance to feathers; the whole head-dress was probably a web of discs, 'feathers' and short chains (Lysons 1817: pl. XXXV, 3). The most complete of the Stony Stratford head-dresses is a further variation on the theme: it is composed of rows of leaves and discs of pressed copper-alloy sheet hanging from a conical finial, with a large vine leaf which would have sat on the forehead of the wearer; the finial has extra holes, perhaps for pins to hold it in place (Lysons 1817: pl. XXXIV).

Diadems are simpler in design but usually carry quite elaborate ornament. A small copper-alloy fitment from the temple site at Ivy Chimneys, Essex, shows a male head wearing a peaked and decorated diadem (Fig. 23; Webster 1999: pl. XXI, A, fig. 62, 70). The five from Hockwold-cum-Wilton are all alike, a broad band with three raised lobes at the front; one end of the back can slide inside the other to adjust the fit. The three lobes were all originally decorated with applied silver plaques with smaller ornaments attached above them; the surviving plaques show either a figure holding a bent stick, perhaps a long-handled smith's mallet, or a *cantharus* with little birds perched on the handles (Toynbee 1962: pl. 140; British Museum 1964: pl. XXV). The two diadems from Cavenham Heath are similar in design, with tall lobed fronts, but have lost all their applied decoration, of which only scars remain. The larger and more ornate one has an oval hole in the centre which probably once held a gem or piece of glass, and two shallow loops which could have held additional ornaments such as feathers or leaves (Layard 1925: pl. XXVII, figs. 1–2; Toynbee 1962: pl. 141). The three diadems from Deeping St James in Lincolnshire are probably of third-century date (Painter 1971); though incomplete and crumpled, they are clearly decorated with round and triangular pierced holes. Discoloration round some of the holes indicates applied borders which may have clasped settings of gems or glass.

Sceptres, symbolic of authority and status, have been recovered from several sites, and are likely to have been carried in processions (Henig 1984: 138); there were probably at least twenty in the Wanborough dedication deposit (Bird 1994). Very few of them survive to their full length but those that do are around 90–95 cm long; as with head-dresses, there is considerable variety of type. A small number consist of a narrow shaft of iron or copper alloy with copper-alloy handles, sometimes with narrow fittings set along the shaft. Two from a burial, possibly of a priest, found near Brough-on-Humber, carry helmeted copper-alloy busts, probably of Mars (Corder and Richmond 1938), while fragments from the Felmingham Hall Hoard include a copper-alloy handle in the shape of Hercules' club and a knobbed terminal in the shape of a leaf or spearhead (Gilbert 1978: fig. 7, A–C; fig. 8, B). A sceptre-shaft with an iron core from Stonea carried a bust of Minerva (Johns 1981: fig. 10). A variation on this type was found at Wanborough, a wooden shaft set in thin cylinders of cast copper alloy which would have appeared to be solid metal; the joins in the cylinders were held by small collars (Bird 1994: no. 31).

The majority of recorded sceptres had a wooden shaft covered with spirally wound strips of copper-alloy sheet fixed with small tacks; not surprisingly, given the thin metal, more handles and terminals survive than bindings. There are three main types of upper terminal: human or divine

heads, birds and animals, and a second 'handle' matching the lower terminal. Normally the terminals are of copper alloy, but a crudely modelled head
from Gloucester, probably from a sceptre, is of sheet gold on a lead core
(Green 1976: pl. XXV, c). Four bearded heads resembling second-century
emperors come from East Anglia, and Henig suggests a link between the
deity and the imperial *Numen* (1984: 138; Toynbee 1962: pls. 2–5); no
shafts survive for these, but one comes from Willingham Fen, where other
wooden-shafted sceptres were found. A further sceptre, which carries an
image of a deity but has lost its upper terminal, is the larger 'mace' from
Willingham Fen. A collar, which probably sat below the top, includes a
figure of Jupiter, a solar wheel, a dolphin and an eagle, and the lower handle is in the shape of Hercules' club (Green 1976: pl. X, a; Henig 1984:
fig. 63).

The only animal head identified as a sceptre crest is a wolf, though
Henig notes the possibility that some model boars may also have been
so used (1984: 141). The birds are all species associated with deities, or
having religious or chthonic connotations: an owl and a raven or crow from
Willingham Fen (Henig 1984: fig. 62), ravens or crows from Felmingham
Hall, Colchester and York (Gilbert 1978: fig. 4, D; Green 1976: pl. XXI, i;
1978: pl. 70) and peacocks from York (Green 1978: pls. 71–2). An eagle from
Farley Heath may also have stood on a sceptre (Bird 2007a: fig. 21, 81). The
evidence for sceptres with a handle at each end, sometimes combined with
intermediate collars, comes from Wanborough; here, the surviving spiral
binding strips have a rib along one edge, presumably to hold them securely
in place (Bird 1994: nos. 10–39). The sceptre binding from Farley Heath is
of similar size to the Wanborough examples but is decorated for much of
its length with crudely punched images, including animals, birds, symbols
and figures associated with the Celtic Jupiter, the smith-god and perhaps
the Celtic Mars. The handle is formed from a narrow piece of iron, spirally
twisted and attached to the shaft with an iron nail (Goodchild 1938; Bird
2007a: figs. 19–20, 78). The sceptre fittings from a ritual deposit at Frensham
in Surrey were made entirely of spirally twisted iron, perhaps again round a
wooden core, and they are decorated with iron studs (David Graham, pers.
comm.).

Ritual vessels and implements

The instruments used in offerings and sacrifices are often depicted on the
sides of altars, such as the altar to Antenociticus from Benwell (Plate 50).

The vessels usually comprise a one-handled jug or flagon and a dish, a patera, which may have a handle and/or a raised boss in the centre of the floor; these were used for ritual purification and for offerings. Copper-alloy flagons frequently have religious or mythological motifs on the handles, such as the figure of Hercules from Welshpool (Toynbee 1962: pl. 133); made of sheet metal, they often survive only as handles and fragments, as with the handle base from the Farley Heath temple which shows a cupid in the role of Perseus holding the Gorgon's head, a powerful apotropaic charm (Bird 2007a: fig. 25, 104). Pewter flagons were among the vessels found in the sacred spring at Bath (Henig *et al.* 1988: figs. 5–7), which also included silver, copper-alloy and pewter *trullae*, handled bowls similar to paterae but deeper, with dedications to Sulis Minerva on the handles (*RIB* II.2, 2414.33, II.2, 2415.60 and II.2, 2417.5–8; Henig *et al.* 1988: figs. 8–11); other *trullae* have religious themes on the handle, as the silver example from Capheaton, Northumberland (Henig 1984: fig. 48). A handle-less copper-alloy patera from South Shields is dedicated to Apollo Anextiomarus (*RIB* II.2, 2415.55; Henig 1984: fig. 56). Some paterae have narrow handles terminating in heads of deities or animals (Toynbee 1962: pls. 126–7); this type was copied more cheaply in London by potters who also made flagons and spouted bowls, and the surfaces are finished with a mica-rich slip which gives a golden metallic sheen (Marsh 1978a: types 1–3, 32 and 46; Seeley and Drummond-Murray 2005).

Other vessel types, some of them bearing votive dedications, may also have been used in rituals and processions as well as in displays of the temple plate. The two-handled *cantharus* is shown regularly on mosaics and sculpture, associated with images of the fountain of life (cf. Toynbee 1962: pl. 209, from Verulamium); a copper-alloy handle with incised 'feather' decoration from Farley Heath is probably from a vessel of this type (Bird 2007a: fig. 25, 105) and there is a complete silver example from the Water Newton Hoard of Christian plate (Hartley *et al.* 2006: no. 200). Hanging bowls, probably used as lamps, are recorded in copper alloy at Farley Heath and in facet-decorated silver at Water Newton (Bird 2007a: fig. 25, 107; Hartley *et al.* 2006: no 197). A long-handled silver strainer, perhaps for wine, was found at Water Newton (Hartley *et al.* 2006: no. 204), and a copper-alloy ladle, a *cyathus*, the handle terminating in a duck's head, apparently comes from Farley Heath; this is an archaic type and emphasises the possible long survival of ritual objects (Bird 2007a: fig. 26, 109). Other vessel types have definite Iron Age antecedents, including one with swing handles, usually referred to as a 'bucket' (cf. Henig 1984: 18); normally all that survives is the handles or mounts, which can be in the form of heads of men or animals, often bulls (Allason-Jones and McKay 1985: nos. 35–7, from Coventina's Well; Green 1978: pls. 78–80). The most unusual ritual vessel found so far is the silver casket and strainer from the London Mithraeum, decorated with scenes of griffin-hunting (Shepherd 1998: figs. 208–10).

The sacrificial implements were usually an axe and a long-bladed triangular knife, as shown on an altar from Chester (*RIB* 448) and the altar from Benwell (Plate 50). A copper-alloy flagon from Carlisle has a scene of sacrifice on the handle: at the left a soldier, perhaps a statue of Mars, in the centre a boy, half-kneeling and holding a small animal as an offering, and at the right a robed priest raising a knife (Plate 52; Henig 1984: fig. 57). These tools are sometimes made of copper alloy rather than the more efficient iron; Henig notes that this is probably an archaism with ritual significance, and cites a copper-alloy cleaver from the temple at Muntham Court and an axe, partially modelled in the form of a bull, found near Canterbury (1984: 131). Copper-alloy knives were found at Muntham Court and at Nettleton (Green 1976: pl. XXV, g; Toynbee 1982: fig. 63, 2), and the latter site also produced a cleaver and knives of iron (Wedlake 1982: figs. 98–9). A pair of copper-alloy shears from Wanborough may have been used to cut a symbolic offering of hairs from the sacrificial animal (Bird 1994: fig. 34, 61; Henig 1984: 33).

Other implements have been recorded which belong to the rites of oriental cults. Finds from the London Mithraeum included a reinforcing lath made of antler from a composite oriental bow, an unsharpened blade, a fine jet handle in the style of a sword handle and perhaps a catapult bolt (Shepherd 1998: 176; figs. 176, 55; 207, 3; 232, 20). Mithraic rites of initiation involved ordeals in which such weapons were probably used, and a decorated pottery jar from a mithraeum in Mainz shows an initiation which includes the use of an oriental bow (Huld-Zetsche 2004). A copper-alloy clamp found in the Thames at London Bridge was probably used in the castration of aspiring priests of Cybele, imitating the self-mutilation of Attis; it is decorated with busts of Cybele and Attis, with busts of the deities of the week, and with the heads of horses, bulls and lions (Henig 1984: fig. 44).

Lighting and incense

Lighting with lamps or torches played an important role in ritual, but lighting equipment is surprisingly uncommon on British temple sites: Eckardt cites only sixty-five examples, of which twenty-three are associated with oriental cults, and not all of these are from the actual shrines (2002a: 96–7).

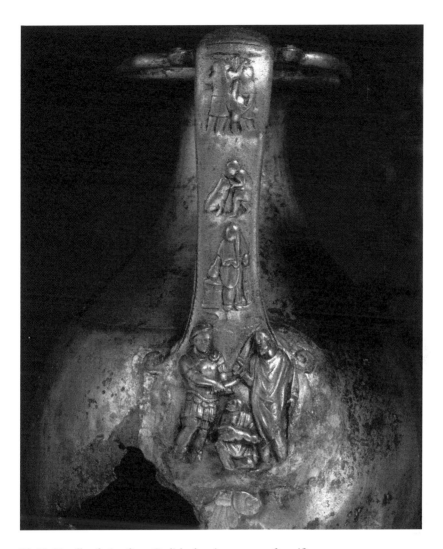

Pl. 52 Handle of a jug from Carlisle showing a scene of sacrifice

This may be further evidence for processions as the main ritual activity. Pottery lamps, particularly pre-Flavian picture lamps, are rare at temples, as indeed are the Spanish amphoras that would have carried the oil to fuel them (e.g. Leach 1993: 238), though such lamps, particularly those decorated with religious and mythical motifs, may well have been chosen for personal devotion at home and for use in domestic or workplace shrines (see also Chapter 7).

Candlesticks occur more frequently at temples; they are usually made of metal, and iron tripod candlesticks are recorded from Nettleton, Uley and Lydney (Fig. 16(b); Wedlake 1982: fig. 96, 9; Henig 1993c, fig. 149, 1–2; Wheeler and Wheeler 1932: fig. 23, 191–2). Zoomorphic candlesticks include a pewter one in the form of a stag from the Bath spring (Henig *et al.* 1988: fig. 7, 22, pl. IX) and copper-alloy cockerels from Lydney and Nettleton (Fig. 16(d); Wheeler and Wheeler 1932: fig. 20, 98; Toynbee 1982: pl. XXXI, a). A miniature stone altar from Piercebridge has a socket in the top, and may have been a votive candlestick (Green 1978: pl. 124). The temple at Harlow in Essex had an ornate fitting from a rare composite candelabrum in copper alloy (Gobel 1985: fig. 44, 63). It is possible that the little enamelled copper-alloy stands, which could be stacked in tiers of two or three, and copper-alloy dodecahedra may have been used to hold candles, perhaps of a special votive type (Plate 45; Henig 1984: 128, fig. 53; British Museum 1964: fig. 40, 5).

There is more evidence for lighting equipment from the oriental cults, particularly Mithraism (Eckardt 2002a: 96); the Mithraeum at Caernarfon, for instance, had twelve pottery lamps of the 'Firmalamp' type and a socketed candlestick (Boon 1960: 167, pls. XV, a, and XVI), and there was an open lamp from London (Shepherd 1998: fig. 174, 40). An iron candlestick was found at Carrawburgh (Plate 34) and a copper-alloy one immediately outside the London Mithraeum (Richmond and Gillam 1951: pl. XV, b; Shepherd 1998: fig. 207, 2). Finds from mithraea throughout the Empire show that lighting was important in the rites, and was used to create dramatic effects. An altar at Carrawburgh shows Mithras-Sol, the rays of his crown pierced to shine from the light of a lamp placed in a niche behind (*RIB* 1546; Toynbee 1962: pl. 75), while an altar at Rudchester has two rough niches cut in the back, probably for lights to illuminate the cult relief behind it (*RIB* 1398; Gillam and MacIvor 1954: fig. 9). A second Rudchester altar has four smaller sockets round the central focus, possibly to hold candles (*RIB* 1395; Gillam and MacIvor 1954: fig. 6). A tall pottery chimney with decorative piercing, a type that was used over lamps or censers, came from the triangular temple at Verulamium, which was probably dedicated to one of the oriental cults (Henig 1984: fig. 80); part of such a chimney was found at Farley Heath (Bird 2007a: 67), and a tall pierced vessel from the Rudchester Mithraeum probably served a similar purpose (Gillam and McIvor 1954: fig. 12).

An important feature of ritual was the offering of incense and perfumes, a valuable bloodless sacrifice and a means of mediation between gods and men. Henig records three small Bacchic incense or perfume containers, *balsamaria*, of copper alloy, including one from Carlisle (1984: 137; Green 1978: pl. 23). Incense was usually burned in pottery censers, made in a relatively coarse ware to withstand the heat of hot charcoal. A particularly fine pair from Coventina's Well carry dedications to the goddess (*RIB* II.4, 2457.2–3; Allason-Jones and McKay 1985: nos. 143–4); a smaller version, inscribed XI, was found at Nettleton (*RIB* II.4, 2457.6; Toynbee 1982: fig. 59, 374), and Henig suggests that a ceramic vessel from Uley, in the shape of a small altar, may have served the same purpose (1993b). The most usual form is the tazza, a carinated bowl on a narrow pedestal, decorated with frilled or rouletted bands (e.g. Seeley and Drummond-Murray 2005: fig. 134). The distribution of tazzas at 2–12 Gresham Street, London, suggests that virtually every house had one, for use in domestic ritual and purification rites (Rupert Featherby, pers. comm.). Incense was also offered on altars, and iron altar-shovels would have been used, such as the one from the Carrawburgh Mithraeum (Richmond and Gillam 1951: fig. 4, pl. XVB). One type of incense was produced by burning cones of the Mediterranean stone pine, which give off a strong resinous scent; cones have been recovered from several shrines, including the Carrawburgh Mithraeum, where there was also a stone bunker containing incense made from cones and hazelwood charcoal (Richmond and Gillam 1951: figs. 2, 4, pls. IIB, IIIA, XVB). Model terracotta pine-cones were found at Rapsley in Surrey, one of the sites that has also produced sherds of a female head-pot with mural crown (Bird 2002a; Bird 2004: fig. 70, pl. 10).

Music and sound

Religious ceremonies were regularly accompanied by musical instruments and sometimes by bells and rattles. Images of Roman sacrifices usually include a musician playing a pair of pipes, *tibiae*, as shown on the dedication stone from Bridgeness on the Antonine Wall which depicts a *suovetaurilia*, the traditional sacrifice of a pig, a sheep and a bull (Plate 55; *RIB* 2139; Henig 1984: fig. 32). Finds of instruments are rare, but there is the mouth-piece of what was probably a trumpet, a *tuba*, from Lydney (Wheeler and Wheeler 1932: fig. 16, 47) (see also Chapter 10). Other instruments, including tambours, flutes and cymbals, were used in the cults of Bacchus, Cybele and Sabazius, but none has apparently survived in Britain; a narrow stone altar from Gloucester bears a relief of Attis playing a pan-pipe, a syrinx (Toynbee 1964: pl. XLII, a). Bells were seen as having the power to drive away evil spirits; they have been found on temple sites, for example at Wanborough (Bird 2007b: fig. 33, no. 51), and in votive deposits such as Coventina's Well (Allason-Jones and McKay 1985: nos. 66–7). The socketed candle-holder from the Mithraeum at Caernarfon apparently had bells hanging from the cross-piece and may have been carried in the rituals (Boon 1960: pl. XVI).

The best-known Roman rattle is the sistrum, a metal frame fitted either with sliding horizontal bars or with fixed bars and metal discs; it is particularly associated with the worship of Isis, and also of Mithras. No exact parallels have apparently been found in Britain, but there are two iron rattles from London which consist of a short handle with a rectangular plate pierced respectively by four and seven holes, fitted with rings on which bells or discs would have hung (Green 1976: pl. XXII, g, h); a damaged iron example with two surviving holes from the temple at Brigstock in Northamptonshire may be of this type (Green 1976: pl. XXV, a). The other identified rattles seem to be connected with native religion. Those from the ritual hoards at Felmingham Hall and Stony Stratford are formed of two joined copper-alloy hemispheres attached to a short handle, presumably once containing loose pellets (Gilbert 1978: figs. 6C, 8A; Lysons 1817: pl. XXXVI). Socketed copper-alloy pole-tips in the shape of four-bladed spearheads have the base of each blade pierced for a ring which probably carried bells or metal discs; there are examples from Felmingham Hall and from the Brigstock temple (Gilbert 1978: fig. 3, A; Green 1976: pls. IX, i; XXV, b).

Votive offerings and vows

Many of the smaller objects considered below were the gifts of worshippers either seeking or repaying favours received from the gods. Some may have been deposited at household or roadside shrines rather than at temples, and other sites were also seen as providing access to the divine. Watery places such as wells, springs and pools were particularly associated with healing and fertility. Despite the industry along its banks, the Walbrook in London received a wide range of offerings, including human skulls, pipeclay 'Venus' figurines, face-pots and triple vases, weapons, tools, keys and jewellery (Merrifield 1995); the dependence of so many on the stream for their livelihood may have been an additional reason for its veneration. Wells that had gone out of use might have been filled in a rite of termination, like one in Southwark that contained a whole antler, shoes and triple vases (Marsh 1978b: 223–5). There is evidence for man-made pits being treated in the same way; the fill of a group of industrial pits in Southwark included dog bones, shoes, writing tablets and complete pots, one of them decorated with smiths' tools (Dennis 1978: 304–7). Much deeper shafts seem to have been excavated specifically for ritual purposes, perhaps reaching into the underworld to ensure the fertility of the land; they were filled with a variety of material, much of it in the form of animal and plant remains but often including metalwork and shoes (Ross 1968). Some buried hoards of iron objects probably also had a ritual nature (see Chapter 3).

Dedicatory plaques have been recovered from a number of sites. Some show a deity, such as the silver Cocidius plaques from Bewcastle or the copper-alloy plaque with a mask of Apollo from Nettleton (Green 1978: pls. 60–1; *RIB* II.3, 2432.3; Toynbee 1982: fig. 61). Holes are sometimes made in them to enable them to be affixed in or around the temple, and it is possible that the plain dome-headed studs found on temple sites were used for this purpose. An incised stone plaque dedicated to Mars comes from Newton, Powys (*RIB* II.4, 2453.3). Mask-like plaques include a silver Neptune and a much cruder tin head from the Bath spring (Henig 1984: figs. 66–7). Fine feathers or leaves, usually of silver and sometimes gilded, recall the feather-like imagery noted above on vessels and head-dresses; these can be simple, carry a dedication, or show images of deities, such as Mars Alator from the Barkway Hoard; the Water Newton Hoard included several Christian examples (Henig 1984: figs. 4 and 52; Toynbee 1978). There are no signs of attachment on the feathers, which may have been propped on a shelf. An apparently unique enamelled plaque from the Thames at London includes Bacchic motifs and was probably a votive deposit in the river (Hutchinson 1986: 142, fig. 6).

Small statuettes, usually of copper alloy, vary enormously in quality; some of the finest, such as the Venus and Mars figures from Verulamium and Lincolnshire (Toynbee 1962: pls. 18–19) may have been decorative rather than purely religious, but many relatively crude figurines were probably made deliberately for sale as votives (Henig 1984: fig. 23). The ploughman in the Piercebridge model drives a team consisting of a cow and a bull, not the most suitable pairing for the work and probably intended as an offering for the fertility of the land (Plate 17; Henig 1984: 29; Toynbee 1962: pl. 60). Small copper-alloy busts of deities, sometimes fitments from larger objects, are also found (Toynbee 1964: pl. XVII, a–d). Figurines made of fine pipeclay were imported from Gaul and the Rhineland; the most popular are the 'Venus' figures, sometimes set in a little shrine, and the nursing-mother images of Dea Nutrix, both probably connected with fertility and childbirth (these figurines have a much wider distribution than was apparent when Jenkins first studied them, but see Jenkins 1957; 1958; 1978). Pipeclay and copper-alloy figurines of animals and birds could be interpreted as toys (see Chapter 10), but the range appears confined to creatures associated with cults, such as Mercury's cockerel and goat, the horse-and-rider figures linked to Mars, animals with healing connotations such as snakes and dogs, and boars and bulls, particularly three-horned Celtic bulls (Henig 1984: fig. 14; Green 1976: pls. IV, h; XIX, a; XX, e; XXI, d; 1978: pls. 74, 87). Miniature objects also feature as votive gifts, standing in for their full-size counterparts; they are frequently bent or broken, 'killing' them in order to dedicate them. They include model weapons and tools, usually of copper alloy, such as spears, tools, particularly axes, *caducei*, altar-shovels and wheels (Henig 1984: fig. 70; 1993a: figs. 89–90; Green 1976: pls. IX, e–h; XXVIII, g, j–n). Miniature pots are also found, including a large group from Uley (Woodward and Leach 1993: figs. 117–19); again, these are probably symbolic of larger vessels, and may have held token offerings of food or liquid (see also Chapter 10).

Other offerings are more personal, objects that would not necessarily be recognised as religious if the context did not indicate it; again, these may have been damaged or broken in order to free them of their earthly links. Brooches (as is discussed in Chapter 9) occur in quantity at many shrines, and some types, such as horse-and-rider, sandal-sole and axe-head plate brooches, seem to be concentrated on religious sites and were probably made deliberately as votive gifts (Johns 1996: 174, 178; Henig 1984: fig. 71). Rings could also carry dedications to deities and were probably votive (*RIB* II.3, 2422.20–1, 28, 52), while gemstones with religious imagery are regularly found at shrines. Other jewellery items, hair pins, and toilet and cosmetic items may have been the gifts of women, donated in the hope of healing or safety in childbirth; pins with heads in the shape of deities or axe-heads may also have been made as votive gifts. Models of body parts, such as the ivory breasts from the Bath spring or the copper-alloy arm from the Springhead complex, were either thank-offerings following a cure (Henig 1984: figs. 74–6) or a reminder to the deities as to which part of the body needed assistance. Shoes are found in deposits, a very personal gift that carried the 'imprint' of the donor and may have incorporated a sense of linking the upper and lower worlds (van Driel-Murray 1999). Craft and agricultural tools and such items as lead weights, all found regularly on temple sites, were probably given in the hope of acquiring favour, skill and good fortune in daily life and business (e.g. Bird 2007a: figs. 28–30).

There is considerable evidence to indicate that vows, or 'contracts' with the gods, were drawn up and deposited at shrines. Sites such as the Bath spring and the Uley temple have produced inscribed lead tablets which promise gifts to the deity in return for revenge or the return of stolen property; the offender is often luridly cursed (see Chapter 6; Henig 1984: 142–5; Tomlin 1988; 1993). While there are as yet no surviving wooden writing-tablets which deal with religious matters, finds of copper-alloy seal-boxes at religious sites do indicate their presence. The votive deposit at Great Walsingham produced a considerable quantity of such seal-boxes (Bagnall Smith 1999: figs. 4–5), while several shrines, including Nettleton, have produced iron and copper-alloy writing *stili* (Wedlake 1982: fig. 103). The presence of these finds indicates that writing was carried out at shrines, and there were probably scribes present to help those who needed it (see also Chapter 6). Among the evidence for Egyptian cults in Britain is a copper-alloy inlay in the shape of an ibis head from the probable religious site at Chiddingfold (Bird 2004: 133, pl. 3); the ibis was sacred to Thoth, patron of writing and medicine, and such an inlay may well have come from a box of writing or medical materials.

Finally, it should be noted that offerings need not necessarily be of Roman date, nor indeed actual artefacts. A Bronze Age stone axe-hammer was among the contents of Coventina's Well (Allason-Jones and McKay 1985: no. 27), and Neolithic polished stone axes, apparently regarded as 'thunder-stones', have been recorded at temple sites (Oakley 1965b: 118; Henig 1984: 188–9). The temple at Farley Heath produced a number of copper-alloy weapons of Bronze Age date, perhaps a hoard that had been found and dedicated (Bird 2007a: 32; Poulton 2007: 125–7). Fossil sea-urchins (echinoids) and sponges, derived from the Chalk, have been found at all three Surrey temples, and Wanborough also produced beach pebbles from the south coast (Bird 2007a: 33; Graham 1936: 99; Poulton 2007: 125–7; Williams 2007: 250–2); the fossils have been plausibly identified with the Druidic 'snake-stones' recorded by Pliny the Elder (Oakley 1965a: 15–16; 1965b: 117–19). Other materials, such as nuts, fruit, wood and fur, have sometimes been recorded from deep shafts (Ross 1968), and grain was probably offered on a clay stand found in a corn-drying kiln at Crookhorn, Hampshire (Henig 1984: 173), but these rarely survive on habitation or temple sites. Textiles would also have had a place in ritual deposits: on one of the Uley tablets a woman offers to Mercury one-third of a linen cloth if he will get it back from the thief who stole it (Tomlin 1993: 121, Tablet 2).

The home

The traditional Roman home held a shrine, a *lararium*, to the household gods, the *Lares* and *Penates*, and traces of such shrines have been found at

Silchester and Verulamium (Henig 1984: 168–9). A number of figures of *Lares* are recorded from Britain (Toynbee 1964: pl. XX, a), but the shrine might also accommodate other deities venerated by the household, and hold images representing departed ancestors. Several of the houses at 2–12 Gresham Street, London, had face-pots (Rupert Featherby, pers. comm.), and these may have been used as ancestral busts. Henig has suggested that hair pins with female heads may have served as ancestral images (1977: 359), and perhaps such objects as jet portrait pendants could also be so used (Allason-Jones 1996: 24–5). The house itself was often protected by a foundation deposit, usually involving a pot (Green 1976: pl. XXVI, c). Box-flue tiles used for heating systems were ultimately plastered over, and so some of the hidden motifs on them may have had protective power, notably the stag and hound images on tiles made at Ashtead, Surrey, which also occur on local cult items such as the Farley Heath sceptre binding (Bird 2004: pl. 8). Antefixes attached to tile roofs sometimes had apotropaic images, and these seem to have been particularly favoured by the military (*RIB* II.4, 2458.1; Toynbee 1964: pls. XCVIII–XCIX). Further protection might be provided by the presence of bells and phallic images, and there is evidence from Pompeii that both were used to guard the home and workplace (Ward-Perkins and Claridge 1976: no. 216).

Personal protection

As well as worshipping and making offerings at sacred sites and around their homes and workplaces, the people of Roman Britain used amulets and charms to avert personal harm or sickness, and to promote good fortune. These often took the form of jewellery which was both talismanic and ornamental. The gold necklace from Backworth has both solar wheel and lunar crescent ornaments, and the Snettisham jeweller's hoard included silver wheel and crescent pendants (Johns 1996: figs. 5.5–6). There are ear-rings in the talismanic shape of Hercules' club (Johns 1996: fig. 6.2), while hair pins might terminate in an image of a goddess, particularly one associated with fertility and well-being, such as the pins from London showing, in silver, Venus and, in bone, Fortuna and Isis (Plate 37; Johns 1996: figs. 6.8–10).

   Rings and bracelets for both sexes often used the healing and regenerative imagery of snakes (Johns 1996: figs. 3.4–6, 5.23); other rings might carry messages wishing good fortune or a blessed life (*RIB* II.3, 2422.5, 14–15). A large number of gemstones from Britain show religious and mythological motifs, and many of their owners would have associated the power of the image with their personal seal (Plate 43; Henig 1984: figs. 86–9). Small rings for children, such as a gold example from London, carried the phallus, a universal charm against harm (Henig 1984: fig. 92); another powerful talisman was the Gorgon's head, found on such ornaments as a copper-alloy *phalera* from Farley Heath and a jet pendant from Strood (Bird 2007a: fig. 24, 84; Henig 1984: fig. 91). Such amulets gained even greater force by being made from materials perceived to have magical and apotropaic power, such as amber, jet, coral, gems and crystal (Puttock 2002: 99–105).

Other, rather heavier, charms seem to have been hung from straps, perhaps from soldier's gear and also to protect riding horses and draught animals. A copper-alloy terminal from Farley Heath is in the shape of Hercules' club (Bird 2007a: fig. 17, 74), but more often these pendants take the shape of a phallus or the *mano fica*, a thumb grasped by the fingers and aimed against hostile forces; they are usually of copper alloy, but one group of phallic roundels is cut from antler burrs (Green 1976: pl. XXV, d, e, h, pl. XXVI, a; 1978: pls. 139–40). This protection could also extend to vehicles: a linchpin from Chelsham, Surrey, has a copper-alloy head with phallic tip (Bird 1997), while an axle-cap from Lullingstone is in the shape of a lion's head (Meates 1987: fig. 30, 148). Other activities where religious symbolism might be invoked to protect or aid include business and crafts: a number of steelyard weights are in the shape of deities, such as the bust of Isis from London (Toynbee 1964: pl. XXII, a), while craft tools might bear an image of Minerva (Henig 1984: 179).

Conclusion

This chapter has concentrated on those objects which were made for religious use, or have been found in recognisably ritual contexts. It is important to remember, however, that any object or deposit might have had a religious significance which may not be immediately apparent to the excavator; we still know very little about the daily rites and superstitious habits which would have been followed by the majority of people in Roman Britain. Habitation sites in the north, for instance, regularly produce a group comprising a broken quern, pottery and a broken glass armlet, which now seems to represent a ritual of departure rather than a normal domestic assemblage (Allason-Jones 2009); the significance of such groupings can often only be recognised when a number of similar finds are identified. Many deposits include items such as animal bones or chunks of building material whose significance is frequently elusive; it is possible that the building material stood as a miniature of the home, asking for protection or for a blessing on a new structure (David Bird, pers. comm.). In a world where the fertility of crops and animals was crucial, and where medical knowledge was often lacking or inadequate, hopes for divine aid may well have been bound up in the most humble of materials.

H. E. M. COOL

Funerary contexts provide objects with one of their best opportunities to tell their stories. They were deposited deliberately and, if we are lucky, they will not be much disturbed. This chapter explores how we can listen to these stories. It will not focus on particular types of finds and their typologies, as more detailed information will be found elsewhere in this volume. Nor will it attempt to provide an exhaustive overview of the range of finds that can be expected in Romano-British cemeteries; that is available in Robert Philpott's book *Burial Practices in Roman Britain* (1991). Instead it looks at the roles material culture played in funerary ritual and how these can be explored.

The chapter is divided into three parts. The first is an overview of the nature of the funerary rites practised in Roman Britain, the types of contexts finds can be expected to come from, and the different roles they played during the funeral. The second part looks at some ways of maximising the amount of information they can provide. The final part attempts to answer the question why the dead were thought to be in need of things.

The nature of Romano-British burial

During the Roman period the dead were dealt with in two ways: the body could be burnt (cremated) or it could be buried (inhumed). Funerals where cremation was the burial rite leave more complex archaeological remains than do inhumation burials, as is discussed in detail by McKinley (2000) and Weekes (2005). The burning of the deceased provides an opportunity to place items on the pyre to be burnt with the body (pyre goods). The pyre itself can become the burial site, in which case it can be referred to as a bustum burial, though these are rare in Roman Britain where it was more normal to gather the calcined bones (sometimes with fragments of pyre goods), place them in a pottery jar or other vessel (Plate 53) (urned burial) and deposit these in a grave with, or without, additional vessels and other items that were not burnt (grave goods). The bones could also be placed loose on the floor of the grave, or in an organic container which does

Pl. 53 Glass container reused as a cinerary urn, from Carlisle

not survive, but whose former presence can be deduced by the compact distribution of the bones (unurned burial).

A recurring feature in many Romano-British cremation cemeteries is that the amount of human bone in the urned burials rarely approaches the full weight of bone a cremated body would yield. It is clear that as well as the formal deposition of the urned or unurned burial, the debris from the pyre (burnt and broken fragments of pyre goods as well as pieces of bone and ash) was often deposited separately. This material (redeposited pyre debris) could be included in the fill of the grave or it could be deposited in other features.

It has to be said that, until recently, anyone reading most reports of Romano-British cremation cemeteries would look in vain for any differentiation between pyre and grave goods and for information about what was happening to the pyre debris. This is because Romano-British studies have always lagged behind other periods, and indeed other areas of the Empire, in recognising the important role pyre goods play in reconstructing funerary ritual. Philpott, reviewing the published evidence up to 1989, noted that pyre debris was not normally incorporated into the grave fill (1991: 8). This view definitely seems to have arisen because of how archaeologists excavated and recorded cremation cemeteries, rather than the actual state of affairs. Cremation cemeteries were seen as unproblematic, tidy deposits of urns with their grave goods, and everything was published as a formal burial. This can make it difficult to assess what was going on in a cemetery if it was excavated and published prior to the 1990s (and occasionally later!). If the contents of the 'graves' have been well catalogued, then it is possible to reassess them. A good example of this is the cemetery at King Harry Lane at Verulamium, in use during the first half of the first century (Stead and Rigby 1989: 274–397). It was dug during the late 1960s and early 1970s and the post-excavation work was carried out during the 1980s. In the report, the deposits are regarded as graves and the objects in them as grave goods. The quality of the catalogue entries, however, makes it possible to reassess the evidence and identify the formal burials and the pyre debris contexts (Cool 2006: 162, 250, data set for Table 16.3). Unfortunately this is not always the case, so older reports of cremation cemeteries always have to be interrogated with some care.

Understanding the processes items may have been through prior to deposition is important as it may influence the interpretations given to them. A Dea Nutrix pipeclay figurine found in fragments in a cremation urn at Canterbury was interpreted as having been ritually smashed prior to deposition, and a link was made with Romano-Gallic religious practice (Jenkins 1958:

41–2). Subsequently it was used as evidence of a Romano-Celtic belief that the smashing of objects released their life force to accompany the deceased to the Underworld (Alcock 1981: 51). Whilst all this may indeed be correct, a more prosaic reason may be that the fragmentation was due to the item having been on the pyre. A number of pipeclay figurines associated with cremation burials show damage, which could be interpreted in this way (Cool 2004a: 401), so such a role for the Canterbury figurine would not have been exceptional. The question why this item was thought particularly appropriate for this individual would still have to be asked, but the current interpretations of it would not be sustainable.

Where the burial rite is inhumation, there is less evidence of the ceremonies that may have preceded the actual placing of the deceased in the grave. People who are inhumed may be given grave goods, but there is no equivalent of pyre goods in the archaeological record to allow us to explore the early stages of the funeral in the same way that we can for cremation burials.

Funerary activity clearly did not cease with the placing of the remains in the grave. Visiting the grave at intervals after the funeral is attested in the Roman world, just as it has been in many societies. The festival of the Parentalia was a time to visit the cemetery and make offerings to the dead, but such ceremonies could be carried out at other times of the year as well (Toynbee 1971: 63–4). Sometimes this activity is vividly attested, as at a grave at Caerleon where a lead pipe enabled the mourners to pour libations directly on to the calcined bones (Toynbee 1971: 52, pl. 14). Visiting the dead continued in the Christian world of late antiquity, even if local bishops disapproved. St Augustine, writing of events in the late fourth century, recalls his mother visiting cemeteries in Milan with baskets of food and cups of wine to share with other pilgrims whilst honouring the saints buried there (Augustine VI.2). These activities by the grave-side can sometimes be detected by comparing the nature of the finds assemblages from the graves and other features directly associated with burial, with the contemporary finds from surface features. At the cremation cemetery at Brougham it could be shown that the pottery assemblage from the surface features was very different from the grave good assemblage, and this was plausibly interpreted as reflecting the preparation and consumption of meals by the grave-side (Evans in Cool 2004a: 364).

There may also be features in cemeteries that give every appearance of being a grave but which contain no evidence of a human occupant. There are various ways of interpreting these. It may be that they are memorials or cenotaphs for individuals whose remains were taken elsewhere (McKinley

2000: 43). Where the features contain vessels, it may be that these mark the end of a period of grave-side ceremonies. The practice of placing whole vessels in deposits as a rite of termination can often be seen on settlement sites (see, for example, Fulford 2001), and it would not be surprising if this pattern of behaviour spread into the funerary realm as well. A third alternative is that cemeteries, being places of the dead, sometimes attracted activity of a less savoury nature associated with magical rites. A pit in a cemetery at Clare, Street, London, seems a likely candidate for this sort of activity as it contained a bizarre assemblage of the skeletons of a heron, large numbers of frogs or toads, and some shrews and voles, with two flagons placed above (Merrifield 1987: 36); a combination that certainly brings to mind the, admittedly much later and fictional, scene where the witches brew up a potion to allow Macbeth to see the future (Shakespeare *Macbeth* Act 4, Scene 1). A group of three pots in the cemetery at Baldock contained a lead *defixio*, cursing an individual named Tacita (Westell 1931: 290, no. 308). As is to be expected of an excavation in the 1920s, there is no specific mention of cremated material in any of the groups excavated, so it is not possible to say whether the curse was included in a formal burial or a deposit without traces of a body. That it was part of a magical rite there can be no doubt: not only was the text written backwards, with unusual letter forms for added potency, but it was also pierced by nine holes, several still retaining their iron nails, to 'fix' the curse.

The preferred rite for the early Roman period was cremation, with inhumation becoming more fashionable in the later Roman period, a change seen across the western Roman world in the second century AD (Morris 1992: 52–61). Naturally there were exceptions to this. In Dorset, for example, a late Iron Age tradition of inhumation had developed and this continued to be practised by the Durotrigians into the early second century (Davies *et al.* 2002: 124). In the north of the country cremation burial was still preferred in the third century (see, for example, Lambert 1996: 87–125; Cool 2004a), and some people were still being cremated in the south during the third and fourth centuries as well (Philpott 1991: fig. 19; more could now be added). In the Eastern Cemetery at London, for example, 159 cremation burials were identified, of which 6 per cent were definitely of fourth-century date (Barber and Bowsher 2000: Table 9). The change in rite would have had an impact on the display element of a funeral. Both rites could involve processions to the cemetery as the mourners accompanied the corpse, providing an opportunity for display; but once at the cemetery, inhumation, by its very nature, is a more private affair as the number of mourners that can gather round the grave and see what is going on is limited.

Cremation, by contrast, generally involved lifting the deceased on a pyre for all to see. Quite how spectacular such a scene could be is made clear by the description of the cremation of the Emperor Septimius Severus in York in AD 211. Dio Cassius (LXXVII) describes how Severus, dressed in military uniform, was placed on the pyre with his sons and soldiers running around it as a mark of respect, the soldiers throwing gifts upon it before it was set alight. The bones were placed in an urn of precious stone and taken back to Rome. It is interesting to reflect that somewhere in York there must be a most spectacular deposit of pyre debris, alas so far undiscovered. Herodion (IV.2) then picks up the story in Rome and describes what happened next. An effigy of the emperor on a bier was placed on a lower storey of a five-storey edifice, full of brushwood and aromatic spices. The pyre was hung with gold-embroidered drapery, ivory carvings and paintings. After ceremonies involving elaborate processions, the whole was torched and an eagle released from the top storey to symbolise the flight of the Emperor's soul to heaven. It is a scene that occurs on various coin reverses, where statuary can also sometimes be seen on the lower storeys (Toynbee 1971: 60–1, pls. 15–16).

Admittedly this was a description of an apotheosis and not a normal funeral, but various features can be matched in the archaeological record, if on a smaller scale. At Brougham some people were cremated with horses (Bond and Worley in Cool 2004a: 314–15, 325), and it is difficult to see how this could have been achieved without the pyre having a complex structure probably including tiers. Burnt bone fittings, almost certainly from biers or funerary couches, attest to the fact that some corpses were placed on the pyre in elaborate settings (Eckardt 1999: 77; Greep in Cool 2004a: 273–82). It is clear that some pyres were lavishly furnished with both objects and offerings of food. A bustum burial in Southwark, that attracted much media attention owing to the suggestion that its occupant may have been a female gladiator, clearly had a pyre covered with animal and vegetable offerings including a chicken, stone pine, figs, dates and a large amount of barley and wheat (Mackinder 2000: 12). Melted vessel glass is common in cremation cemeteries, and where this retains features that allow the vessel to be identified, they are frequently found to be flasks for perfumed oils (see, for example, Jones 2002: colour pl. 7), attesting to the habit of having perfumes and other sweet-smelling items incorporated into the pyre or poured over it and its occupant (see Herodian IV.2; Pliny the Younger *Ep.* V.16).

This display element, with its public destruction of the pyre goods, as opposed to what might be considered the more private disposal of grave goods in both cremation and inhumation burials, should always be remembered when evaluating the richness of a burial. A comparison of a late-third-century cremation burial at Brougham and a later-fourth-century inhumation from the Eastern Cemetery at London makes this clear (Cool 2004a: 133–4, Grave no. 122; Barber and Bowsher 2000: 206–8, Grave no. B538). Both of the deceased were adults, and the London individual was a male. He was provided with two glass flasks, wore a gilded copper-alloy crossbow brooch on his right shoulder and had an elaborate chip-carved belt under his left shoulder. Given that crossbow brooches and this sort of belt appear to be markers of official and military rank (see Chapter 9; Swift 2000b: 43), there is no difficulty in identifying this man as an individual of some distinction. The person buried at Brougham, by contrast, seems to have been a fairly anonymous sort of person if only the evidence of the grave goods is studied. There was a jar used as an urn, a colour-coated beaker and a samian dish: a very common assemblage at this cemetery. The pyre goods, however, included a silver crossbow brooch. It is not known whether crossbow brooches had quite the same association with rank in the later third century as they were to have in the fourth century, but what is known is that silver brooches were always very rare. This can clearly be seen at Richborough, where the largest assemblage of crossbow brooches from a British site has been recovered: only one of the fifty-eight was silver (Bayley and Butcher 2004: 106–20, nos. 269–326). A good case could be made that the apparently anonymous Brougham individual may have been of higher status than the London man.

Approaches to funerary finds

Having established the nature of funerary practice in Roman Britain and the roles objects played, the question arises of how best to approach studying a finds assemblage from a cemetery. Here the specialist responsible for the primary identification, cataloguing and reporting faces something of a dilemma. The publication they will produce will be the primary record mined by most subsequent studies, as it is rare for people to have the opportunity and resources to re-examine the material. We have already seen how many reports of cremation cemeteries can no longer answer the sorts of questions that might be posed now because the people who wrote them had not realised the complexity of the funerary process. The questions people tend to ask of any aspect of the past are always changing to follow intellectual fashion. This can be seen from a quick survey of some of the key publications relating to Romano-British burial studies. A conference on burial held in 1974 was typical of its time; it tried to establish what patterns existed and explored questions of ethnicity, religious beliefs and affiliations (Reece 1977). Philpott's study conducted in the 1980s was concerned with all of these things but added social status to the mix (1991: 228–35). By the late 1990s it was clear that areas of interest that had been addressed for some time in the prehistoric and other disciplines were starting to spread into Roman burial studies, a process that was to be ongoing (see Parker Pearson 1999 for an excellent overview of such approaches in other areas). A conference held in 1997 continued to be interested in social status, ethnicity and religion, but also pursued questions of funerary ritual (Pearce, Millett and Struck 2000). A conference held in 2000 laid much greater emphasis on the individual, with contributions by human bone specialists. There was a continued interest in funerary ritual, and this extended to the placing of the dead in the landscape. Identity became a topic of interest for the first time at the expense of social status and ethnicity, as was discussed at an unpublished conference called 'The Study of Romano-British Funerary Practice: Dead or Alive?' which was held at the Society of Antiquaries of London in November 2000 (though it is to be suspected that the concept of identity covers a multitude of sins, including those topics). Judged by the annual proceedings of the Theoretical Roman Archaeology Conference since 2001, funerary ritual and the placing of the dead continues to be a fruitful area of study; but there is a growing interest in how cemeteries were used and the dead were perceived. This suggests that in future there may well be greater interest in what was going on in the cemetery other than burial. To explore this it will probably be necessary for the material regarded as residual and unstratified to be studied to a greater extent than is currently the case.

Whilst guessing what questions people might be interested in even a few years into the future is difficult, the following approaches should provide a robust data set for the current questions to explore, and possibly also for a few that people have not yet thought to start asking with any regularity.

Given the improved osteological evidence that is now available for both cremated and inhumed bone, the age and sex of the individual that the item is found with should always be the first thing to be inspected. The time has long since passed when it can be automatically assumed that necklaces and bracelets indicate that the deceased was a female or that military equipment means that the body was a male. This may indeed be the case, but there are a small but growing number of counter-examples that provide useful insights into Romano-British society and a better understanding of some of the artefacts involved. The Catterick *gallus* is a case in point. This was the inhumation of an adult who was found wearing a necklace, two bracelets and an anklet (Fig. 24; Wilson 2002a: 176–8; 2002b: 109, no. 8; 177, nos. 1–3; 384, no. 952; see also 41–2). The skeleton was securely identified as that of a male aged 20 to 25 years. Various features of the burial were unusual, such as the wearing of an anklet and the two stones that had been placed in his mouth. It was argued that various aspects of the ornamentation matched how the literary sources described the transvestite priests of Cybele who castrated themselves in her service, and it was suggested that this individual might well have been one of them; a suggestion that proved contentious in some quarters. Similar distinctive beaded jet bracelets to that found with the Catterick individual have been found in the burials of two other adult males, both of which showed some unusual features in their burial rite, and one of which also had a necklace (Ashford: Booth, Bingham and Lawrence 2008: 128, pl. 3.15; Brougham: Cool 2004a: 243–5, no. 307). The sex of other individuals found buried with such bracelets is unfortunately unknown as they were found many years ago (Ospringe: Whiting 1926: 146, Group LXII; Whiting, Hawley and May 1931: pl. LVII, fig. 2; Verulamium: Wheeler and Wheeler 1936: 210, no. 48, fig. 45; York: *RCHM Eburacum* 1962: 94, burial iv.k(vi)). As the evidence currently stands, such bracelets were appropriate for males who were different in some way; though whether they were all as different as the young man from Catterick appears to have been is open to question. If they did form part of some priestly regalia, then it might perhaps provide the context for such beads being present in France where jet and shale are otherwise rare (Allason-Jones 1996: 28, no. 28). It would also raise questions about them when they are isolated finds on settlement sites.

Having established what, if any, the age/sex associations are for individual types of artefacts, it is useful to see if the interpretation of these can be aided by a consideration of the associations other types of finds show. The case of attitudes towards drinking practices amongst the third-century community at Brougham is a good example of this. The analysis of the cremated bone had allowed many of the individuals to be aged and sexed to varying degrees; and it became very apparent that the whole funerary ritual was very strongly structured by the age and sex of the deceased, as the associations could be explored statistically to show that they could not have come about by chance (Baxter in Cool 2004a: 469; Cool and Baxter 2005).

Amongst the metal pyre goods that fell to the lot of the small finds specialist were fragments from large copper-alloy vessels known as Hemoor buckets (Mould in Cool 2004a: 374). The osteological evidence suggested these were accompanying adult females. Meanwhile the glass specialist was

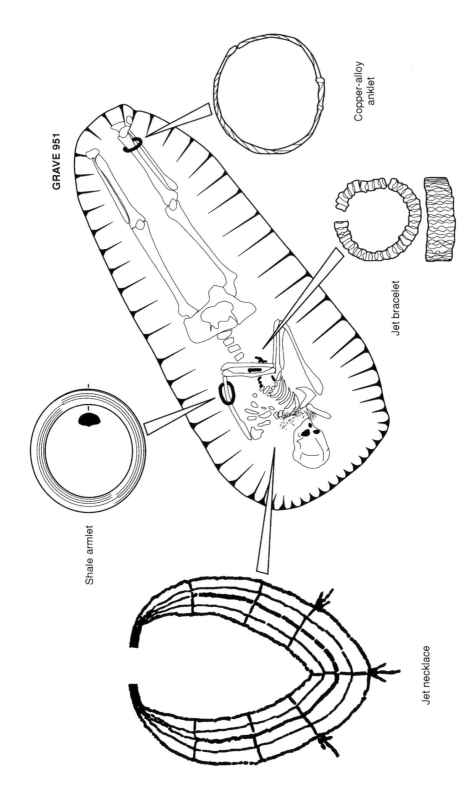

GRAVE 951

Copper-alloy anklet

Jet bracelet

Shale armlet

Jet necklace

Fig. 24 Reconstruction drawing of the burial of the Catterick *gallus*

dealing with drinking vessels deposited as grave goods; these could be shown to be definitely the preserve of adult males (Cool 2004a: 367–8, 371). Both the drinking vessels and the Hemoor buckets were clearly elements of drinking sets similar to that carved on the interior of the Simpelfeld sarcophagus Cool 2006: fig. 15.1); this shows the jugs to hold the wine and water, the large buckets needed to mix these and the glass vessels to drink them from. In themselves, both of the sex associations are interesting, as was the presence of Hemoor buckets, given they are very rarely recovered from Britain. When the different sex associations of the buckets and glasses are put together though, a vivid picture emerges. It would clearly appear that at Brougham women mixed the drinks and men drank them: this may be tediously stereotypical, but one must, perhaps, just concede that sometimes stereotypes reflect reality.

Naturally the integration of the finds with the stratigraphy is central. At the simplest level, knowing whether jewellery was worn or deposited as a separate pile beside the corpse has been used as a clue to ethnicity (Clarke 1979: 364–7). The layout of items in a grave can also be useful indicators of how the objects themselves were regarded, and sometimes suggests that a particular type of persona for the deceased was being presented to the world by the people burying them. Some burials, apparently of elite members of the native British community during the later first and second centuries, illustrate this very clearly.

Nearly two hundred years ago a group of six second-century barrows were excavated at Bartlow (then in Essex, now in Cambridgeshire) (Gage 1834; 1836; 1840; Gage Rokewode 1842). The burial rite had been cremation, with the bones normally being placed in glass bottles which were placed with grave goods in wooden chambers inside the barrow. In four of the burials there were copper-alloy jug and *trullea* sets – these were the vessels used in the Roman period in polite circles for hand-washing, before both sacrifice and dining (Nuber 1972); that they were seen as a set by the Bartlow mourners is made clear by the fact that in each case the vessels were found together, with the jug placed either in or on the *trulleum*. This in itself does not mean that they were being used in a 'Roman' way, but the other contents of the graves suggest they were (summarised in Cool 2006: Table 17.11). In two cases there were sets of vessels appropriate for polite dining, and in a third the goods included strigils and oil flasks, appropriate for a visit to the baths (see Plate 49), and a folding stool of the type used by magistrates and senior soldiers. Such goods could be read as those of someone who was being presented as an officer and a gentleman within the Roman world. An early-second-century cremation burial at Stansted, where the layout of the various goods is recorded, makes it clear that the various different elements of the grave goods were seen by the mourners as having different roles (Fig. 25; Havis and Brooks 2004: 217–27; Cool 2006: 194–5, fig. 17.3). The cremated bones had been placed unurned on a pewter tray with the goods placed around them. To the south were a group of tablewares relating to eating and dining, to the west were the food items themselves, whilst to the north were the items associated with hand-washing (jug and *trulleum*) and bathing (bath saucer).

It might be thought that the stratigraphic relationships of pyre goods, being normally redeposited, would have less to tell us; but it is becoming apparent that this is not necessarily correct. Experimental work has shown that pyres collapse slowly downwards with little lateral spread, and that at the end of the process the remains of the body being burnt will lie in their correct anatomical relationship on a bed of wood ash (McKinley 1997: 134). As there tends to be relatively little disturbance, if the deceased was wearing items such as glass bead necklaces or items of metal jewellery, the bones may well retain melted traces of them. It is also clear that even though the burnt bone and pyre goods will have been gathered from the pyre and placed in an urn, useful information can still sometimes be deduced about where on the pyre objects were placed if the contents of the urn are carefully excavated under laboratory conditions.

A third-century burial recovered at Birdoswald demonstrates this (Wilmott, Cool and Evans 2009: 281–8). The contents of the urn were excavated in spits and were found to include many burnt fragments of decorated bone inlays. Previously it had been assumed that these came from boxes. This seemed an unlikely interpretation here, given the large quantity recovered, in itself only a subset of the amount that had actually been on the pyre. The human bone in the urn consisted of all parts of the skeleton, though with a bias towards the larger elements. This was interpreted as hand collection direct from the pyre site, rather than gathering material from a pile after the remains had been raked together. The inlays had presumably been gathered at the same time, and it was significant that they were as evenly distributed throughout the urn as the human bone. This indicated that whatever they had decorated had been widely spread across the pyre; had it been a box on one part of the pyre, then it might have been expected that the fragments would have been found in a more concentrated area within the urn. The degree of burning on the fragments varied widely; again this argued for them having come from different parts of the pyre. All the different strands of the evidence suggested that they were most likely to have come from a decorated bier. Though elaborate funerary couches were

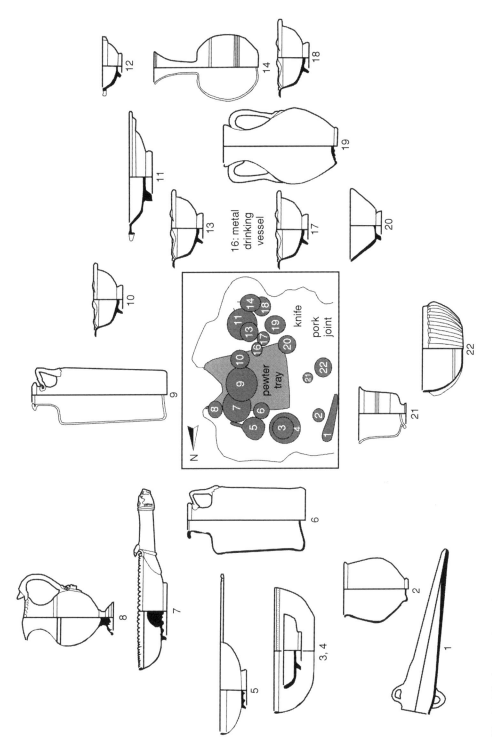

Fig. 25 The layout of an early-second-century AD cremation burial at Stansted

in use in the first century BC and first century AD (Caravale 1994: 33–66; Eckardt 1999: 77), elaborately decorated biers had not been suspected in the third century, despite similar inlays being found in other funerary contexts (Greep in Cool 2004a: 274). That this interpretation could be suggested in the case of the Birdoswald burial was only because of the very close integration of the study of the micro-stratigraphy within the urn and that of the human bone and the inlays themselves.

Finds found in burials are drawn from the finds available to the community as a whole, and a useful avenue to explore is whether or not the material chosen for the dead is typical of what was used in life, or whether only a subset was chosen for them. The best way to explore this initially is to treat the finds in the same way as one would an assemblage from a settlement site, i.e. summarising the material according to the basic functional categories, following the approach pioneered by Nina Crummy when publishing the finds from Colchester (Crummy 1983). Some of the categories, such as building materials and the waste from craft activity, are clearly not appropriate for funerary finds; but there is no reason why items associated with many of the other functional categories could not have been used either as pyre or grave goods. Structuring the analysis by the Crummy functional categories has the advantage that it should highlight any discrepancies between what was thought appropriate for the dead and what the living were using at the same time. The approach advocated by some authors, where the functional categories are based on the grave and pyre goods themselves (Barber and Bowsher 2000: 17, building on the approach of Clarke 1979: 145), risks missing or ignoring such discrepancies.

Such an approach depends on having contemporary domestic assemblages with which to compare the funerary one. Given that the way in which material culture was used and manipulated varied in different areas, the comparison really has to be made with assemblages derived from the community of whom the dead were a part, or at least with those from similar communities in the same region. This, of course, is not always possible, but where it can be done it can produce some interesting insights.

The Roman town of Chichester has seen sufficient excavation to enable us to know what was common and what was rare at different periods. It also has a cremation cemetery at St Pancras, parts of which were dug during the 1930s and the 1960s. The publication of this suffers from all the drawbacks outlined earlier, in that there is no clear demarcation between formal burials and pyre debris deposits, and it is not really possible to re-analyse these retrospectively from the published data (Down and Rule 1971: 89–122). A total of 315 deposits appear to be related to the cremation cemetery in use during the last third of the first century and the second century. The majority of the grave goods are vessels, but other items are also present. Of these, lamps are by far the commonest, occurring in twenty-nine deposits (just under 10 per cent), whilst brooches, the commonest other find, occurred in only four.

These figures are really quite remarkable when compared with the contemporary incidence of these items amongst the living in the town; there, brooches were common (Mackreth in Down 1989: 182–94), while lamps were very rare, with only two having been recorded from the excavations (Down 1981: 160, fig. 8.25, no. 25; 1989: 213, fig. 27.15, no. 4). This would suggest that what was deemed necessary for the dead was very different from what was important for the living. The incidence of the lamps in the St Pancras cemetery has formed part of a study exploring lighting in Roman Britain. In that it was shown that the lamps tended to be in the 'richer' graves, defining 'richness' by the number of items in the grave. The cemetery also displayed a wider range of lamp types than that seen elsewhere. In this the St Pancras usage differed from that seen in the contemporary cemeteries at Colchester, where lamps were found across a wider range of graves (Eckardt 2002a: 112, figs. 50–1). The Colchester funerary use very possibly reflects the fact that lamp use amongst the living at this period was common (Eckardt 2002a: 61). The people who lived in Chichester and Colchester were likely to have been very different. Chichester was a *civitas* capital and its inhabitants were predominantly of native stock. Colchester was founded as a *colonia* in AD 49 and certainly in its early days would have been a predominantly immigrant community. The level of lamp use amongst the living very possibly reflects this. Why then the high usage in death at Chichester? Given the possible association with the richer elements of society, was this a conscious imitation of what was perceived of as a 'Roman' rite, or did the provision of light in the grave have a very different significance to the bereaved of Chichester than it did in Colchester? These questions could only really be explored if data relating to the age and sex of the deceased, the nature of the deposits, etc., was available; but the patterns seen at Chichester do show the value of not exploring finds from cemeteries in isolation. Different insights and questions arise when they are compared with what the living found a use for.

The habit of concentrating on what is actually found in a cemetery almost as a closed world, rather than seeing it as part of the wider pattern of material culture use, probably explains why some very strange patterns have not often been commented on. Amongst Romano-British finds assemblages from domestic sites, items of personal adornment and dress always tend to

Table 3 The incidence of brooches in first-century funerary contexts at Pepper Hill

Deposit type	With burnt brooch	With unburnt brooch	Without brooch	Total
Pyre site	1	1	4	6
Bustum	–	–	2	2
Urned cremation burial	–	–	14	14
Unurned cremation burial	–	1	20	21
Cremation-related deposit	–	–	7	7
Inhumation	–	3	67	70
Total	1	5	114	120

form the largest functional class. Similar items form a very high proportion of finds from funerary contexts. Half of Philpott's discussion of grave furnishings, for example, is devoted to them (Philpott 1991: 128–75). Items such as bracelets and bead necklaces are very common in fourth-century graves, and this need not cause much surprise as it is clear from site finds that these were popular ornaments at that time. In the first and second centuries, brooches are common site finds, yet they are rare as finds from burials. Philpott found about sixty cremation burials with brooches, with the south-west of England only producing four instances (Philpott 1991: table 25). The people who lived in that area seem to have been particularly heavy users of brooches in life, so the latter fact is quite remarkable.

Whilst more recent excavations have added to the total of brooch graves, the pattern of brooch deposition being rare has continued. During the excavations in advance of the Channel Tunnel Rail Link (CTRL) in Kent, an area of a cemetery was excavated at Springhead. This, unusually, mixed both cremation and inhumation burials throughout its life. This excavation had all the benefits of modern practice, such as an extensive sieving regime to recover even very small fragments of finds, and a thorough understanding of the types of contexts that could be expected (Anon. 2000; Biddulph forthcoming). Table 3 summarises the various deposit types that can be dated to the first century and itemises the number of brooches recovered. Currently unpublished work on other CTRL and related sites in Kent has shown that that pattern of brooch use there in the second century may have deviated from what appears normal for the rest of the country, but in the first-century brooches seem to have been just as vital a part of the costume as they were elsewhere. Given the figures in Table 3, they were clearly not regarded as vital for the costume worn to the pyre or the grave, possibly reflecting how the corpse was being dressed.

Why did the dead need things?

Speculations on the answer to this question could occupy a large volume. The dead, of course, do not bury themselves, so a better question would be 'why did the bereaved think things were wanted?' In as far as the material discussed in this volume goes, the bereaved did not think they were required in most cases. Examples of soldiers buried with their equipment, or of craftsmen buried with their tools, are extremely rare. A grieving husband might depict his wife on her tombstone as a respectable matron with spindle, distaff and wool, as for example Barates and his wife Regina at South Shields (Plate 54; *RIB* 1065, pl. XV), but few felt it necessary to include such equipment with them on the pyre or in the grave. As just discussed, the inclusion of even basic functional items of clothing, such as brooches, appears to have been the exception rather than the rule. Graves with objects in them always tend to attract more attention than those without, but in many cemeteries the sort of finds discussed in this volume are rare. At the Eastern Cemetery in London, 550 inhumation burials were excavated but only seventy-seven (14 per cent) had grave goods other than vessels, generally either shoes, jewellery or coins (Barber and Bowsher 2000). In many cemeteries it is exceptional for the deceased to have anything in the grave with them other than vessels, and often not even those. So a better form for the question would be 'why was it thought a minority of people had need of things in the grave?'

Sometimes there does appear to be a religious, or at least superstitious, reason. Where there is a single coin, this can plausibly be interpreted as ensuring the deceased had the money to pay Charon's fee for the boat ride they would take in the Underworld. Shoes, as identified by their iron fittings, are a relatively common grave good from the second century onwards, and may have been even commoner given that many styles of shoes were not nailed (see Chapter 2). Shoes could well relate to a belief that the soul had to go on a journey (see Philpott 1991: 170–3 for discussion). In the Pepper Hill cemetery it was possible to see shoes taking on a new role. In the first century, shoes were burnt on the pyre but none was deposited whole; that started to happen in the second century, when shoes were placed as grave goods in both cremation and inhumation burials, but by then had ceased

Pl. 54 Tombstone of Regina at South Shields

to be a pyre good. This pattern would indicate that shoes were beginning to take on a more symbolic role.

Another trigger for the deposition of grave goods appears to be the age of the deceased. Study of the number of items deposited in the fourth-century cemeteries at Lankhills, Winchester, and Butt Road, Colchester, showed that individuals aged between 8 and 12 years received the most grave goods (Gowland 2001: 159). These were generally pieces of jewellery of types which, when they were found with the sexed adults, could be shown to be associated with females. At these cemeteries, girls on the verge of adolescence were deemed to have special needs, possibly because they had died before they could become wives and mothers. Possibly the jewellery represents the dowry for the wedding they would never have, just as some young girls of similar age were buried with their dolls and treasures which otherwise would have been dedicated to the gods before their wedding (Martin-Kilcher 2000). A burial at the Eastern Cemetery in London clearly belongs to this tradition, as the child, aged between 5 and 12 years, was buried with an ivory doll, three Venus figurines and other unusual items a child might treasure (Barber and Bowsher 2000: 186–9).

Children in general seem to have been thought in special need of grave goods. In cemeteries where grave goods are generally rare it is often found that they have a disproportionate share. At Brougham, grave goods other than vessels were very rare, but an infant was provided with a bell. Where bells have been found in graves, they are generally associated with children and it is to be assumed that they were playing a role in driving off evil spirits (Cool 2004a: 401).

Given that the normal pattern is for grave goods to be an exception in Romano-British cemeteries, the presence of an unusual number of grave goods may be an indication that it was felt necessary to mark out a particular identity for an individual or group. That is what the objects with the adolescent girls are doing. Other identities may relate to ethnicity or status. Many of the high-status native burials of the later first and second centuries include items that overtly indicate adherence to a Roman way of life (items associated with writing, bathing and sacrifice) as though for these individuals it was important to signal this aspect of their life. This sort of burial disappears in the later second century, so it was clearly felt that the elite no longer needed to be differentiated in this way. Why this should be the case clearly deserves much closer scrutiny than it has hitherto received.

Scientific analysis can sometimes confirm that the occupant of a richly furnished grave is indeed foreign. The young woman dressed in cloth of gold and buried at Spitalfields, London, had spent her youth in southern Europe (Swain and Roberts 2001: 12). Such analysis can also complicate matters considerably. The classic example of ethnicity being expressed in burial was seen at the Lankhills cemetery, where a small group of late-fourth-century individuals were richly provided with grave goods that marked them out from the bulk of the population, both in the way they were arranged on the body and in the grave and sometimes because they were of non-British origin (see Chapter 9). Both the arrangements and the types of artefacts suggested these people might be Pannonians (from modern Hungary) (Clarke 1979: 377–89; Swift 2000b: 69–77). Recent scientific analysis of their teeth has shown a more complicated picture. Most of them may indeed have been foreign but they were certainly not all coming from the same place, whilst two foreign individuals were buried according to the native pattern (Evans *et al.* 2006). Of course the finds may be expressing multiple identities or less obvious ones than mere ethnicity. Were the girls at Lankhills primarily given richly furnished graves because they were 'Pannonian' or because they were adolescents? Was the Spitalfields woman buried so richly because she was possibly Spanish or because, judged by one of her glass flasks, she may have been an adherent of Bacchus (Cool 2002)?

We will probably never know the answers to these questions, but that should not stop us asking them; and the fact that we can ask them reflects an increasing understanding of the complexity of the ways in which material culture was used in Roman Britain. In the poem 'An Arundel Tomb', Philip Larkin meditates on how the passage of time means the ability to read what a monument meant to the mourners is lost: all the modern viewer can do is look. As archaeologists we can take a less pessimistic view, and aim to read and not just see, and in this way the finds can tell their stories.

Pl. 55 Inscription from Bridgeness showing the *suovetaurelia* at right, with preliminary libation and musician

Bibliography

Alcock, J. A. (1966) *Life in Roman Britain*. London.

  (2001) *Food in Roman Britain*. Stroud.

Alcock, J. P. (1981) 'Classical religious belief and burial practice in Roman Britain', *Archaeol. J.* 137 (1980): 50–85.

Alföldi, A. (1935) 'Állatdíszes kerékvetö-fejek kelta-römai kocsikról', *Archeologiai Ertesitö* 48: 190–216.

Allason-Jones, L. (1979) 'Two unrecognized Roman surgical instruments', *Archaeol. Aeliana* 5th ser., 6: 239–41.

  (1985) 'Bell-shaped studs?', in M. C. Bishop (ed.), *The Production and Distribution of Roman Military Equipment: Proceedings of the Second Roman Military Research Seminar*. BAR Int. Ser. 275. Oxford: 95–108.

  (1988) 'Small finds from turrets on Hadrian's Wall', in Coulston (1988a): 197–233.

  (1989) *Ear-rings in Roman Britain*. BAR Brit. Ser. 201. Oxford.

  (1991) 'Small objects from the western end of mound B', in D. A. Welsby and C. M. Daniels (eds.), *Soba: Archaeological Research at the Medieval Capital on the Blue Nile*. British Institute in Eastern Africa Memoir 12. London: 126–65.

  (1992) 'An intaglio from High Rochester', *Arma* 4.2: 19–20.

  (1995) '"Sexing" small finds', in P. Rush (ed.), *Theoretical Roman Archaeology: Second Conference Proceedings*. Aldershot: 22–32.

  (1996) *Roman Jet in the Yorkshire Museum*. York.

  (1999a) 'Gilding the black lily', *Roman Finds Group Newsletter* 18: 11–12.

  (1999b) 'Health care in the Roman north', *Britannia* 30: 133–46.

  (2001) 'What is a military assemblage?', *J. Roman Military Equip. Stud.* 10 (1999): 1–4.

  (2002a) 'The jet industry and allied trades in Roman Yorkshire', in Wilson and Price (2002): 125–32.

  (2002b) 'Small finds', in M. Snape and P. Bidwell (eds.), *The Roman Fort at Newcastle upon Tyne. Archaeol. Aeliana* 5th ser., 31: 211–32.

  (2005) *Women in Roman Britain* (2nd edn). York.

  (2007) 'Small objects', in W. H. Hanson (ed.), *Elginhaugh: A Flavian Fort and Its Annexe*. Britannia Mon. Ser. London: 396–443.

  (2008) 'Finding significance in the finds', in P. Bidwell (ed.), *Understanding Hadrian's Wall*. Arbeia Society J. Mon. Kendal: 41–7.

  (2009) 'Some problems of the Roman Iron Age in N England', in W. H. Hanson (ed.), *The Army and Frontiers of Rome*. J. Roman Archaeol. Supp. Ser. 74. Portsmouth, RI: 218–24.

Allason-Jones, L. and Bishop, M. C. (1988) *Excavations at Roman Corbridge: The Hoard.* English Heritage Archaeol. Rep. 7. London.

Allason-Jones, L. and Jones, J. M. (2001) 'Identification of "jet" artefacts by reflected light microscopy', *European J. Archaeol.* 4.2: 233–51.

Allason-Jones, L. and McKay, B. (1985) *Coventina's Well: A Shrine on Hadrian's Wall.* Chollerford.

Allason-Jones, L. and Miket, R. F. (1984) *Catalogue of the Small Finds from South Shields Roman Fort.* Soc. Antiq. Newcastle upon Tyne Mon. Ser. 2. Newcastle upon Tyne.

Allen, D. (1998) *Roman Glass in Britain.* Princes Risborough.

Allison, P. M. (2004) *Pompeian Households: An Analysis of the Material Culture.* Monograph 42 Cotsen Institute of Archaeology, University of California. Los Angeles.

Allison, P., Fairbairn, A., Ellis, S. and Blackall, C. (2004) 'Extracting the social relevance of artefact distribution in Roman military forts', *Internet Archaeol.* 17.

Anon. (2000) 'Springhead Roman Cemetery', *Current Archaeol.* 14.12: 458–9.

Anon. (2006) 'Spring 2005 lecture series – lecture 1 "The Newstead ironwork: a Reappraisal"', *The Trimontium Trumpet* 20: 3.

Anon. (n.d.) *Archaeology in Chester since 1970 Exhibition.* Chester.

Anstee, J. (1967) 'Scythe blades of Roman Britain', *The Countryman* Winter: 365–9.

Applebaum, S. (1987) 'Animal husbandry', in Wacher (1987): 504–25.

Arthur, P. and Marsh, G. (1978) *Early Fine Wares in Roman Britain.* BAR Brit. Ser. 57. Oxford.

ATB 1973: *After the Battle* Issue 1.

ATB 1976: *After the Battle* Issue 15.

Atkinson, J. (1979) 'The bronze finger from Carvoran', *Archaeol. Aeliana* 5th ser., 7: 241–2.

Austen, R. G. (1934) 'Roman board-games', *Greece and Rome* 4: 24–34, 76–82.

Bagnall Smith, J. (1999) 'Votive objects and objects of votive significance from Great Walsingham', *Britannia* 30: 21–56.

Bailey, D. M. (1976) 'Pottery lamps', in D. Strong and D. Brown (eds.), *Roman Crafts.* London: 92–103.

 (1980) *A Catalogue of the Lamps in the British Museum,* Vol. II: *Roman Lamps Made in Italy.* London.

 (1988) *A Catalogue of the Lamps in the British Museum,* Vol. III: *Roman Provincial Lamps.* London.

 (1996) *A Catalogue of the Lamps in the British Museum,* Vol. IV: *Lamps of Metal and Stone, and Lampstands.* London.

Baker, P. (2002) 'The Roman military *valetudinaria*: fact or fiction?', in R. Arnott (ed.), *The Archaeology of Medicine.* BAR Int. Ser. 1046. Oxford: 69–79.

Baker, P., Forcey, C., Jundi, S. and Witcher, R. (eds.) (1999) *TRAC 98. Proceedings of the Eighth Annual Theoretical Roman Archaeology Conference.* Oxford.

Baldwin, R. (1985) 'Intrusive burial groups in the Late Roman cemetery at Lankhills, Winchester: a reassessment of the evidence', *Oxford J. Archaeol.* 4: 93–104.

Balsdon, J. P. V. D. (1962) *Roman Women: Their History and Habits.* London.
(2002) *Life and Leisure in Ancient Rome.* London.

Barber, B. and Bowsher, D. (2000) *The Eastern Cemetery of Roman London Excavations 1983–1990.* MoLAS Mon. 4. London.

Barrett, A. A. (1978) 'Knowledge of the literary classics in Roman Britain', *Britannia* 9: 307–13.

Bateman, N., Cowan, C. and Wroe-Brown, R. (2008) *London's Roman Amphitheatre. Guildhall Yard, City of London.* MoLAS Mon. 35. London.

Bayley, J. and Budd, P. (1998) 'The clay moulds', in Cool and Philo (1998): 195–222.

Bayley, J. and Butcher, S. (1995) 'The composition of Roman brooches found in Britain', in S. T. A. M. Mols, A. M. Gerhartl-Witteveen, H. Kars, A. Koster, W. T. Th. Peters and W. J. H. Willems (eds.), *Acta of the 12th International Congress on Ancient Bronzes Nijmegen 1992.* Nederlandese Archeologische Rapporten18. Amersfoort: 113–19.
(2004) *Roman Brooches in Britain: A Technological and Typological Study based on the Richborough Collection.* Rep. Comm. Res. Soc. Antiq. London 68. London.

Bayley, J., Mackreth, D. F. and Wallis, H. (2001) 'Evidence for Romano-British brooch production at Old Buckenham, Norfolk', *Britannia* 32: 93–118.

Beagrie, N. (1989) 'The Romano-British pewter industry', *Britannia* 20: 169–91.

Belarbi, I. and van Ossel, P. (2003) 'Les épingles à tête anthropomorphie stylisée: un accessoire de la coiffure feminine de l'antiquité tardive', *Gallia* 60: 319–68.

Bell, R. C. (1960) *Board and Table Games from Many Civilizations.* London.

Bellhouse, R. H. (1954) 'Roman sites on the Cumberland coast', *Trans. Cumberland Westmorland Antiquarian & Archaeol. Soc.* 54: 28–55.

Bennett, J. and Young, R. (1981) 'Some new and some forgotten stamped skillets and the date of P. Cipius Polybius', *Britannia* 12: 37–44.

Bennett, P., Frere, S. S. and Stow, S. (1982) *Excavations at Canterbury 1.* Gloucester.

Bennett, P., Riddler, I. and Sparey-Green, C. (2010) *The Roman Watermills and Settlement at Ickham, Kent,* Canterbury.

Berriman, A. E. (1956) 'The Carvoran "modius"', *Archaeol. Aeliana* 4th ser. 34: 130.

Betts, I., Black, E. W. and Gower, J. (1994) A corpus of relief-patterned tiles in Roman Britain. *J. Roman Pottery Stud.* 7. Oxford.

Biddulph, E. (forthcoming) *The Roman Cemetery at Pepper Hill, Southfleet, Kent.* CTRL Integrated Site Report Series, Archaeology Data Service. http://ads.ahds.ac.uk/catalogue/projArch/ctrl/index.cfm.

Bidwell, P. T. (1980) *Roman Exeter: Fortress and Town.* Exeter.
(2001) 'A probable Roman shipwreck on the Herd Sand at South Shields', *Arbeia J.* 6–7 (1997–8): 1–23.

Biggs, N. L., Lloyd, E. K. and Wilson, R. J. (1976) *Graph Theory 1736–1936.* Oxford.

Bird, D. G. (2004) *Roman Surrey.* Stroud.

Bird, J. (1986) 'Samian ware', in L. Miller, J. Schofield and M. Rhodes (eds.), *The Roman Quay at St Magnus Wharf: Excavations at New Fresh Wharf, Lower*

Thames Street, London, 1974–78. London Middlesex Archaeol. Soc. Spec. Pap. 8: 139–85.

(1994) 'Other finds excluding pottery', in O'Connell and Bird (1994): 93–132.

(1996) 'A Romano-British priestly head-dress from Farley Heath', *Surrey Archaeol. Collect.* 83: 81–9.

(1997) 'A Romano-British linch-pin head from Chelsham', *Surrey Archaeol. Collect.* 84: 187–9.

(2002a) 'A group of mural-crowned cult pots from south-east England', in Genin and Vernhet (2002): 301–11.

(2002b) 'Samian wares', in D. Lakin (ed.), *The Roman Tower at Shadwell, London: A Reappraisal.* MoLAS Archaeol. Stud. Ser. 8. London: 31–48.

(2007a) 'Catalogue of Iron Age and Roman artefacts discovered before 1995', in Poulton (2007): 34–68.

(2007b) 'The brooches and non-ferrous small objects', in Williams (2007): 208–21.

(2008) 'The decorated samian', in Bateman, Cowan and Wroe-Brown (2008): 135–42, 184–7.

Bird, J., Chapman, H. and Clark, J. (eds.) (1978a) *Collectanea Londiniensia: Studies in London Archaeology and History Presented to Ralph Merrifield.* London and Middlesex Archaeol. Soc. Spec. Pap. 2. London.

Bird, J., Graham, A. H., Sheldon, H. L. and Townend, P. (eds.) (1978b) *Southwark Excavations 1974–1978.* London and Middlesex Archaeol. Soc. and Surrey Archaeol. Soc. Joint Publication 1. London.

Bird, J., Hassall, M. and Sheldon, H. (1996) *Interpreting Roman London: Papers in Memory of Hugh Chapman.* Oxbow Mon. 58. Oxford.

Birley, A. (1997) *Security: The Keys and Locks.* Vindolanda Res. Rep. New Ser. IV, *The Small Finds*, Fascicule II. Greenhead.

(2002) *Garrison Life at Vindolanda: A Band of Brothers.* Stroud.

Birley, E. (1936) 'Marcus Cocceius Firmus: an epigraphic study', *Proc. Soc. Antiq. Scotland* 70: 363–77.

(1951) 'The prefects at Carrawburgh and their altars', *Archaeol. Aeliana* 4th ser., 29: 45–51.

(1966) Review of *RIB* in *J. Roman Stud.* 56: 226–31.

(1986) 'The deities of Roman Britain', *Augstieg und Niedergang der Römisch Welt* II.18: 3–112.

Birley, E., Birley, R. and Birley, A. (1993) *Vindolanda Research Reports, II: Reports on the Auxiliaries, the Writing-Tablets, Inscriptions, Brands and Graffiti.* Greenhead.

Bishop, M. C. (1986) 'The distribution of military equipment within Roman forts of the first century AD', in Unz (1986): 717–23.

(1988) 'Cavalry equipment of the Roman army in the 1st century AD', in Coulston (1988a): 67–195.

(1989) 'O Fortuna: a sideways look at the archaeological record and Roman military equipment', in van Driel-Murray (1989a): 1–11.

(1990a) 'Two cavalry fittings from Castleford, West Yorkshire', *Arma* 2.2: 28–31.

(1990b) '*Legio V Alaudae* and the crested lark', *J. Roman Military Equip. Stud.* 1: 161–4.

(1991) 'Soldiers and military equipment in the towns of Roman Britain', in Maxfield and Dobson (1991): 21–7.

(1992) 'The early imperial "apron"', *J. Roman Military Equip. Stud.* 3: 81–104.

(1999) '*Praesidium*: social, military, and logistical aspects of the Roman army's distribution during the early Principate', in Goldsworthy and Haynes (1999): 11–118.

(2002) *Lorica Segmentata I: A Handbook of Articulated Roman Plate Armour.* J. Roman Military Equip. Stud. Mon. 1. Chirnside.

(2004) *Inveresk Gate: Excavations in the Roman Civil Settlement at Inveresk, East Lothian, 1996–2000.* Edinburgh.

Bishop, M. C. and Coulston, J. C. (2006) *Roman Military Equipment from the Punic Wars to the Fall of Rome* (2nd edn). Oxford.

Blagg, T. F. C. (1980) 'The sculptured stones', in Hill, Millett and Blagg (1980): 125–93.

(2002) 'Architectural and other stonework from Catterick Bypass and Catterick 1972', in Wilson (2002b): 286–303.

Blair, I. and Hall, J. (2003) *Working Water: Roman Technology in Action.* London.

Bland, R. and Johns, C. (1993) *The Hoxne Treasure: An Illustrated Introduction.* London.

Bliquez, L. J. (1994) *Roman Surgical Instruments and Other Minor Objects in the National Archaeological Museum of Naples.* Mainz.

Blyth, P. H. (1999) 'The consumption and cost of fuel in hypocaust baths', in DeLaine and Johnston (1999): 87–98.

Boeselager, D. von (1989) 'Funde und Darstellungen römischer Schreibzeugfutterale zur Deutung einer Beigabe in kölner Gräbern', *Kölner Jahrbuch* 22: 221–39.

Böhme, H. (1974) *Germanische Grabfunde des 4 bis 5 Jahrhunderts.* Münchner Beiträge zur Vor- und Frühgeschichte 19. Munich.

(1986) 'Das Ende der Römerherrschaft in Britannien und die angelsächsische Besiedlung Englands im 5 Jahrhundert', *Jahrbuch des Römisch-Germanischen Zentralmuseums Mainz* 33: 469–574.

Böhme-Schönberger, A. (1997) *Kleidung und Schmuck in Rom in den Provinzen.* Stuttgart.

Boon, G. C. (1960) A temple of Mithras at Caernarvon-Segontium, *Archaeol. Cambrensis* 109: 136–72.

(1977) 'A Graeco-Roman anchor stock from North Wales', *Antiq. J.* 57: 10–30.

(1983) 'Potters, oculists and eye-troubles', *Britannia* 14: 1–12.

(1974) *Silchester: The Roman Town of Calleva.* London.

(1991) '*Tonsor humanus*: razor and toilet-knife in antiquity', *Britannia* 22: 21–32.

Booth, P., Bingham, A.-M. and Lawrence, S. (2008) *The Roman Roadside Settlement at Westhawk Farm, Ashford, Kent, Excavations 1998–9*. Oxford.

Bowman, A. K. (1994) *Life and Letters on the Roman Frontier: Vindolanda and its People*. London.

Bowman, A. K., Brady, J. M. and Tomlin, R. S. O. (1997) 'Imaging incised documents', *Literary and Linguistic Computing* 12.3: 169–76.

Bowman, A. K. and Thomas, J. D. (1983) *Vindolanda: The Latin Writing Tablets*. Britannia Mon. Ser. 4. London.

(1994) *The Vindolanda Writing Tablets: Tabulae Vindolandenses II*. London.

(2003) *The Vindolanda Writing Tablets: Tabulae Vindolandenses III*. London.

Bowman, A. K. and Tomlin, R. S. O. (2005) 'Wooden stilus tablets from Roman Britain', in A. K. Bowman and M. Brady (eds.), *Images and Artefacts of the Ancient World*. Oxford.

Božič, D. (2001a) 'Über den Verwendungszweck einiger römischer Messerchen', *Instrumentum* 13: 28–30.

(2001b) 'Note sur les plumes à écrire romaines', *Instrumentum* 14: 27–8.

(2002) 'A Roman grave with writing implements from Ljubljana (SI)', *Instrumentum* 16: 33–6.

Božič, D. and Feugère, M. (2004) 'Les instruments de l'écriture', *Gallia* 61: 21–41.

Bradley, R. (1998) *The Passage of Arms* (2nd edn). Cambridge.

Brailsford, J. W. (1951) *Guide to the Antiquities of Roman Britain*. London.

Branigan, K. (1971) *Latimer: Belgic, Roman, Dark Ages and Early Modern Farm*. Chesham.

(1977) *Gatcombe: The Excavation and Study of a Romano-British Villa Estate 1967–76*. BAR Brit. Ser. 44. Oxford.

Breeze, D. J. (1974) 'Ploughmarks at Carrawburgh, on Hadrian's Wall', *Tools and Tillage* 2.3: 188–90.

Breeze, D. J., Close-Brooks, J. and Ritchie, J. N. G. (1976) '"Soldiers'" burials at Camelon, Stirlingshire, 1922 and 1975', *Britannia* 7: 73–95.

Brickstock, R. J. (2000) 'The coins', in A. Birley and J. Blake (eds.), *1999 Excavations, Interim Report*. Greenhead: 27–9.

(2004) *The Production, Analysis and Standardisation of Romano-British Coin Reports*. Swindon.

(forthcoming) *Hollow Banks, Scorton: The Coins*, Northern Archaeological Associates.

(in prep). *The Rudchester Hoard Re-discovered*.

British Museum (1964) *Guide to the Antiquities of Roman Britain* (3rd edn). London.

Brodribb, A., Hands, A. and Walker, D. (1978) *Excavations at Shakenoak*, vol. V. Oxford.

(2005) *Excavations at Shakenoak Farm*. Oxford.

Brodribb, G. (1987) *Roman Brick and Tile*. Gloucester.

Bruckner, A. and Marichal, R. (eds.) (1979) *Chartae Latinae Antiquiores*, Part X, Germany I. Zurich.

Buckley, D. G. and Major, H. (1990) 'Quernstones', in Wrathmell and Nicholson (1990): 105–20.

(1998) 'The quernstones', in Cool and Philo (1998): 241–7.

Burgers, A. (2001) *The Water Supplies and Related Structures of Roman Britain*. BAR Brit. Ser. 324. Oxford.

Burnett, A. (1991) *Interpreting the Past: Coins*. London.

Bushe-Fox, J. P. (1949) *Fourth Report on the Excavations of the Roman Fort at Richborough, Kent*. Oxford.

Butcher, S. (1974) *Nornour*. Isles of Scilly Museum Publication 7. St Mary's.

(1993) *Nornour*. Isles of Scilly Museum Publication 7 (2nd edn). St Mary's.

Butler, R. M. (ed.) (1971) *Soldier and Civilian in Roman Yorkshire: Essays to Commemorate the Nineteenth Century of the Foundation of York*. Leicester.

Caravale, A. (1994) *Museo Nazionale Romano: Avori ed Ossi*. Rome.

Carcopino, J. (1941) *Daily Life in Ancient Rome*, ed. H. T. Rowell, trans. E. O. Lorimer. London.

Carnap-Bornheim, C. von (1999) *Archäologisch-historische Überlegungen zum Fundplatz Kalkriese-Niewedder Senke in den Jahren 9 zwischenn. Chr. und 15 n. Chr. Rom. Germanien und die Ausgrabungen von Kalkriese*. Osnabrück: Landschaftsverband Osnabrücker Land. E.v. (1999): 495–508.

Caruana, I. (1987) 'A wooden ansate panel from Carlisle', *Britannia* 18: 274–7.

Casey, P. J. (1984) *Roman Coinage in Britain* (2nd edn). Princes Risborough.

(1986) *Understanding Ancient Coins: An Introduction for Archaeologists and Historians*. London.

Casson, L. (1960) *The Ancient Mariners: Seafarers and Sea Fighters of the Mediterranean in Ancient Times*. London.

(1994) *Travel in the Ancient World*. Baltimore.

Cerulli Irelli, G. (1977) 'Una officina di Lucerne fittili a Pompeii', in H. Carandini (ed.), *L'instrumentum domesticum di Ercolano e Pompei nella prima età Imperiale*. Rome: 53–72.

Chapman, H. (1980) 'Wood', in D. M. Jones (ed.), *Excavations at Billingsgate Buildings 'Triangle', Lower Thames Street, 1974*. London Middlesex Archaeol. Soc. Spec. Pap. 4. London: 128–31.

Charlesworth, D. (1969) 'A gold signet ring from Housesteads', *Archaeol. Aeliana* 4th ser., 48: 39–42.

(1973) 'The Aesica Hoard', Archaeol. Aeliana 5th ser., 1: 225–34.

Cheesman, C. (1994) 'The coins', in O'Connell and Bird (1994): 31–92.

Cheesman, G. L. (1914) *The Auxilia of the Roman Imperial Army*. Oxford.

Civali, A. (2003) 'Pompeii', in P. G. Guzzo (ed.), *Tales from an Eruption: Pompeii, Herculanium, Oplontis*. Milan: 90–182.

Clark, A. and Nicholas, J. F. (1960) 'Romano-British farms south of the Hog's Back', *Surrey Archaeol. Coll.* 57: 42–71.

Clarke, D. V. (1970) 'Bone dice and the Scottish Iron Age', *Proc. Prehist. Soc.* 36: 214–32.

Clarke, G. (1979) *The Roman Cemetery at Lankhills (Winchester)*. Winchester Studies 3. Oxford.

Clarke, S. and Jones, R. (1994) 'The Newstead pits', *J. Roman Military Equip. Stud.* 5: 109–24.

Clay, C. (2004) 'Iconoclasm in Roman Chester: the significance of the mutilated tombstones from the North Wall', *J. Brit. Archaeol. Assoc.* 157: 1–16.

Cleere, H. (1977) 'The *classis Britannica*', in D. E. Johnston (ed.), *The Saxon Shore*. CBA Res. Rep. 18. London: 16–20.

Clutton-Brock, J. (1992) *Horse Power: A History of the Horse and the Donkey in Human Societies*. Cambridge, Mass.

Coles, J. M. C. and Simpson, D. D. A. (eds.) (1968) *Studies in Ancient Europe: Essays Presented to Stuart Piggott*. Leicester.

Connolly, P. (1991) 'The Roman fighting technique deduced from armour and weaponry', in Maxfield and Dobson (1991): 358–63.

Connolly, P. and van Driel-Murray, C. (1991) 'The Roman cavalry saddle', *Britannia* 22: 33–50.

Cool, H. E. M. (1983) 'A study of the Roman personal ornaments made of metal'. Ph.D. thesis, University of Wales, Cardiff (unpublished).

(1991) 'Roman metal hair pins from southern Britain', *Archaeol. J.* 147: 148–82.

(2002) 'Bottles for Bacchus?', in P. Webster and M. Aldhouse-Green (eds.), *Artefacts and Archaeology: Aspects of the Celtic and Roman Worlds*. Cardiff: 132–51.

(2004a) *The Roman Cemetery at Brougham, Cumbria: Excavation 1966–67*. Britannia Mon. Ser. 21. London.

(2004b) 'Some notes on spoons and mortaria', in B. Croxford, H. Eckardt, J. Meade and J. Weekes (eds.), *TRAC 2003: Proceedings of the Thirteenth Annual Theoretical Roman Archaeology Conference*. Oxford: 28–35.

(2005) 'Roman stone mortars – a preliminary survey', *J. Roman Pottery Stud.* 12: 54–8.

(2006) *Eating and Drinking in Roman Britain*. Cambridge.

Cool, H. E. M. and Baxter, M. J. (2005) 'Cemeteries and significance tests', *J. Roman Archaeol.* 18: 397–404.

Cool, H. E. M. and Philo, C. (eds.) (1998) *Roman Castleford Excavations 1974–85*, Vol. I: *The Small Finds*. Wakefield.

Cool, H. E. M. and Price, J. (1987) 'The glass', in G. W. Meates (ed.), *The Roman Villa at Lullingstone, Kent II*. Maidstone: 123–5.

Cooley, A. (ed.) (2002) *Becoming Roman, Writing Latin? Literacy and Epigraphy in the Roman West*. J. Roman Archaeol. Supp. Ser. Portsmouth, RI.

Cooper, D. (1998) *Coins and Minting*. Princes Risborough.

Copley, M. S., Bland, H. A., Rose, P., Horton, M. and Evershed, R. P. (2005) 'Gas chromatographic, mass spectrometric and stable carbon isotopic investigations of organic residues of plant oils and animal fats employed as illuminants in archaeological lamps from Egypt', *The Analyst* 130: 860–71.

Corder, P. (1943) 'Roman spade irons from Verulamium and elsewhere', *Archaeol. J.* 100: 224–31.

Corder, P. and Richmond, I. A. (1938) 'A Romano-British interment, with bucket and sceptres, from Brough, East Yorkshire', *Antiq. J.* 18: 68–74.

Coulston, J. C. N. (ed.) (1988a) *Military Equipment and the Identity of Roman Soldiers: Proceedings of the Fourth Roman Military Equipment Conference.* BAR Int. Ser. 394. Oxford.

(1988b) 'Three legionaries at Croy Hill', in Coulston (1988a): 1–29.

(1989) 'The value of Trajan's Column as a source for military equipment', in van Driel-Murray (1989a): 31–44.

(2001) 'The archaeology of Roman conflict', in Freeman and Pollard (2001): 23–49.

(2004) 'Military identity and personal self-identity in the Roman army', in de Ligt, Hemelrijk and Singor (2004): 133–52.

(2005) 'Military equipment and the archaeology of Roman conflict' in Jilek (2005): 19–32.

(2007a) 'Art, culture and service: the depiction of soldiers on funerary monuments of the 3rd century AD', in L. de Blois and E. Lo Cascio (eds.), *The Impact of the Roman Army (200 BC–AD 476): Economic, Social, Political, Religious and Cultural Aspects.* Proceedings of the Sixth Workshop of the International Network *Impact of Empire.* Leiden and Boston.

(2007b) 'By the sword united: Roman fighting styles on the battlefield and in the arena', in B. Mollow (ed.), *The Cutting Edge: Archaeological Studies of Violence and Weaponry.* London.

Crawford, M. (1974) *Roman Republican Coinage.* 2 vols. London.

Croom, A. T. (2007) *Roman Furniture.* Stroud.

Croxford, B. (2003) 'Iconoclasm in Roman Britain?', *Britannia* 34: 81–95.

Crummy, N. (1979) 'A chronology of Romano-British bone pins', *Britannia* 10: 157–63.

(1983) *The Roman small finds from excavations in Colchester, 1971–9.* Colchester Archaeol. Rep. 2. Colchester.

(1998) 'New Roman toy?', *The Colchester Archaeologist* 11: 34.

(2000) 'Roman ? military cart fitting from eastern England', *Instrumentum Bulletin* 12: 19.

(2003a) 'The metalwork', in M. Hinman, *A Late Iron Age Farmstead and Romano-British Site at Haddon, Peterborough.* Cambridgeshire County Council Archaeol. Field Unit Mon. 2/BAR Brit. Ser. 328. Oxford: 108–14.

(2003b) 'Other types of wax spatulae from Britain', *Lucerna* 25: 14–17.

(2004) 'The small finds and bulk metalwork', in K. Orr (ed.), *An Archaeological Excavation at 1 Queens Road, (Handford House, now 'Handford Place'), Colchester, Essex, February 2003–April 2004.* Colchester Archaeol. Trust Rep. 323 (developer report, to be published online). Colchester.

(ed.) (2005) *Image, Craft and the Classical World: Essays in Honour of Donald Bailey and Catherine Johns.* Monographies Instrumentum 29. Montagnac.

(2006a) 'Six honest serving men: a basic methodology for the study of small finds', in R. Hingley and S. Willis (eds.), *Roman Finds: Context and Theory.* Oxford.

(2006b) 'The small finds and bulk metalwork', in 'Excavations on Roman Ermine Street at the New Restaurant Facility, GlaxoSmithKline, Ware' by L. O'Brien with B. Roberts, *Herts. Archaeol. Hist* 14 (2004–5): 3–30.

(2006c) 'Worshipping Mercury on Balkerne Hill', in P. Ottaway (ed.), *A Victory Celebration: Papers on the Archaeology of Colchester and Late Iron Age – Roman Britain Presented to Philip Crummy.* Colchester: 55–68.

Crummy, N., Crummy, P. and Crossan, C. (1993) *Excavations of Roman and Later Cemeteries, Churches and Monastic Buildings in Colchester, 1971–88.* Colchester Archaeol. Rep. 9. Colchester.

Crummy, N. and Eckardt, H. (2003) 'Regional identities and technologies of the self: nail-cleaners in Roman Britain', *Archaeol. J.* 160: 44–69.

Crummy, P. (1984) *Excavations at Lion Walk, Balkerne Lane, and Middleborough, Colchester, Essex.* Colchester Archaeol. Rep. 3. Colchester.

(1993) The cemeteries of Roman Colchester, in Crummy, Crummy and Crossan (1993): 257–75.

(1997) *City of Victory: The Story of Colchester – Britain's First Roman Town.* Colchester.

(2005) 'The circus at Colchester (*Colonia Victricensis*)', *J. Roman Archaeol.* 18.1: 267–77.

Crummy, P., Benfield, S., Crummy, N., Rigby, V. and Shimmin, D. (2007) *Stanway: An Elite Burial Site at Camulodunum.* Britannia Mon. Ser. 24. London.

Cunliffe, B. (1972) 'Late Iron Age metalwork from Bulbury, Dorset', *Antiq. J.* 52: 293–308.

(1984) *Roman Bath Discovered* (2nd edn). London.

(1988) *The Temple of Sulis Minerva*, Vol. II: *The Finds from the Sacred Spring.* Oxford Univ. Comm. Archaeol. Mon. 16. Oxford.

Cunnington, M. E. and Goddard, E. H. (1934) *Catalogue of Antiquities in the Museum of the Wiltshire Archaeological and Natural History Society at Devizes II.* Devizes.

Curle, J. (1911) *Newstead: A Roman Frontier Post and Its People.* Glasgow.

(1913) 'Notes on some undescribed objects from the Roman fort at Newstead, Melrose', *Proc. Soc. Antiq. Scotland* 67: 384–405.

(1932) 'An inventory of objects of Roman and provincial Roman origin found on sites in Scotland not definitely associated with Roman construction', *Proc. Soc. Antiq. Scotland* 66: 277–400.

Curwen, E. C. (1937) 'Querns', *Antiquity* 11: 133–51.

(1941) 'More about querns', *Antiquity* 15: 15–32.

Davies, J. L. (1987) 'A bronze vehicle mount from Trawscoed, Dyfed', *Britannia* 18: 277–8.

Davies, R. W. (1970) 'A note on the hoard of Roman equipment buried at Corbridge', *Durham Univ. J.* 1970: 177–80.

Davies, S. M., Bellamy, P. S., Heaton, M. J. and Woodward, P. J. (2002) *Excavations at Alington Avenue, Fordington, Dorchester, Dorset, 1984–87.* Dorset Natur. Hist. Archaeol. Soc. Mon. 15. Dorchester.

Davy, N. and Ling, R. J. (1982) *Wall-Painting in Roman Britain.* Britannia Mon. Ser. 3. Gloucester.

DCMS (2002) *Portable Antiquities Annual Report 2000–2001.* Department of Culture, Media and Sport. London.

de Caro, S. (1996) *The National Archaeological Museum of Naples.* Naples.

Déchelette, J. (1904) *Les vases céramiques ornés de la Gaule romaine.* Paris.

(1914) *Manuel d'archéologie préhistorique, céltique et gallo-romaine,* vol. 11.3: *Second age de fer ou époque de la Tène.* Paris.

Degbomont, J. M. (1984) *Hypocaustes: le chauffage par hypocause dans l'habitat privé.* Liège.

de Jersey, P. (1996) *Celtic Coinage in Britain.* Princes Risborough.

DeLaine, J. (1988) 'Recent research on Roman baths', *J. Roman Archaeol.* 1: 11–32.

DeLaine, J. and Johnston, D. E. (eds.) (1999) *Roman Baths and Bathing.* J. Roman Archaeol. Supp. Ser. 37, Portsmouth, RI.

de Ligt, L., Hemelrijk, E. A. and Singor, H. W. (eds.) (2004) *Roman Rule and Civic Life: Local and Regional Perspectives. Proceedings of the Fourth Workshop of the International Network Impact of Empire (Roman Empire 200 BC – AD 476).* Amsterdam.

dell'Orto, L. F. (1992) *Rediscovering Pompeii.* Rome.

den Boesterd, M. H. P. (1956) *Description of the Collections in the Rijksmuseum G. M. Kam at Nijmegen V: The Bronze Vessels.* Nijmegen.

Dennis, G. (1978) '1–7 St Thomas Street', in Bird *et al.* (1978b): 291–422.

Derks, T. and Roymans, N. (2002) 'Seal-boxes and the spread of Latin literacy in the Rhine delta', in Cooley (2002): 87–134.

Dieudonné-Glad, N. (2002) 'Des plumes à écrire en fer? Projet d'enquête', *Instrumentum* 16: 30.

Down, A. (1981) *Chichester Excavations V.* Chichester.

(1989) *Chichester Excavations VI.* Chichester.

Down, A. and Rule, M. (1971) *Chichester Excavations I.* Chichester.

Doxiadis, E. (1995) *The Mysterious Fayum Portraits: Faces from Ancient Egypt* (paperback edn 2000). London.

Dudley, D. (1968) 'Excavations on Nornour, Isles of Scilly, 1962–6', *Archaeol. J.* 124: 1–64.

Dunabin, K. M. D. (1993) 'Wine and water at the Roman *convivium*', *J. Roman Archaeol.* 6: 116–41.

(2003) *The Roman Banquet: Images of Conviviality.* Cambridge.

Dungworth, D. D. B. (1997) 'Roman copper alloys: analysis of artefacts from North-
    ern Britain', *J. Archaeol. Sci.* 24: 901–10.

    (1998) 'EXRDF analysis of copper-alloy samples', in Cool and Philo (1998): 117.

Earwood, C. (1991) 'Objects of wood,' in Holbrook and Bidwell (1991): 275–8.

    (1993) *Domestic Wooden Artefacts in Britain and Ireland from Neolithic to Viking
    Times.* Exeter.

Eckardt, H. (1999) 'The Colchester "child's grave"', *Britannia* 30: 57–89.

    (2002a) *Illuminating Roman Britain.* Monographies Instrumentum 23.
    Montagnac.

    (2002b) 'The Colchester lamp factory', *Britannia* 33: 77–93.

    (2005) 'The social distribution of Roman artefacts: the case of nail cleaners and
    brooches in Britain', *J. Roman Archaeol.* 18: 139–60.

Egan, G. (1998) *The Medieval Household: Daily Living c.1150–c.1450.* Medieval Finds
    from Excavations in London 6. London.

Elderkin, K. (1930) 'Jointed dolls in antiquity', *American J. Archaeol.* 34: 471.

Ellis, P. (2000) *The Roman Baths and Macellum at Wroxeter: Excavations by Graham
    Webster 1955–85.* English Heritage Archaeol. Rep. 9. London.

Ellis, S. (1994) 'Lighting in Late Roman houses', in S. Cottam, D. Dungworth,
    S. Scott and J. Taylor (eds.), *TRAC 94: Proceedings of the Fourth Annual Theo-
    retical Roman Archaeology Conference.* Oxford: 65–71.

Espérandieu, E. (1966) *Recueil général des bas-reliefs, statues et bustes de la Gaule
    romaine.* Farnborough.

Evans, J. (1894) 'On some iron tools and other articles formed of iron found at
    Silchester in the year 1890', *Archaeologia* 54: 139–56.

Evans, J. (1987) 'Graffiti and the evidence of literacy and pottery use in Roman
    Britain', *Archaeol. J.* 144: 191–204.

Evans, J., Stoodley, N. and Chenery, C. (2006) 'A Strontium and Oxygen isotope
    assessment of the immigrant population from Lankhills by comparison with
    native Roman burials', *J. Archaeol. Sci.* 33.2: 265–72.

Evershed, R., Berstan, R., Grew, F., Copley, M., Charmant, A., Barham, E., Mottram,
    H. and Brown, G. (2004) 'Formulation of a Roman cosmetic', *Nature* 432: 35–6.

Fagan, G. G. (1999) *Bathing in Public in the Roman World.* Ann Arbor.

    (2006) 'Bathing for health with Celsus and Pliny the Elder', *Classical Quarterly*
    56.1: 190–207.

Faulkner, N. (2006) 'Suddenly there was a face staring back at me', *Current Archaeol.*
    202: 543–7.

Ferguson, J. (1970) *The Religions of the Roman Empire.* London.

Ferris, I. M. (1985) 'Horse and rider brooches in Britain: a new example from
    Rocester, Staffordshire', *Trans. S. Staffs. Archaeol. Hist. Soc.* 26: 1–10.

Feugère, M. (1995) 'Les spatules à cire à manche figuré', in W. Czysz *et al.* (eds.),
    *Provinzialrömische Forschungen: Festschrift für Günter Ulbert zum 65. Geburt-
    stag.* Espelkamp: 321–38.

    (2002) *Weapons of the Romans.* Stroud.

(2004a) 'Penknives from Newstead: writing accessories', *Lucerna* 26: 9–12.

(2004b) 'L'*instrumentum*, support d'écrit', *Gallia* 61: 53–65.

Feugère, M. and Garbsch, J. (1993) 'Römische Bronzelaternen', *Bayerische Vorgeschichtsblätter* 58: 143–84.

Feugère, M., Künzl, E. and Weisser, U. (1985) 'Die Starnadeln von Montbellet (Saône-et-Loire). Ein Beitrag zur antiken und islamischen Augenheilkunde', *Jahrbuch des Römisch-Germanischen Zentralmuseums* 32: 436–508.

Feugère, M. and Lambert, P.-Y. (eds.) (2004) 'L'écriture dans la société gallo-romaine: éléments d'une réflexion collective', *Gallia* 61: 1–192.

Fink, R. O. (1971) *Roman Military Records on Papyrus*. Cleveland.

Fischer, T. (1991) 'Zwei neue Metallsammelfunde aus Künzing/Quintana (Lkr. Deggendorf, Niederbayern)', in J. Garbsche (eds.), *Spurensuche: Festschrift für Hans-Jörg Kellner zum 70. Geburtstag*. Kallmünz: 125–75.

Fitzpatrick, A. (1991) '*Ex radice britanica*', *Britannia* 22: 143–6.

Foster, R. H. and Knowles, W. H. (1915) 'Corstopitum: report on the excavations in 1914', *Archaeol. Aeliana* 3rd ser., 12: 227–86.

Fowler, P. J. (1978) 'The Abingdon ard-share', in M. Parrington (ed.), *The Excavation of an Iron Age Settlement, Bronze Age Ring Ditches and Roman Features at Ashville Trading Estate, Abingdon (Oxfordshire) 1974–76*. CBA Res. Rep. 29. London: 83–8.

Fox, C. (1946) *A Find of the Early Iron Age from Llyn Cerrig Bach, Anglesey*. Cardiff.

Fox, G. E. and Hope, W. H. St. J. (1901) 'Excavations on the site of the Roman city of Silchester, Hants. in 1901', *Archaeologia* 57: 229–56.

France, N. E. and Gobel, B. M. (1985) *The Romano-British Temple at Harlow*. Gloucester.

Freeman, P. W. M. and Pollard, A. (2001) *Fields of Conflict: Progress and Prospect in Battlefield Archaeology*. BAR Int. Ser. 394. Oxford.

Frere, S. S. (1972) *Verulamium Excavations I*. Rep. Res. Comm. Soc. Antiq. London 28. London.

Frere, S. S., Roxan, M. and Tomlin, R. S. O. (1990) *Inscriptions of Roman Britain II Instrumentum Domesticum* Fasc. 1. Oxford.

Frere, S. S., and Tomlin, R. S. O. (1991a) *Inscriptions of Roman Britain II Instrumentum Domesticum* Fasc. 2. Oxford.

(1991b) *Inscriptions of Roman Britain II Instrumentum Domesticum* Fasc. 3. Oxford.

Friendship-Taylor, R. and Jackson, R. (2001) 'A new Roman gladiator find from Piddington, Northants.', *Antiquity* 75: 27–8.

Fulford, M. G. F. (1975) *New Forest Roman Pottery*. Oxford.

(1989) 'The economy of Roman Britain', in Todd (1989): 175–201.

(2001) 'Links with the past: pervasive "ritual" behaviour in Roman Britain', *Britannia* 32: 199–218.

Fulford, M., Sim, D., Doig, A. and Painter, J. (2005) 'In defence of Rome: a metallographic investigation of Roman ferrous armour from Northern Britain', *J. Archaeol. Sci.* 32: 241–50.

Gage, J. (1834) 'A plan of barrows called the Bartlow Hills, in the parish of Ashdon, in Essex, with an account of Roman sepulchral relics recently discovered in the lesser barrows', *Archaeologia* 25: 1–23.

  (1836) 'The recent discovery of Roman sepulchral relics in one of the greater barrows at Bartlow, in the parish of Ashdon, in Essex', *Archaeologia* 26: 300–17.

  (1840) 'An account of further discoveries of Roman sepulchral relics in one of the greater barrows at the Bartlow Hills', *Archaeologia* 28: 1–6.

Gage Rokewode, J. (1842) 'An account of the final excavations made at the Bartlow Hills', *Archaeologia* 29: 1–4.

Gailey, A. and Fenton, A. (eds.) (1970) *The Spade in Northern and Atlantic Europe.* Belfast.

Gaitzsch, W. (1980) *Eiserne römische Werkzeuge.* Oxford.

Galloway, P. (1976) 'Notes on descriptions of bone and antler combs', *Medieval Archaeol.* 20: 154–6.

Garbsch, J. (1978) *Römische Paraderüstungen.* Munich.

Gardiner, E. N. (1930) *Athletics of the Ancient World.* Budapest.

Genin, M. and Vernhet, A. (2002) *Céramiques de la Graufesenque et autres productions d'époque romaine: nouvelles recherches. Hommage à Bettina Hoffmann.* Archéologie et Histoire Romaine 7. Montagnac.

Gilbert, H. M. (1978) 'The Felmingham Hall hoard, Norfolk', *Bull. Board Celtic Stud.* 28.1: 159–87.

Gillam, J. P. (1958) 'Roman and native, A.D.122–197', in I. A. Richmond (ed.), *Roman and Native in North Britain.* Edinburgh: 60–90.

Gillam, J. P., Harrison, R. M. and Newman, T. G. (1973) 'Interim Report at the Roman fort of Rudchester, 1972', *Archaeol. Aeliana* 5th ser., 1: 81–5.

Gillam, J. P. and MacIvor, I. (1954) 'The temple of Mithras at Rudchester', *Archaeol. Aeliana* 4th ser., 32: 176–219.

Gilliam, J. F. (1967) 'The deposita of an auxiliary soldier (P. Columbia inv. 325)', *Bonner Jahrbucher* 167: 233–43.

Gilson, A. (1978) 'A doctor at Housesteads', *Archaeol. Aeliana* 5th ser., 6: 162–5.

  (1981) 'A group of Roman surgical and medical instruments from Corbridge', *Saalburg Jahrbuch* 37: 5–9.

  (1983) 'A group of Roman surgical and medical instruments from Cramond, Scotland', *Medizinhistorisches J.* 18: 384–93.

Glob, P. V. (1951) *Ard og Plov I Nordens Oltid.* Aarhus.

Gobel, B. M. (1985) 'Bronze small finds', in France and Gobel (1985): 82–91.

Goethert, K. (1997) *Römische Lampen und Leuchter.* Trier.

Goethert-Polaschek, K. (1985) *Katalog der Römischen Lampen des Rheinischen Landesmuseums Trier.* Mainz.

Goldsworthy, A. and Haynes, I. (eds.) (1999) *The Roman Army as a Community.* J. Roman Archaeol. Suppl. Ser. 34. Portsmouth, RI.

Goodchild, R. G. (1938) 'A priest's sceptre from the Romano-Celtic temple at Farley Heath, Surrey', *Antiq. J.* 18: 391–6.

Gosden, C. (2005) 'What do objects want?', *J. Archaeol. Method and Theory* 12: 193–211.

Gowland, R. (2001) 'Playing dead: implications of mortuary evidence for the social construction of childhood in Roman Britain', in G. Davies, A. Gardner and K. Lockyear (eds.), *TRAC 2000: Proceedings of the Tenth Annual Theoretical Roman Archaeology Conference London 2000.* Oxford: 152–68.

Graham, J. (1936) 'A Romano-Celtic temple at Titsey', *Surrey Archaeol. Collect.* 44: 84–101.

Grasby, R. D. and Tomlin, R. S. O. (2002) 'The sepulchral monument of the procurator C. Julius Classicianus', *Britannia* 33: 43–75.

Grassmann, H.-C. (1994) 'Wirkungsweise und Energieverbrauch antiker Römischer Thermen', *Jahrbuch des Römisch-Germanischen Zentralmuseums Mainz* 41.1: 297–321.

Green, M. J. (1976) *A Corpus of Religious Material from the Civilian Areas of Roman Britain,* BAR Brit. Ser. 24. Oxford.

(1978) *A Corpus of Small Cult-Objects from the Military Areas of Roman Britain.* BAR Brit. Ser. 52. Oxford.

(1992) *Dictionary of Celtic Myth and Legend.* London.

Greep, S. (1983) 'Early import of bone objects to south-east Britain', *Britannia* 14: 259–61.

(1991) *The Archaeology of Canterbury V (The Marlowe Car Park).* London.

(1994) 'Antler roundel pendants from Britain and the north-western provinces', *Britannia* 25: 79–97.

(1998) 'The bone, antler and ivory artefacts', in Cool and Philo (1998): 267–85.

(2003) 'Bone styli', *Lucerna* 24: 11–12.

Grew, F. O. (1980) 'Roman Britain in 1979: I. Sites explored', *Britannia* 11: 346–402.

Grew, F. O. and Griffiths, N. (1991) 'The pre-Flavian military belt: the evidence from Britain', *Archaeologia* 109: 47–84.

Guido, M. (1978) *The Glass Beads of the Prehistoric and Roman Periods in Britain and Ireland.* London.

(1979) 'The beads', in Clarke (1979): 292–300.

(ed. M. Welch) (1999) *The Glass Beads of Anglo-Saxon England 400–700.* Woodbridge.

Guildhall Museum Catalogue (1908) *Catalogue of the Collection of London Antiquities in the Guildhall Museum* (2nd edn). London.

Guirard, H. (1989) 'Bagues et anneaux à l'époque romaine en Gaule', *Gallia* 46: 173–211.

Guzzo, P. G. (ed.) (2003) *Tales from an Eruption: Pompeii, Herculanium, Oplontis.* Milan.

Haigh, D. and Savage, M. J. D. (1984) 'Sewingshields', *Archaeol. Aeliana* 5th ser., 12: 33–147.

Hall, J. and Wardle, A. (2005) 'Dedicated followers of fashion? Decorative bone hairpins from Roman London', in Crummy (2005): 173–9.

Hamilton, J. S. (1986) 'Scribonius Largus on the medical profession', *Bull. History Medicine* 60: 209–16.

Hansen, H.-O. (1969) 'Experimental ploughing with a Dostrup ard replica', *Tools and Tillage* 1.2: 67–92.

Hanson, A. (2006) 'Roman medicine', in D. S. Potter (ed.), *A Companion to the Roman Empire*. Oxford: 492–523.

Hanson, W. S. and Conolly, R. (2002) 'Language and literacy in Roman Britain: some archaeological considerations', in Cooley (2002): 151–64.

Harris, E. and Harris, J. R. (1965) *The Oriental Cults of Roman Britain*. Études Préliminaires aux Religions Orientales dans l'Empire Romain 6. Leiden.

Harris, W. V. (1980) 'Roman terracotta lamps: the organization of an industry', *J. Roman Stud.* 70: 126–45.

  (1989) *Ancient Literacy*. London.

Hartley, B. (1954) 'A fragment of samian ware from York with a figure in "cut-glass" technique', *Antiq. J.* 24: 233.

Hartley, E., Hawkes, J., Henig, M. and Mee, F. (2006) *Constantine the Great: York's Roman Emperor*. York.

Hartmann, M. (1986) *Vindonissa*. Windisch.

Hassall, M. and Sheldon, H. (1996) *Interpreting Roman London: Papers in Memory of Hugh Chapman*. Oxbow Mon. 58. Oxford.

Hassall, M. W. C. and Tomlin, R. S. O. (1994) 'Inscriptions', *Britannia* 25: 293–314.

  (1996) 'Inscriptions', *Britannia* 27: 439–57.

Hattatt, R. A. (1987) *Brooches of Antiquity*. Oxford.

Haverfield, F. J. (1918) 'Roman Leicester', *Archaeol. J.* 75: 297–321.

Havis, R. and Brooks, H. (2004) *Excavations at Stansted Airport, 1986–91*, vol. I: *Prehistoric and Romano-British*. E. Anglian Archaeol. Occ. Pap. 107. Chelmsford.

Hawkes, C. F. C. and Hull, M. R. (1947) *Camulodunum: First Report on the Excavations at Colchester 1930–1939*. Oxford.

Hawkes, S. and Dunning, G. (1961) 'Soldiers and settlers in Britain: 4th–5th century', *Medieval Archaeol.* 5: 1–70.

Hayward, K. M. J. (2006) 'A geological link between the Facilis monument at Colchester and first-century army tombstones from the Rhineland frontier', *Britannia* 37: 359–63.

Heinz, W. (1996) 'Antike Balneologie in späthellenistischer und Römische Zeit. Zur medizinischen Wirkung Römischer Bäder', *ANRW* II, 37.3: 2411–32.

Henig, M. (1970) 'Zoomorphic supports of cast bronze from Roman sites in Britain', *Archaeol. J.* 127: 182–7.

  (1977) 'Death and the maiden: funerary symbolism in daily life', in Munby and Henig (1977): 347–66.

(1978) *A Corpus of Roman Engraved Gemstones from British Sites.* BAR Brit. Ser. 8 (first published in 1974). Oxford.

(1984) *Religion in Roman Britain.* London.

(1993a) 'Votive objects: images and inscriptions', in Woodward and Leach (1993): 88–112.

(1993b) 'Ceramic altar', in Woodward and Leach (1993): 147.

(1993c) 'Candlesticks', in Woodward and Leach (1993): 201–3.

(2005) 'A light to lighten the gentiles: witnessing change in the Roman Empire', in Crummy (2005): 213–22.

Henig, M., Brown, D., Baatz, D., Sunter, N. and Allason-Jones, L. (1988) 'Objects from the sacred spring', in Cunliffe (1988): 5–54.

Henig, M. and King, A. (eds.) (1986) *Pagan Gods and Shrines of the Roman Empire.* Oxford Univ. Comm. Archaeol. Mon. 8. Oxford.

Hicks, J. D. and Wilson, J. A. (1975) 'Romano-British kilns at Hasholme', *E. Riding Archaeologist* 2: 67–9.

Hill, C., Millett, M. and Blagg, T. (1980) *The Roman Riverside Wall and Monumental Arch in London.* London Middlesex Archaeol. Soc. Spec. Pap. 3. London.

Hill, J. (1997) 'The end of one kind of body and the beginning of another kind of body? Toilet instruments and Romanization in Southern England during the 1st century AD', in A. Gwilt and C. Haselgrove (eds.), *Reconstructing Iron Age Societies.* Oxford: 96–107.

Hillman, G. (1981) 'Reconstructing crop husbandry practices from charred remains of crops' in Mercer (1981): 123–62.

Hinton, D. (2005) *Gold and Gilt, Pots and Pins: Possessions and People in Medieval Britain.* Oxford.

Hobbs, R. (2005) 'Why are there always so many spoons? Hoards of precious metals in Late Roman Britain', in Crummy (2005): 197–208.

Hodgkin, T. (1892) 'Discovery of Roman bronze vessels at Prestwick Carr', *Archaeol. Aeliana* 2nd ser., 15: 159–66.

Hodgson, N. (2005) 'Destruction by the enemy? Military equipment and the interpretation of a late-third century fire at South Shields', in *Archäologie de Schlachtfelder – Militaria aus Zerstörunghorizonten. Akten der 14. Internationalen Roman Military Equipment Conference. Carnuntum y Jahrbuch.* Vienna: 207–16.

Holbrook, N. and Bidwell, P. (1991) *Roman Finds from Exeter.* Exeter Archaeol. Rep. 4. Exeter.

Holmes, S. (1995) 'Seal-boxes from Roman London', *London Archaeologist* 7.15: 391–5.

Holwerda, J. (1931) 'Een vondst uit den Rijn bij Doorwerth', *Oudheidkundige Mededelingen* 12 suppl.: 1–26.

Huld-Zetsche, I. (2004) 'Der Mainzer Krater mit den sieben Figuren', in Martens and De Boe (2004): 213–27.

Hüser, H. (1979) 'Wärmetechnische Messungen an einer Hypokaustenheizung in der Saalburg', *Saalburg Jahrbuch* 36: 12–30.

Hutchinson, V. (1986) 'The cult of Bacchus in Roman Britain', in Henig and King (1986): 135–45.

Jackson, R. (1983) 'The Chester Gladiator rediscovered', *Britannia* 14: 87–95.

(1985) 'Cosmetic sets from Late Iron Age and Roman Britain', *Britannia* 16: 165–92.

(1986) 'A set of Roman medical instruments from Italy', *Britannia* 17: 119–67.

(1988) *Doctors and Diseases in the Roman Empire*. London.

(1990a) 'Roman doctors and their instruments: recent research into ancient practice', *J. Roman Archaeol.* 3: 5–27.

(1990b) 'Waters and spas in the classical world', in R. S. Porter and W. F. Bynum (eds.), *The Medical History of Spas and Waters*. Medical History Suppl. 10. London: 1–13.

(1990c) 'A new collyrium stamp from Cambridge and a corrected reading of the stamp from Caistor-by-Norwich', *Britannia* 21: 275–83.

(1992) '*Staphylagra, staphylocaustes,* uvulectomy and haemorrhoidectomy: the Roman instruments and operations', in A. Krug (ed.), *From Epidaurus to Salerno: Symposium held at Ravello, April 1990. PACT* 34. Rixensart: 167–85.

(1993) 'The function and manufacture of Romano-British cosmetic grinders: two important new finds from London', *Antiq. J.* 73: 165–9.

(1994) 'The surgical instruments, appliances and equipment in Celsus' *De medicina*', in G. Sabbah and P. Mudry (eds.), *La médecine de Celse: aspects historiques, scientifiques et littéraires.* St Étienne: 167–209.

(1995a) 'The composition of Roman medical *instrumentaria* as an indicator of medical practice: a provisional assessment', in P. J. van der Eijk, H. F. J. Horstmanshoff and P. H. Schrijvers (eds.), *Ancient Medicine in its Socio-cultural Context*, vol. 1. Clio Medica 27. Amsterdam and Atlanta, Ga.: 189–207.

(1995b) 'A Roman healer god from Sussex', *British Museum Mag.* 23: 19–21.

(1996a) 'Eye medicine in the Roman Empire', *ANRW* II, 37.3: 2228–51.

(1996b) 'A new collyrium-stamp from Staines and some thoughts on eye medicine in Roman London and Britannia', in J. Bird, M. Hassall and H. Sheldon (eds.), *Interpreting Roman London: Papers in Memory of Hugh Chapman.* Oxbow Mon. 58. Oxford: 177–87.

(1997a) 'An ancient British medical kit from Stanway, Essex', *The Lancet* 350: 1471–3.

(1997b) 'Eye diseases in the Greco-Roman world', *British Museum Mag.* 28: 23–5.

(1999) 'Spas, waters and hydrotherapy in the Roman world', in DeLaine and Johnston (1999): 107–16.

(2002) 'Roman surgery: the evidence of the instruments', in R. Arnott (ed.), *The Archaeology of Medicine*. BAR Int. Ser. 1046. Oxford: 87–94.

(2003) 'The Domus 'del chirurgo' at Rimini: an interim account of the medical assemblage', *J. Roman Archaeol.* 16: 312–21.

(2005a) 'Circumcision, de-circumcision and self-image: Celsus's "operations on the penis"', in A. Hopkins and M. Wyke (eds.), *Roman Bodies: Antiquity to the Eighteenth Century*. London: 23–32.

(2005b) 'Holding on to health? Bone surgery and instrumentation in the Roman Empire', in H. King (ed.), *Health in Antiquity*. London and New York: 97–119.

(2006) 'Colchester, cosmetic sets and context', in P. Ottaway (ed.), *A Victory Celebration: Papers on the Archaeology of Colchester and Late Iron Age–Roman Britain Presented to Philip Crummy*. Colchester: 105–12.

(2007) 'The surgical instruments', in Crummy *et al.* (2007): 236–52.

(2009) 'The surgical instrumentation of the Rimini *domus*', in S. DeCarolis (ed.), *Ars Medica. I ferri del mestiere. La domus 'del chirurgo' di Rimini e la chirugia nell' antica Roma*. Rimini: 73–91.

(forthcoming) *Cosmetic Grinders: An Illustrated Catalogue and Discussion of a Type Unique to Late Iron Age and Roman Britain*. British Museum Res. Pap. London.

Jackson, R. and Leahy, K. (1990) 'A Roman surgical forceps from near Littleborough and a note on the type', *Britannia* 21: 271–4.

James, S. (2005) 'The deposition of military equipment during the final siege at Dura-Europos, with particular regard to Tower 19 countermine', in Jilek (2005): 189–206.

Jarrett, M. G. and Wrathmell, S. (1981) *Whitton: An Iron Age and Roman Farmstead in South Glamorgan*. London.

Jenkins, F. (1957) 'The role of the dog in Romano-Gaulish religion', *Latomus* 16: 60–76.

(1958) 'The cult of the *Dea Nutrix* in Kent', *Archaeol. Cantiana* 71: 38–46.

(1978) 'Some interesting types of clay statuettes of the Roman period found in London', in Bird, Chapman and Clark (1978a): 148–62.

Jenkins, I. (1985) 'A group of silvered-bronze horse-trappings from Xanten (Castra Vetera)', *Britannia* 16: 141–64.

Jessop, B. F. (1954) 'Excavation of a Roman barrow at Holborough, Snodland', *Archaeol. Cantiana* 68: 22–30.

Jilek, S. (ed.) (2005) *Archäologie der Schlachtfelder: Militaria aus Zerstörungshorizonten. Proceedings of the Fourteenth Roman Military Equipment Conference (ROMEC XIV)*. Vienna.

Jobey, G. (1978) 'Burnswark Hill', *Trans. Dumfriesshire Galloway Natur. Antiq. Soc.* 53 (1977–8): 57–108.

Johns, C. M. (1981) 'A gold votive leaf and a bust of Minerva from Stonea', in Potter (1981): 101–4.

(1982) 'Finds from a late Roman burial from Stour Street, Canterbury', *Antiq. J.* 62: 361.

(1995) 'Mounted men and sitting ducks: the iconography of Romano-British plate-brooches', in B. Raftery, V. Megaw and V. Rigby (eds.), *Sites and Sights of the Iron Age: Essays on Fieldwork and Museum Research Presented to Ian Mathieson Stead*. Oxford: 103–9.

(1996) *The Jewellery of Roman Britain: Celtic and Classical Tradition*. London.

(1997) *The Snettisham Roman Jeweller's Hoard*. London.

Johns, C. and Potter, T. (1983) *The Thetford Treasure*. London.

Jones, A. H. M. (1964) *The Later Roman Empire, AD 284–602* (2 vols.). Oxford.

Jones, B. and Mattingly, D. (1990) *An Atlas of Roman Britain*. Oxford.

Jones, D. M. (1980) *Excavations at Billingsgate Buildings 'Triangle', Lower Thames Street, 1974*. London Middlesex Archaeol. Soc. Spec. Pap. 4. London.

Jones, M. (1981) 'The development of crop husbandry', in M. Jones and G. Dimbleby (eds.), *The Environment of Man: The Iron Age to the Anglo-Saxon Period*. BAR Brit. Ser. 87. Oxford: 95–127.

(1989) 'Agriculture in Roman Britain: the dynamics of change', in Todd (1989): 127–34.

Jones, M. J. (2002) *Roman Lincoln*. Stroud.

Jørgensen, L., Storgaard, B. and Gebauer Thomsen, L. (2003) *Sieg und Triumpf: Der Norden im Schatten des Römischen Reiches*. Copenhagen.

Jundi, S. and Hill, J. D. (1998). 'Brooches and identities in first century AD Britain: more than meets the eye?', in C. Forcey, J. Hawthorne and R. Witcher (eds.), *TRAC 97: Proceedings of the Seventh Annual Theoretical Roman Archaeology Conference*. Oxford: 125–37.

Károly, G. (1890) 'Okori kocsik helyreállitása', *Archeologiai Ertesitö* 10: 97–126.

Keim, J. and Klumbach, H. (1951) *Der Römische Schatzfund von Straubing*. Munich.

Kent, J. (1977) 'Coinage and currency', in J. Kent and K. Painter (eds.), *Wealth of the Roman World*. London: 159–62.

Kenyon, K. M. (1935) 'The Roman theatre at Verulamium', *Archaeologia* 84: 213–61.

(1948) *Excavations at the Jewry Wall Site, Leicester*. London.

(1954) 'Excavations at Sutton Walls, Herefordshire', *Archaeol. J.* 110: 1–87.

Kilbride-Jones, H. (1938) 'Glass armlets in Britain', *Proc. Soc. Antiq. Scotland* 72: 366–95.

King, D. (1986) 'The petrology, dating and distribution of querns and millstones in the counties of Bedfordshire, Buckinghamshire, Hertfordshire and Middlesex', *Univ. London Inst. Archaeol. Bull.* 23: 65–126.

Köhne, E. and Ewigleben, C. (2000) *Gladiators and Caesars: The Power of Spectacle in Ancient Rome* (English edition ed. R. Jackson). London.

Korpela, J. (1987) *Das Medizinalpersonal im antiken Rom*. Helsinki.

Koster, A. (1997) *Description of the Collections in the Provincial Museum G. M. Kam at Nijmegen XIII: The Bronze Vessels II. Acquisitions 1954–1996 including Vessels of Pewter and Iron*. Nijmegen.

Kudlien, F. (1986) *Die Stellung des Arztes in der Römischen Gesellschaft*. Stuttgart.

Künzl, E. (1983) *Medizinische Instrumente aus Sepulkralfunden der römischen Kaiserzeit*. Bonn.

(1995) 'Medizin der Kelten. Ein archäologischer Forschungsbericht', in R. Bedon and P. M. Martin (eds.), *Mélanges Raymond Chevallier*, Vol II: *Histoire et archéologie*. Tours: 221–39.

(1996) 'Forschungsbericht zu den antiken medizinischen Instrumenten', *ANRW* II, 37.3: 2433–2639.

(1998) 'Instrumentenfunde und Ärzthäuser in Pompeji: die medizinische Versorgung einer Römischen Stadt des 1. Jahrhunderts n. Chr.', *Sartoniana* 11: 71–152.

(2005) 'Aesculapius im Valetudinarium', *Archäologisches Korrespondenzblatt* 35: 55–64.

Künzl, E. and Künzl, S. (1993) 'Der Fund von Neupotz', in E. Künzl (ed.), *Die Alamannenbeute aus dem Rhein bei Neupotz.* Mainz: 473–505.

Lalou, E. (ed.) (1992) *Les tablettes à écrire de l'antiquité à l'époque moderne.* Turnhout.

Lambert, J. (1996) *Transect through Time: The Archaeological Landscape of the Shell North-Western Ethylene Pipeline.* Lancaster Imprints 1. Lancaster.

Lambrick, G. and Robinson, M. (1979) *Iron Age and Roman Riverside Settlements at Farmoor, Oxfordshire.* Oxford Archaeol. Unit Rep. 2. CBA Res. Rep. 32. London.

Langslow, D. R. (2000) *Medical Latin in the Roman Empire.* Oxford.

la Niece, S. (1983) 'Niello: an historical and technical survey', *Antiq. J.* 63: 279–97.

Lawson, A. J. (1975) 'Shale and jet objects from Silchester', *Archaeologia* 105: 241–75.

Lawson, G. and Wardle, A. (1998) 'A Roman pipe from London', *LAMAS: Trans. London Middlesex Archaeol. Soc.* 39: 35–6.

Layard, N. F. (1925) 'Bronze crowns and a bronze head-dress, from a Roman site at Cavenham Heath, Suffolk', *Antiq. J.* 5: 256–65.

Leach, P. (1993) 'Pottery', in Woodward and Leach (1993): 219–49.

Leahy, K. (1980) 'Votive models from Kirmington, South Humberside', *Britannia* 11: 326–30.

Leeds, E. T (1933) *Celtic Ornament in the British Isles, down to 700 A.D.* Oxford.

Leibundgut, A. (1977) *Die Römischen Lampen in der Schweiz.* Berne.

Lepper, F. and Frere, S. S. (1988) *Trajan's Column: A New Edition of the Cichorius Plates.* Gloucester.

Liversidge, J. (1955) *Furniture in Roman Britain.* London.

(1968) *Britain in the Roman Empire* (1st edn). London.

(1973) *Britain in the Roman Empire* (2nd edn). London.

(1977) 'Wooden furniture fragments' in Rogerson (1977): 204–6.

Lloyd-Morgan, G. (1977) 'Roman mirrors in Britain', *Current Archaeol.* 5.11 (no. 58): 329–31.

(1981) *Description of the Collections in the Rijksmuseum G M Kam at Nijmegen. X: The Mirrors.* Nijmegen.

Loeschcke, S. (1919) *Lampen aus Vindonissa.* Zurich.

Lyne, M. A. B. and Jefferies, R. S. (1979) *The Alice Holt/Farnham Roman Pottery Industry.* CBA Res. Rep. 30. London.

Lysons, S. (1817) *Reliquiae Britannico-Romanae; Containing Figures of Roman Antiquities Discovered in Roman Britain*, Vol. II. London.

McCarthy, M. R. (2000) *Roman and Medieval Carlisle: The Southern Lanes. Excavations 1981–2*. Department of Archaeological Sciences, Univ. Bradford Res. Rep. 1. Carlisle.

McCarthy, M., Bishop, M. and Richardson, T. (2001) 'Roman armour and metalworking at Carlisle, Cumbria, England', *Antiquity* 75: 507–8.

Macdonald, G. and Park, A. (1906) *The Roman Forts on the Bar Hill, Dumbartonshire*. Glasgow.

McGrail, S. (1990a) 'Boats and boatmanship in the late prehistoric southern North Sea and Channel region', in McGrail (1990b): 32–48.

(1990b) (ed.) *Maritime Celts, Frisians and Saxons*. CBA Res. Rep. 71. London.

(2004) *Boats of the World*. Oxford.

MacGregor, A. (1976) *Finds from a Roman Sewer System and an Adjacent Building in Church Street, York*. York.

(2001) *Bone, Antler, Ivory and Horn* (Croom Helm reprint; 1st edn 1985). London.

MacGregor, M. (1962) 'The early Iron Age metalwork hoard from Stanwick', *Proc. Prehist. Soc.* 28: 17–57.

(1976) *Early Celtic Art in North Britain*. Leicester.

Mackay, D. (1949) 'The jewellery of Palmyra and its significance', *Iraq* 11.2: 160–87.

Mackinder, A. (2000) *A Romano-British Cemetery on Watling Street*. MoLAS Archaeol. Stud. Ser. 4. London.

McKinley, J. I. (1997) 'Bronze Age "barrows" and the funerary rites and rituals of cremation', *Proc. Prehist. Soc.* 63: 129–45.

(2000) 'Phoenix rising: aspects of cremation in Roman Britain' in Pearce, Millett and Struck (2000): 38–44.

Mackreth, D. F. (1986) 'The brooches', in D. Gurney (ed.), *Settlement, Religion and Industry on the Fen-Edge: Three Romano-British Sites in Norfolk. E. Anglian Archaeol.* 31: 61–7.

MacMullen, R. (1982) 'The epigraphic habit in the Roman Empire', *American J. Philol.* 103: 233–46.

Maiuri, A. (1953) *Roman Painting*, trans. S. Gilbert. Geneva.

Major, H. (2002) 'Roman decorated iron styli', *Lucerna* 23: 2–5.

Manderscheid, H. (2004) *Ancient Baths and Bathing: A Bibliography for the Years 1988–2001*. Portsmouth, RI.

Mann, J. C. (1984) 'A note on the "Modius Claytonensis"', *Archaeol. Aeliana* 5th ser., 12: 242–3.

(1985) 'Epigraphic consciousness', *J. Rom. Stud.* 75: 204–6.

Manning, W. H. (1964) 'The plough in Roman Britain', *J. Rom. Stud.* 54: 54–65.

(1966a) 'A hoard of Romano-British ironwork from Brampton, Cumberland', *Trans. Cumberland Westmorland Antiq. Archaeol. Soc.* 66 2nd ser., 1–36.

(1966b) 'Caistor-by-Norwich and the Notitia Dignitatum', *Antiquity* 40: 60, 62.

(1966c) 'Bronze models from Sussex in the British Museum', *Antiq. J.* 46: 50–9.

(1970) 'Mattocks, hoes, spades and related tools in Roman Britain', in Gailey and Fenton (1970): 18–29.

(1971) 'The Piercebridge ploughgroup', *Brit. Mus. Quarterly* 35: 125–36.

(1972a) 'Ironwork hoards in Iron Age and Roman Britain', *Britannia* 3: 224–50.

(1972b) 'The iron objects', in Frere (1972): 163–95.

(1972c) 'The method of manufacture of Roman-British woolcombs', *Antiq. J.* 52: 333–5.

(1976) *Catalogue of Romano-British Ironwork in the Museum of Antiquities, Newcastle upon Tyne.* Newcastle upon Tyne.

(1984) 'The iron objects', in *Verulamium Excavations*, vol. III. Res. Rep. Comm. Soc. Antiq. London: 83–106.

(1985) *Catalogue of the Romano-British Iron Tools, Fittings and Weapons in the British Museum.* London.

(2006) 'The Roman ironwork deposits from the fort at Newstead', *Bayerische Vorgeschichtsblatter* 71: 15–32.

Manning, W. H., Price, J. and Webster, J. (1995) *The Roman Small Finds: Report on the Excavations at Usk, 1965–1976.* Cardiff.

Marsden, A. (2001) *Roman Coins Found in Britain.* Witham.

Marsden, P. (1965a) 'A boat of the Roman period discovered on the site of New Guy's House, Bermondsey, 1958', *Trans. London Middlesex Archaeol. Soc.* 21.2: 118–31.

(1965b) 'The County Hall ship', *Trans. London Middlesex Archaeol. Soc.* 21.2: 109–17.

(1990) 'A re-assessment of Blackfriars Ship 1', in McGrail (1990b): 66–74.

(1994) *Ships of the Port of Roman London.* English Heritage Archaeol. Rep. 3. London.

Marsh, G. (1978a) 'Early second century fine wares in the London area', in Arthur and Marsh (1978): 119–223.

(1978b) '8 Union Street', in Bird *et al.* (1978b): 221–32.

Martens, M. and De Boe, G. (eds.) (2004) *Roman Mithraism: The Evidence of the Small Finds.* Archeologie in Vlaanderen Monografie 4. Brussels.

Martin-Kilcher, S. (2000) '*Mors immatura* in the Roman world – a mirror of society and tradition', in Pearce, Millett and Struck (2000): 63–77.

Massart, C. (2003) 'Au-dela du bijou, le pouvoir du symbole: les amulettes en forme de lunule et de phallus', in Sas and Thoen (2003): 101–4.

Mattingly, D. (2004) 'Being Roman: expressing identity in a provincial setting', *J. Roman Archaeol.* 17: 5–25.

Mattingly, H. and Sydenham, E. A. (eds.) (1923–94) *Roman Imperial Coinage* (10 vols.). London.

Maxfield, V. (1986) 'Pre-Flavian forts and their garrisons', *Britannia* 17: 59–72.

Maxfield, V. and Dobson, M. (eds.) (1991) *Roman Frontier Studies 1989.* Exeter.

Maxwell, G. (1990) *A Battle Lost: Romans and Caledonians at Mons Graupius.* Edinburgh.

May, T. (1904) *Warrington's Roman Remains.* Warrington.

  (1922) *The Roman Forts at Templeborough near Rotherham.* Rotherham.

  (1930) *Catalogue of the Roman Pottery in the Colchester and Essex Museum.* Cambridge.

Meates, G. W. (1987) *The Roman Villa at Lullingstone, Kent II: The Wall Paintings and Finds.* Maidstone.

Megaw, J. V. S. (ed.) (1976) *To Illustrate the Monument.* London.

Mercer, R. (ed.) (1981) *Farming Practice in British Prehistory.* Edinburgh.

Merrifield, R. (1965) *The Roman City of London.* London.

  (1987) *The Archaeology of Ritual and Magic.* London.

  (1995) 'Roman metalwork from the Walbrook – rubbish, ritual or redundancy?', *Trans. London Middlesex Archaeol. Soc.* 46: 27–44.

  (1996) 'The London hunter-god and his significance in the history of Londinium', in Bird *et al.* (1996): 105–13.

Millett, M. and McGrail, S. (1987) 'Archaeology of the Hasholme logboat', *Archaeol. J.* 144: 69–155.

Morel, J.-M. A. W. and Bosman, A. V. A. J. (1989) 'An early Roman burial in Velsen I', in van Driel-Murray (1989a): 167–9.

Moritz, L. A. (1958) *Grain Mills and Flour in Classical Antiquity.* Oxford.

Morley, N. (2005) 'The salubriousness of the Roman city', in H. King (ed.), *Health in Antiquity.* London and New York: 192–204.

Morris, C. (1990) 'Wooden finds', in Wrathmell and Nicholson (1990): 206–30.

  (1998) 'The wooden artefacts,' in Cool and Philo (1998): 335–46.

Morris, I. (1992) *Death-Ritual and Social Structure in Classical Antiquity.* Cambridge.

Mould, Q. (2002) 'Iron objects from Catterick Bypass (Site 433)', in Wilson (2002a): 82–99.

  (2004) 'Hobnails and shoes', in Cool (2004a): 391–2.

  (2006), 'Leather' from Colchester Garrison Alienated Land Sites. Unpublished report submitted to Colchester Archaeological Trust, February 2006.

  (2010a) 'Pewter vessels', in Bennett *et al.* 2010: 241–3.

  (2010b) 'Knives', in Bennett *et al.* 2010: 223–7.

Muckelroy, K., Haselgrove, C. and Nash, D. (1978) 'A pre-Roman coin from Canterbury and the ship represented on it', *Proc. Prehist. Soc.* 44: 439–44.

Munby, J. and Henig, M. (eds.) (1977). *Roman Life and Art in Britain.* BAR Brit. Ser. 41. Oxford.

Nash-Williams, V. E. (1932) 'The Roman Legionary Fortress at Caerleon in Monmouthshire. Report on the excavations carried out in the Prysg Field 1927–9', *Archaeol. Cambrensis* 87: 48–104.

  (1950) *The Early Christian Monuments of Wales.* Cardiff.

Nayling, N. and McGrail, S. (2004) *The Barland's Farm Romano-Celtic Boat.* CBA Res. Rep. 138. York.

Neal, D. S. (1974) *The Excavation of the Roman Villa in Gadebridge Park, Hemel Hempstead 1963–8.* Rep. Res. Comm. Soc. Antiq. London 31. London.

Neal, D. S. and Cosh, S. R. (2002) *The Roman Mosaics of Britain. I: Northern Britain Incorporating the Midlands and East Anglia.* London.

(2006) *The Roman Mosaics of Britain. II: South West Britain.* London.

Neal, D. S., Wardle, A. and Hunn, J. (1990) *Excavation of the Iron Age, Roman and Medieval Settlement at Gorhambury, St Albans.* English Heritage Archaeol. Rep. 14. London.

Nenova-Merdjanova, R. (1999) 'Roman bronze vessels as part of *instrumentum balnei*', in DeLaine and Johnston (1999): 131–4.

Neville, R. C. (1856) 'Description of a remarkable deposit of Roman antiquities of iron, discovered at Great Chesterford, Essex, in 1854', *Archaeol. J.* 13: 1–13.

Niblett, R. (2001) *Verulamium.* Stroud.

Nielsen, I. (1993) *Thermae et Balnea: The Architecture and Cultural History of Roman Public Baths.* Aarhus.

Nuber, H.-U. (1972) 'Kanne und Griffschale. Ihr Gebrauch im täglichen Leben und die Beigabe in Gräbern der Römischen Kaiserzeit', *Bericht der Römisch-Germanischen Kommission* 53: 1–232.

Nutton, V. (1986) 'The perils of patriotism: Pliny and Roman medicine', in R. French and F. Greenaway (eds.), *Science in the Early Roman Empire: Pliny the Elder, His Sources and Influences.* London and Sydney: 30–58.

(2004) *Ancient Medicine.* London.

Oakley, K. (1965a) 'Folklore of fossils, part I', *Antiquity* 39.153: 9–16.

(1965b) 'Folklore of fossils, part II', *Antiquity* 39.154: 117–25.

O'Connell, M. and Bird, J. (1994) 'The Roman temple at Wanborough, excavations 1985–1986', *Surrey Archaeol. Collect.* 82: 1–168.

Ogden, J. (1982) *Ancient Jewellery.* London.

Oldenstein, J. (1976): 'Zur Ausrüstung römischer Auxiliareinheiten', *Bericht der Römisch-Germanischen Kommission* 57: 49–284.

Oliver, A. (2000) 'Jewellery for the unmarried', in D. Kleiner and S. Mathisen (eds.), *Claudia II: Women in Roman Culture and Society.* Austin, TX: 115–24.

Öllerer, C. (1998) 'Römisches Schreibgerät vom Magdalensberg', *Carinthia* 188: 121–55.

O'Neil, H. E. (1945) 'The Roman villa at Park Street, near St. Albans, Hertfordshire: report on the excavations of 1943–45', *Archaeol. J.* 102: 21–110.

Pace, B. (1955) *I Mosaici di Piazza Armerina.* Sicily.

Padley, T. G. (2000) 'The finds', in McCarthy (2000): 93–121.

Padley, T. G. and Tomlin, R. S. O. (1991) 'The writing tablets', in T. G. Padley and S. Winterbottom, *The Wooden, Leather and Bone Objects from Castle Street, Carlisle: Excavations 1981–2.* Cumberland Westmorland Antiquarian Arch. Soc. Res.Rep. Fasc. 3. Kendal: 209–18.

Painter, K. S. (1971) 'Roman bronze crowns from Deeping St James, Lincolnshire', *Antiq. J.* 51: 319–21.

Parfitt, K. (1995) *Iron Age Burials from Mill Hill, Deal.* London.

Parker, A. J. (1992) *Ancient Shipwrecks of the Mediterranean and the Roman Provinces*, BAR Int. Ser. 580. Oxford.

Parker Pearson, M. (1999) *The Archaeology of Death and Burial.* Stroud.

Paulsen, P. (1992) *Die Holzfunde aus dem Gräberfeld bei Oberflacht und ihre kulturgeschichtliche Bedeutung.* Stuttgart.

Payne, F. G. (1947) 'The plough in Ancient Britain', *Archaeol. J.* 104: 82–111.

Peacock, D. S. (1977) 'Bricks and tiles of the *Classis Britannica*: petrology and origin', *Britannia* 8: 235–48.

(1987) 'Iron Age and Roman quern production at Lodworth, West Sussex', *Antiq. J.* 67: 61–85.

Pearce, J. (2004) 'Archaeology, writing tablets and literacy in Roman Britain', *Gallia* 61: 43–51.

Pearce, J., Millett, M. and Struck, M. (eds.) (2000) *Burial, Society and Context in the Roman World.* Oxford.

Perez-Arantegui, J. (1996) 'Analysis of the products contained in two Roman glass *unguentaria* from the colony of Celsa, Spain', *J. Archaeol. Sci.* 23: 649–55.

Perrin, J. R. (1990) *Roman Pottery from the Colonia.* The Archaeology of York. The Pottery 16/4. London.

Petts, D. (2003) *Christianity in Roman Britain.* Stroud.

Phillips, E. J. (1977) *Corpus Signorum Imperii Romani: Great Britain I.1 Corbridge, Hadrian's Wall East of the North Tyne.* Oxford.

Philpott, R. (1991) *Burial Practices in Roman Britain*, BAR Brit. Ser. 219. Oxford.

Piggott, S. (1953) 'Three metal-work hoards of the Roman period from southern Scotland', *Proc. Soc. Antiq. Scotland* 87 (1951–3): 1–50.

(1959) 'The *carnyx* in Early Iron Age Britain', *Antiq. J.* 39: 19–32.

Pirling, R. (1971) 'Ein Bestattungsplatz gefallener Römer in Krefeld-Gellep', *Archäologisches Korrespondenzblatt* 1: 45–6.

(1977), 'Die Ausgrabungen in Krefeld-Gellep', *Ausgrabungen in Rheinland* 77: 138–40.

(1986), 'Ein Mithräum als Kriegergrab', in Unz (1986): 244–6.

(1997) *Das Römisch-Frankish Graberfeld von Krefeld-Gellep 1975–82.* Stuttgart.

Pitt-Rivers, A. H. L. (1887) *Excavations in Cranborne Chase I.* Printed privately.

(1888) *Excavations in Cranborne Chase II.* Printed privately.

(1892) *Excavations in Cranborne Chase III.* Printed privately.

(1898) *Excavations in Cranborne Chase IV.* Printed privately.

Pitts, L. F. (1979) *Roman Bronze Figurines of the Catuvellauni and Trinovantes*, BAR Brit. Ser. 60. Oxford.

Pitts, L. F. and St. Joseph, J. K. (1985) *Inchtuthil: The Roman Legionary Fortress.* London.

Potter, T. W. (1981) 'The Roman occupation of the central Fenland', *Britannia* 12: 79–133.

Poulton, R. (2007) 'Farley Heath Roman temple', *Surrey Archaeol. Collect.* 93: 1–147.

Price, J. (1988) 'Romano-British glass bangles from E. Yorkshire', in J. Price and P. Wilson (eds.), *Recent Research in Roman Yorkshire*. BAR Brit. Ser. 193. Oxford: 339–66.

(1995a) 'Glass bangles', in Manning, Price and Webster (1995): 99–104.

(1995b) 'Glass beads', in Manning, Price and Webster (1995): 105–12.

Price, J. and Cottam, S. (1998) *Romano-British Glass Vessels: A Handbook*. York.

Pritchard, F. A. (1986) 'Ornamental stonework from Roman London', *Britannia* 17: 169–89.

Pugsley, P. (2003) *Roman Domestic Wood*. BAR Int. Ser. 1118. Oxford.

(2005) 'The origins of medieval vessel turning', *Antiq. J.* 85: 1–22.

Puttock, S. (2002) *Ritual Significance of Personal Ornament in Roman Britain*. BAR Brit. Ser. 327. Oxford.

Quinnell, H. (2004) *Trethurgy: Excavations at Trethurgy Round, St. Austell: Community and Status in Roman and Post-Roman Cornwall*. Truro.

Raepsaet, G. (2002) *Attelages et techniques de transport dans le monde gréco-romain*. Brussels.

Rahtz, P. A. and ApSimon, A. (1962) 'Excavations at Shearplace Hill, St. Nicholas, Dorset, England', *Proc. Prehist. Soc.* 28: 289–328.

Reece, R. (1970) *Roman Coins*. London.

(1977) *Burial in the Roman World*. CBA Res. Rep. 22. London.

(2002) *The Coinage of Roman Britain*. Stroud.

Reece, R. and James, S. (2000) *Identifying Roman Coins: A Practical Guide to the Identification of Site Finds in Britain* (2nd edn). London.

Rees, S. E. (1979) *Agricultural Implements in Prehistoric and Roman Britain*. BAR Brit. Ser. 69. Oxford.

(1981) 'Agricultural tools: function and use', in Mercer (1981): 66–84.

Reuter, M. and Scholz, M. (2004) *Geritzt und Entziffert: Schriftzeugnisse der römischen Informationsgesellschaft*. Stuttgart.

Richards, D. (2000) 'The ironwork', in M. Fulford and J. Timby, *Late Iron Age and Roman Silchester: Excavations on the Site of the Forum-Basilica 1977, 1980-86*. Britannia Mon. Ser. 15. London: 360–79.

Richmond, I. A. (1947) 'The Roman city of Lincoln', *Archaeol. J.* 103: 26–56.

(1968) *Hod Hill*, vol. II: *Excavations Carried Out between 1951 and 1958 for the Trustees of the British Museum*. London.

Richmond, I. A. and Gillam, J. P. (1951) 'The temple of Mithras at Carrawburgh', *Archaeol. Aeliana* 4th ser., 29: 1–92.

Ricken, H. and Thomas, M. (2005) *Die Dekorationsserien der Rheinzaberner Reliefsigillata*. Materialen zur Römisch-Germansichen Keramik 14. Bonn.

Riha, E. (1986) *Römisches Toilettgerät und medizinische Instrumente aus Augst und Kaiseraugst*. Augst.

Ritchie, J. N. G. (1974) 'Iron Age finds from Dun an Fheurain, Gallanach, Argyll', *Proc. Soc. Antiq. Scotland* 103: 100–12.

Ritterling, E. (1912) 'Das frührömische Lager bei Hofheim im Taunus', *Annalen des Vereins für Nassauische Altertumskunde und Geschichtsforschung* 40: 1–416.

Roberts, C. and Cox, M. (2003) *Health and Disease in Britain: From Prehistory to the Present Day*. Stroud.

Roberts, M. and Swain, H. (eds.) (2001) *The Spitalfields Roman* (2nd edn). London.

Robinson, H. R. (1975) *The Armour of Imperial Rome*. London.

Roe, F., Boyle, A. and Early, R. (2000). *Excavations at Springhead Roman Town, Southfleet, Kent*. Oxford Archaeol. Unit. Occ. Pap. 1. Oxford.

Rogerson, A. (1977) *Excavations at Scole, 1973*. E. Anglian Archaeol. Rep. 5. Gressenhall.

Rook, T. (1978) 'The development and operation of Roman hypocaust baths', *J. Archaeol. Sci.* 5: 269–82.

(1992) *Roman Baths in Britain*. Princes Risborough.

Röring, C. W. (1983) *Untersuchungen zu Römischen Reisewagen*. Coblenz.

Ross, A. (1968) 'Pits, shafts and wells – sanctuaries of the Belgic Britains', in Coles and Simpson (1968): 255–85.

Ross, A. and Feacham, R. (1976) 'Ritual rubbish? The Newstead pits', in Megaw (1976): 230–7.

Rostowzew, M. (1903) *Tesserarum Urbis Romae et Suburbi Plumbearum Sylloge*. St Petersburg.

(1905) *Römische Bleitesserae: ein Beitrag zur Sozial- und Wirtschaftsgeschichte der Römischen Kaiserziet*. Beiträge zur alten Geschichte 3. Leipzig.

Rottländer, R. C. A. (1992) 'Der Brennstoff Römischer Beleuchtungskörper', *Jahresberichte aus Augst und Kaiseraugst* 13: 225–9.

Royal Mint (2006) www.royalmint.com/RoyalMint/web/site/Corporate/Corp_british_coin age/CoinDesign/1pCoin.asp.

Rule, M. (1990) 'The Romano-Celtic ship excavated at St Peter's Port, Guernsey' in McGrail (1990b): 49–56.

Salza Prina Ricotti, E. (1978/80) 'Cucine e quartieri servili in epoca Romana', *Rendiconti Atti della Pontificia Academia Romana di Archeologia* 51.2: 237–94.

Sas, K. (2004) '"Military" bracelets in Oudenburg: troop movements, origins and relations in the Litus Saxonicum in the 4th century AD', in F. Vermeulen, K. Sas and W. Dhaeze (eds.), *Archaeology in Confrontation: Aspects of Roman Military Presence in the Northwest*. Ghent: 343–78.

Sas, K. and Thoen, H. (eds.) (2003) *Schone Schijn: Romeinse juweelkunst in West-Europa/Brillance et prestige: la joaillerie romaine en Europe occidentale*. Leuven.

Sauer, E. (2000) 'Alchester, a Claudian "vexillation fortress" near the western boundary of the Catuvellauni, new light on the Roman invasion of Britain', *Archaeol. J.* 157: 1–78.

(2005) 'Inscriptions from Alchester: Vespasian's base of the Second Augustan Legion(?)', *Britannia* 36: 101–33.

Schenk, D. (1930) *Flavius Vegetius Renatus: die Quellen der Epit. rei militaris*. Klio Beiheft 22. Leipzig.

Schlüter, W. (1993) *Kalkriese – Römer im Osnabrücker Land*. Archäologisch Forschungen zur Varusschlacht. Bramsche.

(1999) 'The battle of the Teutoburg Forest: archaeological research near Kalkreise near Osnabrück', in Schlüter and Wiegels (1999): 125–60.

Schlüter, W. and Wiegels, R. (eds.) (1999) *Rom, Germanien und die Ausgrabungen von Kalkriese*. Bramsche.

Scobie, A. (1986) 'Slums, sanitation and mortality in the Roman world', *Klio* 68.2: 399–433.

Sconocchia, S (1983) *Scribonii Largi Compositiones*. Leipzig.

Scott, I. R. (1990) 'Ironwork from Well 1', in Wrathmell and Nicholson (1990): 197–206.

Seaward, M. R. D. (1993) 'The environmental material', in R. Birley (ed.), *Vindolanda*, vol. III: *The Early Wooden Forts: Preliminary Reports on the Leather, Textiles, Environmental Evidence and Dendrochronology*. Hexham: 91–119.

Seeley, F. and Drummond-Murray, J. (2005) *Roman Pottery Production in the Walbrook Valley: Excavations at 20–28 Moorgate, City of London, 1998–2000*. MoLAS Mon. 25. London.

Shaffrey, R. (2003) 'The rotary querns from the Society of Antiquaries' excavations at Silchester 1890–1909', *Britannia* 34: 143–74.

(2006) *Grinding and Milling: A Study of Romano-British Rotary Querns and Millstones made of Old Red Sandstone*. BAR Brit. Ser. 409. Oxford.

Sharpe, J. L. (1992) 'The Dakhleh tablets and some codicological considerations', in Lalou (1992): 127–37.

Shepherd, J. (1998) *The Temple of Mithras, London: Excavations by W. F. Grimes and A. Williams at the Walbrook*. English Heritage Archaeol. Rep. 12. London.

Shirley, E. (2001) *Building a Roman Legionary Fortress*. Stroud.

Shotter, D. and White, A. (1990) *The Roman Fort and Town of Lancaster*. Univ. Lancaster Occ. Pap. 18. Lancaster.

Sim, D. and Ridge, I. (2002) *Iron for the Eagles: The Iron Industry of Roman Britain*. Stroud.

Simpson, C. (1976) 'Belt buckles and strap-ends of the Later Roman Empire: a preliminary survey of several new groups', *Britannia* 7: 192–223.

Simpson, G. and Blance, B. (1998) 'Do brooches have ritual associations?', in J. Bird (ed.), *Form and Fabric: Studies in Rome's Material Past in Honour of B. R. Hartley*. Oxford: 267–79.

Smith, R. A. (1918) 'A peculiar type of Roman bronze pendant', *Proc. Soc. Antiq. London* 2nd ser., 30: 54–63.

(1922) *British Museum Guide to Roman Britain*. London.

Sommer, M. (1984) *Die Gürtel und Gürtelbeschläge des 4 und 5 Jahrhunderts im Römischen Reich*. Bonner Hefte zur Vorgeschichte 22. Bonn.

Spain, R. (1984) 'The second-century Romano-British watermill at Ickham', *Kent Hist. Technology* 9: 143–80.

(1993) 'A possible tide mill', Kent Archaeol. Soc. Pap. 5. (www. kentarchaeology.org.uk, accessed July 2007).

Stanfield, J. A. and Simpson, G. (1958) *Central Gaulish Potters*. London.

Stead, I. M. (1967) 'A La Tène burial at Welwyn Garden City', *Archaeologia* 109: 1–63.

(1995) 'The metalwork', in Parfitt (1995): 58–111.

Stead, I. M., and Rigby, V. (1986) *Baldock: The Excavation of a Roman and Pre-Roman Settlement 1968–72*. London.

(1989) *Verulamium: The King Harry Lane Site*. English Heritage Archaeol. Rep. 12. London.

Steensberg, A. (1936) 'North West European plough types of prehistoric times and the middle ages', *Acta Archaeologica* 7: 244–80.

(1942) *Ancient Harvesting Implements*. Copenhagen.

Stein, R. (2004) 'Roman wooden force pumps: a case-study in innovation', *J. Roman Archaeol.* 17: 221–50.

Stevenson, R. B. K. (1957) 'Native bangles and Roman glass', *Proc. Soc. Antiq. Scotland* 88: 208–21.

Stout, A. (2001) 'Jewellery as a symbol of status in the Roman Empire', in J. L. Sebesta and L. Bonfante (eds.), *The World of Roman Costume*. Madison, WI: 77–100.

Straker, V. (1987) 'Report on grain', in P. Marsden (ed.), *The Roman Forum Site in London*. London: 151–3.

Struck, M. (2000) 'High status burials in Roman Britain (first–third century AD) – potential interpretation', in Pearce, Millett and Struck (2000): 85–96.

Sumner, G. (2002) *Roman Military Clothing (1) 100BC–AD200*. Oxford.

Susini, G. (1973) *The Roman Stonecutter: An Introduction to Latin Epigraphy*. Oxford.

Swain, H. and Roberts, M. (2001) *The Spitalfields Roman*. London.

Swan, V. E. (1992) 'Legion VI and its men: African legionaries in Britain,' *J. Roman Pottery Stud.* 5: 1–33.

Swift, E. (2000a) *Regionality in Dress Accessories in the Late Roman West*, Monographies Instrumentum 11. Montagnac.

(2000b) *The End of the Western Roman Empire*. Stroud.

(2003) 'Late Roman necklaces and bracelets', *J. Roman Archaeol.* 16: 336–49.

(2004) 'Dress accessories, culture and identity in the late Roman period', *Antiquité Tardive* 12: 217–22.

(2006) 'Constructing Roman identities in late Antiquity: the north-west frontier', *Late Antique Archaeology 3, Social and Political Archaeology of Late Antiquity*. Leiden.

(2009) *Style and Function in Roman Decoration: Living with Objects and Interiors*. Farnham.

Tassinari, S. (1993) *Il vasellame bronzeo di Pompei I–II*. Soprintendenza archeologica di Pompei cataloghi 5. Rome.

Thevenot, E. (1968) *Divinités et sanctuaires de la Gaule*. Paris.

Todd, M. (ed.) (1989) *Research in Roman Britain.* Britannia Mon. Ser. 11. London: 127–34.

Tomlin, R. S. O. (1979) 'Graffiti on Roman bricks and tiles found in Britain', in A. McWhirr (ed.), *Roman Brick and Tile: Studies in Manufacture, Distribution and Use in the Western Empire.* BAR Int. Ser. 68. Oxford: 231–51.

(1988) *Tabellae Sulis: Roman Inscribed Tablets of Tin and Lead from the Sacred Spring at Bath.* Oxford; also published as Part IV (*The Curse Tablets*) of Cunliffe (1988): 59–260.

(1991) 'Inscriptions from Roman Britain in 1990', *Britannia* 22: 293–311.

(1992) 'The Twentieth Legion at Wroxeter and Carlisle in the first century: the epigraphic evidence', *Britannia* 23: 141–58.

(1993) 'The inscribed lead tablets: an interim report', in Woodward and Leach (1993): 113–30.

(1996a) 'The Vindolanda Tablets' [review article of Bowman and Thomas 1994], *Britannia* 27: 459–63.

(1996b) 'A five-acre wood in Roman Kent', in Bird *et al.* (1996): 209–15.

(1997) '*Sede in tuo loco:* a fourth-century uterine phylactery in Latin from Roman Britain', *ZPE* 115: 291–4.

(1998) 'Roman manuscripts from Carlisle: the ink-written tablets', *Britannia* 29: 31–84.

(2002) 'Writing to the gods in Britain', in Cooley (2002): 165–79.

(2003) '"The girl in question": a new text from Roman London', *Britannia* 34: 41–57.

(2004) 'A Roman will from North Wales', *Archaeol. Cambrensis* 150: 143–56.

(2008) '*Paedagogium* and *Septizonium:* two Roman lead tablets from Leicester', *ZPE* 167: 207–18.

(forthcoming) 'The book in Roman Britain', in *The Cambridge History of the Book,* vol. I.

Tomlin, R. S. O, and Hassall, M. W. C (2003) 'Inscriptions' in *Britannia* 34: 361–82.

(2004) 'Inscriptions', *Britannia* 35: 335–49.

(2005) 'Inscriptions', *Britannia* 36: 473–97.

(2006) 'Inscriptions', *Britannia* 37: 467–99.

Tongue, J. (2004) 'Seal boxes from Britain', *Lucerna: Roman Finds Group Newsletter* 27: 23–40.

Torbrügge, W. (1972) 'Vor- und Frühgeschichtliche Flußfunde. Zur Ordnung und Bestimmung einer Denkmälergruppe', *Bericht der Römisch-Germanischen Kommission* 51–2: 3–146.

Toynbee, J. M. C. (1962) *Art in Roman Britain.* Oxford.

(1964) *Art in Britain under the Romans.* Oxford.

(1971) *Death and Burial in the Roman World.* London. 1996 reprint Baltimore and London.

(1978) 'A Londinium votive leaf or feather and its fellows', in Bird, Chapman and Clark (1978a), 129–47.

(1982) 'Bronze, ivory and iron objects recovered from the floor of the later improvised shrine', in Wedlake (1982): 143–50.

(1986) *The Roman Art Treasures from the Temple of Mithras*. London Middlesex Archaeol. Soc. Spec. Pap. 7. London.

Toynbee, J. M. C. and Wilkins, A. (1982) 'The Vindolanda horse', *Britannia* 13: 245–51.

Tufi, S. R. (1983) *Corpus Signorum Imperii Romani: Great Britain* I.3. Oxford.

Turner, R. (1999) *Excavations of an Iron Age Settlement and Roman Religious Complex at Ivy Chimneys, Witham, Essex 1978–83*. E. Anglian Archaeol. Rep. 88. Chelmsford.

Turner, R. C., Rhodes, M. and Wild, J. P. (1991) 'The Roman body found on Grewelthorpe Moor in 1850: a reappraisal', *Britannia* 22: 191–201.

Tyers, P. (1996) *Roman Pottery in Britain*. London.

Tylecote, R. F. (1961) 'The Roman Anvil from Sutton Walls, Herefordshire', *Trans. Woolhope Natur. Field Club* 38: 56.

(1962) *Metallurgy in Archaeology*. London.

(1986) *The Prehistory of Metallurgy in the British Isles*. London.

Unz, C. (ed.) (1986) *Studien zu den Militärgrenzen Roms III*. Stuttgart.

Unz, C. and Deschler-Erb, E. (1997) *Katalog der Militaria aus Vindonissa: Militärische Funde, Pferdegeschirr und Jochteile bis 1976*. Bruges.

Vanderveen, B. H. (1969) *The Observer's Fighting Vehicles Directory World War II*. London and New York.

van Driel-Murray, C. (1987) 'Roman footwear: a mirror of fashion and society', in D. E. Friendship-Taylor, J. M. Swann and S. Thomas (eds.), *Recent Research in Archaeological Footwear*. Assoc. Archaeol. Illustrators Surveyors Techn. Pap. 8: 32–4.

(1989a) *Roman Military Equipment: The Sources of Evidence. Proceedings of the Fifth Roman Military Equipment Conference*, BAR Int. Ser. 476. Oxford.

(1989b) 'The Vindolanda chamfrons and miscellaneous items of leather horse gear', in van Driel-Murray (1989a): 281–318.

(1990) 'New light on old tents', *J. Roman Military Equip. Stud.* 1: 109–37.

(1993) 'The leatherwork', in van Driel Murray *et al.* (1993): 1–75.

(1999) 'And did those feet in ancient time . . . Feet and shoes as a material projection of the self', in Baker *et al.* (1999): 131–40.

(2001a) 'Vindolanda and the dating of Roman footwear', *Britannia* 32: 185–97.

(2001b) 'Technology transfer: the introduction and loss of tanning technology during the Roman period', in M. Polfer (ed.), *L'artisanat romain: évolutions, continuités et ruptures (Italie et provinces occidentals)*. Monographies Instrumentum 20. Montagnac: 55–67.

(2002) 'The leather trades in Roman Yorkshire and beyond', in Wilson and Price (2002): 109–23.

van Driel-Murray, C., Wild, J., Seaward, M. and Hillam, J. (1993) (eds.) *Vindolanda Research Reports*, New Ser. vol. III: *The Early Wooden Forts. Preliminary*

Reports on the Leather, Textiles, Environmental Evidence and Dendrochronology. Hexham.

Voinot, J. (1999) *Les cachets à collyres dans le monde romain.* Monographies Instrumentum 7. Montagnac.

Von Boeslager, D. (1989) 'Funde und Darstellungen Römischer Schreibzeugfutterale zur Deutung einer Beigabe in Kölner Gräbern', *Kölner Jahrburch* 22: 221–39.

von Mercklin, E. (1933) 'Wagenschmuck aus der Römischen Kaiserzeit', *Jahrbuch des Deutschen Archäologischen Instituts* 48: 84–176.

Wacher, J. (1975) *The Towns of Roman Britain.* London.

  (ed.) (1987) *The Roman World.* London.

Wainright, G. J. (1971) 'The excavation of a fortified settlement at Walesland Rath, Pembs.', *Britannia* 2: 48–108.

Ward, J. (1903) *The Roman Fort at Gellygaer in the County of Glamorgan.* Cardiff.

Wardle, A. (1998) 'Roman London: recent finds and research', in B. Watson (ed.), *Roman London: Recent Archaeological Work.* JRA Supplement Ser. 24. Portsmouth, RI: 83–9.

Ward-Perkins, J. and Claridge, A. (1976) *Pompeii AD 79.* Bristol.

Washburn, D. (1999) 'Perceptual anthropology: the cultural salience of symmetry', *American Anthropologist* 101.33, 547–62.

Watts, S. (1996) 'The rotary quern in Wales: Part 1', *Melin J. Welsh Mills Soc.* 12: 26–35.

Waugh, H. and Goodburn, R. (1972) 'The non-ferrous objects', in Frere (1972): 114-62.

Webster, G. A. (1960) 'The Roman military advance under Ostorius Scapula', *Archaeol. J.* 115: 49–98.

  (1969) *The Roman Imperial Army.* London.

  (1971) 'A hoard of Roman military equipment from Fremington Hagg', in Butler (1971): 107–25.

  (1978) *Boudica: The British Revolt against Rome AD 60.* London.

  (1980) *The Roman Invasion of Britain.* London.

  (1999) 'Bronze (copper alloy), silver and gold', in Turner (1999): 79–96.

Webster, J. and Cooper, N. (1996) *Roman Imperialism: Post-colonial Perspectives.* Leicester Archaeol. Mon. 3. Leicester.

Wedlake, W. J. (1982) *The Excavation of the Shrine of Apollo at Nettleton, Wiltshire, 1956–1971.* Rep. Res. Comm. Soc. Antiq. London 40. London.

Weekes, J. (2005) 'Reconstructing syntheses in Romano-British cremation', in J. Bruhn, B. Croxford and D. Grigoropoulos (eds.), *TRAC 2004: Proceedings of the Fourteenth Annual Theoretical Conference Durham 2004.* Oxford: 16–26.

Welfare, A. (1995) 'The millingstones', in Manning, Price and Webster (1995): 214–37.

West, S. (2005) 'Turners Hall Farm', *Current Archaeol.* 198: 268–75.

Westell, W. P. (1931) 'A Romano-British cemetery at Baldock, Herts', *Archaeol. J.* 88: 247–301.

Wheeler, R. E. M (1930) *London in Roman Times*. London.

(1946) *London in Roman Times* (2nd edn). London.

Wheeler, R. E. M and Wheeler, T. V. (1928) 'The Roman amphitheatre at Caerleon, Monmouthshire', *Archaeologia* 78: 111–218.

(1932) *Report on the Excavations of the Prehistoric, Roman and Post Roman Site in Lydney Park, Gloucestershire*. Rep. Res. Comm. Soc. Antiq. London 9. Oxford.

(1936) *Verulamium, a Belgic and two Roman Cities*. Rep. Res. Comm. Soc. Antiq. London 11. Oxford.

White, K. D. (1967) *Agricultural Implements of the Roman World*. Cambridge.

(1972) 'The Great Chesterford scythes', *Proc. Hungarian Agric. Museum*: 77–92.

(1975) *Farm Equipment of the Roman World*. Cambridge.

Whiting, W. (1926) 'The Roman cemeteries at Ospringe. Description of the finds continued', *Archaeol. Cantiana* 38: 123–51.

Whiting, W., Hawley, W. and May, T. (1931) *Report on the Excavation of the Roman Cemetery at Ospringe, Kent*. Rep. Res. Comm. Soc. Antiq. London 8. Oxford.

Wild, J. P. (1970) 'Button-and-loop fasteners in the Roman provinces', *Britannia* 1: 137–55.

Wilkes, J. (2005) 'The Roman Danube: an archaeological survey', *J. Roman Stud.* 95: 124–225.

Williams, D. (2007) 'Green Lane, Wanborough: excavations at the Roman religious site, 1999', *Surrey Archaeol. Collect.* 93: 149–265.

Willis, S. (2005) 'The context of writing and written records in ink: the archaeology of Samian inkwells in Roman Britain', *Archaeol. J.* 162: 96–145.

Wilmott, T. (1991) *Excavations in the Middle Walbrook Valley*, LAMAS Spec. Pap. 13. London.

(1997) *Birdoswald: Excavations of a Roman Fort on Hadrian's Wall and Its Successor Settlements 1987–92*. English Heritage Archaeol. Rep. 14. London.

(2009) *Hadrian's Wall: Archaeological Research by English Heritage 1976–2000*. London.

Wilmott, T., Cool, H. and Evans, J. (2009) 'Excavations at the Hadrian's Wall fort of Birdoswald (*Banna*), Cumbria: 1996–2000', in T. Wilmott (ed.), *Hadrian's Wall: Archaeological Research by English Heritage 1976–2000*. English Heritage Res. Rep. London: 203–395.

Wilson, D. R. (1969) 'Roman Britain in 1968', *J. Roman Stud.* 59: 176–206.

Wilson, P. R. (2002a) *Cataractonium: Roman Catterick and Its Hinterland. Excavations and Research, 1958–1997*. Part 1. CBA Res. Rep. 128. York.

(2002b) *Cataractonium: Roman Catterick and Its Hinterland. Excavations and Research, 1958–1997*. Part 2. CBA Res. Rep. 128. York.

Wilson, P. and Price, J. (2002) *Aspects of Industry in Roman Yorkshire and the North*. Oxford.

Winterbottom, S. (1989) 'Saddle covers, chamfrons and possible horse armour from Carlisle', in van Driel-Murray (1989a): 319–36.

Wiseman, J. (2005) *Hide and Seek: The Archaeology of Childhood.* Stroud.

Woodward, A. and Leach, P. (1993) *The Uley Shrines: Excavation of a Ritual Complex on West Hill, Uley, Gloucestershire 1977–9.* English Heritage Archaeol. Rep. 17. London.

Woodwood, P. J., Davies, S. M. and Graham, A. H. (1993) *Excavations at Greyhound Yard, Dorchester, 1981–4.* Dorset Natur. Hist. Archaeol. Soc. Mon. Ser. 12. Dorchester.

Worrell, S. (2004) 'Finds reported under the Portable Antiquities Scheme', *Britannia* 35: 316–34.

Wrathmell, S. and Nicholson, A. (eds.) (1990) *Dalton Parlours Iron Age Settlement and Roman Villa.* Yorkshire Archaeol. 3. Wakefield.

Wright, M. E. (2002) 'Querns and millstones,' in Wilson (2002b): 267–85.

Wright, R. P. and Hassall, M. W. C. (1973) 'Inscriptions', *Britannia* 4: 324–37.

Wright, R. P. and Richmond, I. (1955) *Catalogue of the Roman Inscribed and Sculptured Stone in the Grosvenor Museum, Chester.* Chester.

Wyke, M. (1994) 'Woman in the mirror: the rhetoric of adornment in the Roman world', in L. Archer, S. Fischler and M. Wyke (eds.), *Women in Ancient Society.* London: 134–51.

Yegül, F. (1992) *Baths and Bathing in Classical Antiquity.* Cambridge, Mass. and London.

Zanker, P. (1988) *The Power of Images in the Age of Augustus.* Ann Arbor.

Zelle, M. (2000) *Colonia Ulpia Traiana: Götter und Kulte, Führer und Schriften des Archäologischen Parks.* Xanten 21. Cologne.

Zienkiewicz, J. D. (1986) *The Legionary Fortress Baths at Caerleon II: The Finds.* Cardiff.

Index

Printed in Great Britain
by Amazon

47852166R00212